Peter Biddlecombe is a travel-hardened businessman. His much-acclaimed first book, *French Lessons in Africa*, described his travels through French-speaking Africa, and has been followed by eight more gloriously funny accounts of global business trips: *Travels With My Briefcase*; *Around the World – On Expenses*; *I Came, I Saw, I Lost My Luggage*; *Very Funny – Now Change Me Back Again*; *Faster, They're Gaining*; *A Nice Time Being Had By All*; *Never Feel A Stranger* and *The United Burger States of America*, all of which are available from Abacus Travel.

He is the first travel writer to have visited and written about over 170 different countries.

Faster –
They're Gaining

PETER BIDDLECOMBE

An *Abacus* Book

First published in Great Britain in 1998
by Abacus
Reprinted 2002

Copyright © 1998 by Peter Biddlecombe

The moral right of the author has been asserted.

A CIP catalogue record for this book
is available from the British Library.

ISBN: 0 349 11062 X

Typeset by Solidus (Bristol) Limited
Printed and bound in Great Britain
by Clays Ltd, St Ives plc

Abacus
An imprint of
Time Warner Books UK
Brettenham House
Lancaster Place
London WC2E 7EN

www.TimeWarnerBooks.co.uk

CONTENTS

INTRODUCTION

Doctor Livingstone only had lions and journalists to worry about. Now, I'm by no means a big traveller. I mean, I've only visited 117 countries so far, not like some people I know, who travel so much they have friends round on Friday nights to show them slides of the weekends they spend at home. But even with my limited experience, I tell you there are a million things I'd like to run away from.

Like looky-loo check-in bags with brains like an airline meal who look as though they can not only scramble eggs with their tongue but are fully paid-up members of the World Headache Council as well. Like slugabed air hostesses who give you the impression they don't believe in taking survivors. Like gonzos who turn up for a quick overnight trip with half a dozen fancy designer imitation suitcases that look more like camp handbags than real luggage.

Then there are guys with money belts, or rather pansy pouches, especially those who insist on wearing them in countries which have a far, far lower crime rate than we do as well as those awful dunderheads with a size 8 face on a size 4 body who are always working out their change. 'Seventy-three from hundred and fifty is thirty-three. Plus three. Divide by twenty-one over four and a half to give you good old British pounds and it's ... Cheats. Cheats. They've cheated me again.'

And off they go to create hell over, what, tuppence halfpenny, if that.

But whatever you do, don't think I'm prejudiced. My philosophy in life is simple. If I like it, I drink it; if not, I hate it.

I'll tell you who else gives me the trots more than a bucket of curry in a back street in downtown Madras. Fat ladies and kids you know about, but I've now got some new ones as well.

Elderly French women with horrible tiny little dogs tucked inside their handbags. I got a flight once from Seville to Madrid. Sitting next to me was this French woman and her disgusting little dog. She not only looked as though she was smeared with some repulsive insect repellant, she smelled like it as well. The dog, I mean. At least, I hope it was insect repellant.

People who keep wanting to look at everything you've got. Coming home from Damascus once, I got stuck with some slaphead who kept wanting to look at everything I had: my papers, my books, the label on the wine bottle, the inside of my miserable pack of peanuts, everything. In fact, at one stage I thought he was going for the label inside my shirt as well.

And, of course, people who do nothing but talk, talk, talk. At present the airlines are obsessed with non-smoking flights. I reckon they should introduce non-speaking flights. Just imagine the joy of crossing the Atlantic without some guy sitting next to you going on and on and on about double glazing or the latest sprinkler systems for your office. I mean, why should I be stuck next to someone from Cape Town to Brussels – including a refuelling stop at Rome – with whom I would not be seen dead anywhere else in the world? It's not fair.

Now, I know I'm just a mere beginner when it comes to dragging myself around the world, but you wouldn't believe the number of times I've been lectured for hours on end on hotels, bars, cocktails, taxis, fax machines and why ZoZo's is the best nightclub in Maputo. Actually, it isn't, but I'm not telling you which one is. Normally when it comes to anybody recommending me anything, I've got a simple response. Ignore it. They usually don't know what the hell they're talking about.

Once on a trip to Minsk I met the world's greatest hotel expert. He told me to go and stay at some famous hotel in the middle of town. I'm not saying it was bad, it's just that every day I was there I carved another notch on my brief-case. But it did have its advantages. On the final day I didn't have to carry my suitcase down to reception: the cockroaches had already done it for me. I say cockroaches, they were more like tortoises.

Now, in spite of what you may think, I don't usually take an instant dislike to people, but once in the States I got a flight from Minneapolis-St Paul. I was sat next to this stripe-suited doo-wop who kept trying to do press-ups in his seat before the engines had even started. It was a short flight and I didn't have a whole lot of time to spare, so I decided there and then to immediately hate his guts.

God help me if he then didn't go on and on and on about how he had to have three daily injections of radish juice; how he could turn any hotel room into his own mini-gym in the time it took me to wipe out a bottle of champagne. The bath, he made a base for push-ups. A chair, he used as a bar for something he called, I think, tricep dips, whatever the hell they are. Cushions were hurdles. Phone books were his weights. As for leg lifts and jumping jacks, they didn't require anything at all. As if that was not agonising enough, he then insisted on showing me the contents of his briefcase. Now there are many things in this world I'm interested in. There are also many things I am not interested in, and I must tell you that the contents of other blokes' briefcases is way up there alongside recipes for spinach roulade and why the Internet is going to dominate world trade. But this guy's briefcase was a revelation. It contained:

24	soluble aspirins
1	spoon for rehydration
5	gauze swats
1	roll of zinc-oxide tape
2	cotton buds
2	lancets
1	syringe: 5ml
2	syringes: 2ml
2	blue needles
2	tins of Elastoplast
$\frac{1}{2}$	ton malaria tablets
2	clean sheets
1	pillowcase with pretty flowers all the way round the edge
1	teddy bear
1	pair of rubber gloves

Could I say a word? I couldn't even ask if I could move to another seat.

But the problem doesn't end when you get off the plane. If anything, it gets worse. First, there are the expats who are invariably the kind of people you would emigrate to avoid. They either keep on about living 'Chez Johnny Foreigner' or they drag on about Kashmir. Or Burma. Or Kenya. Or anywhere.

'It was '47. Just back from Blighty. Whole lot went up. Whizz bang. What? Did I tell you?'

Did he tell me? He's told me about it almost as many times as he told me about some colonic depth-charge he'd had in the local knacker's yard to clear his sinuses or whatever.

But worst, worst, worst of all are the tourists who travel the world with their jars of homemade marmalade wrapped up inside their Marks & Spencer carrier bags but never leave England. Take them anywhere, show them anything, tell them anything – they are not interested. They are only interested in getting back to their hotel rooms, where they can secretly brew another cuppa with tea they smuggled in from England because they didn't want to risk touching anything foreign.

Worse still, they are devaluing and destroying the places they are not visiting: the pyramids; the ancient city of Pompeii; the Taj Mahal; Ayuttaya, the ancient capital of Thailand. A whole string of eighteenth-century wooden churches in Russia. The Morgan Lewis Sugar Mill on Barbados, the last remaining wind-driven sugar mill in the Caribbean. They and many, many more places, are being destroyed not by people who love and honour and respect them, but by people who are totally indifferent to them. You've only got to listen to what they say about them.

'Give it five years, it'll be just like Blackpool.' (Walking along the Great Wall of China.)

'Did I tell you the trouble I have with my sweet peas?' (On the cable car to Table Mountain.)

'An egg cup. I must have an egg cup. Don't tell me in the whole of Brazil there's not one egg cup. I can't eat an egg without an egg cup.' (Having a picnic in Machu Picchu.)

'Never eat fish more than ten miles from the sea.' (Strolling along the creek in Dubai.)

'Mark my words, someone will have a runny tummy tomorrow morning.' (In the restaurant in Raffles Hotel, Singapore.)

'Never touch the salad. They might have washed it in the local water.' (Surveying Victoria Falls.)

'I'm not saying I didn't like it, it's just that when I was in India …' (Gawping at a painting in the Prado.)

'You can never pluck a louse from your head using a single finger.' (Shuffling through the Medici Chapel in Florence.)

Case proven?

About the only bunch of tourists I've ever enjoyed meeting was a big Welsh group I bumped into in Buenos Aires who were on their way to Patagonia. And that was only because whenever they went anywhere, the wild, red-faced leader would holler out at the top of his voice, 'Dragons roll.' It was hilarious.

I tell you, on the odd occasion between meetings when I've had a few seconds to spare to see the local sights, I've only got to catch a glimpse of a group of tourists in the distance and it gives a whole new meaning to the phrase Terror Incognita. I make no apologies. In the old days, I would pretend to be French and go around insulting everybody, because the crazy thing is, the Brits don't object to French whine. But not any more. Now I turn and run. Because I'm convinced that if I don't turn and run, it won't be long before I'm the one being chased by the men in white coats.

Peter Biddlecombe
In Luang Prabang. On the banks of the Mekong River. In northern Laos. Still looking over my shoulder.

MOSCOW

Gee whizz. You think trying to make a living back home is difficult, you should try Russia. There everything is impossible. Even walking down the street or answering the telephone is a drama, let alone being paid. Being paid! That's the biggest laugh of all. Because as far as I could discover, nobody – well, nobody apart from the big guys – has been paid literally for three, four, five, six months, maybe more. Factory workers, miners, doctors, nurses, schoolteachers, professors, musicians, the Army, the Navy, the Air Force ... it's unbelievable. In fact some people, who presumably are being paid, estimate that there is over US$7 billion owing throughout the country in unpaid salaries and wages to over a quarter of the whole workforce. The other thing that amazes me is petrol. You can hardly find any, yet Russia is the second largest oil-producer in the world.

Russia in the old days I could have accepted, no problem. The absolute dictatorship. The strict party line. Brainwashing. The total ban on discussion and debate, unquestioning obedience. The wrong word at the wrong time and you're a dead man. Which, let's be honest, is a bit like being married. But Russia today is unbelievable. Now, don't get me wrong – I'm not a rouble-rouser. What with *glasnost* and *perestroika* I know they've had a couple or three million little problems to deal with. Like the

7

spectacular break-up of the old Communist regime, the collapse of the Soviet Union, the loss of the Cold War, the sudden appearance of fifteen new independent states, nine years of continuous economic shrinkage and the opening of the biggest McDonald's in the world, just round the corner from the old red-painted English Club, which, in its day, blackballed not only Leo Tolstoy but Aleksandr Pushkin as well. As if that were not enough, they then slammed the whole thing into reverse. Virtually overnight they went from being a strict Stalinist command economy where the state, alongside Lambeth Council and the National Health Service, was the biggest employer in the whole of Western Europe with a stranglehold on everything, to rip-roaring devil-may-care the-World-Bank-will-pick-up-the-tab capitalism.

But did it have to be as bad as this? Because, make no mistake about it, the changes the Russians have had to go through have been tremendous. The effect on their lives has been cataclysmic. From being helpless and defence-less nonentities, the poor individual Russians have had suddenly to adjust to the fact that everybody is now somebody and however many stars or pips they have on their shoulders, they've all got to fight their own fight. For bread, for water, for the most basic living conditions. Today, tomorrow and probably every single day for the rest of their lives. The result is that the whole place looks like one enormous car-boot sale.

On practically every street corner, from opposite the old KGB headquarters on Lubyanka Square, where the tour guides brag that today the same number of people who go in come out again at the end of the visit, along the length of Starry Arbat Street, the pedestrian-only shopping street where Pushkin once lived, you see nothing but the biggest-selling imports in the country: lightweight aluminium trestle tables. I say imports because, whatever the figures say, the Russians can't/don't/won't make anything any more. And piled on top of these tables is everything you can think of: lumps of stale bread; piles of potatoes and cabbages; chunks of what looks like cake, thirty-year-old maps of Belgium; bits of uniform; old Madonna CDs and Michael Jackson cassettes; a Morris Oxford handbook, paintings of the Red Square; stacks and stacks of homemade potato vodka; long, thin bits of metal with electric plugs on the end which, when heated, are all most families have to keep warm in temperatures that can drop as low as minus 50. And, of course, those flipping Russian dolls. One I saw for sale on a row of trestle tables outside Moscow State University – from which you can see the whole city, including Mikhail Gorbachev's new house – was made up of all the Russian presidents. I looked inside the Yeltsin doll, but there was no vodka. So I didn't buy it – it was obviously fake. And standing, sitting, falling asleep, dying behind the tables is a complete cross-section of Russian society. Hairy old women wrapped in dozens of tatty, paper-thin coats, red, white and blue with the cold. Ancient old soldiers who look as though they've just got back from seeing off the French at Borodino. Fat old babushkas. Weak, pathetic men who could be anything from fifteen to fifty. And, of course, students, all of them hoping against hope that they will be able to put off the day of reckoning maybe just another twenty-four hours. And if they can, whether they'll be able to change their roubles into dollars fast enough.

It's the same story in shops and offices and factories, though I didn't go into many shops, on the basis that since I avoid them when I'm at home, there's no way I'm going into them when I'm away. However, I must admit that seeing the shops on Maxim Gorky Street was a moving experience. In the 1930s it would literally have been a moving experience. In order to widen the street for the non-expected growth of the Russian car industry, most buildings either side were just flattened. A few, however, were actually hoisted on to giant rollers and literally pulled back 50 or 100 yards. The ones I did spot might have looked like a wet Wednesday afternoon in Wigan, but at least they had something to sell, which is in itself a vast improvement on the old days. Even GUM, which runs the length of Red Square, looked decidedly GLUM – the L, of course, standing for Lenin, who nationalised it in 1921. From the outside, it looks like any other dilapidated government office, like, say, the Ministry of Technology. The entrances are filthy, doors are hanging off the hinges; there's no lighting, no displays. Everything is dark and dank and dismal. Inside, it's only marginally better. The main walkways are clean and functional and there's the occasional stall selling flowers or ice-creams, but it's a million miles away from even your average run-down shopping centre or mall in the West. The shops themselves are a different matter. Most of them are your average shops for your average poor, desperately hungry, down-at-heel Muscovite: Christian Dior, Estée Lauder, Galeries Lafayette, Karstadt and I can't remember how many others. Buy an ice-cream from a stall outside on the streets and it will cost you the equivalent of a half-day's pay for the average Muscovite, so you can imagine how busy it gets.

Behind GLUM, which was originally called VTR until Lenin came along, is the old business area of Moscow where different trades and professions occupied different streets and different buildings. Today it's a crumbling jumble of filthy back streets. collapsing buildings, frail old churches, overgrown gardens, rusty iron staircases, locked, barred and barricaded courtyards and struggling, pathetic shops.

I have, however, been to lots of factories in and around Moscow. Now, I'm not normally soft, and especially not about factories, but honestly, they would break your heart. There's nothing there: no glass in the windows, no doors on the hinges. If they have any machines they are completely clapped out. Half, maybe more, are not working at all. There are thick puddles of oil oozing all over the place. Birds fly in and out of holes in the roof. It's unbelievable. One factory in particular I remember visiting. The whole place was falling apart, but there at the end of this vast machine shop was a huge old-style ten-storey-high mural depicting Lenin, complete with velvet-collared overcoat blowing behind him in the wind, surrounded by slogans proclaiming 'Power to the Soviet. Peace to the People. Land to the Peasants.'

'Of course, nobody believes it any more,' everybody told me, slightly shamefacedly. 'It's just tradition, that's all. Like you have pictures of the Queen.' Well, there's no denying that.

The other thing I always find still stuck on the walls when I'm wandering around Russian factories are their old, yellowing civil-defence posters: What Happens When a Nuclear Bomb explodes? What Size Gas Mask Do You Need? How to Evacuate the Factory. How to Build an Underground Shelter. Safety Procedures. Ways to Seal Your Home from Radioactivity. Building an Underground Shelter Under Your Street. These guys, believe me, took their civil defence seriously. To them a nuclear war was a matter of when, not if. Many people have told me how at school every week they had civil-defence classes, how they were taught to put on a gas mask and shown how to build a tunnel. One woman, a personnel manager, remembered that at her school the teachers actually made the pupils build a tunnel all the way round the main school building and out into the street to connect with the main tunnel in the area. Another manager who was in charge of so-called production told me that at his school, not only did they dig tunnels, they learned to shoot as well. Not just the boys, the girls as well. 'It's silly when I think of it now,' he laughed. 'But at the time we all took it seriously.'

Whole towns and villages would have regular monthly training sessions. 'It was nothing unusual,' he said, 'for us all to be out in the countryside. Then suddenly you would hear the sirens, and you would have to run back to town quickly to the nearest shelters.'

'And if you didn't run?' I wondered.

'Then the police would come and see you,' he grinned.

You also come across horrifying stories of people struggling to survive. I went into one factory on the outskirts of Moscow which looked like a bomb site. The floor was, as usual, covered in oil about an inch thick and there was hardly a pane of glass in the building. Less than, I guess, a quarter of the machines were working. Those that were were chuntering away. One tiny, wiry old man who looked as though he'd spent half his life in the Gulags told me that to try to make ends meet he had started organising dog fights on a patch of ground near where he lived in western Moscow.

'But isn't it against the law?' I couldn't help asking.

'The Police, they come as well,' he said. 'We make money. Dogs use their energy. We eat.'

I went to visit an old friend in one of the enormous seventeen-storey towerblocks around Moscow known as Khrushchoby after Nikita Khrushchev, who apparently, on being shown a string of designs, simply stubbed his finger on one at random. 'This one,' he said. And that was it – the Khrushchoby was born. Before you could say, 'Excuse me, don't you think they're a touch hideous?' there were thousands of them all over the Soviet Union. 'Go into a Khrushchoby anywhere in Russia, the door is always in the same place, the windows are in the same place, even the light switch is in the same place,' my friend's wife complained.

Next door lived an Academician, a member of the prestigious Russian Academy of Science. And I mean next door: he was living in one room. Next door to him was a bus-driver. Upstairs was a bunch of schoolteachers sharing another single room. None of them had been paid for way over six months. They were able to survive only because the bus-driver had an aunt in the country who kept them supplied with cabbages.

It was exactly the same story at the huge, sprawling Kupavinsky Naval Base just outside Moscow. In the old days the Navy were the chosen few. They had plenty of food and all the vodka they could drink. Now defending the country doesn't count, they're more interested in defending themselves and their families. The only thing that counts is moonlighting. One officer I met, who looked more like a dustman than a sailor, told me he had a full-time job as a security guard at a factory near the old airport. 'Full time?' I asked. 'But I thought you said you were a naval officer.'

'I must eat,' he grunted.

The commander of an army anti-aircraft unit near Cherepovets, about 250 miles north of Moscow, had gone a stage further. He had set up in business selling off bits of the Army. When I was there he was advertising their stock in his local newspaper, trying to sell decommissioned ground-to-air missiles to farmers as scarecrows. One evening outside The Banner of Labour Mig-29 factory in north Moscow, I actually saw guys coming straight out of the gates carrying what looked like empty lunchboxes, ambling casually a couple of hundred yards across to a van and piling them all on top of one another in the back. Except they weren't empty lunchboxes. They were 5-kilogram ingots of raw aluminium. For their trouble they got US$50 in cash. Which, when you remember that they are being paid less than US$35 for a full month's work, makes you wonder how the place is still standing.

If you check out some of the kiosks you find on practically every street corner in Moscow, you'll see that they're not selling sweets and cans of Coke and yesterday's newspapers. Well, not just sweets and cans of Coke and yesterday's newspapers. They're the sharp end of an enormous metals-smuggling operation. Copper, nickel, zinc, titanium, special steels, even live radioactive materials – they deal in everything. Why do you think the first thing the Russians did after the Wall came down was to go for the statues of Marx and Lenin and all the others? Because they wanted to celebrate their freedom? Come on, these guys are Russians. They were after the bronze. The same thing happened with 100 kms of bronze and copper telephone cables that disappeared literally from under the nose of post and telecommunications officials in St Petersburg. It was dug up and sold before they even thought of picking up the phone and calling the police.

But at least the guys behind these scams are able to survive, not like the poor guys digging the Krasnodonskaya extension to the Moscow Metro in the far south-east of the city. They had to barricade themselves in the tunnels and practically starve themselves to death to get paid – and they were only asking for 70 per cent of what they should have been paid eight months earlier. To be fair, some companies unable to pay their workers any money have been giving them some of the goods they produce instead – like tins of rotten meat, bags of manure, boxes of matches, used ball bearings or toilet paper. This doesn't always work out: one company in Voronezh, a violently pro-Communist stronghold deep in the south of Russia, practically had a revolution on their hands when they started handing out their products instead of wages. They were bra manufacturers.

One factory I was not unhappy to see closing down was the huge Aviakor plant at Samara, which was responsible for trying to build the Tupolev-154, the workhorse of Russian airlines. I say trying to build, because since 1993 it has been involved in more deadly crashes than I've had lousy airline meals.

It's the same story in hospitals. If you're lucky enough to get into a hospital, you not only have to supply all your own bandages and medicines and syringes and bed linen, you also have to pay for your own food as well. Up front, in cash. It's no wonder the famous so-called Street of Life – which begins with a maternity hospital and goes on to include every other kind of hospital you can imagine to cope with every possible disease it's best not to imagine – ends with a cemetery: the famous Second Division cemetery for the guys who were not quite important enough to be buried in the Kremlin. Even the Central Clinic, the big prestigious hospital where President Yeltsin had his operation, couldn't survive unless patients paid their way. Up front, in cash. Maybe the reason why his operation was delayed for so long was that the Russian government had a struggle trying to find the cash to pay for it.

Still not convinced? OK, what about this, then? The Russians can no longer even produce vodka. Kristall, the company which made the famous Stolichnaya (You remember those good old days? A chunk of salty fish, a lump of rye bread and a slug of iced Stolichnaya?) is now well and truly on the rocks. Bust. Bankrupt. Smashed out of its tiny mind. Shortly after, it must be admitted, they had installed a load of brand-new, shiny Italian production equipment, but, let's be honest, that's just a detail. The brewers, however, seem to be doing well – at least, there were always long, long queues outside all the brewers I saw. One afternoon on my way back from a meeting I stopped off at this tiny, poor, little wooden

house with a mere sixteen rooms, which once belonged
to a man who preached the simple life and was, at one
time, home to his cantankerous old wife, eight children,
fourteen servants, a grand piano from Zimmerman's and a
genuine, still-working British bicycle. It was Leo Tolstoy's
very own Moscow pad. Outside was this enormous queue.
I reckoned that the time I got in I would have had time to
read *War and Peace* at least once, if not twice. Then I
realised that the people weren't queuing up to go in the
house. They were queuing up for the brewery next door.

As a result, before you could say, 'A pint of the best,' I
was treading the very boards the Great Man himself had
trod. Well, I say treading the boards: as befits any tiny,
poor, little wooden house in Russia, I hardly set foot in the
place before a bunch of babushkas pounced on me with
this enormous pair of overshoes that looked like a cross
between half the country's carpet production for a week
and a platypus on heat. How my cardboard-soled cheap
Marks & Spencer rejects could do more damage than eight
children, fourteen servants, an old British bicycle and a
cantankerous old wife, I do not know, but as there were
more of them than there was of me, and as we're all
democrats nowadays, I gave in.

For the next twenty minutes or so I flip-flopped around
the dining room with its heavy mahogany furniture. The
table was set for dinner, Tolstoy's place, surprisingly, at the
side of the table rather than at the head. Obviously a true
man of the people, even in his own home. Either that or he
couldn't stand sitting next to his wife. Upstairs I flip-
flopped into what looked like a lounge complete with
grand piano. I even heard Tolstoy himself reading one of
his own works, written when he was twenty and recorded
fifty years later. Which is about the length of time it still
takes to get any decent literature on to a cassette. I saw his
study, where, in order to save the cost of buying a pair of

spectacles, he had great chunks sawn off the legs of his chair so he could get closer to the paper on the top of the desk. Not just a great writer, then, but a DIY genius as well. Outside on the landing were all the boots and shoes of cantankerous old wife, children and servants, which he repaired himself. There was also his old Rover bicycle, which he got when he was sixty-seven years old. When he actually ordered it none of the old babushkas could tell me, but as sixty-seven is not the usual age to take up cycling, my guess is that he ordered it when he was seventeen and that, being British, it was a little late being delivered. Finally, as I flip-flopped my way out, there, still hanging up on the wall by the front door, was the poor man's great, big, expensive, luxury, fur coat.

As I struggled to escape from the overshoes, I saw that the crowd was still there. 'Well, somebody's got some money,' I said to my driver. 'If they can queue up like that for beer.'

'They are not queuing up for beer,' he replied. 'They are queuing up to get money back on the bottles they collect on the streets.'

If life is tough for the ordinary ex-comrade, just think what it's like for the wheeler-dealers, the shakers and movers who make little bits of the system work. There's no way they can invest and expand and build up their businesses, because as soon as they get any money, it's gone. Either on essentials like video-players, champagne, perfume, the various delights on offer in Tverskaya Street in the shadow of the Kremlin - which all in their own way involve a different form of Russian roulette - or the far more upmarket, far more exciting and far more expensive dolls whose policy seems to be, in traditional Russian style, to grin and bare it. Or, failing that, it goes straight into their back pocket. Not once did I come across a single Russian businessman who was putting money back into Russia. Instead they were putting it into

Switzerland or Finland or Cyprus, or anywhere but where it should have been going. Which is one hell of a recommendation for Russia, and one hell of an incentive for foreign businessmen to invest in the country. Again and again and again I was told, 'We started off poor, we will probably end up poor. Why not spend it when you have it? This is Russia.'

In the lobby of the Ukraine Hotel, one of Stalin's seven wedding-cake wonders of Moscow, a mysterious man in a brown jacket and grey trousers surrounded by hordes of over-eager heavily built young men in black leather jackets said to me, 'I was born in a one-room flat. I will probably die in a one-room flat. That is our system.'

I asked him what he did for a living. He said that he bought Russian Migs and then sold them on to an American guy for US$800,000.

'Who does the American guy sell them to?'

'Countries in South America.'

'For how much?'

'For an extra US$2 million. He always takes US$2 million commission. It is good business.'

Another Russian I met, who had a face that looked as though it had been blasted sideways by a Kalashnikov at point-blank range, strangely enough didn't want to talk about business. Instead, as we walked up and down outside the plush, extravagant art-nouveau Hotel Metropol, all he wanted to do was to talk about guns. 'Some people like a Beretta 92FS. But for me they're too light. They're a lady's gun. I prefer a .45. I've always got a .357 revolver, but I hardly ever use it.'

Everybody, but everybody, is living not just for today, but for this morning, for this afternoon, for this evening. Long-term planning is tomorrow morning – early. And no wonder. The country itself, the whole of the once-mighty Russian Empire that at one time produced more steel per capita than the United States, more tractors per 1,000 people than Germany and enough bombs to blow us all to kingdom come, has less than £2 billion in currency reserves. GEC, thanks to Lord Weinstock, has more than that in petty cash. For the poor the whole place is one huge battlefield, and for the rich one huge firing-range. I admit I don't have experience of many battlefields – well, apart from trying to entertain the in-laws at Christmas. But, believe me, Moscow is one. It's Paris by day and New York or, I suppose, Marseilles, by night. It is long, broad, sweeping avenues and boulevards and huge squares and enormous buildings by day, but by night, there is more than a whiff of cordite in the air. The streets are practically flowing with blood.

If you think the triads in Hong Kong or the Yakuza in Japan are bad, you should see Moscow. There are supposed to be over 3,000 organised gangs in the city, each one heavily armed with guns and bombs and even rocket-launchers. The murder rate, which has trebled since *perestroika*, is currently running at around 20 per cent per 100,000 inhabitants – double the number of killings in the US, whose record I always thought (well, maybe apart from Colombia's), was the worst in the world. In fact, it's got so bad that you can't consider yourself a fully fledged, 100 per cent-genuine innocent, law-abiding Muscovite unless you've got one black eye, a swollen lip, you're clutching your rib cage and you are about to keel over into the gutter in a pool of blood. You think I'm exaggerating. One woman, an interpreter in one of the companies I visited, told me that her children have problems getting to sleep at night unless there is a gun-fight or an explosion outside in the streets. What's more, some contract killers, who claim they operate for as little as 10,000 Finnish marks – barely US$5 a hit – are so popular that they are becoming personalities in their own right and, would you believe, regularly give press interviews and appear on television.

Go into an office. That alone is an achievement: many offices have had hand grenades stuck to the door – touch it and you're a dead man. If you manage to get inside and are still alive, you can't help but notice all the sophisticated little touches, like metal grilles and steel shutters and huge metal doors all over the place. First, make certain you haven't got a gun or a bomb taped to your inside leg. Secondly, make certain nobody else in going to burst in after you and blow the whole place to smithereens. Once you get inside, along the corridors, you'll hardly be able to move for gun-carrying heavies in rubber boots and flak jackets checking for anti-personnel mines and exploding briefcases. Wander in to see the manager or the director, and he is as likely to be priming his pump-action shotgun as playing with his PC.

Go into a bar or a restaurant. Practically everybody is frisked. If it's a halfway respectable place, and you've got a gun – and most Russians have – you are given a choice: put it in a special locked box and claim it on the way out, or find another bar or restaurant. Unless, of course, you're wearing an expensive Armani suit, have half a dozen rings on each finger and are surrounded by a couple of dozen guys in black leather jackets, all waving mobile telephones in the air. Then it's straight to the best table, and did you say you wanted one bottle or two of Dom Perignon? If you hit on a bar or restaurant which doesn't frisk you, stay there. You'll have one hell of a time. You'll end up either getting bombed out of your mind on cheap, industrial vodka, discussing the finer points of *Giselle* with a string of dancers moonlighting from the Bolshoi and singing catchy tunes like 'From Irkutsk to Brighton Beach' at the top of your voice, or in the gutter outside with your insides hanging out, courtesy of the Sointsevo boys. Either way, it'll be a night to remember.

If that's not risky enough for you, try something really way out. Wander down the street. Either people will ignore you or they'll keep bumping into you. Me, they keep bumping into. Which either means they think I have that hangdog look of a Russian just back from the camps, so what difference does it make, or they're trying to relieve me of my wallet, my small change, my glasses, my watch, my— 'Hey! Watch out! Whatdyathinkyadoing?' And be careful of bus shelters, they're a favourite spot for bombs. Especially the ones down Kutuzovsky's Prospekt, the road President Yeltsin takes every morning on the way to his office in the Kremlin. Practically every one has had a bomb left in it at some time or other, usually at the time Yeltsin happens to be passing. And that lorry parked by the kerb. Take care. Lorries have suddenly started exploding all over the place. Maybe this is the next one. Even if lorries don't have bombs in them, they can still be dangerous. Hardly a day goes by without armed guards and drivers of huge container lorries being overpowered in broad daylight by gangs of highly armed, ruthless thugs. During one trip a lorry was stolen almost opposite the hotel I was staying in.

'What was in it?' I asked the bell captain, who seemed to know everything. 'Gold? Silver? Cigarettes?'

'No,' he said. 'Mars bars.'

And litter bins. Litter bins are another problem. Not because they are a favourite hiding place for bombs and guns – that would be too obvious. All the same, whatever you do, don't look inside a litter bin in Moscow. There is more likely to be a dead body inside it than anything else. One bank manager, an American, told me that in the bins close to his office they recently discovered three bodies, all decapitated with their hands tied behind their backs.

If you want to get the flavour of Moscow and do something really dangerous and reckless and death-defying, there's no shortage of opportunities. Like crossing the road. Any road: a small back street, a main highway, the fifty-seven-lane Leningradsky Prospekt. It's like trying to cross the M1. The traffic, I swear, accelerates from 102 to 152mph in order to hit you. If they miss they're not worried – they know there are another 2.5 million clapped-out Ladas and Zils, not to mention the gloriously named Gigolis, equally determined to get you. If you survive, it won't be for want of trying on their part. It's just a statistical blip. They'll get you next time.

On the other hand, you could get a cab, hire a car or even accept a lift in somebody else's. Not only do you risk being smashed to a pulp in some unbelievable car crash, there's a better than evens chance that you'll either see some other poor guy splattered all over the road or you'll be kidnapped, cut up into little bits and fed to the bears prancing up and down Starry Arbut Street, which is virtually Moscow's Left Bank.

Then, of course, there's car-jacking. A Swedish business-man told me he had been a victim of a car-jack. He was driving through Moscow early one morning in his armoured Mercedes and pulled up at the lights near Red Square. As he stopped, three heavies, all in regulation black leather jackets, grabbed the doors. He was bundled out and thrown in the back seat, one heavy on either side of him. The leader leaped into the driving seat, then started cursing. He'd never seen an automatic car before and he didn't know how to drive it. The Swedish guy was then bundled out of the back seat and into the driving seat, and told to drive like hell for somewhere on the outskirts of Moscow. The heavies were obviously on the run and needed a getaway car.

'Gee,' I said, 'you were lucky. Anything could have happened. You could have been shot up by the police, you could have been thrown in jail, you could have been...'

'I know,' he said. 'I've still got my car.'

So what about just sitting in the car doing nothing? No way. Sit in the car and do nothing and you're just as likely to be shot in the stomach. After one guy, I was told, was shot in the stomach, the gun jammed – typically Russian – so he was stabbed as well.

You could take the Metro, join the throng of people careering from one station to another to another scared out of their wits that another bomb is going to go off. Into the booking hall you rush, up to the hole in the wall with the grubby net curtains. You hand over your 1,500 roubles – which is roughly the equivalent of two shirt buttons – grab your greasy, plastic coin, race across to the row of broken-down old stalls and stick the coin in the slot. Then you try like hell to get through before the metal slats snap out and damage your enthusiasm. Down the escalators you go. They are all as old as Lenin's grandmother but are somehow still working, unlike our super-modern ones at Victoria Station. On to the platform – about the size of an aircraft hangar with trains running practically non-stop on either side – you slouch. Into the train you leap. It is invariably packed whatever the time of day. Quick, here's the station already. Dash for the escalator. This one is as old as Lenin's grandmother's grandmother, but still it's working. Through the barriers and out of the exit. Phew, made it. But some poor guys down the line at Tulskaya Station, about three miles south of the Kremlin, didn't; neither did some guys outside Kolkhoznaya Station on the inner ring road, where one evening there was a real Wild West, or rather Wild East, shoot-out. Two men came hurtling out of the station. One man shot the other. A policeman standing nearby fired, and the gunman shot him as well. And then, of course, there was the American guy who put together the Radisson–Slavjanskaya Hotel deal, Paul Tatum. He made it to Kievskaya Station. A hail of bullets from a sub-machine-gun and it was all over.

If you don't think the Metro is dangerous enough, take the ordinary train. Not only are passengers regularly beaten up and robbed, but whole trains are hijacked – especially if they're carrying precious raw materials or, more important even than that, cigarettes. Three times the top-secret, heavily guarded train delivering cigarettes between Moscow and Kazakhstan has been held up and virtually stripped clean by armed robbers. A Finnish businessman told me that whenever he went anywhere by train in Russia he always carried a piece of rope with him. My mind boggled. I know Russian train journeys always take a long time, even if you're only going to the next station, but I didn't realise they took so long that you had to go to such lengths to make your own amusement.

'To hang yourself before they get you?' I wondered.

'No,' he said. 'To tie together the doors of your compartment so nobody else can get in.'

Believe me, everyone you meet has a story to tell about being robbed or beaten up or mugged or having seen somebody else being robbed or beaten up or mugged. Not once, or even twice; often three, four, five times. It's like going to a dinner party back home and hearing people talk about the number of times their houses have been broken into.

You are not much safer indoors. You open the door of your flat, a bomb explodes, you bleed to death in the doorway. One Irish banker told me no sooner had he moved into his new apartment and got his feet under his word-processor than there was a knock at the door. Outside was a little old lady. She said she had just moved out and asked if she could come in to fetch some long-lost family heirloom she'd left behind. Before you could say, 'There's one born every…', wham, he was face down on the floor, hands tied behind his back, and, crash, they were taking the place apart.

'Did you call the police?' I asked.

'No point. He was off duty that night,' he shrugged.

Even if you decide you've had enough, you can't take any more, you want to sell up and move out, you're still not safe. Before you move out people will come round claiming they're interested in buying or renting your room, flat, house or *dacha* in the country. Once inside the door, before you can say, 'subject to surveyor's report', they'll be drawing a gun on you and ransacking the place. Even President Yeltsin's doctor's in-laws were beaten and stabbed to death in their apartment in the not particularly dangerous Rublyovskoye Chaussee. Not particularly, that is, until they were killed. Now it is as dangerous as everywhere else, and everybody in the area is as scared as everybody else in Moscow. It's not even safe to go to the funerals of people who have been killed: a bomb is as likely to go off there as outside a Metro station.

In short, visiting Moscow is unlike visiting any other city in the world. Instead of pointing out the sights, the locals point out where people have been gunned down, killed, shot accidentally; where people have been beaten up, a friend of a friend attacked, where bodies were found in litter bins, which litter bins were destroyed ...

One day I was having an expensive Russian expense-account lunch – cabbage pie and a glass of *kvas*, lukewarm non-alcoholic beer made from fermented bread – in the Russkoye Bistro, the Russian equivalent of McDonald's, in Tverskya Street, near the huge 6,000-room Russia Hotel, when a young Russian guy leaned across and asked me what was the most important day in the Russian calendar.

'Er, er, er,' I said tactfully.

It turned out to be Tuesday 20 December 1996. It was the first day that year, he said that nobody had been murdered.

At the same time, I must say, in all fairness, that when they're not mounting full-scale, armed, vicious attacks on little old ladies selling fruit and vegetables at some open-air market in Istra, about 40 miles west of Moscow, the authorities are taking dramatic decisive steps to combat the situation. They've started distributing leaflets to foreign businessmen telling them to fix steel doors to their apartments, not to go to work the same way every day and to stay off the streets at night. Which is fantastic, because now there are no problems getting tickets for the Bolshoi. Not like the old days, when you virtually had to put your name down for a ticket before you were shipped off to Siberia for twenty years and hope to good-ness your name had got to the top of the list by the time you got back. There are safety instructions everywhere – in fact, there are probably as many safety instructions in Moscow today as there were once political slogans.

In banks, there are more safety notices than they have roubles in the safe. 'Carry your purse or wallet as close to your body as possible, preferably in an inside pocket that closes with a zipper. If you keep your purse in a handbag or shoulder bag, please make sure it is well down inside the bag.'

'Always keep your cheques in a separate place from your cheque card. Check regularly to make sure your cheques and card are still there.'

'If possible do not use cash to pay for items. Keep a note of the numbers of the cheques you have written and keep receipts from purchases made by credit card.'

In restaurants, there are more signs than there are items on the menu. 'Take your wallet, camera and other valuables with you to the table.' You mean I've got to take that bottle of Cheval Blanc 1947 to the table? Hell, they'll all want a glass. 'Avoid dense crowds.' You mean I've got to check their IQs as well? 'If you are pushed in a crowd, turn round immediately and look to see who pushed you.' If he's smaller than you, poke him in the eye. If not, empty your wallet there and then. Believe me, it's the safest thing to do, unless, of course, you like being beaten up.

In car-hire offices, you can hardly see the signs for all the bars and grilles all over the place. 'Always lock your car. Never leave the key in the car. Make sure that the sunroof and all the windows are closed. Turn the lights off.' What else do you want me to do? Take the engine with me? 'Do not leave valuables in your car. Remember, even a locked door at a supervised garage is not a guarantee that no one will break into your car.' So what's the point in me spending half the day and a bucketful of roubles trying to find a supervised garage?

In hotels, they're even worse. There's a plague of the things. 'Do not take all your money with you when you go for a walk.' I never do. If I did, I couldn't walk. 'Never leave your luggage unattended on the pavement in front of the hotel or in the hotel lobby – neither when you arrive nor when you depart.'

Even the bathroom of the hotel was so full of warnings that I could hardly get in there to check I still had a bit of enamel left on my teeth after drinking a string of cheap-flavoured vodkas at an open-air bar outside the huge Dynamo sports stadium. 'Please watch your step when exiting bath.' Why? Are they lying in wait behind the pile of dirty washing to jump out and grab my valuables? And then the sign that solved, once and for all, all my problems in Moscow: 'A rubber bath mat has been provided for your safety.' Wow. Who would have guessed, in these days of science and technology, that a simple rubber bath mat would be the answer to all my safety problems. Other people might have their Kalashnikovs and their Berettas and their .45s, but now I could walk the mean streets of the city at any time of the day or night without fear or favour. I had my rubber bath mat with me.

If you don't fancy the idea of carrying your rubber mat with you wherever you go, you have three alternatives: pray, get a gun or form your own private army. As for the rights and wrongs of praying, getting a gun or forming your own private army, forget it. Ethics, I remember an old East End debt-collector telling me years ago, 'is somewhere east of London'. Praying, though, is obviously something the Muscovites believe in. Take the Kremlin, for example. It's full of churches. In fact, I reckon there are more churches in the Kremlin than there are in the Vatican. If you're an icon addict like me, the Church of the Assumption is a dream. It also graphically pins down the turning point in Russian history. Right in the front are the first two seats ever provided in a Russian church – for the Tsar and Tsarina, to save them having to stand throughout the hours-long service.

Next door, on Red Square, is St Basil's which, with all its multicolored onion-shaped cupolas, looks like a Disney-world reject. The domes are onion-shaped because the wife of good old Ivan the Terrible, who built it, was a Muslim. Even so, she acted and behaved very much like a Christian wife: she did nothing but moan, moan, moan all the time about how she missed seeing her mother and the rest of her family and friends back home. So, for the sake of some peace and quiet, even a guy like Ivan the Terrible had to make a gesture. He decided to build her a glorious mosque. But, because he knew women judge everything by its appearance, outside it looks like a mosque but inside it's a Christian church. So pleased and grateful was he to the architect for getting his wife off his back and, at the same time, doing such a fantastic job, that he showed his appreciation in the only way he knew. He blinded him. Whenever I go there I can't help but wonder what the place would be like if his wife had been English. Probably all bowler hats and Laura Ashley and hundreds of cats.

As it is, inside it's a complete jumble. Underneath every dome is a separate altar, each with its own sanctuary. The problem is they are all so so tiny. Not one, I reckon, is bigger than a billiard table. On top of that, everything is crumbling and falling to pieces. What's more, to get from one altar to the next you have to climb one tiny staircase after another, squeeze along tiny corridors then virtually abseil back to earth again. A church for old people and families it is not. More like a church for mountaineers and rock-climbers.

Tucked away in odd corners all over Moscow are still more churches. And as if there were not enough of them already, they're even racing to rebuild their Cathedral of Christ the Saviour, a symbol of pre-revolutionary Russia. It was originally financed by the Romanovs, only to be blown up by Stalin in 1931 to make way for some enormous Palace of the Soviets which was going to be higher than the Empire State Building and boast a statue of Lenin on top bigger than the Statue of Liberty. It was not to be: the ground was too soft, and couldn't take the weight, so instead the site lay virtually untouched until Khruschev decided to build some kind of weird-looking swimming pool on it, connected to some kind of spring. Today, just two years after work began, the cathedral is nearing completion, its deep gold dome already glittering in the sunshine. The amazing thing is not only that it is being built entirely from private funds – not one kopek has come from the public purse – but that it is being built so quickly. Naturally, I thought this was living proof that the Russians were turning back to God, but one of the workmen told me it was because they were being fed with all the vodka they wanted provided they finished on time.

If, instead of prayer, you prefer to put your trust in firearms, getting a gun is easy. An ordinary pistol, say a gas pellet-firing Makarov, you can buy as easily as a bottle of vodka, if not more easily, for around US$100, from shops all over Moscow. For something a little more sophisticated, or for your automatic, sub-machine-gun and tank requirements, all you have to do is take a trip to Tula, the paratroopers' garrison town just outside Moscow which the gravel-voiced next president of Russia, General Lebed, used to represent in Parliament, and where most light Russian armaments are manufactured. Say that I sent you. For intercontinental ballistic missiles, suitcase size, complete with either atomic, hydrogen or nuclear warheads, try the Commander out at Cherepovets. Even taking the Russians' own figures at face value, of the 132 ICBMs that were manufactured, eighty-four have gone walkabout, so he should have no problem finding the odd one for you. Just tell him you want them to scare away the crows, he'll understand.

As for your final option, forming your own private army, it's not as impossible as it sounds providing you've got some good contacts with the old 9th (Personal Security) Department of the KGB. Lots of people have done it. Take the Association of Bankers. They have a hectic programme, not organising whist drives and charity golf matches and ladies' nights, but trying to arrange not to be killed. Every year 100, 200, 300 maybe 1,000 businessmen are murdered in Moscow. Traders, shopkeepers, bankers – especially bankers. It's got so bad, I was told, that Moscow is the only city in the world where bankers don't complain if there are any holes in agreements they are asked to sign in case they end up having a few holes drilled into their backs instead. In the last three years, according to one banker, forty-seven members of the association had been shot and killed, most of them arriving home from work. One evening I was driving down

Novokuznetsky Street, a once grand street full of old houses and even older families, when three cars, a Volvo, a big Mercedes 600 with smoked glass and another Volvo, hurtled past, then suddenly swung across the middle of the road and slammed on their brakes. Out of the two Volvos jumped four men apiece, dressed in black and waving guns and mobile phones all over the place. They virtually formed a guard of honour between the Mercedes and one of the houses. Except they were facing out, not in, and swinging their guns around. The door of the Mercedes opened and out stumbled an elderly, heavy, white-haired old man who hobbled like mad to the door of the house.

'Must be a banker,' my driver grunted. 'They always travel like that.'

If you don't want to go to the trouble of setting up your own private army, you could always hire somebody else's. Official estimate of the Russians themselves is that there are over 2,000 to choose from, so you can guess what the real figure must be. It is obviously a good thing for the economy because, for all the mayhem and violence, it shows that they have at least got things moving and are beginning to develop a service sector. One security company advertising 'armed guards and bodyguards, engineering security improvements and a wide range of information services' told me that for £30 an hour I could hire a machine-gun-toting female bodyguard who would be prepared to act as a personal secretary or chauffeur, or both, and, if necessary, would lay down her life for me. I thought that was a bargain. Most people I know wouldn't cross the road to talk to me for less that £3,000. She could also, the salesman went on, undertake 'special assignments'.

One of the side-effects of all this violence, of course, is that in Moscow the last thing anybody who's got a job worries about is working hard and being loyal and devoted and scrambling their way slowly up the corporate ladder. All they do is go out and hire a hitman to eliminate the competition. They tell him what they want done, he does it and they pay him. If he's a friend, it's probably just a matter of a bottle of vodka. If he's a professional, maybe a couple or three thousand dollars. And hey presto, they're the new managing director. So much easier, don't you think, than dragging yourself through Henley Management Centre or, God help us, some American business school.

OK, so now you've got your protection, but you've still got to go outside into the real-life Russia. But don't worry, you'll be quite safe, providing you follow some basic rules steppe by steppe.

First, if you're a businessman moving in business circles, you must look inconspicuous. There's no alternative, I'm afraid, you're just going to have to get a very big, very fast bullet-proof Mercedes 600 as well as a scruffy, dirty, clapped-out old Volvo. The Mercedes is for your body-guards, the Volvo is for you. Well, you want to survive, don't you? In the Mercedes, if you really want to merge with the crowd, you also put a young man in a white suit and a blonde. Forget all that PC nonsense: any business-man worthy of his expense account must have a blonde. It's the Russian way of getting lost in a crowd.

Second, you must know all the tricks. Bribery and corruption I know about – you can't have anything to do with Africa and not be an expert at it. But Russia is unbelievable. It's not that it's everywhere, or that everybody is up to it, it's just that they have a genius for it – which, I suppose, is not surprising, seeing that they produced such a classic as Gogol's *Dead Souls*. Whatever you do, you mustn't upset the system. So here, for your eyes only, is Biddlecombe's complete guide to Russian bribery and corruption – in other words, who to bribe and with how much.

Policeman, traffic, for the avoiding of aggro: US$10 a time, say ten times a week. Total: US$100.

Police officer, for the avoiding of being arrested on some trumped-up charge and dragged down the police station for a couple of days: US$500, say once a week. Total: US$500.

Junior civil servant, for getting rubber stamps on bits of paper: US$1,000, say two to three times a week. Total: US$2,000.

Senior civil servants, customs officials, police inspectors: anything from a plain brown envelope and a language course in Oxford for his kids to a couple of sleek Mercedes.

Export licences: senior civil servant rates multiplied by two, maybe more. Especially if you use Export Dodge 27: instead of filling in the forms and specifying exactly the rare strategic metal you're exporting, you make up technical-sounding Mickey Mouse names like metallian-iallicum and carborunalidium, and you'll get the licence just the same.

Customs officer, for looking the other way and leaving his rubber stamp on the desk: $25 a month. Along the border with the Baltic republics: US$20, or maybe even less.

Then there are everyday matters, like dealing with the ordinary police. They stop you in the street, and come up to you waving their truncheons. They shout, they scream, they damn you to Hell and beyond. Finally you agree a price – 200, 250, 300 or whatever. You count it out slowly into his hand... 298 ... 299 ... 300. They practically give you a big slobbering kiss. Three hundred roubles? No, 300 cigarettes. Don't you know anything about Marxist economic determinism?

Or the right way to park. In Prague you park by taking a parking ticket off another car and putting it on yours.

That way you know you won't get your own ticket. In
Moscow you park the KGB way, with the windscreen-
wipers pointing up at the sky. You can laugh, but in the
old days this was the KGB's way of telling the local police
they were in the area and to lay off handing out the fines.
All I can say is that it works. I do it the whole time in
Moscow. I park in all the wrong places at all the wrong
times of the day and night. Even when I park in a no-
parking area the wrong way round in a one-way street
down near the sprawling Gorbanovski market just south
of the Moscow river (where, incidentally, for around
30,000 roubles or £3 you can always get videos of films
weeks before they open in the UK), nobody stops me or
even attempts to approach me. Try it yourself and see.
Should you get caught, just pretend you're an old KGB
officer. It's easy, all you do is put on a haughty upper-class
English accent and patronise the policeman like mad. For
some reason or other, all the top KGB guys I've come
across speak with perfect Cambridge accents and keep
saying 'actually'. If you ask a scruffy old taxi-driver how
long it takes to get to Red Square and he turns round and
says, 'Well, taking everything into account, it should take
about twenty minutes, actually,' you've got him.

Once I was wandering around some back street near
Kiev Station looking for some office or other and I hit the
jackpot with a real live KGB colonel. Ex, of course. I asked
this shabby-looking guy by the side of the road selling
paintings of St Basil's Cathedral if I was heading in the
right direction. He looked me straight in the eye and
replied in a booming common-room voice, 'Indubitably.'

Third, know thine enemy. I don't mean the in-laws or
traffic wardens or the police, or any one of the dozen-odd
secret-service organisations that have replaced the KGB. I
mean the guys with the real power: the – don't say I told you
– Mafyia. They're all over the place. They look like weight-

lifters who've hit the bottle and gone to seed. They've all got black leather jackets and a collar and tie and spend all day leaning casually against their Mercedes 600s or one of those huge American stretch limos eating ice-cream. Some say the Russian Mafyia was born in the concentration camps. No way. It came about as a direct result of eating too much Italian ice-cream. Go anywhere in Russia today, and you'll see nothing but old women in black, sitting in dusty courtyards looking after millions of babies, and fellas eating ice-cream. So how do they pay for the ice-cream?

First of all there are the scams. You want to park your car in your own car park. No problem. It'll be safe all day – providing you pay the unofficial car-park attendant US$10 for the privilege. What do you mean? Why should you pay some unofficial car-park attendant US$10 a day for parking in your very own personal car park? OK, don't. But don't blame me if you come back this evening and find all the windows mysteriously smashed, the paintwork smothered in scratches and three of the tyres missing.

You want the car of your dreams tomorrow morning. If you dream sensible dreams, no problem. Dream crazy, way-out dreams like owning a big BMW and you could be forced to wait as long as, say, two weeks or maybe even three. The reason it takes so long is that, depending on the make, the car will have to be lifted in either Germany or France or the Netherlands. It then has to be assembled in a convoy with others and driven all the way to Moscow.

'Why convoys?' I wondered.

'To ensure they don't get stolen. There are lots of gangsters on the way who will do anything to steal a car.'

Of course. Fancy not thinking of that in the first place. So how much does it cost?

'About US$3,000,' one dealer told me.

'What do you get?'

'A Nissan Sunny.'

'Gee,' I said. 'That's cheap. I'd have thought cars in Moscow would—'

'For the bribes,' he explained.

Somebody, after all, had to lift the car. The convoys have to be organised. Drivers have to be paid, and customs officials sweetened. Then there's the insurance, the protection, the guys with the guns. Every convoy has to have its outriders to ensure it gets through. And if you don't buy a car this way, there's virtually no other way of getting one. Unless you know somebody big, or you know somebody medium-sized who knows somebody big. Even then, the odds are against you.

But what happens, perish the thought, if you go through all this, hand over your money and your car doesn't arrive? What do you do? Complain? Write a letter? Go to the police? There's nothing you can do. You just have to start all over again, and pray that the person you have paid to steal your car, drive it illegally into the country and to bribe half a dozen officials in the process will turn up with it. Not, I would have thought, that this is the kind of prayer that gets answered. But you never know, Russia is not like the rest of the world.

Then there's what's known as roof money. Go into a shop, a bar, a restaurant or even a snack bar. One day the food is green, the bread is curling up in front of you, the service is non-existent and the prices horrendous. The next day the food is fresh, service is, well, adequate, and prices are sensible. Nine times out of ten it's because they've started paying their roof money. As a result supplies are somehow miraculously delivered on time. Staff are no longer frightened to come to work. Breakages and damages are suddenly a thing of the past.

A fat old babushka who had a stall near the airport Metro station told me that things are more sophisticated now than when she first started in business. In the old days the men used to come round, usually on a Friday evening, and demand their roof money, 'or else'. Today they are not only much more polite, they even give her an insurance certificate as a form of receipt for her contributions. How much did she pay? She wouldn't tell me. But the owner of a back-street garage confided that his roof money cost him around 0.25 to 0.30 per cent of his turnover. On a turnover of US$100,000 a month, that worked out at US$250 to 300, which was much, much lower than I expected, bearing in mind he was using US$15,000 a month to pay off a bank loan at – are you ready? – 156 per cent interest. Either way he could live with it, which, I suppose, is why the rate is what it is. After all, the Mafyia presumably make their calculations and go for a figure that will yield the maximum for the minimum effort.

I know it's wrong. But you could argue that it is thanks to the Mafyia and the whole grubby system of backhanders that Russia is still at peace and slowly, slowly, slowly improving its standard of living. Because without them, let's be honest, everybody would be struggling to survive on what they were officially paid – or officially not paid. People would not be able to get whatever it was they want – a bottle of vodka, a Mars bar, a couple of gallons of CFCs, a stack of bricks, gas, water, electricity. Yes, even gas, water and electricity.

I met an American oil wheeler-dealer who told me he had bought a *dacha* in Zhukovka on the Rublovo-Uspeyenskoye road, once the street of 100 secret state-owned *dachas* for old party bosses. It was somewhere, he thought, he could retreat to at weekends and get away from the constant everyday struggle for absolutely everything in Moscow. The problem was, when he moved in, nothing was what it seemed. The electricity was illegally connected to the local network. His gas supply came courtesy of his next-door neighbour, who knew nothing about it. The previous owner had just tapped into the neighbour's supply pipe. Water came in much the same way, from somebody else's pipe he found at the bottom of the garden. So was he going to come clean and own up? Was he, hell. If he did, the neighbours might make him pay for all the electricity, gas and water consumed by the previous owner. If he refused, they would all cut him off and he would never, ever be able to obtain his own direct supplies. On top of that, there would inevitably be problems with the electricity, gas and water authorities, the local authority, the taxman and probably the police as well. It was not worth the bother. 'This is Russia,' he said.

With such glorious free enterprise going on all over the place, you would think doing business, real, proper, boring business, would be simple. Nothing could be further from the truth. The Russian way of doing business is not only totally different from our way of doing business, it is totally beyond the scope of any economic textbook ever written as well. 'Doing business with the Russians,' a Frenchman told me once, 'calls for a touch of le Jamesbonderie.' Actually, it calls for one hell of a lot of Jamesbonderie. There's no way you can even consider doing any business in Russia unless you're prepared to do it their way. Or, shrinking violet that you are, get somebody else to carry the suitcase for you.

Take simple things like telephone directories. There are no telephone directories. If you want to telephone somebody, you have to drive across town, ask him for his number, drive back to your place and then call him. Of course, by the time you've done all that, either you've forgotten why you wanted to ring him in the first place or your telephone has been stolen, the wiring ripped out and the copper inside melted down and sold.

Then there are meetings. When you arrange to see somebody you don't merely check when he's going to be in his office or factory, you check when his office or factory is going to be open. Many, maybe most of them, close down for weeks or months at a time. Because there's no work, because there's no money to pay for anything, because nobody has got the courage to do anything about it. One factory I visited had shut down from the middle of December to the middle of February, and again from mid-March to mid-April. And when I say shut down, I mean shut down overnight. There, still on the production line gathering dust, was a string of half-built yellow tractors. Just imagine the problems you're going to have if you get one of these tractors which have been standing around half made for weeks on end.

So what happens when people want to come and see you? No problem, you say, show them in. The difficulty in Moscow is that if door-to-door salesmen turn up at your office and you don't buy whatever it is they're selling, they take off your office door and smash everything inside to pieces. One metal trader told me about a group of seven eager young men who arrived in his office one day. They were selling champagne. He said, 'Thank you, but no thank you. We don't need any—' They immediately set upon him, beat him up, beat up everybody else in the office and wrecked the place – desks, chairs, computers, fax machines, the works. Even a picture of Lenin on the wall and an enormous plaster bust of the great man he kept on his desk in the belief that it would keep him out of trouble.

Another favourite dodge, I learned, is the illegal removal firm which turns up unannounced and removes all the furniture from your home or your office. One international trading company not only had all their furniture taken away but all their computers and files as well. In the middle of the day.

And what about actually running a company? Trouble getting raw materials? And at the right price? No problem. Somebody always knows somebody who knows somebody who can lift anything you want. The biggest single hoist I heard of was 100 lorryloads of wine. At the same time, in a single hit. You want to cut production costs? Somebody knows somebody in the military. You can have oil, petrol, rocket fuel, even radioactive isotopes. Tomorrow evening or the evening after, whichever is more convenient. Competition causing you problems? Don't worry. It can be arranged for a bunch of guys in black leather jackets to walk into your competitor's office and politely tell him to stop selling whatever he's selling and never to go near your customers again. If he's lucky, he'll do as he's told. If he's unlucky they will break down his door at three in the morning.

Then there's all the administration. Like insurance. Take something simple: say your car has been stolen. In any other country you would ring up the insurance company, get the forms, fill them in and forget all about it. In Russia you have to go to the police to get a statement to send to your insurance company, which, of course, costs you. The insurance company then charges you a fee for the costs of handling your claim because you've been stupid enough to let somebody steal your car. For two, three, four months nothing happens. In desperation you then have to go down to the insurance company to look after the clerk handling your claim, otherwise there's no chance you'll ever get your money. Alternatively, you could buy a Volvo. Apparently, nobody bothers to steal a Volvo in Moscow, at least, not an old Volvo. Everybody's after the flashy cars. Perhaps its a worldwide phenomenon: I've got a broken-down, battered old Volvo at home, and I promise you it's the only car that hasn't been broken into at my local railway station.

Now, heaven help us, we come to the banks. Banks, let me tell you, are impossible, but you can't do without them and, boy, do they know it. It can take eight weeks to transfer money from one account in one branch to another account in the same branch. To transfer it to another account of another branch of another bank in another city can take for ever. I'm told that the cheque Lenin made out for that fancy velvet-collared overcoat you see him wearing in all the pictures still hasn't been cleared, and it only had to travel from the Kremlin to the 50-rouble tailor across the street. With inflation running at 30 per cent and more, and that's a day, you can imagine how out of pocket you are by the time you are paid. As for letters of credit… It's a nice sunny day, but they say there's a little rain on the way.

If you manage to endure all this without being reduced to a quivering wreck, there is still no guarantee that your business will survive. Again and again you come across examples of management fraud or looting, as the Russians call it, on a grand, all-embracing, *War and Peace* scale. One big oil company, I heard, in Nizhiny Novgorod – once the closed city of Gorky, it was stuffed full of military hi-tech factories – shipped oil to a major customer for a whole year without sending so much as a single invoice. When it went bust and the investigators moved in, they discovered that the company had substantial assets, enormous earning potential but no money in the bank. And no managing director. He was already sunning himself in Florida.

The big problem, of course, is that the Russians just don't understand even the basic rules of doing business. They have no idea of planning, forecasting, product-development, production, marketing, inflation, cost-control, treasury-management or the most expensive restaurants to go to for lunch. Take some simple business terms. To your ordinary, average Russian businessman they have a completely different meaning than they do to us.

Free economy: you are free to go on producing shoddy goods nobody wants.

Maximum production: when the factory doesn't close for nine months of the year.

Full employment: when 80 per cent of the working population actually works sometimes as much as 50 per cent of the time in the hope, admittedly the faintest hope, that they might get paid as soon as three months later.

Cashflow: what you've got flowing into some bank in Cyprus.

Contracts: the agreed basis of negotiations.

Lease: a lease is only a lease until your landlord finds someone willing to pay a higher rent. Failing that, you'll find that your office mysteriously catches fire. That is bad enough; what is worse is the fire brigade. Unless you get there in time and make all the necessary arrangements, they'll use so much water to put out the blaze that you'll be wishing the whole place had burned down after all.

Fair competition: eliminating your rivals - literally. I know this is what many businessmen would like to do, but in Russia they don't just wish it, they do it.

Loss-making enterprises: companies where the big guys all have big cars, houses in the country - somebody else's country - bank accounts around the world, all the champagne they can drink and a list of complaints about foreign firms being unwilling to invest in them and support them and help them to expand and develop.

Inflation: the creation of employment for government banknote printers by letting them churn out unlimited quantities of roubles to give to companies which complain that they haven't got any money.

As for profits, profits are unprocessed raw materials,

uncompleted projects, start-up capital and the wholly unreasonable thing that foreigners keep on and on and on about wanting before they hand over vast sums of money to be turned immediately into cashflow. Even when Gazprom, the huge Russian oil and gas conglomerate which alone is responsible for 23 per cent of the world's natural gas production, came up with a prospectus to try to raise funds in the West, it was impossible to work out whether they actually made a profit, at least according to standard, boring, run-of-the-mill, 100 per cent reliable Western accountancy standards. What was more, they didn't even bother to throw in a cashflow statement, so anyone who was going to jump in was doing so with one hell of a pinch of Siberian salt. Investing in Russian telecommunications is even riskier. One Western bank which advised people to buy nonetheless concluded with the cheerful little warning: 'An investment in Russian companies is speculative and involves significant risk. Investors must be able to sustain a loss of the entire amount that they invest.'

Now, if you think your nerves can stand it, let me tell you about the Russian stock exchange, which one Russian economist once described as 'a synthesis of the positive aspects of neoclassical theory based on the positive aspects of economic liberalisation and Keynesian ideas and the ideas first proposed by Marx and developed by practitioners in Russia which make it possible for the state to play a positive role in managing the economy'.

There are no share certificates. There is no way of finding out the price of a particular share, apart from ringing up any one of the handful of local brokers and asking how much they would sell it for. There is no way of finding out who owns any shares, because although every company is supposed to have a share register, none of them bother. There is no organisation or body controlling the activities of the exchange. There is no such thing as rules or regulations or even laws controlling the activities of the stock exchange.

In other words, you can buy an old state-owned company, and the government can take the money and stash it away wherever, but it still doesn't mean you've bought the firm. In court case after court case after court case, anti-privatisation campaigners have been able to prove again and again and again that such deals were in fact against the law, because at the time of the sale the new owner did not have all the necessary government approvals. The government then grabs the company back and, this will make you laugh, promises to give you back your money. When GUM, or rather GLUM, was privatised, GUM Trading House, the company issuing the shares, for some reason or another, included the building in which it operated in its list of assets. However, the building didn't belong to them. As a listed, protected, architectural monument, it was owned by the state and managed by the Department of Ancient Monuments. This didn't seem to worry the original shareholders, who saw the value of their holding shoot up sixteen times when it came on to the market.

Government bonds are an even bigger lottery. Trying to discover if you've got a genuine one or not is like trying to establish whether you're holding a genuine bunch of roubles. Except that, with a single bond worth anything from US$250,000 up to a million and maybe more, we're talking big money. It's the same story with your 100 per cent genuine Russian bonds. For example, Russia already has a stack of bonds outstanding in France. Contrary to all the rules and regulations you can think of, they just decided to stop paying interest on them, never mind redeeming them. When they tried to join the Council of Europe, they said they would pay up. They didn't. When they signed the Franco–Russian Treaty, they said they would pay up. They didn't. The bonds are still outstanding.

Now for the real bundle of laughs: tax. Tax anywhere in Russia is a nightmare. In Moscow it's the nightmare of nightmares. First, there's a tax on everything, on the payroll, on property, on investment, on value added, on sales, on profits – if there are any. There is even a tax on the number of times you use the word 'Russia'. And these are just the national taxes. On top of them come all the local taxes as well: on advertising, on printing, even on trees. In some parts of the country, just because some trees are there, they charge you an environment tax. Chop them down and they'll charge you a chopping-down tax as well. There are even various local taxes on cats and dogs – at least, that's the theory.

At the end of the day, however, tax depends on the taxman. A Russian taxman is in a class of his own. Not for him the bowler hat, the pin-striped, slightly shiny suit and all that 'Your obedient servant' nonsense. Instead it's fatigues, flak jackets, balaclava helmets and a bunch of 6-foot six-gun-toting gorillas. When he comes knocking on your office door and throws it open, you know he's there, because everything goes dark. How much you pay, what you pay it on and when – not to mention the small voluntary contribution to some charity based at the local branch of the Credit Suisse in Zürich – is then up to you and him, and whether you want the whole of your office emptied out the window or not. You cannot complain to the tax commissioners about the way he behaves, because Russian taxmen don't work for the state, they work for themselves. In a desperate effort to raise some kind of tax revenue, the government has been forced to go back to what they call *kormlenie,* the mediaeval system which virtually turns your friendly local taxman into an unfriendly local bounty-hunter. He can do what the hell he likes so long as he sends 50 per cent of the take back to Moscow.

One legitimate, straight-up-and-down, 100 per cent honest businessman – an Englishman, of course – told me that one day one of this new breed of taxmen strolled into his office, asked to see his books, flicked through them and promptly fined him US$30 million for keeping the company cash in foreign banks instead of Russian ones. Another, a Canadian, recalled how a bunch of taxmen came to his office and actually took money out of the safe as payment of their taxes. It was only when he asked them to sign some kind of receipt for the cash that he discovered none of them could read or write.

You think I'm exaggerating? Pop into Arrears, the special shop set up in the old Metallurgical Institute by these wheeler-dealer self-employed taxmen, and see for yourself all the goods they've seized from companies unable or unwilling for whatever reason to pay their taxes. Office chairs, telephones, computers, shirts, shoes, jeans. One day, I was told, there was even an old bus for sale – one owner, good condition, no brakes, US$20,000.

'People always ask me if they should do business in Russia,' an elegant old-school Swedish businessman once told me. 'I always say to them, "Pay me US$20,000 and I'll tell you." They pay me US$20,000 and I say to them, "No. You've already lost US$20,000 in Russia, don't lose anymore."' But if you're determined to go ahead, there are only two ways to try to ensure that at least you get some sleep at night. Charge cash, in advance, for absolutely everything. Or set up a joint venture with a reputable Russian company. The only snag is that there don't seem to be any reputable Russian companies, and even if you find one, you're going to be very lucky.

An American I met told me he had set up a joint

venture with a reputable Russian company, splitting everything 50–50. All was going well, all the accounts were coming through on time and nothing could have been better. Until the time came to share out the profits. There was nothing in the bank. One of the accountants had skipped, taking everything with him. 'Go to the Bahamas,' he advised me. 'Invest in pork-belly futures. It'll be a whole lot safer. What's more, their Piña Coladas are better.'

So you can see how difficult it is, amid the trials of doing business in Moscow, to snatch a couple of quick seconds to see the sights between meetings and sampling vodka and cav... I mean assessing and testing various engineering prototypes. Museums I had already seen – I'd been to no end of Russian factories. As for art galleries, I wanted to go to the Tretyakov Gallery, which contains the world's biggest collection of Russian icons, but I couldn't make it. I ended up doing the next best thing: travelling by Metro. If you are brave enough to run the gauntlet of bombs and gunmen, their Circle Line, believe me, is a transport of delight. It's the Victoria and Albert, the Imperial War Museum, the British Museum, the National Portrait Gallery and the Tate all rolled into one.

Start at Belorusskaya Station with its two huge bronzes and go right. Nobody goes left any more – well, apart from the crazy guy in Belorussia. Novoslobodskaya is the place for stained-glass windows. Fantastic. Prospekt Mira for gilt and porcelain, and Komsomolskaya has more mosaics than half a dozen cathedrals. Kurskaya is not so hot, but it's still a million times better than Tooting Broadway on the Northern Line. Taganskaya has a series of huge, white, blue and gold triangles running the length of the station like a row of bishops' mitres left hanging up on the wall while they nip outside for a quick drink.

Paveletskaya, I'm afraid, looks like one big Russian

gents' toilet – or rather, what Russian gents' toilets would look like if they ever got round to building any. Octyabskaya is the opposite, nothing but dark, heavy tiles and funny-shaped bronze torches. A bit like the old District Line. Park Kultury is what you would expect: vast plaques of guys playing chess, peasants dancing in the sunshine, musicians playing away to their hearts' content. All terribly bucolic.

Kievskaya is your Soviet kitsch. One huge mosaic after another, taken direct from Every Revolutionary's Handbook: Lenin in his overcoat, Trotsky in his beard and Stalin in power. Great strapping country girls leaping up to hulking great soldiers and offering them a traditional Russian welcome home. Hulking great soldiers trying to convince young, innocent kids that no, they're not their father. And my favourite, the 'spot the guy who sent 60 million innocent people to their death trying to hide among this crowd of innocent peasants' plaque. In case you can't find him, I'll give you a clue. He's the one from whom the white dove is trying to escape as quickly as possible. The Krasnopresnenskaya is the story of the events leading up to the revolution told in massive panels. Lenin, I swear, is the kid throwing the brick in panel number 8. But I could be wrong – he's not wearing an overcoat.

If you see all the stations you deserve a treat. Before I left for Moscow my wife said to me, 'Whatever you do, don't drink seriously.' So I just had to go to the bar in the Metropol, where, with all the gold and marble and deep brown leather armchairs, the last thing you do is drink seriously, especially if you hit the vodkas.

'I'll have a large Kremlyovskaya.'

'Yes, sir. Straight away, sir. With ice, sir?'

'No, I'll take it chilled.'

'Yes, sir.'

Three large Kremlyovskayas, two small Yuri Dolgorukys and a couple of Kubanskaya chasers later, the waiter asks: 'Excuse me, sir. Would sir like me to call you an ambulance, sir?'

'Nufflinksyatavellysmuchaeisalrightski. Seriouslyski.'

Honestly, it's the only way to forget the problems of doing business in Russia.

Yet in spite of everything, the lying and the cheating, the bribery and the corruption, and all the gangs and all the killings, the new Russia, I'm convinced, is a huge success. Why? Because the fat old lady selling fish in the open-air market at the back of the Little Maidens' Convent is now selling no fewer than seven different types of fish. Next to her, a tiny, fragile old lady with a moustache and about six layers of coats is now offering all kinds of fresh vegetables: potatoes, cabbages, onions, carrots and something that looks like turnips. Alongside her an old man in a paper-thin fur hat is selling meat and sausages. Opposite him an eager young man is selling piles of shoes from Poland. Alongside him, a middle-aged man with broken glasses is selling cheap shirts from China.

Five years ago, under the Communists, this would have been impossible. That's why for me, Russia today is reaching for the Tsars. If you don't agree with me there's this guy I know who'll be more than happy to come round and persuade you to change your mind. And it doesn't matter whether you've got the rubber bath mat from the hotel with you or not. It won't provide for your safety, believe me.

BAKU

Tell me what is going to be one of the richest cities in the world in say twenty or thirty years' time. London? No way. Frankfurt? Perhaps. Shanghai? Maybe. Baku, the capital of Azerbaijan? Almost certainly. Just as it was 100 years ago, when it was the playground of the Nobels and the Rothschilds and scores of other Greek, Jewish and Russian wheeler-dealers and entrepreneurs who turned it into the world's first oil-boom town.

Once the hub of the Ottoman Empire and an important staging post on the Silk Road, Baku was renowned at the time for its hotels and casinos as well as for its mosques and bath houses. It was the rich and fashionable and romantic and mysterious centre of the Caucasus. It was even said to have more beautiful buildings and palaces than Paris. At the turn of the century it was supplying half the world's oil. The Nobel family, one of the major players, not only owned the oil wells, they also built the world's first oil tanker, the *Zoroaster*, to ship the stuff out. Then, because that couldn't move it fast enough, using some of the family's dynamite and a lot of Rothschild money, they blasted the world's first rail and pipeline route all the way to Batumi and the Black Sea. To mark the success of their operations, they built a park for the people of Baku which they called, with the same amazing originality that led them to call their peace prize the Nobel Peace Prize, Nobel

Park. In the centre they built a huge mansion which they called not Villa Nobel, but Villa Petrolea. The Rothschilds, on the other hand, simply built their own oil refinery.

Now Baku is heading that way again, thanks to the enormous influence the Russians had on tiny Azerbaijan for over seventy years. Because it is probably true to say that without their help and dedication and investment, Azerbaijan would have been up there years ago instead of scrabbling around now desperately trying to catch up. At one time even Hitler tried to help them develop their oil industry, but the Germans got stuck in the Caucasus. If they hadn't it's anyone's guess what might have happened, or might be happening now.

The Middle East may be big, Alaska may be big, the North Sea may be big, but the oilfields 100 miles out into the Caspian off Baku are bigger still. So big, in fact, that depending on whether you're talking to some guy from the Ministry of Foreign Affairs stuffing himself with roast sturgeon washed down with gallons of vodka in the Gatiston Palace of Culture, or to a hard-nosed American accountant drinking a can of Coke in a back office in Maj Street, they are capable of producing 3 or 4 billion barrels of oil over the next thirty years worth anything between US$100 and US$150 billion. Maybe even more. Which, if nothing else, will put the Arabs in their place and ensure that we are never ever again held to ransom by an OPEC-inspired price rise.

There is so much oil in and around Baku that you've only got to dig a hole in the ground and whoosh, there it is. 'Why do you think we don't have many trees, only scrubland?' one local wheeler-dealer asked me. As if that's not enough to be getting on with, they've also got around 800 billion cubic metres of gas waiting to be developed as well. Not to mention copper, aluminium and the most important, the most vital, the most essential commodity of all, without which nobody can possibly even think of surviving: caviar.

There's only one problem: Mark Thatcher, who is not exactly your intellectual beluga - more a pot of cold Lincolnshire peas, I would have thought - is offering to help them. And if they need his help, boy, they're in trouble. At least, that's what I was told by this guy in a pair of Levi's, a collar and tie and a black jacket who I found lounging up against a Mercedes with German number plates and a sticker on the windscreen from a garage in Neuss parked outside the Informational Commercial Association, almost opposite the old theatre. Now, I know I know nothing - that's what my wife keeps telling me - but I know one thing: guys in Eastern Europe and central Asia who wear Levi's, a collar and tie and a black jacket and drive around in Mercedes which not only have German number plates but service stickers from German garages still on the windscreen are either secret police or Mafyia. Or, more likely than not, both. So if he says it, it must be true. What's more, for the price of a Turkish beer, he showed me the great wheeler-dealer's Caspian operational headquarters, on condition that I swore an oath of secrecy on the head of Alfred Nobel that I would never reveal it to anyone. So I'm afraid I cannot tell you that it's in a nondescript 1960s council-style block of flats, which would not go down well with Mother, above the Kommersiya Bank in Sheikh Shamil Street, a long, sloping, tree-lined rat run close to the crumbling esplanade and seafront.

As I have a lot in common with Mark Thatcher, naturally I wanted to go and see him to pay my respects. Well, I say we have a lot in common: I crossed the Sahara two and a half times without any problems; he tried it once and got disastrously lost. However, I got bounced by this babushka on the ground floor who looked like a Russian tank in a black dress and a headscarf. 'There, that

proves he's there,' said the friendly man in the black jacket
with the logic that makes the whole of the Caucasus such
an easy region to understand and appreciate.

So we did what any reasonable person would do in the
circumstances. We went looking for him. We asked at the
barber's shop opposite. He hadn't been in there for a short
back and sides. Then at the vegetable stall. They hadn't seen
him. We went to the American poker bar down the street,
where we had another Turkish beer, then to the Kanten
Bar, where we had another. Then the Computer Salonu,
where we had another. Then downstairs to the Café Eden
bar, where we were forced to have another. We asked the
man at the Marlboro cigarette stall outside, who said, no he
hadn't seen him, but did I want to change some money? To
show you how desperate we were, we even staggered
downstairs to the Amerikan Bilardo ve Kafeterya, where I
can't remember what we had. All I know is they kept
asking me if I wanted to change some money.

So no Mark Thatcher. It was bad news for me, but
definitely good news, I thought, for Baku, which already
has most of the basic ingredients for becoming one of the
world's richest cities. Long, open avenues. Huge squares.
Lots of art-nouveau buildings dating back to their last oil
boom in the 1870s. A huge, white marble presidential
palace overlooking the sea. A wide, sweeping bay and a
big, impressive corniche built in the days when the Azeris
had money, could afford to swan off to the French Riviera,
have the time of their lives, come home and then copy
everything they saw. Of course, had they gone to Venice
instead, Baku would probably look a whole lot different.
The level of corruption would probably not be as high,
either. Instead of snatching billions of dollars (one leading
politician, I was told, had already grabbed US$1.5 billion),
they would only be dealing in millions. On top of that, the
sun shines on them practically all year round.

On the other hand, they do have one or two little problems to sort out before they can become one of the world's fun spots. A string of Stalinist 1960s kitsch monstrosities, including two of the worst hotels I think I've ever had the immense pleasure not to have to stay at, and I forget how many empty plinths where once huge statues used to tower over the city. A vast Party headquarters, massive university buildings, huge museums. A million broken pavements with trees growing through the cracks. Pot holes surrounded by shaky bits of road. Vast, empty factories with chimneys held in place by wires pegged into the ground all around them. Long, narrow back streets so choked with rubbish that you can't tell where the rubbish ends and the balconies begin. Thousands of street stalls and street markets run by old ladies in black selling fruit, vegetables and even the occasional carpets with traditional Azeri designs.

One afternoon, racing between meetings, I swung round one corner by a shop called Sweetness and Groceries and saw a mangy, droopy old sheep tethered to a tree – and it wasn't outside a restaurant, either. Another afternoon between more meetings I swung round another corner, by the Ministry of Petroleum, and there in front of me was a huge billboard promoting something called Arcelik. It gave me quite a turn, I can tell you. It also reminded me of one or two people back in London who for some reason or other I don't quite understand have been far more successful than they deserve. Then suddenly you are confronted by a very smart, modern-looking house practically covered in marble. In front of it, an elegant little patio bedecked with trees and umbrellas. A satellite dish fixed to the wall. And inside the family glued to the television. Watching – no, it can't be. Yes, it is. *Dallas.*

Baku also has its fair share of opera houses and theatres and museums and trams and buses, none of which actually work any more, or rather, shouldn't be working any more. The opera houses and the theatres ended their revels years ago and are now crumbling gently into the dust. The trams and buses look as though they ran out of steam, not to mention windows, sticky tape, floorboards, roofs, sides and everything else a million years ago, but are still somehow chugging backwards and forwards, packed to overflowing, morning, noon and night.

All the offices I visited were pure Russia circa 1960: broken tables and chairs; bare boards, or in some cases, bare concrete; narrow, unlit corridors; peeling paint; varnished wall panels; studded, greasy leather doors and mountains of paper all over the place. Telephones are practically non-existent. They are impossible to obtain unless you have anything between US$1,000 and US$5,000. In cash. In a plastic bag. And the right contacts. Which is obviously why there are security guards in every office protecting them as if their lives depended on it. But having a telephone is one thing; getting it to work is another matter altogether. I don't think I ever saw a telephone working in any office the whole time I was there.

The best-kept and most up-to-date place in town seems to be the old mediaeval city. Drive through the gate by the Ministry of Foreign Affairs and you can see where the first handful of Azerbaijan petro-dollars are going to be spent. A lick of paint here, a lump of cement there. A bucket of plaster over there. This could be the Marbella of the Caspian. Wonderful little houses, tiny, twisting streets and alleyways. Little squares, trees, lots of interesting nooks and crannies. Already one or two houses have had the treatment. There are also one or two miniature bars. Nothing spectacular, but at least they've made a start.

However, casting a pall over all this, slap-bang in the centre, is this enormous tower which, as far as I can gather, commemorates the first case of child-abuse in the country. An old Azerbaijani king, so the story goes, fell in love with his daughter. The daughter said, no, not until the tower is built, which is probably what any young Azerbaijani daughter would say in the circumstances. When the tower was built and the father persisted, the girl threw herself off the top and into the sea. An extension of the story has it that the girl's true lover then killed the father, only to discover that - cue music, soft lights, Black Magic chocolates - she was not dead after all. She had been saved by mermaids who returned her to him. Not only was the first modern Azerbaijan poem written about the tower, but the first Azerbaijan ballet was based on it as well. So, whatever you think about them, you can't say they don't believe in recycling.

To me the Azeris themselves are all wonderful, warm-hearted, kind, friendly, generous people. The fact that they're all going to be millionaires or multimillionaires in a couple of years doesn't come into it at all, how dare you think such a thing. You've only got to stop anywhere, look anywhere, go to do anything and a nice, kind, friendly policeman in his grey uniform and peaked cap which always seems too big for him will immediately rush up to you. He smiles, shakes you by the hand and asks you where you come from. And then he smiles, shakes you by the hand and asks you where you come from. Again and again. Until, of course, you realise he's not really smiling, shaking you by the hand and asking you where you are from...

To others, who may not appreciate their finer qualities the way I do, Azeris might create the impression that they're dull and drab and boring, as if either they don't believe their luck that the Russians have finally pulled out, or don't believe that they've struck oil and are shortly going to be one of the richest countries in the world. Or they do and they're worried about whether they're going to see any of it, bearing in mind they've lost US$1.5 billion of it already and things haven't even got going yet. Either way, some people think they're quiet, reserved, almost withdrawn. A bunch of Russians enjoying themselves, in comparison, can give a passable imitation of another world war, especially if they're hitting the vodka. A bunch of Azeris enjoying themselves is a bit like a Rotary Club lunch without the gin and tonic. All very formal, very quiet and very serious. Partly because, I guess, they're out of practice. It takes time to learn how to relax after seventy years of looking over your shoulder and feeling for microphones under the table. The current president, who at one time was one of the big guys in Moscow – he was even considered a rival to Mikhail Gorbachev for the job of first secretary to the Politburo – learned his trade as a Kremlin apparatchik by running the KGB in Azerbaijan, so you can bet your life they had a rough time of it. Partly because, for all that they are southerners, the three Ss as far as they are concerned stand for sun, sea and seriousness. They're not all Muslims, but that Muslim sense of duty and earnestness is still there. Like a bunch of Calvinists on holiday, they know they're there to relax, but they don't know how. And finally, I think, it's because if they've got worries about their past, they've got even more worries about their future.

Sure, there's the oil, but to the south, 100 miles away, is Iran. Along the border many Azeris and many Iranians share the same language. Many have family either side. Many also listen to the Azeri-language radio programmes the Iranians beam across the Caucasus to them, especially the how-to-be-a-mullah Islamic theological courses. In Baku itself there are also lots of Iranian banks, lots of Iranian buses full of lots of Iranians come to do a day's shopping, and of course, lots of Iranian mullahs all over the place peering suspiciously at everything through their thick, heavy glasses. Go and look at the minarets, for example. Most of them, especially in the poor parts of Baku, fly the Iranian flag. Some even have posters and photographs of Ayatollah Khomeini on the walls. The big fear, of course, is that just as the Azeris are about to hit the jackpot and head off for the good life, the militants will spoil their fun, seize power and turn the place into a fundamentalist Muslim state. All things, of course, are possible, but I doubt it. The Azeris might be Muslims or a variation, but their spiritual home seems firmly rooted in the West. Furthermore, the fundamentalists usually score when countries are running downhill, not uphill. And having fought off the influence of the Russians for seventy years, the Azeris are not short of experience in hanging on to their own identity and traditions. The result is that the only women you see in Baku today with their faces covered are the road-sweepers. Not because of their religion, but because of all the dust and rubbish all over the place.

To the west is Turkey. All the good things in Azerbaijan come from Turkey: the beer, most of the decent food, the textiles and, of course, the people themselves. Most Azeris are of Turkish descent; indeed, to many Russians and Eastern Europeans, Azerbaijan is a Turkish Fifth Column. But Turkey is becoming more Muslim. Will it go further? Will it drag the Azeris in its wake? Again, I doubt it. Turkey sees itself firmly as a part of the West, and Azerbaijan will go along with Turkey.

To the north, over the Caucasus are, of course, the Russians. They may have left, but will they come back again? Well, what do you think?

Finally, there are the Armenians, their Christian next-door neighbours, who currently occupy Nagorno-Karabakh, the beautiful, hilly region down in the south-west which was at one time the buffer between the old Ottoman, Persian and Russian empires. Are the Azeris worried about them? Yes, of course they're worried. Nagorno-Karabakh is sovereign Azeri territory and the Armenians had no right to invade it. It was an act of unprovoked aggression. They have no right to be still occupying almost one fifth of the country. Nagorno-Karabakh must be returned, blah blah blah. However, deep down in the deepest beer cellar in Baku in the dead of night, they don't seem to care. It didn't belong to them in the first place: it was a present from Stalin back in 1923, and it was practically full of Armenians anyway. The war lasted seven years, caused around 15,000 deaths and made over a million people homeless. A truce has already held for two years, so why not let it continue, look the other way and get on with the serious business of making money? In any case, even if they are perfectly entitled to try to get their land back, they know there's no way the oil industry and foreign investors are going to sit around and continue to pour money into the country if they do.

Marco Polo was the first outsider to stumble across their oil during his travels way back in the thirteenth century. There was a great fountain of the stuff, he said, which they loaded on to the backs of camels and took back with them to use for lighting as well as to cure all kinds of diseases in men and cattle.

After that the Azeris built up a fantastic string of oil firsts. They were the first to extract oil from offshore wells, around the 1800s; the first to start refining oil industrially, around 1820. The first to develop a process for producing kerosene (around 1830). The first to transport kerosene by sea (around 1840). The first ever to drill an oil well (1844, ten years before the Americans started drilling wells in Pennsylvania). The first to build a kerosene and paraffin production plant (1859) and an oil-distillation plant (1863). They are the holders of the first oil-production record, set in 1875, when a gusher in Balakhanni produced over 300 tons of oil every day for a month. Theirs were the first oil wells to be owned by the Nobels and the Rothschilds (1872). They produced the first lubricating oil in the world (1875). They built the world's first steel oil tanker to ship kerosene, the world's first oil pipeline, to Baku (both in 1877). Azerbaijan was the first country in the world to produce 11.5 million tons of oil while, since you ask, the US was producing barely 1 million tons a year (1899). They were the first to introduce what's known as compressor exploitation of oil (1905) and rotary drilling (1911). The first to use deep-sea pumps (in 1915, fifteen years before the Americans got round to it). Theirs was the first offshore oil ever to be pumped (1924, in Bibi Heybat Bay). Theirs were the first wells to be drilled electrically and the first to use directional turbine drilling (both in 1940, in the Kala and Bail oilfields). They were the first - are you still with me? - to develop an offshore platform (1947, to exploit the Neft Dashlari oilfield). The first to install a deep-water offshore platform (1977). The first to bore the pants off everybody with their list of oil firsts (1998, or whenever you beg, borrow or steal this book. I just know you'll never buy it yourself).

This fantastic string of firsts amazed me when I first discovered it because I had always thought that Azerbaijan was the world's first in a far more important and far more essential industry even than oil: caviar. They might be greasy little fish eggs to you, but let me tell you, there's only one thing that beats a dish of caviar and a bottle of chilled vodka, and that's two dishes of caviar and two bottles of chilled vodka. Providing, of course, it's the right kind of caviar - none of this cheap stuff from Denmark - and providing the vodka is *really* chilled. Whether it's served on silver and glass caviar dishes from Asprey's for £1,000 (or £100, if you are one of the select group of regular customers lucky enough to be invited to one of their secret, after-hours Christmas sales), and whether you have silver spoons or not is neither here nor there. But whatever you do, forget the garnish. The only reason some restaurants push the chopped onion, the parsley and the lemon is to try to disguise the fact the caviar has gone off.

Whenever I'm in Baku, the only way I know to block out that stench of crude oil, not to mention the sulphur that hits the back of your throat as soon as you get out of the plane -- flames from the oilfields light up the midday sky -- is to force myself to go on the strictest possible diet. For breakfast, Turkish beer and caviar. For lunch, champagne and caviar. For dinner, ice-cold vodka and caviar. In between, whenever I get the chance I prop myself up against a bar and ponder the deep, meaningful mysteries of life. Which is better? Caviar with biscuits, no butter? Caviar with biscuits and butter, preferably salty? Caviar with bread, no butter? Caviar with bread and butter? Caviar with Brie? Why do I drive myself so hard? I'll tell you why. When I'm home I'm surrounded by organic yoghurt, giant boxes of muesli, tofu salads, cartons of soya milk and enough E-numbers to stretch from here to Baku and back.

Now, I know that when it comes to caviar everybody goes on about Russia and, if they're not American, Iran. Don't listen to them. After a lifetime's self-sacrifice and dedication I can assure you that the pearly black Azerbaijani caviar is the best of the lot. Black because that's the way it is, not because there's so much oil in the sea that it's started to leak out and affect the fish, although you might be forgiven for thinking that if you saw how it is produced down in Neftchilla, where the Kura River runs into the Caspian. At this end of the business, a luxury trade it is not; it's more a case of caviar emptor. The place is positively seventeenth-century.

There are rusty fishing boats all over the place, many of which will never put to sea again; a ramshackle canning plant; a string of fish farms which look as though between them they couldn't produce an Arbroath smokie, let alone the black pearls so beloved by tsars, shahs, bar girls and African dictators. In New York, it's the caviar for the select few. In some bars there 30 grammes of the best Oscietra sets you, or rather the old expense account, back around US$5,000. Beluga, the rarer white sturgeon, may cost twice that.

In Azerbaijan, it's the opposite. It's the caviar for the general public. If you take a bucket and a handful of dollars to Neftchilla you can have as much as you like of what they call the little black balls. Even in Baku, if you know the right man – usually the one by the third lorry on the right-hand side of the street up near the army barracks at the top of the hill – you can pick up a kilo of Sevruga or Oscietra in a greasy plastic bag for maybe US$20. Down in the town in the market, canned, wrapped and labelled 'Produce of the USSR', it will be US$30 or US$40. Come, come, this is the Caucasus, you know. In Harrods or any other similar Egyptian bazaar it will cost you ten times as much. Beluga caviar, considered by many to be the best because of the size of the eggs and its age, around sixteen to eighteen years old, will cost perhaps three times as much again. In fact, I swear I once saw a kilo of Beluga on sale in Harrods for – are you ready? – £1,600. And of course it's getting more and more expensive all the time, not just because of the demand, but because there is less and less of it around. Indeed, some people maintain that a fish that has been around virtually unchanged for 250 million years – sorry about that, Mr Darwin – could be extinct within twenty-five unless stocks are allowed to replenish themselves.

The problem started, as most problems started, in Russia

with Stalin and his grandiose hydro-electric schemes which, combined with increasing industrial pollution in the Caspian, destroyed nearly 90 per cent of the sturgeons' natural spawning grounds in the Volga River. Now, because there is less and less of the stuff around, and because of the high prices it can command, not only have poachers moved in, but so too has a caviar mafia. In Neftchilla while digging into great buckets of the 'black balls', I was told that as much as 90 per cent of fishing was currently illegal. But there was nothing anyone could do about it. The old USSR and Iran had an agreement not to overfish the already dangerously low level of sturgeon in the Caspian, but since the break-up of the Soviet Union, Russia, Iran, Kazakhstan, Turkmenistan and Azerbaijan have all been overfishing like mad. Furthermore, the precious black pearls have now become something to kill for. I don't mean in London, Paris or New York, I mean in Makhachkala, the capital of Dagestan. The Russian caviar mafia, they told me, had just blown up a nine-storey Russian border guards' barracks, killing sixty-seven people, of whom twenty-one were children, for doing their job and seizing caviar being shipped out illegally from the nearby airport.

'How much caviar?' I wondered.

'About one and a half tons.'

I nearly dropped the tin metal spoon I was using straight into the middle of the bucket. I had not dreamed such quantities were involved. 'So where was it going?' To the United Arab Emirates, they said. Together with fake airway bills.

I reckon it's only with a bucket of caviar in one hand and the dregs of a second bottle of vodka in the other that you are in a condition to appreciate just what is going to happen to Baku. At the moment it takes your breath away – those views, all that oil, everything peeling off and falling into the sea. The oil platforms are crumbling before your eyes, the cables suddenly splashing into the sea. The drilling equipment is literally falling apart bit by bit. Stagger around the run-down wreck of a port and you'll see what I mean. Decaying old ships, abandoned cranes, bits of drilling equipment, and literally hundreds and hundreds of offshore oil platforms entwined with thousands and thousands of kilometres of electric cable, all connected together by giant concrete causeways. A glorious testament to Soviet technology.

Look at the water. Everywhere there's that thick film of oil. Fifty years ago the Russians built a huge offshore complex way out in the Caspian Sea. For fifty years they claimed it was going to be their pride and joy. For fifty years virtually nothing happened. That is, nothing happened except that it leaked and leaked and leaked. Today, if you didn't know the Azeris' skill and expertise in the oil business, you'd think they were so eager to land the damn stuff that they opened all the taps and decided to let it all wash up on the shore rather than go to the bother of piping it back to land.

At least it's not as bad as the radioactive mess the Russians left behind elsewhere. But tomorrow everything may have disappeared, because the Caspian Sea is rising higher and higher every year, fed by the Volga, Europe's longest river. Complete islands have already gone, and flooding, especially on the Russian side, is becoming more and more of a problem. And if the Caspian doesn't wash the lot away, the new oil barons will, before they start pumping, have to clear up the mess themselves. But in spite of having created the mess in the first place and then walking away, the Russians still don't want to let go. The Caspian Sea, they say, is not a sea, it's a lake. Everybody around the lake should, therefore, share in its goodies.

To the Azeris, of course, this is a stab in the Baku. Never, they retorted. The Russians then said they wanted a round table to discuss the matter with all the other countries bordering the Caspian Sea, knowing, of course, that they would have a majority. The Azeris said no. There was only one thing to do if Azerbaijan was to get back to where it was seventy years ago: ignore the Russians and put the whole thing out to tender. Which is what they did. As bidding began, they faced one attempted coup after another. When the bidding was completed, and in September 1994 the huge US$8 billion oil contract of the century was given to a consortium of the twelve biggest oil companies in the world, led by good old BP, came still more coup attempts. Almost the first thing the consortium did was to give the Russian oil company Lukoil a 10 per cent share of the project. There hasn't been a single coup attempt since. Funny, that.

But don't think the Russians are the only ones worried about the Azeri oil. It is so important to the Americans, too, that, as anti-Tehran as they are, they created a special loophole in their own super-tough anti-Iran sanctions to enable some early supplies to be pumped through their arch-enemy's territory to the outside world. Now, isn't that amazing? And what is even more amazing, nobody said a word about it. Not in Congress, not in the Senate, not even on *Larry King Live* on CNN. I wonder why. And no, it wasn't because it went via Arkansas.

However, the most important question of all, and a question with enormous economic and therefore political implications for all concerned, has yet to be answered. Which way will the pipeline go? The easiest, quickest and cheapest option would be to take the shortest, most direct route through Iran or Armenia to Turkey. But this won't happen. The Americans have got this thing about Iran, the Azeris hate the Armenians and the Russians want part of the action, otherwise they'll start throwing their toys out of the cot. Other possibilities are through 900 kilometres of Georgia to the Black Sea port of Batumi, the route originally built by Nobel, the king of Baku oil, or 1,400 kilometres through Russia and Chechnya via an existing pipeline to the giant Black Sea terminal at Novorossiysk, which would, say some people, especially the Russians, cost up to four times less. Another idea put forward, by the Turks, is for the pipeline to go across Georgia to Supsa on the Black Sea with a spur heading overland to Turkey and Ceyhan on the Mediterranean.

So, if you were the Azeris and you had to make a purely economic decision based solely on the merits of the various proposals, which would you choose? That's right! Build two, one through Georgia, the other through Russia. That way they can say they are dependent on neither. If there is trouble with one they can still keep pumping through the other. What they don't add, of course, is that expensive though it will be to have two pipelines, at least it means they will not be at the mercy of the Russians.

As a result, Baku today is a Wild East boom town wait-ing to happen. It's the Great Game all over again. Russia, Iran, Turkey and, of course, the West are all jostling for influence. The place is rumoured to be crawling with spies from everywhere eager to know who is seeing whom, what they are saying and where the next order is going. Who is sleeping with whom is not important – this is the real world. In the little underground bars and alleyways gaggles of Turkish businessmen who have practically got the market sewn up when it comes to small things like washing-up liquid, butter and beer, not to mention cheap shirts, are now going for the big stuff. This is their backyard and they don't see why anybody else should get a look in.

In the Hotel Azerbaijan and the Hotel Abseron, in between taking bets on which pane of glass will be the next to fall out, or, an even riskier bet, when it will be replaced, ever-optimistic or maybe over-desperate Russian businessmen are offering to do deals in wines, precious stones, meat, armaments, weapons – anything to get a share. In the Hyatt Regency, the only decent hotel in town, a secret band of Swiss bankers are buying drinks for all and sundry. I know, because they even bought one for me. And at the other end of the bar I noticed a lone Scotsman waiting for someone to buy him a drink to cash in on Scotland's oil experience.

It's not just in the hotels that deals are being done. In Charlie's, a strange-looking club on the bay where West tries desperately to meet East, your typical big swash-buckling American roustabout, all Stetson and no cattle, goes up to an Azeri civil-servant type. 'Hey, Vitali baby. How's it goin'?' he slaps him on the shoulder.

'Fine. Great.'

He turns to the barman. 'Hey, give him some candy bars. No, let's have some pizzas. Whaddayasay, Vitali? Some pizzas? Yeah, oil on everything. Yeah, who cares. Hey, Vitali, now tell me about those babes, you old son of a bitch.'

Vitali looks him straight in the eye. 'Where are you from?' he asks.

In the nightclubs everybody was doing deals. Including, I was told, selling arms to the Chechnians on the basis that the further away the Russians were, the better. The casinos, which don't normally get going until two or three in the morning, seem more full of bodyguards than bodies being guarded. Apart from mine, of course. And you can bet the integrity of the Americans to stand four-square to their tough anti-Iranian legislation to a picture of the Ayatollah Khomeini that in the mosques and the minarets the mullahs are having a quiet word in the right ear after Friday-morning service. Because tomorrow, oh la la, will be the oil boom to end all oil booms. As they start to develop the Azeri, Chirag and deep-water sections of the Guneshli offshore oilfields; as production elsewhere, especially in Alaska and the North Sea, begins to decline, Baku will be its old self again. Rich, confident, a major player in the world's major market.

It will mean the worries of ordinary Azeris will be over. They will no longer have to live in tiny shacks in factory yards or ten to a room in some Soviet towerblock. Instead they'll be squeezed into luxury flats in Bayswater or Earl's Court, frightened to go out in case they're mugged or beaten up. They will no longer have to risk their lives going to the local hospital. Instead they'll be spending all day queuing up in Harley Street to be ripped off by doctors charging them more for a quick five minutes count-up-to-ten-and-cough routine than the cost of a heart transplant on the National Health. They'll no longer have to eat all the delicious fresh fruit and vegetables sold by fat old ladies sitting by the side of the road all over town. Instead they'll be worrying about their cholesterol levels and lipids and living off organic yoghurt and giant boxes of muesli and tofu salads and soya milk.

Instead of wandering around shops full of empty shelves they'll be fighting their way into Harrods, paying enormous prices for nothing and staggering around massive shopping centres all the way from Miami to Malibu. Instead of fighting to get into First World War buses already packed to overflowing they'll be worrying about where to park their expensive cars without getting them scratched, broken into or lifted. Instead of being able to wander along the corniche, watching people playing billiards under the trees in the open or spending hours on end playing chess with their old buddies at the Veterans' Association Klub, they'll be queuing up for berths in huge yachting marinas overrun by a bunch of Hooray Henrys and Henriettas.

As for Baku, it will be the fun spot of the Caspian. Pipelines will be under the ground instead of on top. Houses will have doors and windows instead of doors or windows. Flats will have curtains instead of no curtains. The local Most Bank will be the Mostest Bank. Taxis will no longer be smashed in on one side only. They'll be smashed in on both sides. Because, instead of tiny little Renaults, everybody will be driving Mercedes at twice the speed. And the streets won't be littered with the occasional wreck, they will be lined with them.

It is all too depressing to think about. So for a real laugh, I decided there was only one thing to do: go and have another look for Mark Thatcher. This time I did what I should have done in the first place. Instead of a suit I put on a pair of slacks. I didn't happen to have a black leather jacket in my suitcase, so got out my blazer instead. The old Babushka, I hoped, wouldn't notice the difference. Then I went up to her, gave her US$10 and asked her straight out which flat he was in. And, of course, in time-honoured Caucasian tradition, she immediately told me.

Up I went and knocked on the door. A young man answered. Inside I could see the usual basic cardboard furniture arranged to suit a reception area or waiting room. I heard a dog barking, a woman's voice with an American accent shouting and screaming in the background. Excited? She sounded as if she was having labour pains. Then – Bang! – the door slammed shut. 'There,' I thought with that impeccable Caucasian logic. 'That proves he is there.'

I only hope he was, because if he was in any government office, he could be setting back their prospects a million years. On the other hand, I suppose he could have got lost on his way from the airport. Do you think I should call his mother?

MINSK

Belarus is the only place I've been where, not to Minsk words, they are turning back the clock with a vengeance. Vengeance being the operative word. Instead of dismantling Communism and all its works and pomps as they are doing all over Eastern Europe, in Belarus they are actually rebuilding it rougher and tougher and harsher than ever before.

Perestroika? *Glasnost*? They want nothing whatsoever to do with it. Mikhail Gorbachev? What was that you said? Wash your mouth out immediately. Their national flag? They've rolled it up and thrown it away. Their national anthem? That's out of the window. And, as for speaking Belorussian, are you out of your mind? The last thing they want is anything as absurd as a separate Belorussian history and culture, let alone identity. For them it's back to the good old days of bear hugs and huge state banquets, non-stop toasts of vodka and never-ending balalaika muzak, enormous hotel dining rooms lit by two tiny 40-watt bulbs, one of which doesn't work, menus that span the gastronomic range from salad cold to salad very cold and pork as sweet and succulent as a pair of old Army boots. Soviet, of course. Not to mention cheap aluminium knives and forks that buckle as soon as you begin to test the softness of an old-style Soviet fried egg.

Believe me, the vast 30-metre-high statue of Lenin

outside the Parliament building has never looked in better condition. Every day, I promise you, they polish it from head to toe. Not out of a sense of duty, or because its their job, but out of pure love and devotion.

Then, of course, there are all the other glorious incidentals without which a genuine Soviet state would not be a genuine Soviet state. Policemen strolling along the streets nonchalantly swinging their truncheons at everybody and everything. Riot police hanging around street corners in their khaki sweaters, black boots and white motorbike helmets just itching for a spot of action. The military swaggering about all over the place in their brand-new drab Soviet-style uniforms, confident that they are part of one of the largest armies in Eastern Europe, backed up by a mere 2,000 tanks, 3,000 armoured vehicles, over 150 combat aircraft and a string of 18 SS-25 nuclear missiles, at one time Russia's most mobile single warhead missiles. Then, of course, the icing on the cake, the real mark of a genuine Soviet state. A big hand, please, for those wonderful guys the KGB.

Everybody else has got rid of them, including the Russians themselves. But not the Belorussians. The KGB are still there, in their headquarters, as large as death. Official, above board. Licensed to do whatever they want to do. Not hidden away in some back street, but standing four-square in the middle of the main shopping street in town, a huge, solid, implacable, scruffy yellow and white building with five storeys above ground, seven storeys below. Still as busy as ever doing what they always did: tapping phones and faxes, beating up people in the street and, of course, knocking people's doors down at four o'clock in the morning. None of their functions have been abolished, none of their activities watered down. In fact, I was told that there are over 150,000 of them in a country of, don't forget, just 10 million people. There is even talk of toughening them up a bit. Wouldn't want them to get too soft, y'know. Although fair's fair, they have shown signs of adapting to these consumer-friendly times. They have just issued a special secret tip-off telephone number to make it easier for people to split on their friends and relatives.

Talk about Le Carré. To find out even this much I had to hang around the big, dark waiting room in Minsk Railway Station for hours on end for a group of young businessmen to arrive. Then, practically in the middle of the night, they made me walk up and down the main platform in the freezing cold, smoke and steam belching out all over the place, before they would say a word. I'm not kidding. When I said they were turning the clock back with a vengeance, I meant it.

In the old days Belarus meant White or rather, Very Pale Russian, as opposed to the thick, hairy, leathery types you get further north. Today, make no mistake, it means Redder than the Reddest Russian. And the reason? Don't say a word – there could be microphones anywhere. It's all the fault of one man, Alexander 'I'm not sharing power with anyone' Lukashenko. Damn. Now I've told you, I'm afraid, if you want to protect your family and friends, you'll have to tear out this page and swallow it whole. Now, this instant. Because I tell you, the guy is a crazy Minsked-up kid. A former boss of a collective farm in Gomel down in the south-east, he swept to power as president in 1994 with a staggering 84 per cent of the vote because he claimed he'd never, ever eaten one of those nasty, capitalist Snickers bars, the hated symbol of everything that people believe has gone wrong with the Soviet way of life since *perestroika*. The biggest pan-Slav nationalist of all time, he was so broken-hearted at the break-up of the Soviet Union that he was the only deputy in the Belorussian Parliament to actually vote against independence for his own country in 1991.

Now he wants to return to the old days. He not only

wants complete economic, political and military integration with Russia, he wants to do things the old Russian way. For him, it's the state, the whole state and nothing but the state. That's all that counts. He wants central control of the economy, he wants currency controls and he wants rigid control of the banks. Private enterprise he believes is theft. Foreigners are evil, and NATO is the devil incarnate. Privatisation? No way. He's even talking of reviewing the state's shareholding in all the big commercial banks, which is government-speak for nationalisation. As if that's not enough, he's taken down the huge plaque outside the Parliament building which was the symbol of their independence. He also wants to ban post-independence schoolbooks and go back to the good old Soviet books instead.

Give him the choice between Belarus being an independent sovereign state and a mere province of the mighty Russian state, and he would unquestionably prefer to be a Russian province, where people do nothing all day long but pick cabbages to try to survive the winter. He simply adores all things Russian – especially the Russia of tight security, wire-tapping concentration camps. And the Russian way of doing things, like disconnecting independent radio-transmitters, which he does about once a month. Like governing by decree, which he does all the time: people must have permission to travel abroad, 75 per cent of all goods on sale in Belarus shops must be locally produced, Internet users must register with the police, goods bought at a government shop must not be resold. Not for nothing is he known as Lucastro. Or rather, not for nothing is he referred to in late-night conversations in the freezing cold at Minsk Railway Station as Lucastro.

He's gooey about Stalin, Felix Dzerzhinsky – the founder of the Cheka, the predecessor of the KGB and a native of Belarus – and Yuri Andropov, the KGB boss who was Gorbachev's predecessor. Yaaagh, that name again. The

Russians he doesn't see as conquerors or in any way an occupying army; instead he refers to them as cousins and brothers. As a result, he still hasn't taken down any of the huge old Communist posters proclaiming. 'We in friendship and unity are strong'. And Hitler? He raves about him, his policies on law and order and even more enthusiastically about his methods of maintaining law and order. 'Hitler created a powerful Germany due to strong presidential power,' he keeps on saying.

But credit where credit is due. In the short time he's been president, Lukashenko has had a major impact on the country. He's stimulated the economy – by boosting imports of video cameras, tapping equipment, listening devices and two-way mirrors. He's dramatically cut costs – by switching off the country's television transmitters whenever anything is screened, even direct from Russia, which he disagrees with. At the same time, to show that he's not in any way against free speech, he has launched a special 'cleaning service' for all the local television stations not under his control. Whenever their equipment needs to be cleaned, he sends in a crack team of technicians to do the job for them, there and then, completely free of charge. The necessity for their equipment to be shut down and cleaned around election times is, of course, purely coincidental.

He's boosted production – of guns, truncheons, barbed wire and banknotes. Especially banknotes. With inflation running at 2,200 per cent a year and still soaring, the machines have been running so long they are practically beginning to melt. He's stopped the *perestroika*-inspired climb in unemployment and created thousands of new jobs – in the police and the Ministry of the Interior, which, according to the last figures, now employs over 150,000 people. He's increased the amount of overtime people can work. If they're skilled, he encourages them to go around day and night beating up old-age pensioners they catch selling foreign newspapers or magazines criticising him – that even included copies of *Izvestia* published in his beloved Russia when it dared to criticise him – and throwing them into the Svislach River, which runs through the middle of town. The copies of the newspapers, that is, although I wouldn't be surprised if many an old-age pensioner doesn't end up in there as well. If they're unskilled workers, he promptly enrols them in AGAP, the crack anti-riot police squad, and lets them loose on all kinds of public gatherings, not merely protest demonstrations, on the pretext that since Belarus is an agricultural economy everybody should be encouraged to be out in the countryside helping to bring in the harvest instead of hanging around street corners shouting silly slogans. Spray a silly slogan on a statue of Dzerzhinsky, let alone Lenin, and it's dogs, chains, beatings and six months in jail before your trial, eighteen months' hard labour afterwards.

There is one group of people, however, to whom he seems determined to give as little work as possible: doctors and nurses. Once, kind-hearted man that he is, when the trades unions were discussing a possible railway strike, he sent ambulances to surround the building where the meeting was taking place. Next he sent the military, and doctors and nurses had another night off. The Army got home early as well.

He has also stimulated the leisure and travel industries – by giving lawyers and judges virtually nothing to do and completely ignoring the members of Parliament, or rather the Supreme Soviet, as he still insists on calling it. So out of practice are the lawyers and judges nowadays that when they get a case to try they muck the whole thing up totally. They actually sentenced a nineteen-year-old-deaf mute to jail for shouting anti-government slogans.

As for MPs, I know that it's generally very difficult to tell when they're working and when they're not working. In

Minsk, the only way you can tell if an MP is working is if you see him drawing up plans for a spot of overseas travel influenced not so much by the president's plan for him to spend more time with his family - Lukashenko has banned all election campaigns, barred candidates from spending more than US$50 on their total election expenses and restricted all but the basic minimum coverage of elections in the press, radio and television on the basis that he could do what they do far more efficiently and far more cheaply anyway - as perhaps by the fact that one day shortly after he was elected, riot police stormed the chamber, beat up all the members of the Opposition, dragged fifty of them out and threw them in prison. Already the leader of the Opposition party in the country, Zenon Poznyak, has fled to, or rather taken a long holiday in the United States. Which shows you just how desperate he was to get out. Others who must have been even more desperate have gone to Canada. Still others, as we speak, are beginning to pack.

As for journalists, many of them have followed the same route, and those who are left hardly do a thing. Most days the newspapers which are still in business here, as opposed to those which are printed next door in Lithuania - *Sarmizdat* is alive and well and being circulated in Minsk - appear with enormous blank spaces all over the front page rather than go to the trouble of printing long, boring articles on corruption in the inner circle surrounding the president and stories about how the presidential security force is busy illegally trans-shipping alcohol to Russia.

But the biggest disaster of all is that the two famous rabbis from Minsk and Pinsk are no longer telling jokes. Not that the Belorussians have stopped telling jokes. It's just that they now tell different types of jokes.

The president is in his beloved Moscow. He is negotiating with Yeltsin. He says he would like to consult his hero, Stalin. Yeltsin says, 'No problem. Calls to Hell are US$1,000 a minute.'

The president comes back to Minsk. He says he wants to call Stalin. 'OK,' his secretary says. 'That'll be US$10.'

'Ten dollars?' he says. 'How come in Moscow it's US$1,000 a minute to call Hell, but here in Minsk it's only $10?'

'Easy,' she says. 'Here it's a local call.'

I'm told by people who've met the president that he staunchly maintains he is a democrat. He has, he says, gone out of this way to encourage as many political parties as possible. At the last count there were over thirty. He has held election after election – local elections, national elections and even a referendum to give people a chance to have their say. What's more, to ensure that everything is above board, he says he always insists that the ballot papers are printed by the only truly independent, trustworthy, objective institution in the country: the presidential administration itself. He has also, he insists, done everything he can to make sure that when elections take place they genuinely reflect the genuine will of the genuine people. Hence his 50 per cent rule, which he claims he discovered in an old Soviet law book: unless 50 per cent of the electorate take part in an election, the election is null and void. Unfortunately, this meant that 120 members of Parliament out of 260 had to be thrown out on their ears for breaking the law, but it was a small price to pay for upholding democracy.

'Mr President, robbers have broken into the Presidency.'

'Did they steal anything?'

'Yes. The results of the next election.'

* * *

In order to further improve his democratic credentials, he sent one of his closest aides, the deputy chief of staff, Colonel Vladimir Zametalin, to observe elections taking place in other parts of the world to study their procedures and organisation so that he could adopt the same approach back home. Of course, the fact that the place Zametalin visited was Iraq and the elections were to confirm Saddam Hussein as president of that country is neither here nor there. At least they have shown a willingness to learn. You can't accuse them of being indifferent to what's going on in the outside world.

> Come the election, everybody is queuing up outside the polling station. A soldier marches along and gives them an envelope to put in the ballot box. An old man opens his envelope.
> 'You mustn't do that,' says the soldier, 'It's a secret ballot.'

My friends on Minsk Railway Station told me that the president likes to keep a note of people's names and addresses. Especially if they're asking him questions about democracy.

Not that the poor Belorussians don't know what it is to suffer. Squeezed between Poland, Russia, the Ukraine and Lithuania, the country has been trampled on and smashed to pieces by Poles, Lithuanians, French and Germans – they suffered more than anybody during the last war – and, of course, the Russians. Especially the Russians. The only time they've ever really known what it's like to be out from under anybody's jackboot was between 1919 and 1920. Consequently they've never really had a chance to establish any kind of national identity, let alone any kind of national institution of their own, such as the Catholic Church in Poland or the Orthodox Church in the Ukraine.

Then, God help us, there was Chernobyl, which affected them far, far more than the Ukraine, even though the Ukraine gets all the publicity. Some reports I've seen say they took 60 to 70 per cent of the fall-out and that up to 2 million people, 20 per cent of the population, and a third of the country, more than 500,000 acres, were contaminated. So as the years go by they will also get more than their unfair share of thyroid cancers, malignant tumours, blood diseases, heart problems and horribly deformed births.

Most Belorussians who were prepared to talk about it, and that was not many, blamed the Russians for making the situation worse.

'At first, the Russians did nothing. They didn't know what to do. Then they sent up a missile to attack the radioactive cloud. What happened? It brought all the radioactivity down to earth. If they hadn't done that we wouldn't have had so many problems.'

'Why didn't you complain? To avoid embarrassing the Russians?'

'Did you say you would like another glass of vodka?'

So if they don't complain about what the Russians did to protect them, do they now beg for help and assistance from world aid organisations? No, they don't. As more and more people suffer from cancer, and as more and more children are born horribly deformed, are they pleading for help? Not at all. Once on a trip to Minneapolis-St Paul in the States, I came across a group of Lutheran businessmen who were doing the usual and organising jumble sales and whist drives and what have you to raise money for the Ukrainian victims of Chernobyl. In addition to money, they were sending out food and medical equipment. They were also bringing these poor kids back to the States for treatment and to be fitted with wigs and hairpieces. When I told them about Belorussia, they didn't believe me. As far as they were concerned, Chernobyl was in the Ukraine and the fall-out fell on the Ukraine.

Wander around the country today, the bits that are not contaminated, and, let me tell you, it's eerie. Like stepping back in time, or living through a non-stop rerun of All Our Soviet Yesterdays. No matter where you go, it's flat and dull, nothing but miles and miles of fields. No walls, no hedges, no ditches. Just fields, decrepit cottages and primitive, primitive farming. Which is just as well, because none of their clapped-out old buses could go anywhere that wasn't flat and dull. I know – I've spent a lifetime on them. First they sort of whine and strain, then the engine coughs and splutters, the gears crunch and the brakes emit this long, piercing whistle. Next the whole thing shudders violently. Finally there's total silence. And that's just pulling away from a bus stop. On the other hand, the buses were so loaded down it was a wonder they could move at all. Not with people: most buses I travelled on were less than half full of passengers. Instead they were loaded down with potatoes, sacks of them. It seemed as if everybody was taking potatoes to everybody else. At some bus stops in the middle of nowhere you could hardly get on or off the bus for sacks of potatoes stacked up in the gangway.

But wherever I went and however I managed to get there, I could see the effects of Mr Lucastro's rule. The price of a litre of milk had doubled. The cost of bus tickets had quadrupled. Electricity had gone up from 1,500 to 28,000 roubles per kilowatt hour. And pensions – the cost of the average pension was about US$40 a month, a healthy US$10 below the poverty line. With inflation at a mere 50 per cent per month, nothing was worth anything any more. What money there was was virtually worthless. People who had any wanted to get rid of it as quickly as possible.

Hotels, at least I think they were hotels, were invariably pitch-black. Talk about two 40-watt bulbs per floor: in most cases there were only two 40-watt bulbs in the whole building. The only way I could find the lift was by heading in the direction of this awful screeching sound a bit like an old, scratchy Red Army band 78. As for the rooms, I'm not certain I ever made it to mine. In Russian hotels I can never find the bath plug; in Belorussian hotels I couldn't even find the bath. Not even when I stumbled upon the typical Russian paper-thin multicoloured towels which a businessman from hell once told me were really worn out tea-towels. The only plugs I located on the whole trip were electrical plugs – and I only found them because they were hanging out of the walls, presumably in an effort to heat up the room.

What shops there were were invariably empty. The shelves were bare and there were hardly any customers around. Even so, you still had to go through the typical Russian routine: queue up for whatever it was they didn't have; queue up to pay for what you bought instead; queue up again to collect whatever it was you didn't want for which you had just been forced to pay through the nose. But whether they were tiny, scruffy village shops or fairly modern town shops (in Belarus that's about 1930), they all seemed to have the latest computers and all the usual point-of-sale equipment. The really modern shops (that's about 1960s) also had abacuses, which the shop assistants used before punching the totals into the computers.

Offices were, well, acceptable – if you're used to cheap, basic, under-furnished Russian offices with lino on the floors and holes in the walls. One office I visited must have been where Lenin's father served his apprenticeship. It was dark and dingy, with funny little lace curtains at the windows which were black with age. All over the place were piles of paper so old they were turning yellow – for the second time. The lino on the floor was a distant memory. There was a telephone, however, locked in a box on the corner of the manager's table. It didn't work.

Factories were the biggest surprise of all. From the

outside they looked like huge government departments, say, the Ministry of Foreign Affairs or the Ministry of Public Works. Inside they were literally dumps. None of them were working full time. They all had problems locating raw materials, getting them delivered, finding customers. And, of course, problems getting customers to pay. Big or small, they were all yearning for the old days when Belarus was a major subcontractor for the Soviet Union with probably the most militarised economy in Eastern Europe. Whatever they produced they could sell. Whatever they sold they got paid for. No hassles.

'We say the Berlin Wall went up, not down,' the manager of a company which made, or rather used to make, transformers, told me. 'This is why all the bad things have come in. If it had gone down, all the good things would have come flying over the top.'

A Belorussian is working in a factory making baby carriages. Every day he steals a different part so that his family can have a baby carriage of its own.

After six weeks his wife says to him, 'It's funny, but whichever way I put the bits together, it still comes out looking like a gun.'

The other thing that struck me was the number of women in senior-management positions. Practically every accountant and economist, as they call them, and finance director was a woman. So many women are now accountants and economists and finance directors that if a man is appointed to such a job, he will be looked upon, one of the women told me, giggling slightly, as a 'weak man'. Which should go down well among the accountancy fraternity in the City.

The only factory I visited that was rushed off its feet was manufacturing television sets. 'You must have a big market, all these television sets you're producing,' I commented to the manager as we wandered up and down the production line.

'Oh no. These are not for sale,' he said. 'The government ordered them. They want to use them to pay for the gas we import from Russia. They are going to try to pay in television sets instead of money because we have no money.'

'You don't mean to say,' I said nervously, 'that they don't work.'

'Not all of them,' he grinned.

Wherever I went, hotels, shops, offices, factories, there was a lot of deep-seated resentment. 'We work hard. Very hard. We have nothing,' a manager in one factory told me. 'There's a young man. He's twenty-one. He has car, he has mobile phone, he has everything. Why?'

That evening I went back with him to his flat. On the way we had to collect his kids from school. 'In the old days, if we were one minute late for school, literally one minute, we had to write a long explanation saying why we were late. Now it doesn't matter. Nobody cares,' he remarked as we waited outside with all the other mums and dads. 'In the old days, when we were young we had to learn everything: philosophy, medicine, biology, the Party history. At ten years old we knew more than American graduates. But today it's different. Children are getting like Americans.'

A teacher goes into a class and asks the kids, 'How tall is President Lukashenko?'

'Five feet seven inches,' shouts out one of the boys in the front row.

'So how do you know?' says the teacher.

'Easy,' says the boy. 'My father is six foot two inches. Every day he puts his hand up to his neck and says, "Lukashenko, I have had him up to here."'

*** *

The following day, out towards Khatyn, where the Graveyard of Villages commemorates no fewer than 185 Belorussian villages completely destroyed by the Nazis, I came across the exact opposite: a group of serious, determined, young people trying to stimulate interest in Belorussian culture. They were teaching each other Belorussian, reading Belorussian books - or at least reading anything they could find written by Jacob Kolas, who is about the only Belorussian who's been able to string a couple of words together in his native language over the last couple of hundred years. They were also studying engravings by Francis Skaryna, who seems to have been the William Blake of Belarus (well, the Polish-Lithuanian Commonwealth, as it was called at the time he was around, but I'm not fussy if you're not).

Pick up any old Bible, if you can find one, in Poland, Lithuania, Russia or even Belarus itself, and the chances are not only was it translated by the Great Man himself, but that he drew all the strange Byzantine Slavonic pictures as well. One particularly enthusiastic young man told me that after the break-up of the old Soviet Union and the general relaxation in everything, he decided he wanted to become a Christian. He wanted his baptism to be conducted in Belorussian, the language of his country, but he couldn't find a priest anywhere in Belarus who spoke it. In the end he went to Vilnius, next door in Lithuania. There in the big, rock-solid Greek temple of a Catholic Church in the centre of town, he found a priest who was prepared to learn enough Belorussian to be able to baptise him.

To raise money for their activities, the youngsters said, they spent their spare time selling traditional prints and paintings. They were dreadful, but I bought a handful. When I finally staggered back to the hotel, negotiated the lift, and found what I hoped was my room, I discovered the truth. I'd come all this way and spent all that money to acquire the most awful, cheap, glittery pictures of cats and dogs printed in, would you believe, Hitchin in Hertfordshire.

On the bus on the way back to Minsk, squeezed between sacks of potatoes, I sat next to an old school-teacher. In many ways, he said, Belarus had at one time been the most Jewish of all the once-Jewish countries in Eastern Europe. Minsk, Pinsk, Vitebsk, Mogilev, Borbrusk, Gormel, all had large Jewish populations. In many cases, they were even in the majority. Weizmann, Shazar, Begin, Peres, Chagall, Soloveitchik and many other famous and influential Jewish figures came from Belorussia. One hundred years ago they made up 13 per cent of the population as a whole; today they were too few to even register as a percentage on the population charts. And, of course, every year they were getting fewer and fewer. The old were dying, the young were leaving, many for the US and Germany, but most to Israel.

On another day and another bus, up in the north-east, towards Vitsebsk, a wonderful old city which once had thirty churches and a glorious history stretching back 1,500 years, I discovered that the Belorussians were trying to persuade the Poles to let them build a highway across the top right-hand corner of their country. This would link them to Kaliningrad and the Baltic. It would be good for them, another old man told me, because it would give them access to the sea; good for Kaliningrad because they would get the increased business in and out; good for Lithuania, because it would mean the end, or almost the end, of virtually non-stop Russian convoys ploughing backwards and forwards between Kaliningrad and the motherland; and finally, of course, good for Poland, because of the project itself as well as the revenues it would produce. But instead of approaching the Poles and trying to put the deal together themselves, the Belorussians asked their big buddies the Russians for help. What did the Russians do? They got on to the Poles and started talking about a Corridor. Which, of course, is the last thing you do with the Poles. To them a Corridor is not a Corridor, it's Hitler demanding access to Danzig. So the chances of the whole thing coming off, the old man told me in a simile understood throughout the world, is about as likely as getting a drink out of your brother-in-law at Christmas. So did the Belorussians get mad with the Russians? What do you think?

This was the uncontaminated bit of Belarus. Wander around the contaminated bit by Chernobyl, or simply talk to people who've wandered around it, and you will be horrified. The worst-affected areas, which were evacuated – on a Belorussian map you will see town after town labelled 'Dead' – they are now using for Army exercises. What could be better? argue the military. Thousands and thousands of acres of empty land, no towns to worry about, no people to get in the way. They can have the time of their lives ploughing across fields, shooting up empty buildings and generally destroying the place. All good practice for the day NATO invades and it's their job to stop them from rolling on to Moscow. You can bet your life, however, that the big guys, the colonels and the generals, will be nowhere near the place. They'll be protecting their genes, not to mention their Levi's, in their *dachas* the other side of the country. It'll be the poor foot soldiers, or I suppose, tank soldiers, who'll have this pleasure.

If that were not bad enough, they're now allowing the old and the infirm back in again on the basis that if they didn't like where they were sent they might as well let them come back to die in peace in their own radioactive homes. It frees up accommodation for other people as well.

But what's a million times worse, what's totally out of this world, is that down on the plutonium-rich farms just downwind of Chernobyl, they are giving a warm welcome to new people actually moving into the area. The local Strelichovo Collective Farm has started advertising the somewhat unique attractions of the region in newspapers throughout areas of the old Soviet Union where there are problems – Azerbaijan, Georgia, Tajikistan and, of course, Chechnya – forgetting, no doubt, to mention that any newcomers will not only spend the rest of their short lives eating, drinking and breathing in radioactive toxins, but on a good day, if they cough up blood they could probably hit the devastated number 4 reactor itself.

Minsk is a bit of a ghost town, too. Nine hundred years ago it is supposed to have been a major trading centre between the Baltic and the Black Sea, but it only hit the big time in 1919, when Guess Who moved in and decided to make it the capital. Come the Second World War, however, most of it was destroyed. Guess Who then decided not only to rebuild it, but on a huge scale, destroying whatever the war had not already destroyed. Minsk was, after all, now the capital of a bigger country. As a result of the war they had grabbed bits and pieces of Poland. They were also a member of the United Nations in their own right and deserved a proper city of their own. The Belorussians agreed, and up went one Stalinist monstrosity after another. You get the impression that it wasn't so much planned as thrown together over the usual boozy dinner of Russian architects.

'Hey, Comradeski. What about a Red Square?'

'*Da.*'

'A big oneski.'

'*Da, da.*'

'And a – what's the word? – Parliamentski building?'

'*Da, da.*'

'And a university on the square.'

'*Da*. I mean *niet*. A university on the square, near the whatdyacallit building, that will mean problemskis. Big problemskis.'

'But we won't be here.'

'OK then, a university on the whatever-it-is-ski.'

'And a KGB building.'

'And a post office.'

'And a GUM department store. Must have somewhere to get my caviar.'

'Hey, we've forgotten.'

'What, another bottle?'

'*Niet*. A palace for the workers.'

'Mustn't forget the Palish of the …'

'All pillars.'

'Big room.'

'Like the Parthenon in Venice.'

'The Parthenon is not in Venice, it's in … it's in … it's in … zzzzzz.'

The result is massive, brutal buildings, enormous squares, streets so wide they are in different time zones and statues everywhere. The main street, dominated by the KGB headquarters at the centre, is a veritable textbook of Soviet architecture. At one end is the trades union headquarters, which looks like the proletarian version of the Parthenon, all pillars and gold. At the other is a vast square, bigger than Red Square in Moscow, they say. On one side is the Parliament building, outside it that great big highly polished statue of Lenin. Facing it is the architects' practical joke, the university, which is, of course, the last place anybody should put a university, especially if they want peace and quiet.

On another corner is the giant 500-room Hotel Minsk, which is famous the world over because it was built in less time than it takes for your coffee or breakfast to arrive in the morning. Khrushchev, turning up in Minsk some time in 1957, didn't like where he had to stay and, as anybody would do in the circumstances, promptly ordered a new hotel to be built there and then. It took them all of three months. Having stayed there a couple of times, all I can say is I'm surprised it took them that long. The Finns are about the only people I know who enjoy staying there. No sooner have they checked in than they are bombed out of their minds on vodka and drifting around all over the place stark naked.

As for the main street itself, it's full of grubby little shops, dusty old offices, something called London Boutique, more towering statues and, of course, the GUM department store. But everywhere there are ghosts: the ghosts of 5,000 Jewish children buried alive by the Nazis in a large trench along Ratomskaya Street; the ghosts of the German prisoners of war who were used as slave labour to build the new Minsk and were simply buried where they dropped. In the foundations, under the floors, between the walls.

Nevertheless, some people, usually Belorussians, claim that today Minsk is the Brussels of Eastern Europe because it is home to all the CIS (Commonwealth of Independent States) institutions that the Russians ran round setting up after the Soviet Union fell apart. Don't listen to them. Belgium has probably been trampled on as many times by its more important neighbours as Belarus, but it is a bundle of laughs compared to Minsk. Believe me, about the only thing to do in Minsk that keeps you warm and doesn't cost a fortune is sitting in front of the gas stove with the door open. Even with everything blazing non-stop the average monthly bill comes to less than a dollar. Admittedly Belarus owes the Russians a fortune for the gas, but so far they have managed to get away with it. As long as they don't find out that too many of their television sets don't work.

Failing that, you could take a look at the place and freeze to death. I decided to start off at the luxury presidential mansion and work my way up from there. As befits a president who sees himself as a man of the people, it is tucked away in a secret park-like setting minutes from the centre of town, protected by both natural and supernatural powers. The natural powers were not exactly inclined towards me. I'd no sooner got out of the car to pay my respects than I was pretty sharply told to get back in again and push offski. The supernatural powers, in the form of a holy spring at the end of the street, did not react to my presence quite so quickly, although they should prove more beneficial in the long run.

President Lukashenko is out fishing with the chief of the Belorussian KGB. They don't get a bite all day long.

Then, just as they're about to go home, the president feels something tugging on his line. He hauls in the fish. It's tiny. He goes to throw it back in.

'No, don't do that,' says the head of the KGB. 'Give it to me.'

The president gives it to him and he starts slapping it and thumping it and banging it on the ground.

'What are you doing?' asks the president.

'I'm trying to get it to tell us where the big ones are,' says the KGB chief.

From then on it was pot luck, I'm afraid. The town that was responsible for producing all the most detailed maps of the whole of the Soviet Union forgot to produce one of itself. I was left, therefore, to my own devices. Everywhere everybody was selling something. All along the pavements, in the subways, in the dark passageways to the Metro, all over the football stadium. 'I thought the government was against private enterprise,' I asked one businessman I met.

'It is,' he said. 'That's why so many people are selling things. They think it will be their last chance.'

What's the difference between a Russian crook and a Belorussian crook?
A Belorussian crook has no money.

I tried the Metro, which was fun, but not as much fun as Moscow or Peking or Samarkand. I got a cab round town, which seemed to be full of nothing but mile after mile after mile of faceless towerblocks. They started at the very edge of the city – on one side of the road was open country, on the other a towerblock – and continued through the middle and out the other side, until suddenly, there, across the road, was open country again. The most modern, the most beautifully designed and the most exciting part of the city was the old town, which is the newest old town in the world. When the Soviet planners realised there wasn't an old town to restore, they did what anybody who relied on the state for pay and privileges over and above the line of duty would do: they proposed to the government that they build a new Old Town.

Known as the Traetskaye Pradmestse, the Trinity Suburb, because it is bound by five streets and criss-crossed by five others, it is the only place where archae-ologists have found anything interesting. Well, I say inter-esting: they found some bits of ceramic dating back to the twelfth century which, even then, were made in Russia. Today it's like walking around a Disneyworld designed by the French – all structure and no substance. The buildings, which certainly look old, are all neat and brightly painted. The little squares are pleasant. The one or two bars look as though they could be fun once you had half a bottle of vodka inside you. But it lacks any kind of buzz, probably because facing it is the memorial to all the desperately young Belorussian soldiers who died fighting on the side of their friends in Afghanistan. Occasionally the reserve breaks down and a whole bunch of guys desert the bars and spend the night drinking themselves out of their minds stretched out around the memorial.

No matter where I went people seemed to be plodding backwards and forwards. In the countryside they seemed to plod for miles, the lucky ones wrapped up in their thread-bare overcoats, the others in virtual rags. In Minsk they plod shorter distances. Hardly anybody talked to anyone else, and those who did were doing so as if they were committing a crime. Nobody was even smiling, let alone laughing.

A couple had a parrot. It kept saying, 'Down with Lukashenko!'

One of their neighbours denounced them to the police. The police arrived, and as the couple saw them coming they put the parrot in the fridge. The police searched the apartment, couldn't find the parrot and left. The couple went to take the parrot out of the fridge. As they opened the door they could hear it saying, 'I love President Lukashenko.'

'What do you mean, you love President Lukashenko?' they said. 'A moment ago you were against him.'

'Yes,' said the parrot. 'But that was before I was sent to Siberia.'

The other ghost which hangs over Minsk is, of course, that of Lee Harvey Oswald, who lived at Vulitsa Kisjaleva 2 and worked as a checker, first grade, in the experimental shop at the Belvar Company, a big armaments plant just round the corner from the Kolas Memorial.

Call me suspicious if you must, but there was no way he was in Minsk for his health. Think about it. Minsk today is not exactly a bundle of laughs; Minsk in Oswald's time, in the 1960s, in the depths of the Cold War, was certainly no party. Living conditions must have been very grim, the atmosphere pretty heavy, the working conditions tough. Today people earn US$20 a month and think they're doing OK. Why did he do it? How did he manage to get a flat? How did he get the job? How did he keep the job? Those were the days, don't forget, when it was impossible to get a visa in and out of the country. It's difficult enough today, but it's a million times easier than it was then. For an American to be living and working in a state industry in Minsk during the height of the Cold War without the knowledge of the KGB, and especially the Belorussian KGB, beggars belief. It's just not possible. Which means, my dear Watson, that he was there with permission.

Why was he there with permission? Because they liked the colour of his eyes? Because they thought they could benefit from his vast experience of American manufacturing technology? Or because they thought that some time or another they could use him? Like it or not, you'd have to say he was there because they thought they could use him. Now the crunch question. Who is 'they', if you see what I mean? The official KGB, or a maverick group either within the KGB or outside it and in competition with the KGB? For what it's worth, my roubles are on a maverick group loyal to Khrushchev. First, I don't believe the KGB, for all the terror and horrors for which it has been responsible, would come up with a plan to assassinate the US president. Second, if it did, it is still a huge bureaucracy, and I cannot see such a huge bureaucracy being able to take that kind of decision. The mavericks, however, had seen Khrushchev humiliated over Cuba, saw the way Kennedy was rubbing salt in his wounds, and decided to take their revenge. Who should they ask to do the deed but this poor guy working in an armaments factory in Minsk? It was perfect.

The Belorussians don't make a fuss about Oswald at all. There is no plaque on the wall, no guided tours, no souvenirs. It's pretty difficult even to find his flat. Maybe it's because the Russians asked them not to embarrass the Americans. Or maybe it's because they think it might give somebody some ideas...

LUXEMBOURG

Forget secrecy, forget reputation, forget stability. Forget language, culture, location. Forget the range of services on offer. When it comes to choosing a tax haven, think only of the important things in life. Sinking bar bonds, high-yielding restaurant growth stocks, exotic option look-back clubs, racing track-certainty currency growth funds, casino-denominated Swiss franc-guaranteed funds, bench-mark thirty-year opera treasuries, non-negotiable theatre derivatives. And as many bonds, government and otherwise, as you think you can endure. I mean, imagine earning a fortune and having to spend the rest of your days yawning all the way to the bank in some god-forsaken tax haven like Luxembourg.

I remember driving one morning all the way from Luxembourg to Brussels. It was like going back to the nineteenth or even the eighteenth century. The only person I saw all the way to the non-existent border was an old lady in black rinsing out a dirty old orange plastic bowl by the roadside. It was 8.30 in the morning, and this was the richest country in the world. In fact the whole place is a perpetual Sunday morning. To look at it's a bit like the Lake District – without the lakes, and without the crowds. I don't think I have ever seen a crowd of anything there, even though they've got the cheapest booze and cigarettes anywhere in Europe. What few people you come across all seem to be old and slow and stolid, no matter what age they are, the kind who, if the speed limit is 50 kilometres an hour, will stick to 40 in case there is a fault in the speedometer.

On the fun, fun, fun index some cities are dead by seven o'clock at night. Luxembourg is dead by seven o'clock in the morning - and that's official. The European Union carried out a survey to find the most boring place in the whole community, and guess which one came out on top? On every other count they don't just come bottom, they fall off the edge of the chart. And no wonder. They don't have any art galleries or sports stadia, there's no opera, no ballet, no concert hall, no nothing.

Around the Grund, the so-called swinging centre of Luxembourg, the only thing that is swinging are all the 'closed' signs. The solitary theatre-restaurant is closed, the jazz club is closed. There are just two people in Scott's Bar. Goodness me, what's gone wrong? There are five people in the Pygmalion, drinking Guinness; another five in the Britannia, drinking mineral water. But four of them are probably carrying out yet another European Union survey to find out how boring Luxembourg is. The only man I've ever come across who actually liked the place - he was a film critic, which tells you how much he knew about reality - told me that it had more Michelin-star restaurants per square kilometre than anywhere else on earth. For the life of me, I couldn't find one, and it was not for want of trying.

For excitement about the only thing they've got - and that's only if you're really desperate - is the Kirchberg or European Château. This is chock-a-block with fun spots such as the European Parliament Secretariat, the European Court of Justice, the European Investment Bank and the European Court of Auditors. Apart from that there are some restaurants on the Boulevard Franklin Roosevelt, which, again, are always closed whenever I go there, and some jewellery shops in the Place D'Armes and on the Avenue Monterey. There is the Place de la Gare and the Avenue de la Gare. Oh yes, I nearly forgot, through the middle of town is this enormous gorge. On one side stand the Grand Duke's Ruritanian Castle and the old town, on the other, some pretty miserable 1960s office blocks. There are no traffic jams, no lager louts, no beggars, nobody sleeping in cardboard boxes, no dog mess. If your dog messes, you put your money into this thing that looks like a parking meter. Out comes a plastic bag, you do your civic duty and – scoop – it's gone. So what do they do with themselves? They sleep. Honestly. It's their favourite pastime. Their second favourite pastime is taking it easy. I'm not kidding: that was the result of yet another poll into the drab lives and boring times of the Luxemburgers.

Luxembourg makes a big thing about being the melting pot of Europe. Don't you believe it. Foreign nationals, who make up a third of the population and half the workforce, know exactly where they stand. Firmly behind the sign saying, 'second-class citizens'. For no matter how much money they pour into the *banques* of Luxembourg they are denied what many people would say are the three basic human rights every man, woman and anonymous deposit-holder are entitled to: the right to vote in local elections; the right to stand for local elections; the right to complain like mad about the people they didn't vote for in local elections. Which means that the whole country at local, village and town level is in the tight grip of a tiny minority of the total population. Some villages are, for example, 60 per cent Portuguese, but their elected representatives are 100 per cent Luxemburgers. So what are they doing about it? Nothing. It's too much effort. In any case, the Luxemburgers won't stay awake long enough to listen to what they've got to say. Consequently Luxembourg looks and feels and behaves like any one of a dozen countries, so the poor foreign guys don't know whether to eat croissants, hang their bedclothes out of the window, have a language crisis or hang around all day waiting for someone to buy them a drink.

Yet to many people it is the centre of the world. Go to St Peter's? Go to Mecca? Even go to Budleigh Salterton? Forget it. Their sole aim in life is to make an annual pilgrimage to the Boulevard Royale, the Avenue de la Liberté or even the Avenue Emile Reuter; their only travelling companion a briefcase, a canvas holdall or a simple plastic bag. For to them Luxembourg is not a country at all. It's a string of banks – it has one bank for every 2,000 inhabitants – and a host of different investment funds, 2,000 at the last count, and still growing. Not that I have any personal experience of this, you understand, as a boring, hard-working, law-abiding British citizen eternally loyal to tax Britannica. If, however, I was suddenly elected a Labour MP and appointed a Treasury minister, I suppose I would very quickly change my mind.

The last time I was there I got a cab from the station. The driver, an Iranian, told me he'd been a teacher in Tehran. When the ayatollahs took over he left – he didn't want his two daughters shrouded in veils for the rest of their lives. First he went to Brussels, seeking a job at the Commission, but no go. He ended up driving taxis. He spent so much time carrying Belgian businessmen to Luxembourg and back so that they could stash their money away from the taxman he decided to stay. 'Boulevard Royale', he told me, 'is the centre of the world. They all come here – doctors, dentists, government people, even taxi-drivers. If you have money in Belgium, Holland or Germany you keep it in Luxembourg. It's better. Everybody is doing it.'

Apparently, all you have to do is saunter into any bank and flip open your briefcase. If you've got two pennies or two dollars or even two roubles to rub together, you're in. No names, no ID, no references. None of this 'What school did your father go to?' nonsense. You just fill in the form. Name? Donald Duck, Mickey Mouse or the Grand Duke Schwarzburg-Rudolstadt III, it doesn't make any difference. If you want to leave it blank, you just leave it blank. Address? Again, that's up to you. Buckingham Palace, Chernobyl-on-Sea. Somerset House, London SW1 or Serious Fraud Office, Elm Street, London WC1. Whatever you want to say. Now close your eyes and count up to ten. You're now a member of one of the most exclusive clubs in the world. And you don't have to restrict yourself to one bank account, either. You want two bank accounts? You can have two bank accounts. You want three? You can have three. Fifty-three? You can have fifty-three. In your own name, in fifty-three different names, no problem, they're yours.

It's not just the big guys in dark glasses who are at it. The banks are just as happy looking after Dutch taxi-drivers, Belgian barmen, German car mechanics, French restaurant-owners and European Union officials running the community's Common Agricultural Policy. I know, because every Dutch taxi-driver, Belgian barman, German car mechanic, French restaurant-owner and European Union official running the community's Common Agricultural Policy I've come across keeps telling me that the only way to make money in this world is to stash it away in some secret bank account in the Boulevard Royale and watch it grow and grow and grow.

One Dutch taxi-driver recalled that when he first went into the Grand Banque de Luxembourg in the Boulevard Royale, he didn't know what to do. 'I go up to the counter. The bank official he says, "Yes?" I say I have half-million dollars, can I put them in bank? The official, guess what he says? He says, "Why not? There is nothing to be ashamed of in being poor." '

From the tax point of view, of course, Luxembourg couldn't be better. No income tax, no capital gains, no stamp duty, nothing. On top of that it's 200 per cent safe, reliable, rock-solid, dyed in the wool, and behind every dodge you can think of to avoid paying any government anywhere in the world anything at all. What's more, you need have no worries that they are going to split on you. I'm not saying that bank secrecy in Luxembourg is tighter than it is in Switzerland, it is just that these guys could convince your own mother you never existed.

Investment recommendation: never in a million years.

If Luxembourg is for Dutch taxi-drivers, Belgian barmen and the rest of them, how about the other European tax havens?

Monte Carlo is, I reckon, for people who made their money the old-fashioned way. In other words, they inherited it. Somerset Maugham used to call it a 'sunny place for shady people'. Today it's a shady place for sunny people. Especially for all those German strippers who seem to be hooked on trading separately the principal and interest on their government bonds and just want to have funds, funds, funds. Every square inch is packed with so many hotels, apartment buildings, banks and office blocks that the sun hasn't got a hope in hell of getting through. But that apart, it's got everything else Luxembourg hasn't. Elegance. Fashion. Untold luxuries. The good life extraordinaire. And the friendliest sharks you could expect to meet anywhere in the world.

'It's Grace Kelly soaked in gin,' an old American banker once told me.

'It's like walking into the pages of *Hello!* magazine,' a young American banker added.

Unbelievably minute – the entire place is smaller than

London's Hyde Park – it has everything the tax exile could possibly want. The Oceanographic Museum with 25,000 books. The Exotic Garden with thousands of cacti. A wonderful Princess Grace Rose Garden with... No, I'm only kidding. It's got some of the best bars and restaurants in the whole universe. The Louis XV in the Hotel de Paris, where a slab of foie gras and a couple of new potatoes in the fantastic baroque dining room will cost you, or the expense account, a cool arm and two legs. It's so exclusive and loaded with so many stars that even Alain Ducasse, their chef, cannot afford to eat there. He dines further down the road in La Meranda in Nice. His favourite dish is boudin, black pudding, dried salt cod or fresh pasta with basil. Or Jacques, or Henri, or Marcel, or, I suppose, whoever happens to be around at the time.

As for something to drink, the Hotel de Paris also boasts, among other things, that it has the biggest hotel wine cellar in the world. It was just my luck that on my one and only visit I was with a couple of clients who insisted on drinking mineral water. Canadians, of course, damn them. If you're worrying about the running costs of the Ferrari, try its little sister, the Hermitage. Once the secret hideaway of the in crowd from Paris, today it seems to be the place for cocktail parties and lots of Chanel-clad women sitting around sipping Perrier.

Talking of entertainment, Monte Carlo has probably the most famous opera house in the world. It is famous not because it's a scaled-down version of the Paris Opera House – it seats just 500 people – but because it was the scene of Nijinsky's legendary leap through the open windows at the premiere of *La Spectre de la Rose*. Whether it would have been equally legendary if the window had been closed is, of course, another matter. If the opera is not your hammer, then never fear. Tell the wife you've got to make a phone call, send her on ahead, dash quickly through the door to the left of the Opera House and you're in the Casino, also one of the most famous of its ilk in the world. Built by the same man who built the Paris Opera and the scaled-down Monte Carlo Opera House next door, this is the real thing. Grand marble entrance halls, soaring ceilings, enormous Bohemian crystal chandeliers, great arched doorways, huge murals of wistful pre-Raphaelite damsels. Tuxedos, women dripping in jewels, some with so many rocks on their fingers they can hardly lift their hands. It is also rumoured to have been the scene of many legendary leaps through open windows, but nobody talks about that. Which is not surprising, because the betting, believe me, is out of this world. Sometimes you see on the green baize tables so many piles of chips, each worth thousands and thousands of pounds, that you wonder how they can shift the lot without the aid of a JCB. But they do, and then it's off to Jimmy's or Parady'z, or even the Sass-Café in the old Lambo – Lamborghini to the likes of you and me – to celebrate the night away.

How do they manage it? Easy. Stroke the knee of the bronze horse carrying Louis XIV outside the Hotel de Paris – it's guaranteed to bring you luck. However lucky you get, contrary to what they sing, nobody has yet broken the bank since they opened for business in 1891, and probably nobody ever will. But you may like to bet on that.

As for the other essential ingredients in the life of a tax exile, Monte Carlo has them as well. Along the Place du Casino and the Boulevard des Molins, your Saint-Laurents and Armanis and Alain Manoukians are two a penny or, I suppose, seven a French franc. What they cost, I have no idea, but then, if you have to ask the price there's no point asking the trustees whether you can go to Monte Carlo. Neither do I know how much anything costs in the Marché de la Condamine on the Place des Armes, the giant

open-air Harrods Food Hall of the place. Like Harrods
Food Hall, they sell a fantastic range of Middle Eastern
delicacies. A Grande Sonnerie is the ultimate status symbol
if you're going to live in Monte Carlo. Now, I know how
much that costs: US$1 million. What is it? A wristwatch.
Which just shows how out of place you would be in
Monte Carlo.

The other big advantage of Monte Carlo, which has one
policeman for every sixty champagne bottles, is that it's
super, super, safe. The hard-up widow of a once mega-rich
businessman can still go out at night for a game of bingo and
walk home afterwards in her fake imitation jewellery
without once attracting the attention of a mugger or
realising that the real stuff was long ago pawned by his
mistress in a back street in Marseilles for the price of a shot
of heroin for her Algerian boyfriend. Apartments arc secure,
especially if they've got Italian marble floors, sound-proof
cushioned walls, bullet-proof windows, a Jacuzzi, six
bathrooms, four bedrooms and cost around US$10 million.
The more expensive ones throw in security cameras and a
couple of guards as well. Traffic, however, can be a problem
at certain times of the year, with gangs of multimillionaires
racing round and round the narrow streets and along the
palm-fringed esplanade practically faster than the speed of
sound. But whenever that happens, everybody locks themselves indoors and wonders why the hell they chose to
come to Monte Carlo in the first place.

That apart, everything is whiter than white. So white
that I reckon it's secretly sponsored by some detergent
company. There is one problem, and it's a big problem. If
you decide to become a Monégasque, you're immediately
barred from ever going into the casino again. You have
been warned.

Investment recommendation: buy. Providing you can get

hold of a Grande Sonnerie, otherwise they'll treat you as, my God, nouveau riche.

Switzerland. Well, yes, I suppose that's a maybe. But it's not exactly fun, fun, fun, is it? In any case, it's not exactly a tax haven, either. Tax rates are about the same as anywhere else. Foreigners have to pay either normal tax on their earnings from their Swiss investments, or cough up a stiff no-questions-asked 35 per cent multiholding tax. And all this secrecy stuff is for the movies. Gone are the days when you could hide behind your lawyer. Today, if these guys suspect you're up to any kind of shilly chalet, they will spill the beans on you as quickly as slice an apple in half on top of your head. Especially if too many people are leaning on them.

Liechtenstein? You've got to be joking. First of all because the capital, Vaduz, is nothing like you imagine. A tiny mountain village way up in the Alps? An enormous, eerie Gothic castle brooding over cowed hordes? A drawbridge? Creaking doors? Bats? Thunder and lightning? Snow swirling around the battlements? Wooden stakes in the graveyard? No way. It's nothing but a collection of open-air cafés and souvenir shops and anonymous office buildings, not to mention an Old Castle Inn and a Super Discount Store. To tell you the truth, it's as bland and antiseptic and squeaky-clean as a Swiss cheese label. Every time I go there I keep hoping to see Julie Andrews come tripping round the corner practising her scales just to liven the place up a bit.

Furthermore - and this I find unbelievable - they don't even have any big, expensive shops. No Guccis, no Givenchys, no Yves Saint-Laurents, no Tiffany's, no big, expensive sports car-dealers. Instead there's a cheap, downmarket Arcade des Modes, an Adrian Huber jewellery outfit and a collection of souvenir shops. The only stores that seem to be doing well are the shop selling a million different types of Swiss Army knives – was I thinking there was only one kind – and the shop selling big, expensive suitcases. Why that should be the case I have no idea. As for fast cars, the only one I've ever seen there was an old Porsche, and that was parked opposite the post office. In the public car park. Surrounded by broken beer bottles.

As for excitement – apart from the three-day Treesonburg Oompah Festival, of course – my only thrill was seeing a sign saying, 'British Motorcycles'. I followed the direction it was pointing and stumbled down a side street. Suddenly, there in front of me – oh, the glories of being British – was a notice proclaiming to the world, 'Royal Enfields. Ariels. Matchless.' I marched proudly up to the door, painted with a huge Union Jack, to the strains, I swear, of 'Land of Hope and Glory'. With a lump in my throat, I knocked on the door. No response. The place had closed down years ago. Because of – how can I say this? – lack of business.

The other thing that puts me off Liechtenstein is that they've just discovered – I have to say this – democracy. Previously everybody followed the so-called Liechtenstein party line, which was whatever the ruler, His Serene Highness Prince Hans Adam II, Duke of Rietburg and Count of Troppau, said or thought. Even when he suggested legalising heroin and cocaine. Now the 14,000 Leichtensteiners, if that's what you call them, want a genuine say in running their own affairs. Until recently the Parliament has virtually always gone along with the Prince, the Duke, the Count or whatever you call him, but now they are electing an opposition party which will actually oppose him. The problem is the possibility of change. The last thing any tax exile or offshore investor wants, apart from a visit by the taxman, is the possibility of change. Today they might just be talking about bland things like painting the road signs with lead-free paint, but tomorrow, who knows what might happen? Prince Hans Adam might decide he's fed up with financing not only his fancy castle but the country as a whole and decide to take off for Luxembourg. Highly unlikely, I admit, but it's not worth the risk.

Zug? Now, that's a much better bet. It's bigger, more organised, more grown up and has a better class of graffiti. On top of that it's actually got a high street as well – and one wide enough to take four lanes of traffic. Side by side. All at the same time. It's got office buildings four and five storeys high which are not, would you believe, banks. And it has shops selling everything the Swiss consider essential for survival: expensive clothes, expensive shoes, expensive jewellery, expensive cars and, of course, expensive suitcases. It also has some proper restaurants, like the Aklin and the Baarerhof, and a proper hotel, the Ochsen, which looks as though it was built out of gold bars with a stack of Toblerones on top as a roof.

The only thing that puts me off is the Schweizerischer-Bank. They were running what I thought was a somewhat unique advertising campaign for a bank supposedly trying to attract foreign investors. Wherever I looked were their posters distinctly featuring the two-fingers sign.

Liechtenstein and Zug do have one thing in common, however. In neither place did I see a single policeman, which could be the most important factor of all.

Investment recommendation: stick to cuckoo clocks. You can always throttle the damn thing if it gets too much for you.

The Channel Islands? Do you really want to spend the rest of your life marooned on a rock with – hic 80,000 alcoholics – forever – hic – having to walk in the street because Alan Whicker has – hic – parked his battered old Bentley on the pavement again? You can tell it's Alan Whicker's, say the locals, because it's covered in parking tickets. Alternatively, there is always the thrill of yet again being thrown out of the Longueville Manor, the only decent restaurant on Jersey, because it's been taken over lock, stock and barrel for the week by another – hic – super tax exile desperately trying to make friends with the locals. Failing that you could spend every waking minute queuing up at your garage pleading with them to yet again decoke the old Ferrari because – hic – you never get the chance of putting the damn thing into second gear.

And if that's not bad enough, do you honestly mean to say you fancy being woken up every morning at five o'clock when they start washing the streets down; spending your mornings wandering around De Gruchy's and Voisin, the two big department stores on the island; your afternoons visiting the Jersey Potter and your evenings proposing toasts to the Duke of Normandy, which, for some reason or other, is what they call the Queen? Not to mention the Norwegians. Whenever I go there the island is practically overrun by Norwegians who, unaccountably, have gone absolutely bananas about *Bergerac*, and insist on being photographed by every street corner, pillarbox and manhole cover they have ever seen on the box.

On the other hand, I suppose it does have its advantages. It's 100 per cent safe. There are no muggings or robberies or break-ins, because to buy anything even as simple as an iron bar or a jemmy, let alone a striped sweater, costs more than anyone could possibly steal in a month of repeats of *Whicker's World*. The only crime on the island, more likely than not, takes place deep inside the million and one banks huddled around the centre of the tiny capital, St Helier, although despite the presence of no fewer than thirteen different police forces on the island, not one has ever been detected. Which might, of course, have something to do with the fact that under their funny French local-government system, the thirteen local magistrates to whom the thirteen different police forces report change every month. So sooner or later everybody gets a chance of being a magistrate and dismissing any cases that are brought against them.

And it's politically stable. Nothing has changed for over 900 years. These were the guys, don't forget, who were responsible for 1066 and all that, which is probably why they call the Queen the Duke of Normandy. It is financially stable. Investors are guaranteed 100 per cent protection, 100 per cent secrecy and, if you're an international firm of accountants, limited liability. Which means there's a limit to the number of times they expect you to risk your life stepping off the pavement and walking in the street because of Alan Whicker's Bentley.

As for the French, forget it. Their influence is *rien*. How do I know? Because the main street in St Helier, the Rue de Derrière, is known as King Street. That's how I know.

Investment recommendation: sell. Especially those woolly jumpers you wear for golf. Hic.

Gibraltar? Come on. Who wants to be stuck on a 5-square-kilometre lump of limestone rock staring at a bunch of Barbary apes? To the Romans it was the gateway to Hell. To Molly Bloom, the most famous daughter ever of any of Gibraltar's military officials, it was simply, 'O Rocks'. To Brits living in the days of Mr Wilson's government, when it was actually against the law to take more than £50 out of the country or visit anywhere outside the sterling area, it was the gateway to Paradise. Like good socialist boys and girls everybody would make for Gibraltar. Once there, it was off with the shoes and socks and whatever else to retrieve the bunch of notes they had loyally smuggled out of the country. Then off to the bank to change the lot into pesetas and off to Spain and the bright lights and the action.

On my first visit to Gibraltar I flew in from Casablanca. Sitting next to me on the plane was one of these merchant-banker types in his pin-striped suit, pin-striped shirt and pin-striped tie. No sooner had he embarked than he settled down in his seat, strapped on his seatbelt and buried his big, thick, strawberry nose in a big, thick, greasy paperback hidden behind a copy of *The Times,* which was unfortunately upside down. He refused drinks. He turned down the quick snack. He didn't even look up when they came round with the duty-frees. When we landed, no sooner had the engines stopped than he was up and away to Aldershot-on-Sea leaving the book and the upside-down copy of *The Times* on the seat behind him. I just couldn't help accidentally glancing at the book. It was Jilly Cooper's *Polo,* which he obviously thought, even so far from home, wasn't suitable reading of the huntin', shootin' and fishin' set.

Originally I intended to spend a couple of days there. I had heard that the pioneers of the great 'exempt company' dodge – I mean concept – were planning to turn themselves into a bit of a tax haven. They were putting up a whole Europort complex with the usual mix of giant office blocks and luxury hotels. Some people were even talking about the place becoming the Hong Kong of the Med. But when I saw we were coming into land not at an airport but on the actual main road to the Spanish border, I decided – no disrespect to the red pillarboxes, the British-style bobbies and the Barbary apes – to pick up my bags and check right back in again. Had we not come in to land on the local railway line I would have stayed. I must have been there for all of thirty – no, I tell a lie, thirty-two minutes. The extra two minutes was the time it took me to flick through Jilly Cooper to decide I didn't want to read it behind either an upside-down or right-side-up copy of *The Times.*

Since then, of course, Gibraltar has developed enormously. It is more than just a tax haven. Apparently, not too many people fancied the idea of living somewhere that was a mix of Moorish, Regency, Genoese and cheap Ministry of Defence shacks with people of British, Spanish, Portuguese and Italian descent. So now it is a major centre for smuggling drugs from Africa into Europe and cigarettes into Spain. So worried are the authorities about the number of ships ploughing backwards and forwards from Morocco loaded with drugs that they've decided there is only one way to stop them. They're going to build a tunnel instead. As far as the cigarette trade is concerned, I'm told that all night and practically all day long as well, the Winston boys, in their black leather jackets, ponytails and dark glasses, are ploughing backwards and forwards in stripped-down speedboats loaded with crates of cigarettes from the eastern beach across the border to Spain.

Use Gibraltar as a tax haven? No way. It would be more trouble than a wagonload of monkeys. Barbary, of course.

Investment recommendation: buy. Cigarettes. Millions of them. From the Winston boys. You'll make millions.

On the other side of the great enemy, Spain, is Andorra, way up in the middle of the Pyrenees. This is more your downmarket, bargain-basement tax haven. The location, however, is spectacular – so spectacular that Andorra doesn't deserve to exist. There you are driving through tiny little villages and hills and valleys and mountains that have obviously been lifted straight off a French cheese label, when suddenly you find yourself in this dreary nondescript little town which seems to be full of nothing but car showrooms, caravan parks, huge billboards advertising cigarettes and masses of strange unknown banks with funny names such as Banca Reig, Credit Andorra and the International Bank of Commerce.

The car showrooms are not your ordinary car showrooms. These sell only your upmarket cars. There is even one selling Rolls-Royces. Yet every time I've been there I've only ever seen one expensive car on the roads, a Porsche. The caravan parks are straight from Hell, with billboards so huge you can hardly see the mountains. As for the shops, they're drab. Even the jewellery shops, which is some achievement. The banks almost make you wish you were poor. In other words, reduced to drinking a bottle of champagne a day. Non-vintage, of course. There is no buzz about the place, no style. It's the kind of place where you see people photographing each other outside those strange-sounding banks. Which, let me tell you, is something you never see in grown-up tax havens like, say, Monte Carlo or the Cayman Islands. What's more, it's always raining.

In the old days, of course, life was simple. Whatever Franco decided, they did the opposite. Franco said, 'No luxury goods in Spain.' Andorra sold luxury goods. Franco said, 'High taxes on this.' Andorra said, 'Forget the taxes.' Once Spain went constitutional and graduated to the European Community, they hit problems. Their only salvation today is to waive the VAT, especially on, as you would expect, booze, fags, perfume and petrol. On everything else – jewellery, electrical goods, clothes – they cut their margins and just hope to goodness they'll make up for it in volume.

As for the important things in life, there's no income tax, no corporation tax and it's small. In fact it's so small that practically all the government offices are in one building, an ordinary-looking three-storey block. When I first went there I thought I was in for a couple of days dragging myself from one government department to another to another. In the event I was finished in a single morning. It was fantastic. But it was still raining. I had a quick look at the swinging centre of town - which, I kid you not, was a field of cabbages - a wander around a couple of banks and a quick drink in a bar round the back of the Novotel. Then I was O-U-T, back to a real country and to some decent eating and drinking.

But don't get me wrong - I like Andorra, no, I love it. It's the only place I know in the whole wide world where French culture has clashed head on with another culture and lost. In theory, it's supposed to be half French and half Spanish. The head of government is supposed to be a job-share between the president of France and the Bishop of Seo de Urgel, a pleasant little town just on the other side of the border. Why the Bishop of Seo de Urgel? Because, don't forget, these señors in Andorra are not Spanish, they're Catalans. And to the fiercely independent Catalans, the Bishop of Seo de Urgel, or any Catalan from anywhere in the world, for that matter, is the equal to any old president of France. And, would you believe, the French agreed.

As a result, no way is this an international tax haven. This is a Catalan tax haven with the French very much *numéro deux*. Go into a bar and order a Cognac in French and you'll be greeted with a glare. Try to buy a bottle of French champagne with French francs. *Mon Dieu,* are you off your *tête*? Introduce yourself to an official in the Ministry of Finance in French and he'll cut you dead in two seconds. It's so wonderful you feel like throwing your beret in the air and kissing everybody. Twice. Once on each cheek. As far as they are concerned the only thing that counts is Catalan. French is nothing, Spanish is nothing.

If you don't fancy learning Catalan, try Polish. Speak Polish, say your family is Polish, even hint that you once spent a weekend in Warsaw and they're all over you. Because during the war they set up some huge international network which helped many Poles escape from occupied France. Even today, they have still not signed a peace treaty with Germany, although it doesn't, of course, stop them selling German cars and German everything else.

As for living there, God help us. Can you imagine it? Mornings you'd be filling in time mooching around the Markut supermarket, studying the grass in the Parc Central and desperately trying not to eat one of those big, chocolate whirly things for breakfast. Afternoons you'd be dragging yourself around the Museum of Miniatures, pretending to buy a Ferrari in yet another showroom, attempting to make coffee at the Hotel Garden last for an hour and a half and practising scrawling Viva Catalonia, on walls. Evenings would be spent watching those cabbages grow, counting the days to the next Andorra International Jazz Festival, making an effort not to crack jokes about the Andorran national football team or their Navy and learning how to blow up walls which have 'Viva Catalonia' scrawled all over them. And, in the rain, of course, which at least means liquidity is not a problem. On the other hand, when it's not raining, it's invariably snowing.

Investment recommendation: fantastic. Providing, of course, you're an umbrella manufacturer. Otherwise forget it.

Vienna? Now there's a real possibility. It's got all the bars and restaurants and casinos and music and opera anyone could wish for. It's also flexible. What am I saying? It's super, super flexible. In some banks, if you want to open an account they don't even want to know your name or your address or even require anything as definite as a signature. I'm no expert on international financial shenanigans – all my money is tied up in champagne – but I seem to remember reading somewhere that you had to be Austrian before any Austrian bank would give you an anonymous Austrian account.

'That's right,' an Austrian bank manager told me. 'You just tell them you're Austrian and mutter a few words in German.'

'But don't they check?'

'Of course not. They want the business, don't they?'

Which is obviously why I'm investing in champagne. And under my own name as well. It is also obviously why Vienna is supposed to be a favourite spot for wheeler-dealers, taxi-drivers, drug barons, destitute ex-members of the KGB, members of the Serious Fraud Office investigating the way the European Community hands out funds in Eastern Europe and Arabs. It was not for nothing that the Austrians bent over backwards to get the OPEC offices based in Vienna.

Investment recommendation: brilliant. Especially if the bank manager lets you use his box at the opera.

Cyprus? If you're Russian, OK. But it is still a divided country and anything could happen. In any case, go anywhere near Cyprus and my old friends Patrick and Mary will be on to you to dig ditches, repair fences and put money into their donkey sanctuary.

Do you know, I don't think I'll bother to earn a fortune. It's just too complicated. Another glass of champagne, please, Michel, mon vieux. Hell. No. I'll have the bottle.

OPORTO

Well, guess what I discovered? Oporto, hailed for generations as the spiritual home of the port trade, the liquid
heaven of every club man in the world and the inventor of
gout, is not really Oporto at all. It's Porto. It's only the
English who insist on calling it Oporto. Goodness knows
why. We don't call Paris Oparis, or Frankfurt Ofrankfurt or
even Dublin, of all places, Odublin. We might, of course, call
Rio O-bloody-Rio because we don't want the wife to think
we actually enjoy going there and being forced to sit on
Copacabana Beach for hours on end sipping pink
champagne and looking at all the... looking at all the sights.
  But that's different.
  Maybe the fact that Porto is called Oporto is Oproofo
Opositivo of the odangers of otrying to do any oworko
after a heavy oluncho. You just tend to forget the
odetailso. 'Wake up, wake up, sir,' some secretary must
have said to the original Mr Taylor or Mr Sandemann or
Mr Ramos and Mr Pinto. 'It's the chairman. He wants to
know where you are. What shall I tell him?'
  'Oh, Porto or some other godforsaken bloody flea pit in
the middle of nowhere. Tell him I'm in a meeting. I'll call
him when... zzzzzz.'
  And it's been obloody Oporto ever since.
  I also discovered – prepare yourself: if you're a port
drinker you're not going to like this – that the centre of the

port trade is not Porto, or even Oporto. It's the Vila Nova de Gaia. Which I will leave you to translate as best you can otherwise I shall be accused of all kinds of things. Porto, or Oporto, is on one side of the River Douro and the Vila Nova de Gaia is the other. And I don't care what all the wine books say, or even what the lord high archbishop of wine Michael Broadbent himself says, the port business is definitely slap bang in the middle of the new town of… I mean the town of the new… you know where I mean.

So how come, my dears, all these fine upstanding, red braces, regimental ties, pin-striped suits and upper-class English accents of the portocracy kept that quiet for so long? No other wine region in the world is ashamed of its origins. In the Napa Valley they say they're in the Napa Valley, not in San Francisco. In Paarl they say they are in Paarl, not in Stellenbosch, or even Cape Town. Even in Graves, of all places, they don't try to hide the fact that their wine is produced in Graves and not in Bordeaux, where presumably there is even less body in the soil. In fact, when you come to think of it, the whole port business is a little, how shall I put it, odd. And I don't just mean all the red braces and pin stripes and all those upper-class English accents.

First there's the drink itself. It's neither one thing nor the other. Neither wine nor brandy. It's both. Thanks to a bunch of original red braces, regimental ties, pin stripes and upper-class English accents who, 300 years ago, realised they would never make a living shipping cheap Portuguese red wine, let alone cheap Portuguese brandy, back to the UK. It's the oldest marketing trick in the book. If you've got two duff products you add them together so that at the annual branch managers' meeting in Orio (branch managers never meet anywhere boring like Brighton or Rotterdam or, God help us, Auckland), you've only got to report one dud in your portfolio.

The port business is also the only drinks business in the world where, as far as I know, the production and blending and storage happens so far apart. In the wine business, the champagne business, the sherry business - damn it, even when in the alcopops business - production and bottling and storage is all carried out at the same place. Not so in the port business. The grapes are grown way up in the rugged Douro Valley. They are then shipped to O(hell, we can't say we're based in Gaia or we'll be the laughing stock of the drinks trade - we'll say we're based on the other side of the river in)porto. It's crazy. Vineyards produce their own wines at their own vineyards, or at least, at the local co-operative. They don't ship the stuff a million miles downstream and make it practically on the dockside. The only reason I can think for the port business to do it this way is that the guys in the fancy braces in Oporto didn't fancy living upstream with the natives. They preferred to stay close to the British hospital, the British school (where they spend ten years doing nothing but learning how to spit out their port so accurately that they can kill a fly at three paces), the British church, the British public convenience in the Passeio Alegre Gardens and, of course, the port, the ships and all those sailors.

Then, when they get the stuff to O(no, I don't have to actually go and visit a vineyard! Why can't I stay here in)porto, why do they insist on calling the warehouse a lodge? Now stand on one leg, wave your leather apron in the air and call me suspicious if you must, but what's wrong with warehouse, storage depot, blending and bottling facility, the works, the plant, the shed or the whatever? Why lodge? Unless, of course, you're thinking what I'm thinking.

And why do they call their holy of holies, the famous Factory House on the Rua Infante Dom Henrique, a factory house when it's neither a factory nor a house? A mortuary, maybe - it's cold enough inside even on the sunniest day and the whole place practically smells of death. The walls are lined with complete collections of *The Times* and Blackwoods going way back to before the beginning of history. Also framed are the latest reports from Waterloo as well as a request in 1809 from the British to French doctors to come and help care for the dying of O(hell, they're dying. Who's going to do the work for us now in)porto. Which, of course, they didn't. And the guys slumped in the chairs - well, who knows? They could be dead, it's difficult to tell. If they are, there's no rush to move them. They're probably so pickled they'll last out at least until the millennium.

Now, I know you think I'm getting paranoid because I haven't been getting my share, but I can assure you that's not true. I might not yet be in the same league as Dr Johnson, who could burn up three bottles a time without even trying, but I'm working on it.

To continue. What would you call the chairman of such an august body as the Factory House? Chairman? Wrong. He's called the treasurer. So what's his job? No, it's to supply the vintage port for the traditional Wednesday lunch. Why traditional? Because it's been held non-stop for the last 150 years? No, because no women are allowed, there's no smoking till 2 pm and everybody has to serve himself from a sideboard, presumably because that's the way you do things in grand houses when you have lots of servants. Wait a minute, you don't think it's that, because of their… attitude, they have problems finding and keeping waiters, do you? And why are the lunches held on Wednesday? To review the week? To catch up on the latest news? To make certain everything is sorted out by Friday? It's because they think there is still no post in England on Sundays, so when they get back to their offices they can go to sleep without worrying about having to deal with news from the old country.

As for their traditional dinners in the dining room with its enormous mahogany table loaded down with Spode and Rockingham, what do you think they do when it's time for the port? They all stagger to their feet as we do, and then shuffle off into another almost identical room, where they slump down again in exactly the same place around another enormous mahogany table to get on with the serious business without being disturbed by the odours of the food which we all find so irritating to our enjoyment of port.

Now tell me, is it me? As a fully paid-up member of the Dr Johnson school of port-drinking, in other words people who would rather curl up in front of the fire with a Noval than with a novel, the thing that has me wondering is why the red braces, pin stripes and upper-class English accents have introduced so many obstacles to the whole simple business of getting bombed out of your mind.

First, the name. Calling it port is crazy. It's like Margaux or Latour or Lafite calling themselves South-West Bord. If they are going to call themselves anything, it should be after the area in which they are really based. Gaia. It would do wonders for their image.

'So what do you fancy tonight, Charles?'

'Shall we try the Gaia Sydney? Do you fancy a touch?'

'What, just the two of us?'

'Yes. Why not?'

'Oh, all right then. I will if you will.'

Club life would never be the same again.

Then they should change the names of the shippers. Taylor's and Ramos Pinto and Barros are OK, but when you hear two men who've spent a lifetime in the tropics talking about what makes their Cockburn's so special, I mean, I ask you. If it were any other product it would have been banned years ago. Except, of course, that the decision would probably have been taken by other men with red braces, pin stripes and upper-class English accents.

And what about the whole business of the candlelit men-only dinners in messes and halls and common rooms the world over? The ritual of passing the port one way and not the other? The continual references to the Bishop of Norwich? The delicate, telling descriptions, the continual references to cracking nuts. The absolute insistence that it should be drunk at the end of a meal, not just with cheese but with Stilton.

Once or twice in France I've tried it – oh, the shame, the embarrassment – as an aperitif. It doesn't seem to work as far as I'm concerned. It's great in itself, but it tends to deaden everything that comes after it. On one occasion I even had a glass of port with my *foie gras*, which is supposed to be a big thing among the French. But again it didn't seem to work for me. In the States, of course, they drink it any time, anywhere and with whatever they damn well like. I've yet to see them drink it with ice, but I'm sure its only a question of time. I only hope I'm there. Preferably in some swish, snobby London club with one of those military-type wine waiters. It would be wonderful. Disastrous for the port, of course, but wouldn't it be fantastic just to see it once? After all, I've practically devoted the whole of my life to the port business. In fact, in my time I reckon I've finished off a good few barrels – not all in one go, of course, although sometimes it felt like it. As a result dates like 1066, 1666, 1943, the wife's birthday mean nothing to me. For me the really great years in history are:

1734: one of the great vintages of the eighteenth century.

1775: the first, real, genuine, 100 per cent port as we know it today.

1797: considered by eighteenth-century experts to be the greatest port ever.

1811: the famous Comet vintage.

1815: the equally famous Waterloo vintage.

1847: the famous mid-nineteenth-century classic.

1863: excellent, excellent, excellent – that's what everybody called it.

1870: but this one they called superlative.

1878: the last of the great phylloxera-free ports.

1884: many people called this the last of the great vintages.

1897: the Royal Diamond Jubilee vintage.

1908: with perhaps a little presumption, this was called one of the great classic wines of the twentieth century.

1927: one of the best ever. Well, that's what they said.

1935: very successful.

1945: the greatest since 1935.

1960: the greatest since 1945.

1963: my first grown-up port. Up until this vintage I was hitting the rough stuff. And I've still got some left.

1966: I bought a lot of this one as well.

1970: and this.

1975: and this.

1977: and, of course, this one too. Especially the Dow's, the Warre's and the Taylor's.

1980: had a bottle the other night. Fantastic. Unfortunately, had to share it with some other people.

1983: will try a bottle maybe next Saturday night.

1985: and a bottle of this the Saturday after.

1992: A very good vintage. Especially for Taylor's and Fonseca. Not, of course, that it had anything to do with the fact they were celebrating their bicentenaries. Wash your mouth out with Californian port.

1994: massive, powerful, slightly flowery, a hint of peppermint. Well, that's what they say, although it'll be a few years yet before we find out.

Believe it or not, I've also devoted many hours of my liver's throbbing life to the Portuguese wine business. Before I started spitting up blood, that is. I don't just mean Mateus Rosé, which tastes like a superb marketing operation, I mean real grown-up wine, red, white and rosé like the stuff they produce in Spain and France and elsewhere. Once, I remember, I even splashed out on a bottle of Quinto do Cotto, one of the most expensive wines you can find in the Douro, and I sat drinking it in this scruffy restaurant while the muzak machine, for some reason, kept playing 'Knock, Knock, Knocking on Heaven's Door'.

But again they don't make it easy for you. Vinho verde means green wine, right? Wrong. It means you drink it young, sometimes just a few days after it has been made. Vinho tinto means red, right? It's actually a dark purply colour and you drink it not from glasses but from dirty great earthenware bowls, preferably in the open air yelling and shouting and screaming at the top of your voice at everybody around you. The perfect accompaniment for family picnics. As for Portuguese brandy, I wouldn't inflict it on a boiler. Use it for stripping paint and it would burn the wood off underneath. All I can say is it's got one hell of a job trying to break through to the big time.

Because of my intense academic interest in the subject, whenever I'm in Oporto I'm always torn between getting soaked outside going snipe-shooting in the marshes or getting soaked inside by visiting and tasting my way through every single wine lodge. Well, apart from Osborne's, which somehow I have never fancied, and I don't see any reason to change my mind just because they are offering free samples. This is not true, of course – there's no way you'd catch me going snipe-shooting. It's just that adding another option makes me look less like a soak.

I am pleased to report that in my view top of the golden-nectar department is Taylor's. It's a bit of a drag up from the river, and a couple of times you wonder whether you've got lost, but it's worth it. It's all very quiet, very reserved, very understated. In other words, typically English. The tasting room is a bit odd. The roof looks like a circus tent which has gone wrong and the showcases don't seem to make the most of their past. In pride of place is a tatty menu showing that Taylor's ten-year-old Tawny was served with petits fours at the Henley Regatta in 1989. As for the staff, the two girls doing their turn when I was there looked as though they would have been happier pushing coke. The guy with them never said a word the whole time. The restaurant was typically English. It opened late, service was slow and, spoilsports, they keep the bottles of port and wine and used glasses on a separate small table so you can't fill the one you're sitting at with so many bottles and glasses there is no more space left. So you just have to stop and go back to work. But that's all detail. The port was fantastic, fantastic, fantastic.

After Taylor's I liked Ramos Pinto. The lodge – that word again – looked more like a château: very elegant, discreet, sandy-coloured. Right on the front facing the river. Their white port was the best I came across. The others were all rich, sweet and full-bodied; their ruby, I think, should be drunk more often. Not to mention their Maria, their Isabella and the rest of their front-office staff. Graham's was also very pleasant. Whitewashed walls, red-brick doorways, vines all over the place. A very pleasant tasting area. Very nice shop. What you would imagine, rich and sweet.

Sandemann's was the big hitter. Very plummy, rich, long-lasting. They had a wonderful location, a square to themselves right on the riverfront and a grand imposing building with markers outside showing the level of flooding they have experienced over the years. It was so grand and so imposing and so popular one immediately felt suspicious. Especially when my guide, a young girl all dressed up in the traditional Sandemann's hat and the traditional Sandemann's cloak, who'd probably drunk nothing stronger than a two-day-old Coca-Cola, kept telling me that in order to stop vintage port from oxidising, I should drink it within thirty-six hours of opening the bottle. Thirty-six hours? On a good night I have problems making it last thirty-six minutes. Then, over a couple of swift tastings before she hit the next tour, she declared that the thing that changed the port industry for ever was the 1920s poster produced by the House of Sandemann of a flapper throwing her arms around the neck of a centaur which, obviously overcome by the attention, was waving his two front legs in the air.

Calem I liked. A long, long building, again on the water-front; a row of trees outside. Understated, reserved, no jazz. Nobody dressed up in hats and cloaks, no stories of flappers and centaurs. Barros I would have liked to have visited, especially as they are a Portuguese port as opposed to a British port, and as a result tend to be neglected by the portocracy. I did try: I went to the lodge, a long, low building that looked a bit like a church, but I arrived at the same time as a busload of kids wearing yellow hats. I'm afraid I ran a mile. There's no way I'm going to visit a wine lodge with a bunch of howling kids.

Down in the sediment, in my opinion, were most of the others. Vasconcellos, up a long alleyway, was like some Dickensian factory – old, dark, dusty. Meister's, even further up the alleyway, resembled a fortress – strong, sturdy, solid. Ferreira looked like a prison, with the wrong kind of bars, whereas Croft and Delaforce could have been military prisons, with strong walls and strict security. Churchill's looked more like Attlee's than anything else. Tiny, insignificant, inconsequential. In fact, it's got nothing whatsoever to do with Churchill, not that they make this immediately obvious. I wonder why? Offley, Diez, Rainha Santa and Forester's, were all straightforward, no nonsense. Get the stuff in, fix it, get it out again.

Fonseca had a sign outside saying 'Visiteurs', so I didn't bother to go in. Damn it, we invented the stuff, we run the show and we drink far more of it than the French. So why can't they at least speak to us in the language we understand: 'Freebies This Way'? Vinicola, which must be the worst possible name for a port, is in a class of its own. The lodge is way the other side of Gaia, but nonetheless it has that port atmosphere – the port of Rotterdam atmosphere. It is a huge, sprawling area with huge tanks everywhere containing over 1 million litres of the stuff. Each. All the time tour buses are driving around the site, passing and overtaking each other. You could get lost there with no problem at all, and that's without any sampling.

As for the world outside the wine warehouses (oh, OK, the lodges), the storage areas and the blending units, Oporto is the only really commercial and industrial town in the country. Lisbon, they say, plays, Coimbra studies, Braga prays. And Porto works. It looks as though it has been treated by the rest of the world in the same way it treats its port: ignored, undisturbed, kept in the dark, left to get on with it. It is all heavy, grey granite, shaky terracotta roofs, baroque churches, tiny, dirty alleyways, cobblestones, iron balconies dripping with washing, old British telephone boxes, dirty grey skies, women selling fresh sardines out of plastic buckets in the streets and massive art-deco buildings dripping with thousands upon thousands of blue ceramic tiles. The tiles in the railway station are a million times more impressive than all the tiles in the Museu do Azulejos, the famous tile museum in Lisbon, including its 20-metre-wide panorama of Lisbon from the river before the great earthquake of 1755.

Across the Douro are three spectacular bridges, two iron, one modern and concrete. One of the iron bridges, the Dona Maria Pia, was designed by Eiffel. Indeed, I was told that it had become so shaky that if you stood on a boat underneath when the Lisbon to Oporto express rumbled across it, you were likely to get an eyeful of nuts and bolts. So they changed the train from a heavy locomotive to a lightweight one, and instead of letting it race across the thing they prohibited it from going any faster than 8mph. I bet you wouldn't have come up with that solution, either.

Another thing that's odd about trains in Portugal is that for some reason they are not allowed to pull away from the platform, or even trundle slowly through some sleepy station in the middle of nowhere, without some guy furiously jumping up and down waving a red flag at them. Which, of course, is disconcerting at first, especially when you're heading towards Oporto and Eiffel's rickety old bridge. Then, of course, as with most things – like your wife saying left when she means right, and you turning straight into the path of a 40-ton container lorry – you get used to it and after a while you don't take any notice. Nevertheless, once or twice I will admit I thought we got dangerously close to some scruffy kids running along the side of the track towards that flipping bridge.

As for the Oportors themselves, they are not at all the kind of people you would expect to find living on top of 100 million litres of port. Happy and laughing and joking they are not. Probably because they've never got over the great siege of 1832, when they were forced to eat not only their cats but their rats as well, while the biggest loss the British had to endure was the magnolia grandiflora in the grounds of the Taylor's wine lodge. Depending on who you share a bottle of Taylor's 1966 with, they are known as either *Tripeiros* or *Alfacinhas*. *Tripeiros* means not day-trippers but tripe-eaters. Forget the 1927, 1945 or even the 1960, they like nothing better than to sit down and tuck into three or four bucketfuls of their favourite dish, tripas a mode do Porto: a sticky mess of tripe, red beans and garlic sausage. And *Alfacinhas*? Boozers? Drunks? Alcoholics? No, it means lettuce-eaters. Why they should be called lettuce-eaters beats me – I can't think of anything less likely. I couldn't find anybody who could give me a sensible reason, either.

Tripe-eaters or lettuce-eaters, the thing that struck me about them was their feet. I don't think I've ever been anywhere in the world where so many people seem to have so many problems with their feet. Practically everybody is hobbling along on some kind of wooden stick, crutch or one of those adjustable aluminium zimmer frames. At first, not surprisingly, I thought that it must be due to some spontaneous outbreak of gout. But it was more serious than that. They had real foot problems. On practically every street corner there was somebody with his leg up begging or, sprawled across the pavement in the early evening sunlight picking the nits off the raw stump of a leg. Again, nobody could give me an explanation.

Had it been their heads it would have been more understandable, because all the time I was there I couldn't help but notice ordinary, sane, sensible-looking people hobbling up to each other and smashing each other on the head with large, multicoloured plastic hammers. They would then smile weakly, turn round and promptly hobble over to somebody else and smash them over the head as well. Once or twice some kids actually smashed me over the head with their damn plastic hammers, which, I can tell you, was not a pleasant experience. Especially after a couple of bottles of that Ramos Pinto white port, which the great Professor Saintsbury, the patron saint of the booze business, dismissed as a 'mere albino'. All I can say is the great professor should knock back a couple of bottles, have his head smashed a couple of times with some dirty great plastic hammer and then tell us if it is still a mere albino. Had I had a couple of bottles of Taylor's 1966 inside me God knows what would have happened to the kids.

Someone told me that the hammering was the way they celebrate their local patron saint's day. But that is stupid:

where else in the world do you commemorate the life of a holy man by going around and instead of loving your neighbour bashing him over the head with a plastic hammer? They don't even do that in New York on St Patrick's Day. They do it every other day of the year instead. Somebody else said it was to stimulate local industry. The Oporto plastic-hammer business wasn't doing too well, and a plastic hammer day boosted sales enormously. Which again seems far-fetched. My theory is that it is a way to see who's been hitting the port and who hasn't. People who have not been hitting the port are then sent home to drink a bottle immediately in order to keep those profits rolling in.

I just adoro the Douro, the river running through the centre of town, which is one long, never-ending sweep of vineyards. The slopes on either side of the world's oldest demarcated wine region are so steep that they say on the way down the Devil is right behind you, but on the way up not even God can help you. Most of the time the water is calm, almost like a mirror. In some places the river is quite narrow - narrow enough for you to throw an empty bottle of port to the opposite bank - in others a good few hundred metres across. Then, suddenly, it swings round a bend and there are ripples on the surface, like those you get when you decant your port into one of those big, two-bottle decanters, the only size of decanter I use. (I mean, are you going to drink the stuff or are you going to drink the stuff?) The ripples become gushes; the gushes become torrents. Then, just as suddenly, everything is calm again. Either side, between the vines, there are little red shacks. Further along is a collection of houses. Now and then, usually at the top of the hill, you see glistening, elegant, white-painted mansions. Just imagine how much pleasure those guys have brought to the world. The pity of it is that most people can only remember half of it, if that. But even that half makes up for everything.

On and on the river goes. Past Peso da Régua, which is a one-bottle town if ever I saw one. Years ago it was virtually the capital of the port business outside Vila Nova de Gaia. Today, apart from one or two lodges, the whole trade has moved to Pinhão, further east and only the sediment is left. Hidden away in the sediment is a scruffy back street named after the famous Baron Joseph James Forrester, the man who practically invented the port business. Which just shows you how much thanks you get when you leave home, go and live in some godforsaken part of the world and help them transform some pretty ordinary grapes into one of the world's greatest and most famous drinks. He should at least have the main square named after him, a statue in the centre and a Joseph James Forrester Day every year when everybody goes around cracking each other over the head with a bottle of port.

Now the river flows on past an enormous hydroelectric dam and into country full to overflowing with all the glory and romance associated with producing one of the world's greatest wines: ground so hard you need dynamite, earth-moving equipment and huge tractors before you can even think of planting a single vine; summers so hot you are practically roasted alive; winters so cold you nearly freeze to death; and in between rain, storms, hailstones the size of tennis balls, not to mention the taxman, VAT forms and visits from the fancy boys in their red braces from Oporto. Everything, it seems, that is good for port is bad for humans.

Pinhão is the place to come for quality, although only in terms of port. And so on to Tua. From Tua you can tua the area, visiting the occasional *quinto*, sampling and sampling and sampling like mad. I didn't have time, but what I did see convinced me that the whole region has been afflicted by one huge collective hangover since the great Waterloo vintage of 1815. Byron went on about its 'beauties of every description, natural and artificial' and swooned about its 'palaces and gardens rising in the midst of rocks, cataracts and precipices'. Not any more. Everything is old-fashioned old-fashioned! I mean historic, a million years out of date and crumbling to pieces.

Explore the Minho Way up in the north bordering Galicia, which many people say is the most beautiful part of the country, and you see nothing but tiny small-holdings, ramshackle old cottages and farmhouses, creaking wooden ox carts bringing in the maize, ploughs and hoes drawn by mules, scrawny chickens, whiskery old women (maybe they're not so old, come to think of it), and kids looking after kids, or rather, small children looking after herds of goats.

The Alentejo region to the south is just as primitive – I mean beautiful – although I am less enthusiastic about the place. Probably because Julius Caesar was once their local governor and, of course, did what all good colonialists do: he left the people alone but stole all their money and natural resources. He used all the gold he grabbed from the local mines to buy his way into Rome and finance his adventures throughout Europe. The way I see it, if Alentejo had not had any gold in the first place I wouldn't have had to spend all those years studying the Gallic Wars when I could have been out enjoying myself and a million kids would not have had to learn all those speeches. As in the Minho, in Alentejo you still come across plenty of places without water, electricity or telephones. There are still boar and deer running around wild, but probably not for long. The area is slowly becoming 'civilised': Lisbon is up the road, and there is a big new highway running through the pine forests of the Serra d'Ossa on to Seville and Spain. More and more people are searching out the local olive groves and vineyards and, of course, the cork forests, which are the largest in the world. They are picking up cottages on the cheap, building tennis courts, stomping across fields and leaving gates open and complaining about the locals who have lived there for generations. All the usual things townies do when they discover the countryside.

But in spite of everything, Portugal is still desperately isolated and behind the times. Out in the countryside women still wear black not only if their husband is dead but even when he's just gone off to Switzerland or Jersey for a job. Apparently there are so many Portuguese working in Jersey that many of the road signs are in Portuguese as well as French and English. There are even some parts of the countryside, especially the Tras os Montes, the three huge mountain ranges up towards the Spanish border, which are so remote that, I was told, even today people there speak a local dialect which is as near as damn it common, everyday Latin.

As for the towns, Portugal, I reckon, is not just the poor man of Europe but the poor man of Africa and Asia as well. Wherever you go you see pathetic reminders and remnants and relics of an empire that once covered the world. For these were the guys, don't forget, who told us where to go, and where we were once we got there. Over 600 years ago good old Henry the Navigator founded the world's first school of navigation and told sailors, map-makers and astronomers what they were supposed to be doing. They organised the first expeditions to Africa, they sailed to India, they discovered Brazil. They were the first to sail around the world. They had enormous colonies in Africa. Today it's all gone. Although now and then you see signs of the old Portugal – stiff-backed colonels in shabby, tatty suits trying vainly to hold on to their past, old dowagers who would have graced the cover of *Vogue* magazine (April 1921 edition) – the fact of the matter is that Portugal has not only lost its compass but all sense of direction as well. But the worst thing of all as far as they are concerned is, of course, that they are way, way, behind their arch-rivals, Spain. I would say they must be at least forty years behind. Everything is very slow, very understated, very quiet, almost very eighteenth century – and in some parts of the country even that's an exaggeration.

Take Braga, for example, way up in the far north. Some days it's practically eleventh or even twelfth century. The religious capital of the country (of all the cities in Portugal, Braga, they say, will be the first to get to Heaven), it boasts so many churches and chapels that the Portuguese often refer to it as their Rome. Its most spectacular feature is the Bom Jesus, just outside of town. Imagine an enormous, imposing fairytale baroque church on top of a hill. Imagine that the face of the hill has been cut away and in its place twelve huge stairways have been constructed, each with its own landing and its own fountain and its own life-sized shrine, all the way up the hill. That is Bom Jesus. Why was it built? Because the archbishop of the time thought it was a good idea. And you don't have to read Trollope to know that whatever archbishops want, archbishops get. Even today you still see people climbing every one of the steps of every one of the twelve staircases on their knees. I climbed the stairs myself (although I'm ashamed to admit that I did it the normal way, on foot, two or three steps at a time followed by half an hour puffing and panting on each landing). What divine revelation did I see when I got to the top? A fat man with two of the oldest box cameras in existence, a moth-eaten toy horse and one of those heavy, ornate, old-fashioned weighing machines proudly proclaiming in neat red letters, 'W. and T. Avery Ltd, Birmingham'. Who says travel broadens the mind?

For genuine nineteenth-century Portugal you could do worse than pop into your nearest factory. Some are superb, and can stand alongside any others anywhere in the world, but some... well, you don't have to go to the Far East or South America to see children working in factories. Indeed, you find them working all over Portugal, in textile plants, in shoe-making and repairing shops, on building sites, in bars and restaurants. And, of course, doing every type of manual work you can imagine, out there alongside the adults. And if they're not working in industry they're working on farms, teasing scruffy-looking donkeys away from the hedgerows or herding goats all over the place.

As for the glories of modern Portugal, the Portuguese still feel they can hold their shaky old heads high, even though if you try to buy a ticket for the equivalent of £20 in a railway station either way out in Tua in the middle of nowhere or in Lisbon itself, the whole place comes to a standstill. Yet what's the most important painting in the country? *The Temptation of St Anthony*, they will proudly tell you, by that well-known Portuguese painter Hieronymus Bosch. Their most revered musician? That's easy. The famous Portuguese conductor Sir Georg Solti, because apparently whenever he conducted anything in Lisbon he got so excited he lost his baton. Their most important exhibition? A display of sculpture from Angola from a million years ago in the Museu Nacional de Ethhologia.

Yet it seems they are determined to maintain their dignity in spite of the truth. They have even gone as far as passing a law stipulating that Portuguese people must have sensible Portuguese names like Vasco or João or Adalberto or Ezequiel or Venceslau or Imaculada. If you have a funny foreign name instead, like Tom, Dick, Harold or, Heaven help me, Peter, it's not just a question of being frowned upon. They declare that you don't exist. Officially or legally, no ifs or buts about it. If you're a baby, you're not allowed to be baptised. If you're a child, you don't get what child allowances there are. If you've managed to survive to adulthood, you don't get whatever adult things you're supposed to get. The whole thing blew up in their face, however, when one of the most senior upstanding generals, who had a string of medals, a wife and the most Portuguese of Portuguese names, turned out not only to be a fraud, but a woman as well.

And these are the guys who make jokes against the Spanish. About their lack of sophistication, their lack of culture. They are rather more quiet about the dramatic progress the Spanish have made, their style, their success and their position in Europe. The Portuguese and the Spanish are about as friendly and understanding towards each other as the British and the French. Anything and everything Spain does is interpreted, reinterpreted and misinterpreted. Spain is five times as large as Portugal. They did it deliberately, the Portuguese say, in order to overshadow them and grab all the tourists and investors before they could get to the promised land. If Spain realigns some river, it's because they want to cut off water supplies to Portugal, destroy the Portuguese agricultural industry and grab the market for themselves. If Spain builds nuclear power stations along the border with Portugal, it's because they want all the nuclear fall-out to drift over Portugal, destroy their tomatoes and infect their women and children. In that order.

If it pours with rain, 'God is a Spaniard,' they say. And when a Spanish horse arrived at their prestigious Alter Stud Farm, which breeds the famous Lusitano thorough-breds, to do his duty, there was a national crisis. The horse-breeders went spare. The Portuguese Federation of Farmers had apoplexy. The Confederation of Industry had a collective heart attack. Was it because this was an affront to their national image? Because the horse would ruin the breed? No way. They were snorting and pawing the ground because they said it would help Spain sell their horses overseas ahead of the Portuguese.

Lisbon is the world capital for athletics. Come on, everybody knows that. In the 1980s, if you wanted to meet any leading athlete you caught a plane to Lisbon, because in Portugal there were no laws against steroids. You just went into a chemist or drug store, bought what you wanted, met all your friends, checked out your prospects for the 100 metres or the 1,000 metres or whatever and got the plane home. The only place you see them now, of course, is in hospitals and nursing homes, being treated for liver cancer.

Indeed, everybody drives as if they've got steroids coming out of their exhaust, which is probably why Lisbon has the highest road-accident rate in the whole of Europe. Especially taxi-drivers, who are all big droopy moustaches and machismo. Lisbon is the only city in the world where I never sit in the front seat next to the driver. Never, ever. Because here suicide seat means suicide seat. In most capital cities they sell T-shirts saying, I ♥ whoever. In Lisbon they have T-shirts saying, 'I drove the Marginal [the coastal highway out to Estoril, the most dangerous road in Europe] and lived'. Not many of them, though, which just proves my point.

Traffic apart (by the way, if you want to go to Estoril take the A5 toll road or, better still, go by train) the rest of it's not up to much, either. Henry Fielding called it the 'nastiest city in the world'. I wouldn't go quite that far, but to me it's more of a war zone than a city. The first time I went there I was completely stunned. I had imagined that Lisbon would be like Madrid or Seville, or maybe Valencia: small, compact, hard-working, serious. I knew Portugal had problems, but I certainly didn't expect Lisbon to be so poverty-stricken. It was so bad it completely put me off my bottle of Warre's 1960.

If people in Oporto have problems with their feet, in Lisbon they have problems with everything: arms, legs, heads, shoulders – you name it, somebody in Lisbon has a filthy bandage half wrapped round it. The other half is undone to show you that whatever it is is genuine. The city also seems to be full of wild-eyed men and women walking the streets screaming at anything that moves, not to mention kids without shoes, women with plastic baskets of laundry on their heads and gypsies, or at least people who look like gypsies, selling sprigs of lavender. You see them everywhere: sleeping in doorways, sitting by the side of the road selling absolutely nothing at all from dirty boxes, stretched out in the gutters, slumped over rickety tables, stacked on top of one another in bus shelters.

Practically every car park has its quota of grubby kids helping motorists find a parking place, then offering their own form of protection service. Some of them are reeling around all over the place, grinning at nothing in particular and running up and down for no reason at all. 'Glue,' I was told. They sniff glue out of plastic bags. Some are even on marijuana.

I was surprised at the number of Africans in Lisbon. I knew the Portuguese once had a vast African empire, but I never realised that so many of them had come to the old country, most of them in pretty miserable circumstances. Those not living on the streets or in shop doorways reside in shanty towns or *bairros de lata* – tin-can houses, as they call them in Portuguese. One, Casal Ventoso, is home to no fewer than 45,000 people, one of the biggest shanty towns and one of the biggest and worst slums in Europe with often as many as twenty to thirty people eating, living and sleeping in tiny, squalid shacks with no facilities.

It seemed as though nothing had been done to it since Vasco da Gama returned from India with his first load of gold and spices or as if the whole city was still struggling

to come to terms with the great earthquake of 1755 -
which, incidentally, inspired Voltaire to write *Candide*.
According to the history books, however, as soon as the
earthquake subsided, the Marquis de Pombal dispatched a
team of architects and designers to Paris with instructions
to copy the Champs Elysées and another team to Brussels
to get them to pay for it. The architects and designers
came home with their plans and built their own Champs
Elysées through the centre of Lisbon - 10 centimetres
wider than the original, which was one in the eye for the
French, and probably the reason why Portugal has
remained Britain's oldest ally for so long. At about that
time a certain Lady Elizabeth Craven visited Lisbon. It was,
she said, nothing but 'Dust. Stinks. Horrid faces. Bells.
Contents of chamberpots. Fleas. Vile cars. Blacks. Bad
water. No good wine.' Well, I've got news for M'Lady
Elizabeth: nearly 250 years later, nothing has changed. If
anything, it's got worse, perhaps because the guys who
went to Brussels are still there, although I understand that
they have been promised an urgent meeting with DG VIII
some time in the next five years.

It is a shame, because Lisbon could be a truly beautiful
city. Built on seven hills facing the River Tagus, it has spectacular views. The old city, the old Moorish and Jewish
quarter, dominated by St Jorge's Castle, is full of courtyards
and mosaic pavements. The new city, dominated, as you
would expect, by the huge Praça do Comercio, the
Commercial Square, opens out discreetly on to the sea. In
between there is a web of tiny streets, steep hills, more
enormous squares, Victorian grocers, washing dripping on
to the streets, sardines being grilled in the open air,
bougainvillaea, orange trees, pillarboxes made by A.
Handyside and Co., Derby and London - you can still see
the name - Edwardian trams, electricity spurting and
flashing and crackling everywhere, with plates sunk into

the floor saying 'Made in Derby, 1870'. And...

Yaaaagh! What's that? A twitch in my left foot. No, it's more than a twitch. It's some enormous shooting P-A-I-N. What the hell... What better souvenir could you have? I think I've got obloody gouto. From obloody Porto.

MADRID

To me Spain is more-ish, or perhaps I should say Moorish.

I've been to factories in and around Valencia, Spain's third-largest city, which at one time was famous for its mediaeval lunatic asylum and the number of mad people wandering the streets. But that's all changed: now they just smear themselves with tomatoes and run around the streets practically stark naked shouting and screaming at the tops of their voices. Somebody told me it had some-thing to do with the tomato harvest. Celebrating a good crop, that kind of thing. I couldn't care less what it is as long as they keep taking the tablets. On the other hand, I hope the idea doesn't catch on. Can you imagine what the *bierfest* would be like in Munich with all those Germans leaping about all over the place covered in nothing but froth? It could turn me teetotal overnight.

I can't remember how many companies I've been to in Castellon, which is, I suppose, the Stoke-on-Trent of Spain. Mañana is definitely not mañana there. Instead it's the *jornada intensiva*. From 8 am to 3 pm, non-stop, six days a week. You can tell they work hard: hardly any of them wear socks. Which shows you how eager they are, once they are awake, to get to work. At one company I went to, anyone who turned up even one minute late had to stand on a wooden box in the centre of the plant as a form of punishment. They did it as well. All the meetings I've been to in offices, in banks, in hotels, started bang on time – some even before the appointed time. On a number of occasions I have spotted the Spanish guys wandering up and down the street outside the office or bank having arrived too early to make certain they were on time. Either that or they were looking for somewhere to buy a pair of socks.

I've also done a fair amount of bombing through countless little villages in blinding white sunshine, every one of them lined with pretty, well-scrubbed, shimmering sandstone houses with immaculate, well-groomed lattice-work verandahs, scaring the hell out of little old ladies in black and sending them scurrying down mysterious little alleyways. And, of course, I've done the *tapas* bars, which to me are worth three olés any day of the week, even though I know that *tapa* is Spanish for a lump of bread you stick on top of your glass of wine to keep the flies off. But believe me, they're fantastic. I've yet to come across a bad one. However, I admit that nine times out of ten you wish you hadn't asked what it was you were eating.

In tiny, almost deserted villages, in the heat of the after-noon when old men and women sit motionless staring at nothing, I've eaten plate after plate of things that look like minced sheep's eyes, *riñones*, minced lambs' ears and minced cows' tongue, all brought direct from the griddle, pink inside with a dash of blood oozing gently from the middle, served with great lumps of tangy *manchego* cheese and washed down with great buckets of Rioja. I've also had prawns, squid served in its own ink, anchovy spines, stuffed mussels, baby octopus, a thousand different kinds of fish eggs, kidneys in sherry, all kinds of strange-looking – and strange-tasting – meatballs, minuscule pigs' trotters, lambs' intestines and all kinds of tails of Spain old and new. You think that's disgusting? These were the people, don't forget, who used to sit around after executions waiting to eat the liver of the poor guys who had just been sent to the gallows.

Once I was doing the rounds with your typical English banker. We went into this bar in a small village where it hadn't rained for four years. Over 25 per cent of their fruit trees had been lost and another 25 per cent were in danger of being lost. 'But do you know,' the barman told me, 'whenever people buy a car around here they still complain if the windscreen-wipers don't work.'

One of the dishes I had there, I remember, looked suspiciously like the lip or tongue of an ox or a cow. With all the bravado and brio and Rioja I could muster, I ate it. The guy I was with, however, visibly shuddered; there was no way, he said, he was going to eat it, because of where it came from. He asked for an egg instead.

In other parts of the country, I've been to towns where blood runs thicker than Rioja and stumbled upon *tapas* bars stacked to the ceiling with barrels. I've been in other bars where you can hardly see the faded bullfighting posters and photographs on the walls for the hams hanging all over the place with their little upside-down umbrellas underneath them to catch the drips. Or at least, the ones not heading for the Costa del Sol. At all hours of the day and practically half the night as well, I've tucked into loaves of warm crusty bread, with slice after slice of *serrano* ham, which is raw, red, chewy and packs a punch you never get with Parma. I've nibbled on *chorizos* which look like marble and gorged myself on my favourite, the *pata negra*, a fantastic ham which comes courtesy of the pigs with the long legs and the black hooves.

I've also done my duty by the Spanish wine industry. I forget how many gallons of the stuff I've shifted – including, I must tell you, barrels of the cheap white wine which, take it from me, was the real inspiration for the flamenco. I mean, why else, if it wasn't for that searing rush of white wine stripping the enamel off their teeth, scouring the insides of their mouths and racing straight towards their feet, would otherwise sensible men and women suddenly leap up and start violently stamping the floor, waving their hands in the air and screaming at the top of their voices? It can't be just to scare the hell out of the rats hiding under the floorboards, can it?

And Madrid, *amigo*, Madrid is fantastico. It's almost a junior, more compact version of Paris. Elegant buildings, wide *avenidas*, or boulevards. Trees everywhere. And lunatic taxi-drivers who always seem to offer you a cigarette as they mount the pavement, dodge between two restaurant tables and crash back on to the road again. 'Itsa cows. Itsa cows,' one driver kept saying to me as we drove up the kerb sending people and tables flying all over the place. To me Madrid has a zing and a buzz and an inexhaustible *energía*. Somehow it always seems to be busy, fast-moving, a thousand things happening all at the same time, all day and all night. I used to think it had something to do with the thin air - Madrid is the highest capital city in Europe - making them all light-headed. Then I thought it was the weather. In the summer it's hot. I've been to offices and factories in and around Madrid where shorts are the order of the day - and I don't mean gin and whisky. I mean it's so hot it makes crossing the Sahara seem like a Sunday-school outing. In the winter, however, it is cold. Very cold. More than 2,000 feet above sea-level, in the middle of that great Spanish plateau, 200 miles from any coast - it's the great bull's-eye of Spain - I tell you, it gets cold. Then, of course, there are the *tapas* bars. *Calamares* fried in batter, baby eels piled high into real, live spaghetti. Chunks of *chorizos* and all those tortillas and peppers. There are supposed to be over 5,000 restaurants and *tapas* bars in Madrid - and every single one of them was Hemingway's favourite, believe me.

I'm not saying I've done them all, but I've done my fair share. What's more, I reckon I hold the world record for seeing more rows and arguments in more *tapas* bars than anybody else in the history of the world. This is because whenever I go to Madrid I do the rounds with a Dutch guy who simply refuses to pay the prices they are charging. Take the beautiful, baroque seventeenth-century Plaza Mayor, which, you would have thought, has seen more than enough excitement and danger, having in its time witnessed everything from bullfighting to the burning of heretics and public executions. No way. You should see the fuss this guy makes every time because he thinks they are charging him tourist prices. Now, I agree that to the Spanish, there's probably very little difference between bull-baiting and tourist-baiting, and that to them Plaza Mayor obviously means, 'If they come into the plaza they must be tourists, so charge them major prices,' but as far as I'm concerned that's just another one of their endearing little Spanish practices. Not to this guy. I reckon he must have been there the day Philip II arrived in town. He's banging his fist on all the zinc counters and slapping the jazzy art-nouveau tiles and scattering all the cards and domino-players in all directions. 'Why you charge me so much?' he shouts at the *camarero* in that serious tone the Dutch reserve for anything to do with money first and religion second.

'We not charge too much!' shouts back the *camarero*.

'Plaza Mayor,' he snorts. 'I am not tourist. I am Madrileño. I not pay tourist prices. I am here when Philippe—'

'You Spanish?' they ask.

'*Sí, sí.* I see Charles III build the Paseo del Prado.'

Down come the prices by half a million pesetas here, three-quarters of a million there, 200 million round the corner. And that's just for the coffee.

It's the same story in the bars in and around the Plaza de la Villa, where you find the town hall. Town hall? This is not a mere building for collecting local government taxes. This is a gorgeous baroque extravaganza. Alongside it is the fabulous Casa de Cisneros with its fantastic collection of Flemish tapestries. In the centre is the patron saint of losers, Don Alvaro de Bazan, the man who lost the Spanish Armada. I always feel the least I can do is pay tribute to one of the great losers of this world. Only in Madrid would they think of putting up a statue to such a man. At home we would just send him to the House of Lords.

And it's the same in and around the Plaza Santa Ana, in front of the Victoria Hotel with all its bulls' heads in the lobby where, like in the Long Bar in Singapore, you're encouraged to throw all the olive pips and debris on to the floor. And the same in all the temporary bars up and down the Casellana Avenue.

Sometimes if I'm in a hurry, or if he doesn't have much time to spare to go from *tapas* bar to *tapas* bar to *tapas* bar, we'll have a quick session. Cocktails and a couple of bottles of *manzanilla* at six in any one of a string of bars around the Puerta del Sol, Madrid's Piccadilly Square, which are always either full of Los Beautis, the beautiful people, or great lumps of ham hanging around the walls, or both. Dinner at ten. A nightcap at twelve in Museo Chicote, a 1940s throwback and another Hemingway favourite. Then it's back to the hotel by 1 am. A quick session for the Spanish, that is. And all the time, because he considers me *mal educado*, he will be lecturing me on Spain. 'It is incredible big. *Sí.*'

'*Sí.*'

'Philip II. He watched the Bourbons build Versailles. He decide to build Versailles lookalike, the great, sprawling Oriente Palace. *Sí.*'

'*Sí.*'

'Charles III. He build the Paseo del Prado, not to mention one sewage works after another. *Sí.*'

'*Sí.*'

'The Spanish. They are not *medio-moros*, half-Arabs. They are Spanish. *Sí.*'

'*Sí.*'

'In Madrid they eat bread and burp chicken. *Sí.*'

'*Sí.*'

He also told me, I don't know how many times, his joke about Charles V. 'Charles V. He speaks four languages. They say to him, "How you know which language to speak?" Charles V, he say, "To my family I speak Spanish. To my diplomats I speak French. To my mistress I speak Italian. And to my horse I speak Dutch." Very good, *sí?*'

'*Sí.*'

On one near-memorable occasion we said our *hasta la vistas* over a cup of hot, treacly chocolate at some choco-latería near the Ritz which is famous for its old masters as well as, presumably, its old mistresses, its droplet chandeliers, its chairs with tassels on the tassels, its marble tiled gold-tapped bathrooms and its exclusive collection of very rare and sophisticated antiques, such as the Duke and Duchess of Windsor, who apparently used to sit in their suite day after boring day looking out of the window, she no doubt cursing non-stop the double standards of the British and he just peering vacantly through the window doing his knitting. I got back to my hotel just in time to check out. I think.

All of which means, I'm afraid, that I've never done the Prado the way Hemingway, the professional drinker, did the Prado. To him, it was apparently the centre of the world. It seems he would stand in front of any painting that caught his fancy for hours on end, which strikes me as odd, especially in a city where there must be nearly 4 million bars, 400,000 nightclubs and bullfights practically every other day during the season. Unless, of course, that macho image was nothing but image after all, and deep down he was really quite shallow like the rest of us.

Now, I'm no expert on art. I have no idea why in *The Bedstead* Rembrandt gave his wife two left arms or where the extra arm came from in Da Vinci's *The Last Supper*. I don't know the difference between *parmigiano* and *parmigianino*, apart from the fact one is a lump of hard Italian cheese and the other one isn't. And no, I don't think Titian's Madonna is too much model and not enough virgin. But either way the Prado is worth the occasional fifteen-, twenty- or even twenty-five-minute trip between *tapas* bars – although not, I would suggest, in the morning, when there are invariably thousands of kids clattering around all over the place, or the afternoon, when the Japanese swarm in and for some reason or other take photographs only of those paintings reflecting some form of suffering.

I've been in art galleries all over the world, but the Prado, I must admit, is different. It's enormous: it covers a good couple of dozen bullrings. It's impressive, like the Rijksmuseum in Amsterdam with all its Rembrandts. And it's packed with goodies. At first, however, I didn't realise it was an art gallery. Go into a gallery or museum in Zambia, for example, and you'll have an art attack. The head of cultural heritage, Mr Iven Nzillah, will practically rip the clothes off your back – something to do, he says, with damp clothing increasing the humidity levels and destroying their national treasures. He also wants people to control the amount of what he calls bio-effluent that he says they emit whenever they go to any of his exhibitions. This, too, he claims is eating away at the national heritage. In the Prado I heard no screams of 'Disgusting!' or 'Rubbish!' or 'Revolting!' or even 'My two-year-old could do better than that!' There were no sounds like 'bluuuuuugh' coming from behind the occasional screen, no smell of formaldehyde, and no bio-effluents, either, as far as I could tell, although I admit it is not a subject upon which I have any particular expertise.

Instead, the Prado has the most fantastic collection of old masters I think I've ever seen. Well, I say old masters – I didn't see any Stubbs or Munnings or even Mark Wallingers, but I may have been mistaken. What I did see were Goyas by the mile, or rather the kilometre. Bartolemé Jureda with his top hat, his cravat and those creepy eyes. La Marquesa de Pontejos and her horrible dog. The Colossus striding across the Pyrenees trying to protect Spain from the French, which I'm surprised is not the standard Eurosceptic's Christmas card. And, of course, the dark, eerie, dramatic *Third of May 1808 in Madrid* with the poor guy, his hands raised in terror like a startled rabbit, facing the firing squad, which I think more than anything proves to me that Goya at least puts the pain into painting. I saw enough royal portraits by the royalist Velázquez to make me seriously think about becoming a republican. I also saw Murillos and El Grecos and works by Tintoretto and Veronese and Rubens and Titian and, of course, Hieronymous Bosch and his puking peasants.

Two paintings, however, stand out: the *Caballero de la Order de Santiago*, by José de Ribera, with his fancy modern sunglasses, and the one painting I think I've ever seen in my life which strikes terror in my soul, Antonio Moro's portrait of his wife. It's chilling, evil, sinister. At the same time, it's the most honest and truthful portrait I think I've ever seen anyone paint of his wife. She has the kind of look you get when you say that unfortunately, through no fault of your own, for the fifty-third year running you're going to have to miss her mother's birthday party because of a pressing engagement at the George V in Paris.

Compared to Madrid, Seville is not just more, well, civil, it is as they say, a *maravilla*, as in, '*Quien no ha visto Sevilla, no ha visto una maravilla*', which, roughly translated, means, 'If you have notta seena Sevilla you wanta your heada examineda.' Because it is absolutely *fantastico*. Lying on the dusty plains of Andalusia, the 'frying pan' of Spain, it was home to Diego, Velázquez and Cervantes (although not voluntarily – he was in prison at the time). It was also, don't forget, the happy hunting ground of Don Juan, some barber or other and a tobacco worker called Carmen who seems to have been an expert in any number of strange Spanish practices. Which reminds me that they also very kindly send us all their sour, inedible oranges, which we desperately try to turn into sour, inedible English marmalade - which, no thank you, not even the Spanish want to eat. It is also, of course, the final resting place of Christopher Columbus - or Cristobál Colón - the patron saint of all management consultants. When he and his crew set out they didn't know where they were going, when they arrived they had no idea where they were, what they did when they were there ruined everybody and everything, and then they came back and demanded more money so that they could go and do the same thing all over again. At least, in Seville they say he is buried in Seville. In Havana, of course, they say he is buried in Havana. In Santo Domingo they say he is buried in Santo Domingo. And you can bet your life some theme park in the States believes he is buried in their back yard. Not, I suppose, that Christopher Columbus cares tuppence where they say he is buried, although I bet, wherever he is, he is as relieved as hell they didn't name America after him. I mean can you imagine bearing that burden for eternity? It would be enough to irritate any colon.

A word of warning, however: if you're going to Seville and you've got a heart condition, don't go over the Easter holiday. I was there once, quite by chance, on an Easter Sunday. I couldn't sleep. Usual problem - my conscience was playing me up. I got up around six, washed and shaved and made one or two discreet calls to reception to try to find out where I was. Around 6.30 am, in the pitch black, I set out to see what I could see. The main street to the river was empty, the Plaza Nueva was empty. I crossed to the far corner, took a left and a couple of rights. Everywhere was deserted, as if nobody knew the city existed. I walked up some narrow alleyway. Everything was locked, barred and bolted. I turned left. My God, I nearly collapsed. Coming towards me, out of the gloom, slowly, slowly, step by step, were a million members of the Ku Klux Klan. Those tall, pointed, white hats which run down over the face with the tiniest of slits for the eyes, those long, white robes trailing the ground. I can tell you, for a moment, it quite turned me over. It was, of course, the start of another one of their traditional Easter processions. All over Easter, the whole city is nothing but solemn, hour-long processions to and from the cathedral, which is the biggest church in the world. There is a certificate on the church noticeboard from the *Guinness Book of Records* saying so. So there.

If you haven't got a heart condition and you want to get one, go during the bullfighting season. There, for three, maybe even four days non-stop, people go from *tapas* bar to bullfight to *tapas* bar to bullfight. They eat in *tapas* bars, they drink in *tapas* bars. They even sleep in *tapas* bars, usually curled up at the bar or slumped across an armchair. Why else do you think there are so many *tapas* bars all over the city?

'Why don't you stay in an hotel?' I asked one guy.

'Why, what is wrong with the *tapas* bars?'

Well, there's a certain logic there, I suppose.

At one time, as a result of its trade monopoly with the Americas, Seville was one of the richest cities in the world. Today things are not so hot. But it's not exactly struggling, either. It is still full of enormous squares, the streets are still lined with *palacios*, many virtually untouched since the sixteenth century, if anything in a city which was home to Don Juan can be called virtually untouched. There are patios everywhere, most of them wild, untamed and a bit over the top, like, I suppose, their other operatic legend. Part of the old mediaeval city remains; so do over one and a half miles of the old mediaeval and pre-mediaeval wall, half a mile more than in Carcassonne in the south of France, although I must admit you don't get the same impression, probably because Seville is so much bigger.

As for the rest of Spain, I like Córdoba, Granada, Ronda. Even Marbella, for an early-morning cup of coffee. You can still see why Córdoba, the birthplace of Seneca, was once the greatest city in Europe and a major centre of learning, of the arts, of science and medicine. From here, the caliphs ruled practically the whole of modern-day Spain and Portugal, apart from the odd one or two Christian enclaves. Their ambassadors covered the whole of Europe as far as the Volga. In terms of Arab power, the caliphs of Córdoba were as important as the caliphs of Baghdad. The Mezquita, or great mosque, should, I reckon, rank alongside the Roman Forum, the Colosseum, the pyramids, Machu Picchu and, course, Angkor Wat as a world heritage site. From the outside, it looks like a series of scruffy warehouses. Inside it is row after row after row of over 900 slender columns above which red and white horseshoe-shaped arches support a beautifully carved ceiling. Even though it has been built on three times and the centre converted into a Christian church, you can still see why it was, in its day, the greatest building in Europe. It just oozes standing and status and reputation and authority.

Equally impressive is the Alhambra, the other great centre of Arab power and art, in Granada, which, between the thirteenth and fifteenth centuries, was one of the most beautiful cities in the whole of the West. Today it is the most visited monument in Spain. The royal palace built by Charles V is supposed to be the only building in the world which is square outside and circular inside. Don't ask me to confirm that. All I saw were touri— I mean people. Everywhere, as far as the eye could see. For all I know it could be a hexagonal triangle outside and a dog's dinner inside – I didn't see a thing. The building next to it is apparently composed of three palaces. The first is a small, primitive, rough-and-ready area for the general public, a bit like a doctor's waiting room. The second, for politicians and diplomats, is a little more spacious, a bit more elegant, a few tiles and mosaics here and there. A bit like a doctor's waiting room for private patients. The third is the real McCoy: luxury apartments, Jacuzzis, Turkish baths, Finnish saunas and facials and massages, the lot. At least, that's what I was told. I didn't get to see it. I was surrounded by a bunch of French tourists who were so interested in what they were seeing that they kept on about which restaurant they were going to for dinner and whether they were going to have scrambled eggs with blood pudding, veal sweetbreads in puff pastry or some unholy stew of woodcock, hare and wood pigeon.

I did, however, catch a glimpse of the royal fountain in the centre of the royal courtyard, which some guide told me was a gift from the Jewish community to their Arab masters. Like hell. The Jews giving presents to their Arab masters? If you ask me, it was all an elaborate ploy by Mossad to get a batch of high-powered microphones inside the palace to pick up every word the Arabs were saying.

I did go round and round Ronda, largely because, for some peculiar Spanish reason, the principal hotel in the centre of town has a policy that if you are having dinner there, they don't want anybody to know about it. Instead of being delivered straight to the front door in the conventional way, I was dumped on the edge of town and had to make my own way into the centre on foot. But, I hate myself for saying it, it was worth it. The bullring, one of the oldest in Spain and a mecca for all aficionados, was a favourite not only of Hemingway but of Orson Welles too. In fact, Orson Welles asked for his ashes to be scattered in the surrounding area after his death. A job they're still busy trying to complete, I should think.

Immediately outside the hotel I discovered an enormous gorge, over 100 metres deep, with first a Roman bridge crossing it, then an Arab bridge and finally a Spanish bridge. With a track record like that, it shouldn't be long before the European Union adds a fourth.

Coastal Spain, the land of such delicate cultural pursuits as *sangria*-vomiting competitions, I don't know at all, apart, that is, from Marbella. The best thing about Marbella is that the worst bits look like Miami and the best bits don't look like Miami. However, I didn't hear anybody asking for a San Mig and I didn't see anybody gesticulating wildly and mouthing, 'Has it got squid in it?' What's more, I could get the *Financial Times*, *Herald Tribune* and *Wall Street Journal* off some shop near the harbour, so I'm not complaining.

I nearly forgot Tenerife. I once spent practically two weeks there. It was like eating, living and sleeping on a coal tip. The beaches are black. OK, so it's volcanic dust or ash or whatever, but that's not how beaches are supposed to look. And it might be 70 miles from Africa and on the same latitude as Luxor, Delhi and the Bahamas, but I tell you, it was covered in dark clouds. I had a raging cold all the time I was there, which is probably why it doesn't exactly stick in the old memory. What does stick in my memory was a holiday brochure for Westerhams Ballena on Gran Canaria I picked up while recuperating in the hotel bar. There, after the telephone number of the local Lufthansa office and the local German doctor, were the personal, private and top-secret telephone numbers of George Bush, François Mitterrand, the Queen, the Pope and even Helmut himself.

I haven't been to Barcelona yet. Or Toledo. Or Bilbao, or Santiago, or Avila, or Málaga, or Cuenca, or Segovia, or Salamanca, or Cáceres. Or even to the Ladybyrds bar in Fuengirola. But I will. Which is what I mean about Spain being Moorish. First, because I'd like to see more places;

second, because I'd like to try to understand the people better. So far as I've been able to establish, the Basques up in the north are stubborn, primaeval, rough and ready and anti anything that's going. Especially Madrid. Every Basque, I reckon, is born hating Madrid - it's in their blood - and government. Any type of government anywhere in the world. Juan Sebastián del Cano, the first man to sail around the world, did so to get away from every type of government he could possibly get away from. Simon Bolivar, the man who led South America to freedom, did so to enable his people to break free of the shackles of Madrid. St Ignatius Loyola, the man who founded the Jesuits, did so to enable people to break free from everything in this world. What do all three have in common? You've got it - they were all Basques. About the only thing they actually like, as far as I can discover, is making money - most bankers and finance and investment experts seem to be Basques - and gathering together behind locked doors in strange, secret societies known as *txokos* in their own language, or *chocos* in Spanish, to cook up enormous buckets of *chorizo* cassoulet for each other. Some meet in cellars or basements, many have their own clubhouse, but wherever they go it will have a massive door, enormous locks and no women. Well, I say no women: I was told women *were* allowed in, but only as cleaners. But even then they are not allowed anywhere near the inner sanctum: the kitchen.

The Catalans way out on the east seem to be more flexible and cosmopolitan. They are prepared to at least talk to Madrid, providing it is on their terms. They would be more than prepared to join any government of whatever shape or colour, providing, again, that it is on their terms. But that doesn't mean to say that for one moment they actually think they're Spanish. Ask a Catalan where he is going on holiday. 'To Spain,' he will say in all innocence. Ask him about immigrants and he'll start going on about Andalusians and Extremadurans and Basques and Galicians. They're even trying to promote their own Catalan clock to stand alongside – note the word alongside – GMT. Ask a Madrileño what time he hits his first *tapas* bar and he'll say 6.30 (am, that is). Wrong, say the Catalans. What he should say is, 'Two quarters of seven.' Ask an Andalusian what time he starts work and he'll say 7.15 (pm, that is). What he should say according to the Catalans, is, 'A quarter of eight.' Last time I was in the area they were even talking about renumbering all the clocks in the province 1, 2, $\frac{1}{4}$, 4, 5, $\frac{2}{4}$, 7, 8, $\frac{3}{4}$, 10, 11 and 12 in order to make things clearer.

Further down the coast, the Valencians are much more relaxed and co-operative and understanding. Except that they insist on speaking Valenciano even though they live in a Castilian-speaking region. Castilians, on the other hand, are not just serious but serious with a strong, almost overpowering, sense of honour and discretion. They believe in what they believe in and will do anything to avoid any compromise on anything. If they want to take you out for a quick lunch from 2 pm to 6 pm then it is a quick lunch. If they insist that dinner is at 11 pm then it is at 11 pm. And if they want to tell you their life story there ain't nothin' you can do to stop them, even if it is -3$\frac{2}{7}$% in the morning, or whatever time the Catalans say it is.

As for the Galicians, I don't know anything about them, probably because they are the most secretive people in the country. Meet a Galician on the stairs, they say, and you'll never guess whether he's going up or coming down. Yet Basques, Catalans, Castilians, Valencians, Galicians, and however many other different types there are, are all fiercely loyal to Spain and everything Spanish. I mean you've only got to meet any one of them and immediately they're on at you about some Spanish magazine called *¡Hola!* And no matter where they come from, there's one thing you never, ever, ever do. You never tell them they've made a mistake. Not unless you want to end up in a *tapas* bar, in a thousand little pieces being served out mixed with sheep's eyes and lambs' intestines.

But wherever I go and whoever I meet in whatever *tapas* bar two things are always nagging away at the back of my mind. The first, obviously, is 'Is this really the lip of a cow I am eating?' The second is 'Why on earth did they blow it?' Get rid of the Arabs, I mean. They had been over-run before, by the Phoenicians, the Greeks and the Romans, but it was the Moors – so called because they had more oil, more money, more executions, more one-handed people and more women per head of the male population than anybody else – who gave the Spanish everything they have: literature, philosophy, mathematics, oranges, algebra, architecture, rice, astronomy, medicine, sugar, all types of construction, irrigation, horses, horsemanship and every kind of spice you can think of. At the time, it was a case of the Moors the merrier. The best part of the Arab world was not the Arab world but Spain. The Arab world was nothing; Spain was everything. Then, of course, Isabella had to go and ruin everything.

In fact, in many ways, I reckon 1492 was a major turning point in European history. Up until then Arabia virtually stopped at the Pyrenees. After that it was downhill all the way – for Spain and, strangely enough, for the Arabs as well. Spain began to slowly fall apart. And they lost that flair for construction, that sense of colour and excitement. The Arabs, too, seemed almost to give up, pull down the veil and stick to their hubble-bubble. You don't agree? Tell me, where in the Arab world was there anything to rival the glory that was Spain up to then? Tell me what the Arabs have done since to rival what they achieved in Spain. Not much, you have to admit. But just imagine what the world would be like today if Isabella had left the

Arabs alone. There would be no America, there would have been no Armada. There would have been no Peninsular Wars, no trying to bloody Boney's nose. Poor old John of Gaunt could have stayed at home instead of traipsing all over Galicia. Nelson wouldn't have been killed off Cape Trafalgar. Spain would be properly organised and run and administered, not like it is today.

If you really want to see a Spaniard, especially one of those super-smooth, slicked-down-hair Spaniards, get his maracas in a twist, ask him how Spain is governed today.

What is the official language of Spain? Spanish. Except in Catalonia, where it is Catalan and in the Basque country, where it is known as Euskera.

Presumably the government in Madrid is responsible for collecting taxes? *Sí*. Except in the Basque country and in Navarre, where for some historical reason, they collect the taxes and whenever they think of it send whatever is left over to Madrid.

How about the police force? Spain must have its own police force? *Sí*. Except, again, in the Basque country and in Catalonia. There they don't only have their own independent police forces, they also have their own separate flashy uniforms. And their own prisons as well.

OK, I understand regional differences and all that. But elections are elections. You must all have elections at the same time? *Sí*. Elections are held in a regular four-year cycle. Except – I knew it! I knew it! – in four regions. There they can hold their elections whenever they want.

But when you have elections you have elections? *Sí*. So what happened last time you had, say, national elections? We elected someone who was implacably opposed to devolution.

So what did he do? He extended devolution more than anybody else had ever done before.

But let's face it, there would be disadvantages if the Arabs were still running the country. No miserable looks coming at you across the breakfast table just because you've got to go off on another trip and can't paint the kitchen ceiling. No mother-in-law pulling a face like the back of a camel because you can't take her for a drive in the country on Sunday afternoon. They would all be covered from head to toe in thick, black, heavy *mantillas*. There would be no breakfast meetings because everybody would be off attending the daily execution or hand-chopping ceremony. There would be no lunches because everybody would be too busy out shopping for Gucci, Versace or Armani. There would be no family dinners because everybody would be in a mad rush to get to the races – the camel races – or to catch the latest opera, *The Berbers of Seville*. Trips to boring old Frankfurt would be long forgotten. Instead Barcelona would be the financial capital of Europe and Byzantium as well as Arabia itself. Come to think of it, there would be very little to do all day, apart from calculating that 10 per cent commission on US$100 million is US$29.5 million and transferring the lot to Vienna. Everything else would be done by people brought in from cheap Third World countries like India, Pakistan, Jordan and the UK.

Of course, there would be no booze. The whole of southern Spain would be planted with orange trees and Jerez would be the biggest orange-juice city in the world. But with a personal harem to look after and a string of Filipino maids to supervise, maybe you wouldn't miss it too much. If you did there would always be the traditional Arab wedding to look forward to, when they take over 100 rooms in a luxury hotel in Paris or New York or even Florida for four days of non-stop boozing. I don't know about you, but I reckon we should sue Isabella for being so stupid and making Spain less Moorish instead of more Moorish and ruining everything. Compensation should run into millions of pounds. Each.

On the other hand, maybe the Arabs didn't leave Spain after all. Maybe they just retreated to Marbella, from where they still own and run the country after all. Why else would there be a Moorish arch at Puerto Banús, the main entrance to the harbour? Why is the place full of Arab banks and Arab offices and huge Arab boats? Why are there palm trees everywhere? Why is every bit of grass shaped like a scimitar? There must be a reason.

PRAGUE

Poor old Vasher.

He was great fun. I didn't see much of him, and in spite of trying a million times, we never managed to do any business together. 'Don't want to risk ruining a beautiful friendship', he used to say. But whenever I did see him, in London or in Prague, he was great company. Always laughing, always joking, always full of ideas. Always drawing up lots of plans and schemes. He also, most important of all, taught me how to drink vodka. Russian-style. A sheet of dirty newspaper, a chilled bottle of vodka, a plate of tiny pieces of bread. A dish of the foulest-smelling, most rotten fish you can imagine. Every time he filled the glasses with vodka we had to take some of the bread, stand up, put one hand behind our backs, eat the bread with the other hand, shout at the top of our voices, '*Na zdrovie!*', and then slug the vodka back in one go.

Mostly he insisted on going to Chinese restaurants to drink vodka, perhaps because he felt they would always run round him, bring him everything he wanted and let him do things his way. Once though, I can just about remember calling on my liver to serve me above the call of duty in that big, circular dining room at the RAC Club in Pall Mall. They made all kinds of fuss to begin with. We couldn't have a bottle to ourselves, it had to be served glass by glass. They couldn't give us the tiny pieces of bread he wanted, we had to have rolls instead. As for the fish, they only had the very best salmon – nothing less at the great RAC Club. And it most definitely was not off. But we went ahead anyway. After three or four glasses it didn't seem to matter what they said or didn't say.

Why the rotten fish? To sober up afterwards, of course. One deep breath and zonk! you were stone-cold sober. The older, the more rotten and the more foul-smelling it was, the quicker it did the trick. Obviously, all a matter of Czechs and balances. Which is presumably why I can remember the Chinese restaurants and not, thank goodness, too much about the RAC Club.

I first went to Chamberlain's 'faraway country' containing 'a people of whom we know nothing' shortly after their Velvet Revolution, the sound of keys still jingling in my ears. I'd no sooner landed than I realised that what he said in his time was perfectly true. Czechoslovakia is all of an hour and a half from London. We call it Eastern Europe although it's west of Vienna. At Christmas the trades unions, not the managers, hand out chocolates to customers. And the people? Well, I've read my Kafka and my Good Soldier Svejk, but honestly I've never met anyone less Bohemian than the Bohemians.

Naturally, I thought they would be happy and laughing and thrilled to bits that at last they were free. Instead they seemed somehow sullen and silent, as if they were suffering from an enormous hangover and were desperately hoping against hope that they hadn't made fools of themselves at the party the night before and that somebody hadn't already sent the photographs to their wife.

As for the 'golden city', it was more the city of grease and grime and soot and smog. Everything everywhere looked dull and depressing and drab and dilapidated, as if it were buried in cobwebs. You couldn't see inside the shops –

which were simply called 'Flowers', 'Shoes', 'Meat', and 'One Veg' – they were so filthy. Which probably didn't much matter, because there was precious little inside anyway. As for the smog, some people maintain that Prague is the most polluted city in Europe after Athens, and that children and trees die younger and locals have more tumours than people in other parts of the country. In fact, it's probably just as well the trees die young because they are needed to build the little wooden kiosks you find all over the city. These are not some fancy Mitteleuropean portaloos. They are do-it-yourself pollution check-up posts. Inside each one is a meter. You check what the meter says, then check the reading against the maximum safety levels stuck up outside. I bet you a Budweiser Pils to a brown-ale shandy the meter reading is higher. If it's way, way over the top, it can cause enormous suffering and inconvenience to a great many people. Jogging is forbidden, children are forced to stay indoors, cars are banned, trams and buses are suspended. Only ambulances and fire engines are allowed to operate. The pollution is so bad that when, after the Velvet Revolution, they launched a whole new series of shiny new coins to mark their first year of independence, within days they had all turned black.

Yet beneath the grease and the grime and the soot and the smog you could just about see why all the books called Prague the 'golden city'. Everywhere there was this unbearable lightness of baroque. Somehow or other the centre had remained virtually untouched for 400 or 500 years. It was like stepping back in time to the seventeenth century. Not only was it still full of glorious buildings and beautiful, hand-painted seventeenth-century ceilings, it was also almost completely unaffected by any wartime bombing. And thankfully, for more than fifty years the Russians did nothing. Well, I say, nothing – they built a six-lane motorway, the *magistrala*, virtually through the middle of town, but apart from that they hardly gave any-thing a lick of paint, let alone a full-scale going over. The result of their neglect and indifference is this magical, glorious mish-mash of every type of building you can imagine: gothic, neo-gothic, nightmare gothic. Renaissance, biedermeir, cubist, art nouveau. Stalinist extreme, Socialist-realist, Khrushchev practical. But the greatest of them all is, of course, baroque. There is so much Baroque in Prague it's the only place in the world where I fall asleep counting cherubs. Admittedly you can hardly walk on the pavements for a forest of rickety scaffolding poles holding everything together, but that doesn't matter.

As for the traffic, the streets were empty then apart from the occasional Skoda coughing and spluttering its heart out the way people cough and splutter their hearts out whenever you tell them a Skoda joke.

What do you call a Skoda convertible? A skip.

What do you call a Skoda with twin exhausts? A wheel-barrow.

See what I mean?

I vaguely remember seeing Prague Castle in the smog with four East Germans who told me they had slipped across the border for a quick beer. East German beer was nothing compared to Czech beer, they said. They dropped in for a quick one whenever they got the chance. It looked like smog, but it could have been Vaclav Havel, the president of Czech chain-smokers, puffing away like mad on one cigarette after another.

We also wandered around St Vitus's Cathedral, a glorious French gothic church. Inside is the chapel of Good King Wenceslas – Good because he left all his jewels to the chapel. The trouble was, an old man told us (I don't think he was Czech – he wasn't smoking like a chimney), they needed seven keys to open the case to get to the jewels. Dubček had one set while he was chairman of the

Federal Parliament from 1990-92. Now that he was dead, nobody knew where it was.

After that, the East Germans said they had had enough culture. They wanted to hit the bars. There was a good one, they told me, in Letenska, which had been brewing away happily on the same site since 1350. But I resisted the temptation. See, I can be serious sometimes. So I slowly picked my way downhill towards the Vltava River all by myself. As I got to the Mala Strana, the Lesser Town, the smog began to clear and I had the shock of my life: I was in a toytown with lots of winding, cobbled streets all painted in pretty, dolly-mixture colours.

Then, suddenly, there was the famous Charles Bridge, the second oldest in Europe, with all the cobweb-festooned seventeenth- and eighteenth-century baroque statues running the length of it on both sides. It was glorious. Why Hasek would want to throw himself off this of all bridges, I don't know, unless, of course, someone told him that a contaminated moral environment was about gentlemen who eat organic vegetables and do not look out of plane windows.

The Stare Mesto, the Old Town, really was an old town: nothing but mediaeval houses and palaces and churches and, of course, in the square – one of the most beautifully preserved baroque squares I've ever seen – the famous gothic town hall which has witnessed everything from Protestants being executed in the fifteenth century to Soviet tanks rolling in in 1968. I was enjoying myself so much that – don't tell anyone – I actually stood and watched the astronomical clock and its twelve apostles who, every day of the year, strut their stuff on the hour between eight in the morning and eight in the evening. The mere fact there are twelve apostles shows you how tolerant and understanding and forgiving the Czechs are. Many people lump them together with the Poles and say they're dull and boring and lifeless like the Brits and the Germans, whereas the Hungarians and the Romanians and anybody else in Eastern Europe who throws a tantrum about nothing at all is like the French, the Spanish and the Italians.

This, I could believe, was the city not just of Kafka and Kundera but also of Alfons Mucha, the man behind all those ornate, opulent, heavily stylised, very snobby and upmarket turn-of-the-century posters and wine lists who many people claim is the most famous Czech artist of all time. I'll drink to that any day. In champagne, of course.

From the town hall I strolled down Wenceslas Square, 60 metres wide, nearly 1 kilometre long. It isn't really a square, more a Champs Elysées without the traffic. Everywhere there were cheap blue neon signs advertising various state-run trading companies and shops selling everything you could possibly want to buy, ranging from Bohemian glass and crystal to Bohemian glass and crystal.

This, of course, is where Jan Palach set fire to himself in 1969 as a protest against the Communist occupation. It is also the place where, in the days before the Velvet Revolution, 300,000 Czechs at a time, braving the cold and jangling their keys, cheered for Vaclav Havel. It couldn't have been more moving if he had written the scene himself, even in his own funny made-up nonsense language, Ptydepe. Come on, you mean you've forgotten *The Memorandum*, his play about office politics and bureaucracy gone mad? Don't worry, I'll send you a memo about it, in triplicate. Then you can file it and forget all about it.

Wenceslas Square might have started out as a horse market but believe me, a quick trot around it today and you've got a pretty good idea of Czech history. The statue of the man himself, Good King Wenceslas. The statue of Jan Hus, who was a pre-Lutheran Luther. On the other side of the Tyn Church, on the ground floor of the gloriously pink Kinsky Palace, is the shop run by Kafka's dad. The gap where the old town hall used to stand until the Germans destroyed it as a farewell present in 1945. The balcony from which Clement Gottwald, probably the most hated man in Czech history, declared the success of the Communist takeover in 1947.

Now it was time for the serious matters of life: eating and drinking. Czech restaurants were at that time probably the worst in the world. Not only were they all state-owned, they were also state-run and state-managed, even down to the recipes. Nothing could be cooked, let alone served, unless it came from some state-published cookbook with a zippy title like *Recipes for Warm Meals*. Change just one ingredient and, by Czech law, the recipe had to be submitted to and approved by the Ministry of Health. So I decided to do as the East Germans had done and hit the bars. The Czechs after all had virtually invented the stuff. Pilsner in Plzen in 1295, lager in 1842. Not surprisingly, they hold the world record for beer consumption. On average every Czech drinks half a litre a day every day of the year.

Forget Kafka and Hasek and Kundera and even the great Mucha: to have ignored the pubs would have been to have ignored their most important single contribution to the world. For Czech pubs are real pubs. Not the pretty-pretty pubs you find in the States, which are about as atmospheric as a warm six-pack and smell like a chemical toilet at the back of a long-distance coach. These are serious, grown-up pubs, dedicated not just to drinking yourself into the ground and imploding your liver but to destroying your brain as well. Sawdust on the floors, spit on the sawdust, and nobody wearing a suit.

I started in the bar the East Germans had recommended. There I had the usual Budwar and Pilsner Urquell in its distinctive green bottle and something called a Gambrinus, which is apparently more popular than the popular Urquell. From then on, for the rest of the day I was in and out of all the pubs in what I think was the Zizkov area of Prague. At any rate there were nothing but number 9 trams running all over the place. Which I thought was another example of Czech humour: number 9 – one over the eight? Oh well, never mind.

Purely out of academic interest, you understand, I then had – or I think I had – a Staropramen, which seemed very much in demand at the time, various Kozel beers and something called a Radegast. My favourites, oratleesht-Ithinkkkzaywere, were a Flek, a dark beer, a bit lighter than a Guinness, and a Kvasnicove, which was very, very strong and very, very dark. The Mestan was also very good, but it took a while to get used to the caramelly taste. In one bar I vaguely remember a professor-type telling me that Czech beer was fantastic because it was made with local tapwater. Which health inspectors had ruled undrinkable because it was so polluted. The one I definitely didn't like was Becherovka, which tasted like medicine.

I ended up in some downstairs bar somewhere or other with two military-looking guys at a table covered with Semtex. At one point one of them got up to buy a round.

'You want to be careful of him,' the other one said to me. 'Ex-KGB. Used to be in charge of breaking people's little fingers. An expert. A real expert.'

Later he went off to get a round himself.

'A word of advice,' the first man said. 'My colleague used to be in the KGB. He specialised in putting needles under people's fingernails.'

The Semtex? No, not the industrial plastic explosive which has guaranteed the Czechs honoured-nation status wherever in the world two or three terrorists gather together. Semtex the drink, made by another Czech brewery called Pinelli, which is supposed to make you explode with energy. I had one sip and it blew my kneecaps off.

By now I was ready to risk all by undertaking probably

the most dangerous mission anybody can attempt in Prague: to have a traditional hearty Czech meal. Hearty because you've only got to look at it and you get a heart attack. It's no wonder they have more heart attacks and die younger than anybody else in Europe. Even more heart attacks than the Poles, which is saying something.

As far as I can tell, Prague is the world capital of *knedliky*, or dumplings. Everything comes with huge, stodgy dumplings practically the size of a football. Our Grandmother's Rabbit. Goulash Old Town-style. Roast Young Duck Old Bohemian-style. Great slabs of meat, huge coils of home-made sausages, enormous piles of odd-looking bones, buckets of lumpy cabbage soup. And whenever I've had a meal there the whole plate has always been buried by an enormous landslide of *sauerkraut.* As if that's not filling enough, for dessert they have cakes and pancakes and *apfelstrudel* the size of a football pitch, all drowned in a rising sea of thick creams and sauces. If all this does not give you a heart attack, one thing definitely will: the bill. Try as hard as I could, there was no way on that trip I managed to spend more than £10 on a single meal, no matter how much I ate or drank.

On the last evening of my visit I had problems getting through the door of the restaurant.

'You should work out,' said an American trying to squeeze past me to get in. He was, I should add, twice my size. But that's the way they are.

The only sensible, practical advice I received was from a Czech banker, who was half my size.

'Big blondes,' he said. 'It's the only way. I'm sorry.'

To look at Vasher you'd have thought he was more British than the British. He had white hair, half-moon glasses and always wore a pin-striped suit, a waistcoat and chain and a red carnation. He also, when I first met him, used to carry a bowler hat and an umbrella. But he wasn't British. He was Czech through and through.

Vasher was born in Prague in 1926. He went to Prague High School. When war broke out he joined the Czech Air Force as a fighter pilot. After the war was over and the Communists were in power, he was invited to join the Czech Foreign Trade Ministry. From there, because he spoke several languages - seven or eight - he was transferred to the Ministry of Foreign Affairs. Throughout the sixties he was chargé d'affaires and then head of chancery in various Czech embassies in Africa.

In August 1970 he arrived in Britain with his wife and three children and was almost immediately granted British nationality. For the next ten years he worked in the City. Well, I say worked in the City - he always said he hardly ever saw the City. He spent anything between five and eight months of the year travelling the world drumming up business for various banks and trade finance houses. But it was in the City of London Club, a depressing shack near Ludgate Circus, that I first met him. We'd both been rambling around Africa for years, we both knew lots of people and we both knew our way around. We thought perhaps we could do business together, but it was not to be. Whenever we met, whether it was in Prague or in London, there was always something far more interesting to talk about.

Once, when I had just got back from Lebanon, he told me about his own visit to Beirut. He was on one of the last flights to land there just as the civil war was getting underway.

'Immediately we landed, the pilot realised what was happening and said we had to leave straight away. As soon as we took off, he said he was heading for Cyprus. But Cyprus wouldn't let us in. Then he said he was going to Prague. Prague! I thought, "My God, if I land in Prague I am a dead man. They will shoot me." I told the crew what would happen to me if we did. They told the pilot so he took us on to Vienna.'

Afterwards we strolled along Fleet Street. It was boiling hot, but Vasher was immaculate as usual in his pin-striped suit and waistcoat, carrying his bowler hat and umbrella.

'Vasher,' I said. 'You're crazy. You're the only man in town with a double-breasted suit and a bowler hat.'

He laughed. 'At the end of my first week in the City I wore a light suit. Nobody said a word all day. Then, as I was leaving, one of my colleagues said, "Vasher, are you going straight to the country tonight?" After that I always, always wear a double-breasted suit.'

My God. Look at what they've done to the place now. Instead of bouncing I reckon they were bounced.

Gone is the grease and the grime and the soot, or at least, most of it. Gone is the smog – or it was the next time I went to Prague. But instead of seeing everywhere the glint of gothic and the beauty of baroque, the bas-reliefs and friezes, the sculptures and the million and one other embellishments hidden for centuries, all I noticed was fancy new office buildings, shiny, pristine shopping malls, a thousand new boutiques, hundreds of hi-fi shops and one, yes one, new Jaguar showroom.

Where before there were beautiful, elegant seventeenth-century buildings, now the façades were being kept while the rest was being knocked down and replaced by fishtank office blocks. The eighteenth-century hand-painted walls and ceilings were being hidden by filing cabinets and stacks of computers.

Where before the streets were dull and lifeless, now they were full of huge, purring Mercedes and stretch limos. Thou shouldst be living at this hour had become a cross between a baroque theme park and a Mitteleuropean Disneyland.

At one big store a young couple were actually living in one of the shop windows. At first I thought it was because of the chronic shortage of decent accommodation created by the enormous influx of tourists, but they were taking part in some tacky capitalist stunt to separate as many ex-Socialists as possible from their hard-earned money. Still, it's a million times better than what you see in the shop windows in Vienna. During one trip there the most talked-about window display in town was the head of the owner. The previous evening her son had stabbed his mother to death, chopped her head off and stuck it in the window of her shop for all the world and King Herod to gawp at.

Hotels in Prague were now permanently overbooked. Flats and single rooms in private houses couldn't be had for love nor money, although I was told that if you were prepared to combine the two there were more possibilities. Even the secret police interrogation centre, where Vaclav Havel was held more times than he said he could remember, had been turned into a tourist hotel. The rooms might be small – just 12 square metres – but I'm told there is no shortage of bars. If you are missing life at home and decide to give it a go, ask for room P6. It's their presidential suite, or rather it was their presidential suite. At £1,500 a month for a tiny three-roomed flat off a court-yard tucked behind the police station in Wenceslas Square, Prague was more expensive than Vienna or even London. And more dangerous. Things are now so bad that the trams play non-stop recordings in three languages warning people against pickpockets. Taxi-drivers fed up with fat-cat tourists refusing to pay all of 24p a mile have even wired up the back seats of their cabs. Anybody who even hesitates about paying the fare, however extortionate, risks getting a quick 240 volts up his back pocket.

Prague Castle was now buried in tourists. Thousands of them. From Germany – especially from Germany – from

Austria, Italy, France, Belgium, Holland, everywhere. The soldiers who would once have been prepared to sacrifice their lives to defend it now merely pose in their new, pretty-pretty red and white chocolate-soldier uniforms. One of the first decisions President Vaclav Havel took after the collapse of fifty years of Communism, apart from having another cigarette, was to commission the design.

For old times' sake I took the same route as I did on my first visit. The Lesser Town was now living up, or rather down, to its name. The cobbled streets were now choked with fat old ladies from Bavaria, tall, thin Huguenots from France and a million kids. As for the little toy-town buildings, I couldn't see them for coaches. Charles Bridge was now the longest and narrowest jumble sale in Europe. Fake-fur hats, Russian dolls, hammer and sickle badges, jars of fake caviar, prints, paintings, arty-crafty souvenirs. And, of course, Kafka T-shirts, Kafka posters, Kafka postcards, Kafka badges and Kafka everything else were piled high on the pavement, on suitcases, on rickety card tables, on anything that didn't move. All around were jugglers, strange-looking guys with strange-looking puppets, snake-charmers, old men playing zithers and what one told me was a water harmonica, not to mention half a dozen local brass quartets, three elderly violinists, two complete baroque ensembles, six jazz bands and a million bored American students of all ages drearily strumming their guitars.

I swear the statues of St Cosmas, St Damien, St Wenceslas, St Vitus and all the others were seriously wondering whether they should follow Hasek's example and throw themselves in the river. In fact some of them looked as though they were already throwing themselves in bit by bit, or else somebody was doing it for them. St Christopher had lost his oar, St Joseph had misplaced a gilded lily. Others were missing fingers, thumbs and various other bits and pieces. Either that or the souvenir-hunters were out in force. Even the Crucifixion had not escaped. Gone also was the golden eagle.

Packing what was left of the bridge was a heaving, sweating, surging, grubby mass of tourist inhumanity to man. Take my advice – although nobody else ever does – if you want to see the bridge for yourself, go between 2.15 and 3.45 in the morning. Preferably on the way back from sampling the beers. And all right, then, just one glass of absinthe. It's the only time you are guaranteed to have the place to yourself.

In the Old Town were all the sophisticated Czechs who couldn't get on the Charles Bridge: sword-swallowers, snake-handlers, puppeteers, smart young men selling Nazi uniforms and all kinds of Communist paraphernalia, frail old ladies dancing around with old-fashioned ruffles round their necks, old men with two ferrets stuck down their trousers.

Wenceslas Square was no longer Wenceslas Square. It was enduring torments worse than anything it had ever experienced in the whole of its long history. As if Prague had not suffered enough, the square had been taken over by millions of Yappies – Young Americans in Prague – who were trying to do a Hemingway, with or without the absinthe, and turn the place into some kind of pre-war Paris. They kept referring to it as Vac Nam. When I first heard this I thought it was some kind of PC-speak for having a vacation from Vietnam. It turned out to be short for Vaclauske Namesti, the Czech for Wenceslas Square.

To help them maximise their Bohemian experience, to capture the authentic atmosphere of a completely different country and a completely different cultural environment, the Yappies have started their own American newspapers and American radio stations and opened American restaurants selling famous traditional Czech specialities such as blueberry cheesecake and banana daiquiris, like the Beef Stew Café, where wannabe novelists, poets, painters, journalists, musicians, English teachers and fat-cat corporate lawyers hang out on Sunday evenings. They've even opened their very own American Hospitality Center, where you can buy popcorn the way Mom makes it back home, as well as get all the latest college and pro football videos.

As well as the Yappies, if you're really unlucky you might bump into another regular, Salman Rushdie, who's made a big thing about not feeling in danger in Prague. Even when riding a number 22 tram. Why should he? Everybody is more interested in Kafka and Hasek and Kundera than in trying to read some long involved story full of impossible names doing impossible things which could seriously damage their health.

The cheap blue neon signs advertising the names of various state-run industries have all gone. Today Vac Nam is covered in gaudy, flashy signs extolling Volkswagen, Philip Morris, Pepsi, Matsushita and Bass, which practically owns Prague Breweries.

In some parts of the Czech Republic, especially east Moravia, the American influence is worse, if that's possible. There people wear blue western shirts, cowboy boots and silver spurs, eat things like poppyseed-paste pie and play country and blue-grass music non-stop. These are the Czechs who discovered, as a result of the Velvet Revolution, that over a million of their ancestors had over the years fled to the States, most of them to Texas. They call themselves Czexans, which I think means 'unfortunate'.

In Prague, instead of freezing to death in the cold and jangling their keys to try to get decent men in power, now the Czechs only seemed interested in waving their credit cards in the air to gain entrance to all the bars and clubs and discos and casinos that have sprung up everywhere. Watching their antics, replacing the secret police, were a motley collection of drug-addicts, uniformed security guards and armed but very incontinent policemen – who, I was told, go to the toilets in the restaurants and fast-food outlets in the square every twenty minutes. Some say they're looking for drug-addicts. Since the war in the old Yugoslavia disrupted the Afghanistan–Pakistan–Turkey–Balkans–Western Europe supply route, Prague has become a major drug centre, especially as smoking pot, though not selling it, is legal there. But I'm not convinced. I reckon they were dodging into the toilets so often to get rid of all the fantastic Czech beer they had drunk before coming on duty.

A lot of the rough, tough, grown-up pubs are prettying themselves up. The sawdust is being replaced by carpets and the beers are giving way to wine – although why anybody would want to drink Czech wine I don't know: it's thinner than water. There are still plenty of bars you wouldn't dare go into – if you weren't wearing a suit, that is. However, there is one bar which maintains the Czech tradition of destroying the brain, and in this case the eyes as well. The Akropolis in Kubelikova has once again started to serve absinthe, which is 80 per cent proof. At first, I admit, I was tempted. I fancied the idea of soaking sugar in the stuff, then setting fire to it and dripping it slowly into the glass. But in the end I chickened out. A string of pink elephants convinced me that after one sip I would probably end up going blind, cutting my ear off and blowing my brains out with a shotgun. Apart from that I thought it might be bad for me.

For me the one innovation that proves above all else how low Prague has plunged in such a short space of time, and how quickly it has abandoned all its age-old traditions, is – I can hardly bring myself to say it – their first vegetarian restaurant. Worse, they have enough customers to keep going until five o'clock in the morning.

A Kosher meal. That was Vasher's way of getting an upgrade wherever he went in the world. He would always book economy, then, when he checked in, looking immaculate in his pin-striped double-breasted suit, his waistcoat and chain and carnation and bowler hat, he would say he was terribly sorry, he didn't want to cause any inconvenience, but he'd forgotten to order a kosher meal. Could they possibly, if it wasn't too awfully inconvenient, blah, blah, blah. It worked every time.

By now he'd set up his own international financial operation. He was into acquisitions, mergers and joint ventures and setting up a string of East–West trade deals. He'd joined a firm of City stockbrokers, become a name at Lloyd's and had a string of directorships. He was a freeman of the City of London, a liveryman, a member of a string of various charitable organisations – at one time he was president of Lions International, the London host club – and a fellow of practically every institute you could think of.

Yet he was spending more and more time in Africa, flying backwards and forwards to Côte d'Ivoire, Gabon and my own favourite, Togo. He had even been made an honorary chief of some big tribe in Nigeria.

As business boomed he was also doing an increasing amount of entertaining. One evening I was invited to his home. It was beautiful, full of nineteenth-century – or what looked like nineteenth-century – paintings, oriental rugs, books and the requisite collections of silver and crystal. Outside the back garden was beautifully landscaped, there were lights and fountains everywhere, and the front lawn was beautifully manicured. The last guest, an African ambassador, turned up late. Arriving in his enormous Mercedes, he skidded to a halt right in the middle of Vasher's immaculate lawn. If he'd had his bowler hat on, I swear he would have thrown it on the ground and jumped up and down on it.

Kafka was right. Prague is 'an old crone with claws'. I've been back to Prague many times now: it's an ideal stopping-off point for the rest of Eastern Europe, the beer is fantastic, the food is great. (I am, of course, speaking as somebody who is married to a vegetarian obsessed with E numbers who thinks there is nothing tastier in the world than a tofu salad followed by veggieburgers.) And in spite of the ever-increasing floods of tourists, it is still a wonderful place.

To survive, you've just got to have a touch of the Good Soldier. You mustn't let them get you down. You must be as cunning, as devious, as sly and as cynical as the best of them, because in Prague nothing is straightforward. Everything is labyrinthine, involved, intricate and exhausting. Like buying a newspaper in the street. Or the sign on the back of one hotel door: 'Guests should announce the abandonment of their rooms before 12 o'clock, emptying the room at the latest until 14 o'clock, for the use of the room before 5 at the arrival or after the 16 o'clock at the departure, will be billed as one night more.'

If you see a notice which says 'Out of Order' or 'Slow' or 'Danger', the chances are it's just a trick to get you to part with your money. A Swedish businessman told me that once, way out in the middle of nowhere, he stopped his car by a road sign in Czech. A traffic policeman immediately fined him because he couldn't understand what it said.

If you want two beers, order one. Whatever you order, you will always be given more than you asked for. It's just the Czech way of making you spend more. In some bar down near the river I once ordered one beer. What I got was two beers and a kangaroo-steak sandwich. And the guy serving me wasn't even Czech. He was a Young Australian in Prague.

If you want to change some money, whether at a bank, at one of the currency shops, with some guys in the street or even at the hotel, check what you are given. It's not unusual for forged notes to be stuck in the middle of a bundle of good ones. If a policeman comes up to you in the street and wants to see your passport and any foreign currency you have, be careful. He could be a crook after your passport to hustle on the black market. How you tell the difference between a real policeman and a crook is for you to work out.

If you want to purchase a Czech company, whatever you do – and I know this sounds stupid – make certain that the guy you are dealing with actually owns it, or at least has the authority of the owners to deal. If not, you could be in for an awful lot of wasted time, trouble and, of course, expense. I know two people this happened to, so there's bound to have been many more.

These guys are dodgers par excellence. It was because of their dodging skills, don't forget, that they survived, or at least most of them did, the last fifty years; that they were not dominated as much or for so long by the Soviets as other countries, and that at the end of the day they emerged in much better shape financially speaking than the rest of Eastern Europe, or at any rate the bit that's not west of Vienna. Between the wars they were the most economically successful and politically stable of all the states which replaced the old Hapsburg empire. In 1937 income per head of population was greater than in Italy, Austria or Switzerland and roughly the same as in France. They had a strong industrial sector and were the eighth-richest nation in the world.

Today, in control once again of their own destiny, the Czechs are still a big, big success. Unemployment is around 3 per cent, even less in Prague. National debt per capita is the region's lowest. Their purchasing power is about the same as Portugal's, which is fantastic when you remember where they have come from, and in such a short time as well. The Czech Republic is the only Eastern European country increasing its manufactured exports to the West. GDP, of which two thirds is generated by the private sector, is a staggering 5.2 per cent. Foreign investment is pouring in, over US$6 billion since 1990. Czech bonds are trading only just above UK levels. The stock exchange is booming and they've just opened a diamond exchange. Already they've got a higher international credit rating than Greece, and all the signs indicate that they will continue growing at a staggering 5 per cent a year for the next fifteen or twenty years. In fact they already meet all the criteria for European Monetary Union that many of the countries already in the EU are struggling to reach.

Yet just ten, twenty, fifty yards off the tourist rat run from the castle through the Mala Strana, across Charles Bridge across the Old Town into Wenceslas Square, is the Prague of ten, twenty, fifty years ago. Old women hobbling about, lonely old men sitting staring out of windows, near-abandoned streets, offices full of piles of dusty papers. Just behind the castle is the Loreto Church, where I discovered the hair-raising story of St Wilgefortis, who prayed to become more like a man. Her prayer was answered. She grew a beard. When her father saw it, he did what any self-respecting father would do in the circumstances. He had her crucified.

One day I caught the end of an organ recital in St James Church, which, I reckon, should hold the world record for cherubs dangling from the ceiling, clambering up pillars and swinging from cornices. And just off the Royal Road in Mala Strana, the Lesser Quarter, is Mozart territory. This is where they filmed *Amadeus,* and where most of the cast stayed. In the evenings they used to hang around the Café Amadeus in the Old Town Square. Oh yes, of course – I nearly forgot – this is where Mozart himself used to stay as well.

St Nicholas Church is probably the largest and finest baroque building in Prague. Here Mozart used to play the organ, and here they held a memorial service for him which was attended by 400, 4,000 or even 4 million people, depending on who you talk to, whereas in Vienna he was completely ignored. Then there is Skorepka Street, where Mozart lived at number 420 for some of the time he was in Prague; the Clementium, near Charles Bridge, which has a special Mozart Hall and jealously guards some of his scores; Strahor Monastery, where he played the organ; and Villa Bertramka in Smichov, which has now been turned into a museum. Here he lived with the Duseks and completed the overture to *Don Giovanni* just minutes before its first performance down the road in the Estates Theatre in 1787.

If you don't fancy eine kleine Mozart, you could try Kafka – unless you feel he's too much of a trial, what with his obsession with his bowels and the fuss he made about being a vegetarian. I reckon that's what killed him. Had he stuck to Our Grandmother's Rabbit, Goulash Old Town-style or even Roast Young Duck Old Bohemian-style, and not started drinking gallons of unpasteurised milk from suspect cattle, he would not have caught tuberculosis and died in 1924, just one month before his forty-first birthday. Especially as he was the grandson of a kosher butcher.

In any event you're practically guaranteed, wherever you go in Prague, that Kafka has been there too. He spent almost his whole life there, and he lived all over the place. In the house next to St Nicholas Church, in Old Town Square, where he was born, in Wenceslas Square, in Old Town Square again, next to the Tyn Church.

I'm ashamed to say that I still have to do all the really important sights: U Fleku, the bar where Hasek used to hang out; Café Slavia, where Charter 77, the human-rights campaign, was born; the Magic Lantern Theatre, where Vaclav Havel and all the others founded the Civil Forum in those heady pre-revolutionary days of November 1989; and, of course, U Maliru, which is reputed to be the most expensive restaurant in the country. But there's absolutely no way you'll ever catch me anywhere near the Jazz Club

Reduta, where Bill Clinton played the sax one night with Havel even though I gather they've now put a big brass plaque on the chair he sat on.

'Please, a nice, neat little scar,' Vasher told the surgeon as he was being wheeled into the operating theatre in Prague. 'Not for me. For the ladies.' He had had a string of bad luck. First he was attacked outside his London home. Then, shortly after the Velvet Revolution, he went back to Prague and was beaten up. He had to be taken to hospital. He'd been attacked before, in Marseilles. 'Five people surrounded me. Five. They asked for my wallet,' he told me. 'I said, Here, take it. Have it. Take what you want.' And in Mombasa he was robbed of everything. 'Naked. I tell you, naked. They took everything. Everything. My wife said, "What can we do?" I said, "What can we do? Nothing. Let's have a drink." I go to the drinks cabinet, but they have taken all my drinks as well.' But the attack in Prague was serious. It took him a long, long time to get over it. He lost a lot of weight. His double-breasted pin-striped suits were hanging off him and he had trouble walking. Things looked bad, but he fought back. Slowly he put on weight, and the suits filled out, but never to their original capacity. Walking became easier, but he never got back that spring in his step. Every month ever after, on the same date as he'd had the operation, he sent twenty-four red roses to the lady surgeon who operated on him. Presumably for giving him a neat little scar, as he requested. For the ladies.

Beyond Prague the Czech Republic is littered with fairy-tale castles, pretty little villages and lots of wonderful mediaeval towns packed with a million exciting things to do such as, according to one tourist-information leaflet I saw, 'Walk to mill. Walk along canal. Walk to hill. Walk to pond. Walk around pond.'

So why can't I be spa-struck and holiday this year in Karlsbad, next year in Marienbad, once the oh-so-civilised playgrounds of the European elite, as well as the likes of Goethe, Schiller, Beethoven, Chopin, Brahms and Karl Marx, who apparently had big digestive problems and as a result found many things hard to swallow. Peter the Great also popped in once for a quick drink of the waters. Then, typically, rushed off to spend the rest of the day working on some local building site. I could have blazing-hot saunas, wander in the woods, sip champagne in the cocktail lounges of the grand hotels and try desperately to pronounce their Czech names, Karlovy Vary and Marianske Lazne.

Unfortunately, the Czech Republic is also littered with lots of filthy old factories, some of which pump out dangerously high levels of potentially cancer-causing radon. This has forced many potential investors to walk away, on how many legs I wasn't told. It is at these factories that I invariably end up. The manufacturing centre of the Austro-Hungarian Empire the Czech Republic may have been, but way out in the sticks they still harvest the crops with scythes and rake everything by hand. They even have road signs banning horse-drawn hay carts from going down certain roads.

The Czech Republic's second city, Brno, is the home of the Bren gun. In fact if it hadn't been for its huge arms industry, Hitler might never have moved in and annexed Moravia and Bohemia and given us all a lot of problems to sort out. Today Brno is still big in arms. It is also the most heavily industrialised part of the country, and it looks it. So does Ostrava, a bleak industrial city if ever I saw one, up in northern Moravia. It is completely dominated by the largest integrated steel and engineering complex in the country – the only steel company in the world founded by an archbishop, Rudolf Jan, who also happened to be one of the Hapsburgs. As you would expect of a Hapsburg, in addition to his church duties he also had his own coalmines in the region as well as in Sweden. He decided he wanted his own smelter as well, and so he went ahead and built one. Today it is the third-biggest company in the Czech Republic. 'You can always tell when you're getting near Ostrava,' my driver told me on my first visit. 'You can see the smoke.'

Ostrava – at one time the steel mill employed over 15,000 people – is like Pittsburg, or any of the steel towns of the old days. Block after block of nondescript flats surrounded by block after block of nondescript factories and workshops. The hotel in the centre of town – the only hotel in the centre of town – was called Steel Hotel. What else? It was like all the other blocks, functional, to the point. No carpets, no telephones, no lifts – and my room was on the tenth floor. But it was cheap: I paid around £20 a night which, I suppose, was good value for money. There were no taxis, either. Not one. That stunned me, because wherever you go in the world – Bamako, Tamanrasset in the middle of the Sahara or even Ashby-de-la-Zouch – there are always taxis. I had to get a message to the factory I was visiting to ask them to come and collect me. When I finally got there, the factory was unbelievable: modern, up to date, everything working, everything in immaculate condition. What was more, they were manufacturing on time, delivering on time and making money. It was the complete opposite of what I had expected, which just goes to prove that, once the Czechs begin to roll, it won't be long before they're the eighth-richest country in the world again.

'Drink to my death. May I die soon.'

The last time I saw Vasher was at the RAC Club. He was on sparkling form. He'd just come back from his house in Spain and was talking about doing deals between Spain

and the Czech Republic. This time – it was the only time –
we didn't stand. We didn't have any bread, either. We just
drank our vodka the straightforward, the ordinary, the
boring way.

'I want to die, Peter,' he suddenly said. 'I want to die.'

He did. A few months later. In Prague.

Poor old Vasher.

VALLETTA

OK, so how do you make a Maltese cross?

Ask him why, if the megalithic temple of Ggantija is the oldest free-standing structure on earth, nobody has ever heard of it.

Well, have you? I hadn't, until I stumbled across it on a hillside just outside Xaghra, after I'd been shipwrecked on the island of Gozo, the second-largest of the three islands that make up Malta.

The pyramids, I've heard of them. Stonehenge, sure, I've come across that, not to mention plenty of other ancient ruins of all shapes and sizes, some closer to home than others. But not these so-called ur-buildings made of huge stones, some 20 feet high, which are supposed to be the bedrock of Western civilisation. To look at them, though, you'd think they were a couple of temples designed by Henry Moore, all curves and strange shapes with great big holes all over the place. Some of the walls are quite high, maybe two or three storeys high. Others are just one stone on top of another. Inside you can see what were probably altar stones and pillars and somewhere to wash your feet, although, as with Henry Moore, you can never be too sure.

To the Gozos, of course, these temples are nothing as exotic as the oldest free-standing structures on earth. They're simply stone buildings thrown together by huge

Amazons who gorged themselves on magic beans and then thought nothing of bounding across the face of the world with a baby under one arm and a 50-ton boulder under the other. Hey, maybe they built Stonehenge as well.

Ask him where Clapham Junction is.

It's near Buskett Gardens in the centre of the island of Malta, a major prehistoric cross-over point for sledges or carts. You can see all the ruts in the rock. They call it Clapham Junction because they say it's like Britain's busiest railway intersection. Ha, ha. Who says the Maltese haven't got a sense of humour?

Ask him when Malta's most famous visitor arrived on the island.

It was AD60. And to mark the event, the Maltese have turned the site into the second-largest holiday area on the island with modern hotels everywhere.

Go to the Veechia Restaurant. Opposite it is a spring which is where, they say, St Paul caused water to gush forth from the rock in order to give his fellow survivors a drink after everything they'd been through. Don't believe them. He was protesting at the prices they were charging for the drinks. Luckily for St Paul, he was able to do something about it. The rest of us have to give in and cough up. Naxxar is where, they say, the guys who rescued everything from the wreck came from, Naxxar, of course, being Maltese for the verb 'to hang clothes out to dry'. Nothing, you notice, about pressing them and folding them: poor old St Paul had to do all that himself.

Call in at Gillieru Restaurant. That's where they lit a bonfire so they could all dry off. Try it today and you'll get arrested. The Grotto in Rabat is the cave where St Paul lived for three months while waiting for the next boat to Rome. Which doesn't say a lot for Maltese hospitality. The least they could have done, you would have thought, was put him up in a three-star hotel, the mileage they were going to get out of him in the coming years. They did in the end build a St Paul Shipwreck Church in Valletta, which is home to not only one of his arm bones, but also part of the column on which he was beheaded. They have also got a gilded statue of him which they carry through the streets of the city on 10 February every year, the day they reckon he was shipwrecked. I must say I feel sorry for St Luke. He went through exactly the same thing as St Paul, but the Maltese don't bother to even mention him.

Ask him how come, if the Order of St John of Jerusalem was launched in order to help pilgrims who fell ill on their way either to or from the Holy Land, they ended up becoming such a ruthless bunch of guys responsible for inflicting so much unspeakable violence on the world?

I mean, something must have gone wrong somewhere along the line. You can't just one day be caring for the sick and the dying and the next be adding to their numbers. Some people would say it was a form of insurance. Instead of rushing around caring for the sick and injured, it is better to ensure that there are no sick and injured in the first place. Attack is better than defence, prevention is better than cure, and all that stuff. But if that's the case, doctors today would be cruising motorways trying to prevent accidents rather than patching up the victims afterwards. My guess is that for the Philippe de l'Isle-Adamses, not to mention grand masters like Manoel de Vilhena and others of that ilk, being a nurse was no fun. They wanted the action and the glory and the order gave it to them.

* * *

Ask him if it's true that the knights of the Order of St John
gave Malta the thumbs-down when they first came across
it.

Poor, miserable, disagreeable. A rock of soft sandstone
with no running water and no wells. Almost insupport-
able, especially in summer. That's what they said. Not that
they had much choice in the matter: they'd been thrown
off the island of Rhodes, together with the hand of St John
the Baptist, one of their most prized possessions, by
Ottoman forces led by Suleiman the Magnificent. Charles
V, the holy Roman emperor, offered them either Malta or
Tripoli, the least prized of his possessions. Malta they definitely didn't want, but Tripoli was worse, even without
Gadaffi. So Malta it had to be.

What did the Maltese have to say about it? Nothing, or if
they did nobody took any notice of them. Charles V merely
told them they would 'receive and consider the said Grand
Master as their true and feudal lord. . .and shall perform and
obey his behests as good and faithful vassals should always
obey their lord'. In other words, like it or lump it.

The knights then turned up and, being good, honest,
God-fearing Christian gentlemen, trampled all over them
and what rights, privileges, culture and customs they had.

Ask him what the Maltese cross stands for.

Some say the four arms represent the four virtues pru-
dence, temperance, fortitude and justice, and the eight
points the eight beatitudes: blessed are the poor in spirit,
blessed are those who mourn, and so on. Others say that
as the Order of St John was virtually run by the French,
the traditional Christian cross wasn't good enough for
them. They just had to have something different. To

become a knight you couldn't just join up: you had to be a Catholic, of aristocratic birth and able to pay up-front for the privilege. Once a member, you were pledged to defend the Church, care for the sick and be loyal to the pope. On death you had to agree to surrender any land or possessions you had to the order.

Ask him why Valletta is called Valletta.

After Grand Master Jean Parisot de la Valette, who led the order to victory over the Turks. After the fall of St Elmo on Malta, during which several knights were beheaded and their bodies raised on planks and thrown in the harbour, La Valette executed every single Turkish prisoner under his command, stuck their heads in his cannons and fired them back across the harbour to the Turks in St Elmo. To stop the Turks ever again capturing the island, he decided to build a fantastic fortified baroque city not merely on St Elmo itself but on the entire rocky peninsula upon which it was based. The foundation stone was laid on 28 March 1566, on the site of Our Lady of Victory. The layout of the city was drawn up by the Vatican architect Francesco Laparelli. That is why it is all straight lines and 90-degree angles, no diversions allowed.

Ask him which of the eight *auberges* built by the knights are still standing.

The Auberge de Castile, which is today the prime minister's office; the Auberge d'Aragon, a government ministry; the Auberge d'Italie, the post office; the Auberge de Provence, the Archeological Museum; and the Auberge d'Angleterre et Bavarie, which houses government offices. The three that have gone are the Auberge d'Allemagne, which is today the site of St Paul's Anglican Cathedral; the

Auberge d'Auvergne, which is now the law courts and the Auberge de France, which, serves them right, is the site of the headquarters of the General Workers Union.

The *auberges* were originally a bit like Oxford colleges. The knights were allocated to different *auberges*, depending largely on which language they spoke. Once installed in their *auberge*, they proceeded to do virtually nothing but eat good food, drink good wine and argue about nothing at all.

Ask him, what is the full name of the Order of St John, where its headquarters is and who runs it.

The Sovereign Military and Hospitaller Order of St John of Jerusalem, Rhodes and Malta. Rome. A Scotsman called His Eminent Highness Fra Andrew Bertie.

Ask him who threw the knights out of Malta.

Napoleon Bonaparte, of course. On his way to Egypt. His old headquarters, the Palazzo Parisio is now the Maltese Ministry of Foreign Affairs. His bedroom is the minister's office. He also grabbed the bejewelled sword that Philip II of Spain had given to La Valette. The silver service which was used to feed the patients in the hospital built by the knights, at the time the most advanced in the whole of Europe, he had melted down – all 3,500lbs of it – to pay for his Egyptian campaign.

Oh yes, and he decreed that overnight the official language of Malta should be French.

Ask him to give us back the documents that Henry VIII signed proclaiming himself head of the Church of England.

* * *

At present they are in the dusty old moth-eaten Biblioteca, the National Library, in Valletta along with 300,000 or 400,000 other books and manuscripts. There's no reason why they should have them: they're part of our heritage not theirs. And no, it's not the same as the Elgin Marbles. That's different: we've got them.

Ask him what earth-shattering event happened in 1802.

The Maltese decided they wanted to be run by the British, after, it must be said, having had a taste of being run by the French. They decided in a Declaration of Rights that they wanted to be brought under 'the protection and sovereignty of the King of the free people, His Majesty the King of the United Kingdom of Great Britain and Ireland'.

Makes you feel good, doesn't it? But don't forget they've still got Henry VIII's proclamation.

Ask him what Operation Substance was.

It was the convoy of food, fuel and military hardware that Britain sent to Malta in July 1941 when the island was practically cut off by the Axis forces from the outside world. Up to then the Maltese had been subsisting on the barest minimum, thanks only to the occasional submarine or light aircraft. If they were going to survive, they needed far, far more. Britain decided to risk all and send in a heavily escorted convoy made up of the *Leinster*, a troop ship, six large, fast cargo ships, two cruisers, a mine-layer and ten destroyers. Following behind them at a distance was another convoy made up of a battleship, a battle cruiser, an aircraft- carrier, the *Ark Royal* and seven more destroyers.

As soon as they reached the Sicilian Narrows they were joined by a string of fighter aircraft from the RAF base on

Malta itself and eight submarines, which were deployed off Naples, Sicily and Sardinia in case the Italians got wind of what was going on and decided to cause trouble. As it happened the Italians did find out and decided to attack by air, sinking one of the cargo vessels and a destroyer. A cruiser was also badly hit and towed back to Gibraltar. On 24 July, the day the convoy arrived in Malta, four Italian motor torpedo boats also attacked the convoy, badly holing one, the *Sydney Star*, which nonetheless managed to limp into Grand Harbour.

The result was that over 65,000 tons of essential supplies were delivered, including 10,000 tons of ammunition, hurricane engines, anti-aircraft guns and all the sugar and coffee and edible oil they wanted. Plus another 2,600 troops.

Ask him when the Maltese got their George Cross.

On 15 April 1942, after they had survived 154 days and 6,700 tons of non-stop bombing. Thanks largely to the tunnels beneath the city of Valletta, some dating back to the stone age, others to the days of the knights. Some people even hid in the original Christian catacombs. The citation, signed by King George VI, said it was to honour Malta's 'brave people' and 'to bear witness to a heroism and devotion that will long be famous in history'.

The Americans, you'll be pleased to hear, took until 7 December the following year to get around to giving the Maltese a mere citation for standing 'alone but unafraid in the centre of the sea, one tiny bright flame in the darkness, a beacon of hope for the clearer days which have come… What was done in this island maintains the highest traditions of gallant men and women who from the beginning of time have lived and died to preserve civilisation for all mankind.'

* * *

Ask him for directions to Strait Street.

Well, where else did you think British troops went on their night off? There's a limit to how much NAAFI tea you can drink. Incidentally, a quick word. She said you should continue taking the tablets.

Ask him what happens every year on 15 August.

They ring the special 10-ton siege bell high above the Grand Harbour to commemorate the 8,000 Maltese and British men and women who died during the siege between 1940 and 1943.

Ask him what happened in Spain in 1983.

The national football team lost to Spain 12-1. The reason, said the Malta Football Association afterwards, was that they had lost 5-0 to Holland only four days earlier. Which, of course, explains everything. How have they done since? They're getting better: they've just lost 6-0 to the Czech Republic and 6-0 to Slovakia.

Ask him why the Maltese are all so fat and dumpy.

Well, it's true, isn't it? The men are all about 5 foot nothing, dark, swarthy and 15 stone. The women, who all seem to be called Loredana or Josette or just plain Mama, are, well, barrels. Sure there's the odd exception, but that's probably got more to do with Count Roger and what he got up to behind the Auberge one night.

Go to an expat party and you hear all kinds of stories. The level of in-breeding, they say, is alarming, especially out in some of the villages, where people can barely grunt, let alone speak, and to where it's difficult to get ordinary people to go out and work, let alone take their families with them. I was told that the government had big problems trying to find an architect who was prepared to go and live in one particular part of the country for just six months to oversee some project or other. They were offering big bucks, a big car and free tickets to Europe and the States every month, but there were no takers. In the end they had to abandon the project.

Ask him why they're as miserable as sin.

You may think the Brits are bad serving in bars and restaurants, but you ain't seen nothing until you've spent a couple of days in Malta. No smiles, no 'please' or 'thank you', no pleasantries, nothing. They give you the menu. They wait, staring at you until you decide. They scribble down the order. Then they're off.

'Excuse me, please could I order some wine?'

They're not interested. The next time you see them is when the plate is plonked down on the table in front of you.

'Excuse me. Some wine? Maltese wine. Is that...?'

Usually it isn't Maltese wine, but on the odd occasion that it is, it's like heaven on earth. Not that you're allowed to choose which particular Maltese wine you get. You just have to be grateful for what you are given.

Time for the bill. They give you the impression they couldn't care less whether you pay it or not. A tip? If you give them something, OK, if not, no problem.

Let me tell you, after a stay in Malta it's a joy to get back to the coffee shop downstairs from the office, where one day they're all over you and the next day they're completely ignoring you and trying to con you out of an extra 35p for a disgusting cup of axle grease.

* * *

Ask him if you can have a turtledove and greenfinch casserole for dinner, or failing that a Maltese finch pie.

The Maltese are almost as bad as the French when it comes to dinner, or even lunch. If it flies, shoot it; if it sings as well, better still. That seems to be their motto. One guy I met on Gozo had practically eaten his way through the *British Book of Birds*. Tits, linnets, wheatears, greenfinches, goldfinches, bullfinches, chaffinches – he had had the lot, and cooked every which way as well. Barbecued, stewed, casseroled, grilled. Was he even slightly ashamed? No way. Birds were birds, they were there to be eaten.

Was there any bird he wouldn't eat?

Not at all. He was looking forward to trying kestrel: a friend of his had lined some up for the weekend.

I thought 'traditional hunting', as they call it, was banned in Malta.

It might be banned, he said, but it was not illegal.

What about five-shot repeater rifles?

'Banned, but you can still buy them.'

Spotlights for night-time hunting?

'Banned, but you can still buy them.'

Electronic bird-callers?

'Banned, but you can still buy them.'

Robin traps?

'Banned, but you can still buy them.'

Even if they really banned everything, it wouldn't make any difference. The Maltese would go back to the old tried and tested method of using birds in cages as bait. They put the cages out in the fields or on the clifftops and surround them with thin, nearly invisible nets borrowed from local fishermen. When migrating birds hear the birds in the cages, they go to investigate and then – zap! – they are caught in the nets.

Enjoy your meal.

* * *

If you're not going to get to share the fresh falcon, ask him about pushchairs full of intestines, live chickens nailed to crosses and rats hung out to dry.

No, it's not a joke. It's what goes on in Gozo during carnival time. Well, in Nadur, to be precise. Everybody turns out in the streets dressed in long robes and hoods or even scruffy old boilersuits with old pillowcases thrown over their heads. Anything, it seems, so long as they're covered from head to foot, full to overflowing with booze and doing something or other to an animal.

One year, apparently, it was turkeys. Everybody turned up with turkeys in various stages of life or death. Another year it was swallows. Everybody brought dead swallows tied to bits of string. Once when the government was trying to introduce various controls on hunting, everyone arrived carrying cages of live thrushes and starlings sprayed red.

Ask him what the next problem with environmentalists is going to be.

Spear-fishing. It's banned in most countries, even in Italy. But that doesn't make any difference to the Maltese. You can go spear-fishing off the coast of Comino any time. Plenty of Italians do it all year round.

Put your name down while there are still some places left.

Ask him why, since the Maltese drive on the left like the British, a rare enough thing in this world, they don't drive like the British in any other respect.

Like driving in the correct lane of a dual carriageway. Like going round a roundabout in a clockwise direction. Like overtaking on the outside. Like not doing three-point turns at the traffic lights in the middle of town. Not that I want to criticise, because, bless them, the Maltese do have British telephone boxes, British letterboxes, a million old British cars – Ford Anglias, Ford Prefects, Morris Minors, Vauxhall Victors – and thousands of old British buses: Bedfords, Leylands, AECs. And outside every police station there is a British blue lamp.

Ask him why Malti, the Maltese language, sounds like a cross between Swedish, Arabic and double pneumonia.

Have you tried listening to it? Have you tried to identify where one word finishes and another begins? It's impossible. I just can't for the life of me understand it. The punctuation is a million times worse. I mean, they have twenty-nine letters in their alphabet, twenty-four consonants and five vowels, and they dot their 'c's, 'g's and 'z's and cross their 'h's. And there's no y.
I'm sure it helps if you're dyslexic.

Ask him why, since Gozo is so pretty, Odysseus had to be kept virtually under lock and key to stop him from running away.

You no sooner arrive on the island – usually by clapped-out Russian helicopter – than somebody is telling you that it is really Ogygia, where the nymph Calypso kept Odysseus holed up for seven years. Oh, the joys of a classical education. A third the size of Malta, the main island, it is more rural, greener and lusher, with drystone walls everywhere. It is also more out of date, out of touch, other-worldly, maybe twenty to twenty-five years behind Malta. A traffic jam on Gozo is when one donkey cart tries to overtake another donkey cart.

I doubt I would have to be chained to the ground to stop me from escaping. But then, we don't know what Calypso was like, do we?

Ask him why the capital of Gozo, Victoria, is still officially called Victoria when everybody refers to it as Rabat.

Victoria was named after Queen Victoria, who graciously condescended to give it city status in 1887 to mark the Golden Jubilee. But everybody calls it Rabat. They did in 1887, and they still do today. Even the litter bins have Rabat written on them. The main street, which boasts a post office, a clutch of banks, two opera houses and the unbelievable nineteenth-century palace of the Bishop of Gozo, they call Republic Street. The main square, which is home to a fantastic semi-circular baroque extravaganza – the local council offices – and the tiny church of St James the Apostle, is called It Tokk, or Independence Plaza. So there's no logical reason for them to keep calling it Victoria.

Ask him why Malta made the Duke of Edinburgh redundant, why Prince Charles is no longer functioning as before and why Lady Diana is attracting the crowds.

The Duke of Edinburgh is the oldest hotel in Rabat, I mean Victoria. Not our Duke of Edinburgh, Queen Victoria's Duke of Edinburgh. Although our Duke of Edinburgh did call in there once for a cup of tea a million years ago. Today it is surplus to requirements. It no longer has a role to play. The hotel, not the. . . you know what I mean. It's locked up, barred and bolted and crumbling to pieces. Out of date, out of touch, left behind by the modern world. The hotel, I mean. Although credit where credit is due: just round the corner I spotted a big poster proclaiming, 'Windsor – Bedding specialists'.

Similarly Prince Charles. Ignored, passed by, irrelevant, overlooked. The bar, I mean, in Valletta. As for the Lady Diana, it was doing a roaring trade catering for all appetites. The snack bar, I mean. By the bus station next to the City Gate, also in Valletta.

Ask him how come, if the massive citadel above Victoria is such a splendid example of the skills of Francesco Laparelli, at one time an assistant to the great Michelangelo himself, they drove a massive hole through the middle of it?

Just imagine. It's like knocking a hole in the Tower of London or Hampton Court Palace. Here is this enormous castle dating back to the seventeenth century towering high above the town. King Philip II of Spain chipped in towards the costs of building it. UNESCO is chipping in towards the cost of restoring and maintaining it. The old entrance is still there, all the palaces and chapels are still there, the mass of tiny back streets and alleyways are still there. So what do the Maltese do? Or rather, what does Miss Agatha Barbara the Barbarian do? She knocks a hole right through the middle of it. Some say it was to give people a better view of the cathedral. Nonsense. I reckon it was to let people see how much parking space there was in front of it. Never mind. For such an unprovoked act of aggression she received her just deserts: shortly afterwards she was made president of Malta.

Ask him why there is this big thing between the Cathedral and St George's.

To me it's crazy. The cathedral, a beautiful seventeenth-century baroque masterpiece, is the cathedral. The Basilica of St George, which dominates the mediaeval area of the city, is the Basilica of St George. But it seems you must be on one side or the other.

The cathedral says it's the cathedral, number one. End of argument. The basilica says, yah boo, it's not a proper cathedral anyway – it hasn't even got a proper dome. What you see is not a dome, it's a trick. It's a painting of the inside of a dome. Look at it carefully and you'll see what I mean.

Apparently the feud began innocently enough. The cathedral and the basilica both founded their own bands to provide music for local processions and saints days. The basilica then decided to build an opera house. Not to be outdone, the cathedral decided to follow suit. Now they are virtually at daggers drawn. If one does something the other criticises it. So how did they sort out who should run the big, prestigious Good Friday processions each year? They didn't. They decided they would take it in turns. So there.

Ask him how the Maltese have managed to keep St George's Basilica in such good condition.

The answer is they haven't. Although the church was built in the seventeenth century, practically the whole of the interior decoration is less than thirty years old. It just goes to show that the art, style and extravagance of the baroque was alive and well and working in Gozo as late as the 1960s. Today the church is sparkling. The dome is almost brand new – and it's a real dome, don't forget. The gilded ceilings are brand new. The altar canopy, a copy of Bernini's in St Peter's in Rome, is virtually brand new.

Ask him why nobody can name the third largest unsupported dome in the whole of Europe after St Peter's in Rome and St Sophia's in Istanbul.

* * *

OK, it's the dome of the church in the tiny village of Xewkija, a village of just 3,000 people. When the parish priest decided that his old church was too small, amazingly, he didn't just build one of those new-fangled churches that look as though they've come straight off a municipal drawing board for bus stations. He decided to go the whole hog and build an exact copy of a Renaissance masterpiece, the Santa Maria della Salute in Venice, no less. You wouldn't think the village had two pennies to rub together from the look of it. Everything is crumbling into the dust. Yet there is this fantastic church.

Ask him why Karmela Grima is more important than St Paul.

Karmela Grima has a basilica while poor old St Paul, in spite of everything he went through, only has a church. What's more, the basilica is Malta's national shrine.

   Back in 1883, Karmela was walking home from the fields one day on the island of Gozo when she suddenly heard voices. She immediately went to fetch some local guy called Frangisk Portelli, whose mother was sick at the time. The two of them knelt down together and prayed to the voices that she would recover. Which, of course, she did. Since then the basilica has been a place of pilgrimage for generations of Maltese. Surviving shipwrecks, striking water from the rock and shaking poisonous vipers into the fire count for nothing as far as these guys are concerned.

Ask him why, if the Maltese consider the people of Gozo to be a bit thick, Gozo has provided more than its fair share of Maltese presidents and archbishops and judges.

* * *

Silent, stupid, mean. That's what the Maltese call the Gozos over a glass of the local Cisk lager in the bars of Valletta. They're nothing but peasants, never happier than when they are tending their tiny fields of wheat and barley or cultivating their thyme and fennel or even just staring vacantly at a mass of wild flowers. The more outrageous will even say that the Gozos are never happier than when somebody is walking all over them. Like when they were overrun in 1551 by a bunch of Barbary pirates, who stormed their island and carried practically everybody off into slavery. The few Gozos who were left fought back, slowly ousted the invaders and began all over again. There is nothing wrong with that, they say. There is also nothing wrong with Gozo providing more than its fair share of presidents, archbishops and judges. Especially if they're silent, stupid and mean.

Ask him why, if there is nothing wrong with Gozo providing more than its fair share of presidents, politicians and judges, they don't shout about it.

He won't answer. He'll mutter something about Gozo being Gozo, and say that what one island does on its own is not important.

Ask him why the ferries between Gozo and Malta are such a mess.

The answer, of course, is the government mucking about with the running of the service. First, the company running the ferries wanted to increase fares. The government said OK. Then because everybody, especially everybody in Gozo, went bananas, they backtracked. Next the company wanted to build three new super-modern ferries. The government said yes, providing they were built in Malta. But that means an extra US$6.5 million, said the company. We can't afford that unless you give us a grant. Back the government went to the drawing board. In the meantime the service goes from bad to worse, fewer and fewer people use it – apart that is from the company's directors, ex-directors and all their families, who have free passes – and it sinks deeper and deeper into the red.

Ask him why the famous Malta drydocks, the biggest business in the country, is in such a mess, in spite of all the government money that has been poured into it. If it is true that most workers only do three hours a day on basic rate, the rest on overtime; that over fifteen years nobody has been fired for inefficiency and that a portrait of a certain well-known politician hangs on the perimeter fence alongside a picture of the Holy Spirit?

Hmmm. Could you repeat the question, please?

Ask him if it's true that political influence is rife throughout the country.

Practically every businessman I met told me that government jobs and government contracts depended more on which party you supported than on whether or not you were the lowest bidder.

'It's everywhere,' one expat said. 'Even if you're only talking about a pot of paint, the contract will go to the guy in the right party.'

'Regardless of cost?'

'Regardless of cost.'

'But that's bound to push up the price of everything.'

'Doesn't matter. It's the party that counts.'

Of course, I didn't go everywhere, but I covered a few

miles and I must say I didn't see any obvious signs of wealth.

'You won't,' another expat informed me. 'That's why life is so difficult for burglars in this country. They can size up twelve houses and they'll all look the same. There's no way they can tell which one has all the gold in it.'

Ask him why there are no trees on Malta. Well, hardly any.

Grass, bushes, drystone walls they've got plenty of, but trees, there are only the odd one or two. Everybody came and saw and plundered. Early man used timber as roofs for his temples, especially the Aleppopine. Next they used up the olive trees. Early farmers then cut down huge areas of trees in order to cultivate the land. The Phoenicians and Carthaginians used timber for shipbuilding and repairing. The Order of St John then cleared huge areas to grow cotton. Finally, of course, whenever they planted anything along came the humble goat and ate it.

Ask him where the Valletta summit meeting between George Bush and Mikhail Gorbachev took place in 1989.

Not in Valletta, that's for certain. Security was for some reason or another judged impossible to control, so the meeting took place aboard a warship in Marsaxlokk Bay.

Ask him why, if the Maltese are really dedicated to the environment and all things bright and beautiful, the rotting remains of a dead cat still lay outside the walls of the local council office in Swiegi two months after it was killed.

Nice weather we've been having lately. Hope it docsn't get too hot, though.

***

Ask him what Sir Walter Scott considered the best interior he had ever seen.

Not Waverley Castle or even the guts of a Norman knight. You mean you haven't read *Ivanhoe*? It was the interior of St John's Co-Cathedral in Valletta. Outside it looks quite plain; inside, even today, it is stunning. The ceiling is shaped like the inside of one long wine barrel. It is divided into eighteen different sections, each devoted to different episodes in the life of St John the Baptist. On either side are twelve beautifully gilded and decorated chapels. The English Chapel is, naturally, modest, discreet and understated. The French, of course, say it's cheap, sparse and mean-looking, but then they would, wouldn't they? The floor is covered in brightly coloured unbelievably ornate stone tombs inlaid with bits of marble depicting all kinds of gruesome things, like skulls and crossbones, skeletons, death in a black cowl. Quite charming.

The gates to the Blessed Sacrament Chapel on the right are made of silver. The story goes that when Napoleon and the French arrived in 1798 the Maltese painted them black to look like cast iron. The French fell for it and left them alone. Maybe the Maltese are not so slow after all.

Ask them why, nearly 200 years after Byron damned Valletta for its 'cursed streets of stairs', they are still, even in the late twentieth century, building steps so shallow you'd have thought it was hardly worth the bother.

So that a knight in full armour can walk up them, stupid. They have to be shallow, otherwise he couldn't swing his legs from side to side to get up on to the next one. Don't you know anything?

In any case, I would have thought Byron, of all people, would have preferred the shallow steps to steep ones.

* * *

Ask him why, since they increased postal charges, there is only one counter open in the afternoons at the post office in Merchants Streets, Valletta, and not six as there were before.

If you'd care to drop me a line I'll send you a reply by return. Provided I can get a stamp, of course.

Ask him why, if carnival time is so important for Malta and helps draw in the tourists, the government keeps promising to provide storage facilities for the floats but has never done so.

It's not as if they're asking for much, is it? All the floats they build themselves out of papier mâché. In their spare time, out of their own pockets. Even if they win a prize, it hardly covers the cost. On top of that all the costumes worn by the troupes of dancers preceding each float have to be designed and made. And if it rains there are no floats for the carnival. Originally the carnival was held in February, but the government moved it to May. Some people say this was because they wanted to kill it off altogether. In May fewer children could take part because they were worried about their exams. Others maintain that in May it would attract more visitors and, therefore, more revenue for the island.

Ask him why, if Malta is truly democratic, there are no caricatures of politicians among the carnival floats. Especially when they keep promising to give people somewhere to store their floats and then go back on their word.

* * *

Seen the forecast for May? They say it's going to be sunny again.

Ask him what is one of Malta's biggest exports.

Potatoes. To Holland. But they also grow tomatoes, onions, capers, wheat, maize, melons and sesame. Interesting, isn't it?

Ask him what's so fantastic about their bread anyway.

Honestly, they rave about it so much you would think it was the greatest thing in the whole world. Virtually the first thing they ask you as soon as you clear Customs is 'Have you tried our bread? Isn't it fantastic? Ah, the smell first thing in the morning!' And so it goes on all day long. Stop someone in the street and ask them the way to the Upper Barrakka, or even to the nearest Pizza Hut, and they'll go on and on about the bread before telling you you're standing right outside a bakery.

Your driver takes you the wrong way round a round-about in the centre of town. A police car skids up alongside you. Before he says a word about you nearly killing three cyclists and a busload of pensioners, the policeman is on about the bread. If you go into a Maltese restaurant they're pushing the bread before the menu, let alone the wine list. Is it any good? Well, I admit it does taste like bread, not like some of the stale cotton-wool stuff you get nowadays. And it *is* crusty. But the greatest thing on earth? No way.

Ask him why there aren't any famous Maltese writers or artists or musicians.

When you think about it, it's odd, especially since Malta has been civilised for thousands of years. It has been at the crossroads of a string of different civilisations. It has been trampled on by a host of great names. It has witnessed enough dramatic events to fill a thousand bestsellers. I did spot one book in a bookshop in Victoria by a local man, Francis Cachia. It was called *Vision and Verification: Variations on Themes of European Unity in Various Narrative Modes*. It was, would you believe, a novel. Which perhaps goes some way to explaining why Maltese books are not exactly bestsellers.

Ask him why the Maltese have to keep playing the oompah and marching up and down all the time.

Wherever I went, wherever I stayed, there was an oompah band. Either practising or warming up or going full tilt. At first I thought it was something to do with carnival time, or the day of the *festa*, which is a combination of the local saint's day, the annual village party day and the day they march up and down all day long blowing mouth organs, playing guitars and blowing their trumpets. If they can do it the same time as everybody else is doing it, so much the better. If not, such being the fierce, independent nature of the Maltese, they'll do it all on their own anyway. Then I thought it was all a plot to drive me mad. But apparently it is just the Maltese way of life. If they can oompah, they oompah. If they have a reason, that's great; if not they just get on with it. The result was I hardly had one decent night's sleep. I was glad to get back to the office to catch up with some shut-eye.

Ask them why they always take their kids with them wherever they go.

I've never known anything like it. Whenever I went to meet any Maltese - at offices, restaurants or bars - they brought their kids with them. I know they're Latins and they love their children and all that, but do they really have to take them absolutely everywhere?

In Gozo, no sooner had I clambered off the shaky old Russian helicopter than I was engulfed by kids, grabbing at my briefcase, climbing all over the car, rushing in and out of the hotel. It was the same story in Valletta. The guy I was meeting for lunch not only turned up with his kids, but he brought his wife along as well. We spent practically the whole time discussing how he gave up this big job in New York to come back to Valletta for the sake of the children. As if I was interested.

Finally, ask him why the Maltese never know the answer to any straightforward, simple, courteous question about their country. Honestly, it makes me hopping mad.

JERUSALEM

1. Lo, and so it came to pass at the eighteenth hour of the second day of the third week of the seventh month that the clouds parted and this enormous winged creature of the sky came to rest on the dirty great runway of Ben-Gurion Airport. And there we stopped and there we waited. And waited. And waited. And waited.

And I'm thinking, 'Oy-oy-oy, and this is why I came all this way?'

But instead of making a fuss, and especially as I'm on my way to break bread in Jerusalem, which I have been told is becoming a Mecca for tourists, I decide all I can do, in the circumstances, cramped into one of those tiny seats at the back of the plane next to the toilets, is to turn the other cheek. Which, I can tell you, I did a number of times. Then, just as I was beginning to think tramping through the middle of the Red Sea and spending forty years wandering around in the desert was probably a darn sight quicker way of getting into the place – Torah, Torah, TORAH – we all schlepped out: all the creepy things of the earth: Munchkins, money-changers, gogs, magogs. Lots. Except for Mrs Lot, of course. Samson, the most hard-hitting and successful journalist in history. It took him only two columns to bring the house down. Not even St Paul Johnson, with all the prayers he has written, could achieve that kind of success. An old guy who was the spitting image of Noah – who, incidentally, is much admired in financial circles because he floated his company when the rest of the world was in liquidation. And as many stiff-necked Amorrhites, Canaanites, Helhites, Pherezites, Hevites and Jebusites as you could shake a stick at. It was like walking backwards into the Old Testament. I was so thrilled I almost threw my *yarmulka* in the air.

But at least we'd arrived. Had I gone by Monarch Airlines, we'd still have been trying to land, because as far as they are concerned Israel doesn't exist. Have a look at their European route map. There's nothing there. Although I noticed that, for some reason, Egypt is included twice, Egypt is included twice. That's chutzpah for you.

Now, I know I've always thought of myself as a thing of beauty and a Goy forever but even I wasn't prepared for the traditional Jewish welcome we received: a solid wall of bullet-proof vests, a forest of Uzi rifles and so many forms to fill in that by the time I had finished the immigration hall was littered with so many crumpled bits of yellow paper that it looked like some cave you might come across near the Dead Sea. It was like having one foot in the modern world and one foot in the *shtetl*.

Outside, the earth, as far as I could see, was without form and darkness was upon the face of the deep. But with my loins girded, my shoes on my feet and my staff back at the office ready to type all my reports for me, I was ready to hit the original Bible belt, a land flowing with silk and money where, I was told, there was no such thing as discrimination against anyone on the basis of race, religion, class or creed – providing you were Jewish.

And so, my life, evening came and morning and the first day passed already.

2. Lo, and so it came to pass on the second day that

I discovered the Promised Land was just that. Promises. Everybody I met kept promising me things.

The lady at the reception desk of the first company I went to visit promised to give me the names of some of the best vineyards whose wines rivalled those of Cana. But she didn't.

As soon as I told the first businessman I met about my plans for the week, he immediately promised to let me have one of his old baseball bats. Not for playing with, stupid. For keeping in the car, just in case.

My driver, who was a real *schtick*-in-the-mud, promised to give me the address of a restaurant which, he said, made the best *latkes* in the universe. All sweet potatoes and carrots or zucchini and cheese. Even better than the ones his momma made. But he didn't. I ended up having a Bonkers Bagel, which looked like a hamburger with attitude and a can of mango juice – kosher, of course – and running for my life after being surrounded by a bunch of guys selling olive-wood nativity scenes in Manger Square, Bethlehem. At first, I must admit, I mistakenly thought it was a Passover bagel, because the guy serving them kept saying to the guy making them, 'Hey, passover that pile of bagels, will you?'

I discovered that Jerusalem is nothing like the Bible says at all. Which I thought was grossly unfair, even if Hilaire Belloc did dismiss the Good Book as 'Yiddish folklore'. I know it's not designed to be a travel brochure, and I wasn't expecting to see signs all over the place saying 'Christ slept here' or, I suppose, 'Christ performed a miracle here'. I hadn't banked on Handel's *Messiah* playing in the background wherever I went or everybody saying things unto everybody else, but you would have thought the city would have been something like its description.

But there were no locusts, no gnats, no flies, no

frogs. Well, apart from the ones in striped sweaters staying at the Sheraton Jerusalem Plaza. When I turned on the tap in my room, something I very rarely do, out came water, not blood. I thought I might stumble across groups of people, six, seven, nine, fifteen or even 5,000, but never thirteen at a time, going around eating loaves and fishes. Doors, I imagined, would open as soon as you knocked on them. And the entire city would be crowded with hordes of blind, deaf, dumb and crippled unfortunates desperate to be cured. No way.

All I saw were people eating bagels, bagels and still more bagels and enormous security gates and intercoms and signs all over the place saying, 'Please push button and identify yourself'. As for the blind, deaf, dumb and crippled, one friendly old rabbi told me that nowadays they scuttled out of the way as soon as anyone mentioned the possibility of a cure because they knew there was no way they could make as much money working for a living as they were getting from social security.

On the other hand, it's probably just as well that Israel was nothing like it is in the Bible, because if it had been I would probably have been wading knee-deep through blood and gore. I know the Old Testament is the Old Testament and the New Testament is the New Testament, but, boy, did those *schmucks* go for the blood and guts. Ten thousand killed here, 20,000 there, another half a million over there. It's a wonder there was anybody left.

Then there were all those sacrifices. You think Jeffrey Archer throws a mean party? These noodriks were way ahead of him. According to the Bible, King David really knew how to schmooze people. When he became King of Israel he hosted a party which lasted three days. Can you imagine the hangover you would get after three days? I know what I'm like after one night.

King Solomon was, of course, much wiser in these matters. He threw parties which lasted only two weeks.

And not for them hot salt-beef sandwiches, bowls of chicken soup or even turkey schnitzels. They laid on the kind of meal I can only fantasise about: legs of cows, half a sheep à la Damien Hirst, two thirds of an ox. I've only got to think about what the menu looked like and my weak, pathetic little white corpuscles are collapsing from exhaustion.

But what staggers me is the practicalities of the whole thing. Have you ever considered the arrangements and the planning and all the movement sheets that would have to be filled in and sent to the Ministry of Agriculture to shift that many cattle? Believe me, the paperwork involved in bringing one old milker home from Haywards Heath Market is enough to generate a full week's work for half a dozen civil servants. Can you imagine

how many Old Testament rainforests it took to set up King Solomon's bash? The fact that the Middle East is nothing but desert today just proves my point.

Then there were all the transport arrangements: the loading and unloading; the pens the cattle would have been kept in; the actual slaughter itself; the number of butchers that would have been needed for hacking and chopping and slicing up the meat; the other guys who would have separated out all the uneatable stuff like the eyes, the ears, the brains, the spinal cord to sell to the Arabs as food; the tanners to handle the skins. Forget the Passover: the entire place must have been running in blood and guts for years afterwards. Which is another reason, I reckon, why today the country is covered in sand and not lush, green pasture.

And that's before you come to cooking and preparing the stuff for the table or, I suppose, the reclining sofa. Just think how many cooks, deputy cooks, sous-chefs and Marco Pierre Whites that would have taken, not to mention all the screaming and yelling in the kitchens. And how many maître d's and waiters would you have needed? It's hard enough trying to find decent staff even for the top-notch restaurants. How these guys did it I'll never know. And they didn't have even one star to their name.

It's my own fault, of course. Instead of spending so much time on the Bible, maybe I should have stuck to something more practical, like the Yellow Pages or the *National Hunt Directory*, but it's too late to worry about that now. I must admit I'm still an Authorised Version/Ronald Knox fan. The Authorised Version for the great rolling set pieces, Ronald Knox for the detail. I like the thees, the thous and the there-fores and the whores and the harlots, if you see what I mean.

'The heavens declare the glory of God: and the firma-ment sheweth his handi-work. Day unto day uttereth speech and night unto night sheweth knowledge.' Fantastic.

I also like all the silly schoolboy passages. Like the fellas going around all day putting their hands under each other's thighs, which I suppose is about all they had the strength to do after shifting that amount of food. Like the secret proof that Shakespeare worked on the King James version of the Bible. You don't know? Well, what's the forty-sixth word of Psalm 46? 'Shake'. And the 46th from the end? 'Spear'. And how old was he when he worked on the Bible? Forty-six. And, of course, the old favourite in the Acts of the Apostles: 'And the lot fell upon Matthias'. Poor guy.

But the trouble is that the Good Book no longer speaketh like the Good Book. Instead it speaketh more like the Pretty Medi-ocre Book, judging by some of the translations and rewrites and general botch-ups I've come across in different parts of the world.

'Physician, heal thyself,' is now 'Doctor, cure yourself.'

'A stranger in a strange land,' has become, would you believe, 'An alien resident in a foreign land.'

And 'Yea, though I walk through the valley of the shadow of death, I will fear no evil,' has emerged, Heaven help us, as 'I may walk through the valleys as dark as death but I won't be afraid.'

Take Psalm 23: 'The Lord is my Shepherd, I shall not want. He maketh me to lie down in green pastures; He leadeth me beside the still waters.'

Fabulous. What do we get today? 'You Lord are my shepherd. I will never be in need. You let me rest in fields of green grass. You lead me to streams of peaceful water and refresh my life.'

And look at how they are pushing us meek guys around. Instead of absolutely guaranteeing beyond any doubt whatsoever that we shall inherit the earth they're only going to let us 'have the land'. Well, let me tell you, if that's all I'm going to get for having been meek all these years, it's not worth the fuss and bother. Inheriting the earth is one thing, but land fetches only about £1,000 to £2,000 an acre down our way. In any case, I've got all the land I want at the moment, thank you. It's the earth I'm after.

Whenever I come across a new translation of the Bible I always check out what for me is the single most important verse of all: Ephesians 5, verse 22: 'Wives submit yourselves unto your own husbands, as unto the Lord,' although my wife doesn't always give me permission. The differences are amazing. Some don't say wives or husbands at all, just partners. Others go on about togetherness. Submitting is out: instead it's 'heed'.

A special women's-only Bible I once had the misfortune to come across in the States – where else? – which claimed to be based on original historical sources, somehow unearthed the following 'facts': that Eve was the number one; that Paradise cramped her style, which is why she wanted her own space; that Mary Magdalene wasn't a prostitute but a social worker, and that, even though Christ was the Son of God and died on the Cross, he was still just your typical male chauvinist pig.

Other translations I've come across are equally stupid. In one, God no longer roared at Eve in the Garden of Eden, 'Woman. What is this that thou hast done?' Instead, he stamped his foot and, no doubt, in a shrill, high-pitched New York accent, whined, 'How could you do such a thing?' And Saul no longer railed against Jonathan, 'Thou son of a perverse rebellious woman.' Instead he waves his limp wrists at him, and squeals, 'You son of a bitch.' I note that God is no longer righteous. He is 'really kind'.

A manger is a feed box, which means we should all have great fun at Christmas singing 'Away in a Feed box'. Swaddling clothes are bands of cloth; shepherds are not 'sore afraid', they're terrified.

In most new translations I've seen Christ hardly gets a mention at all, and when he does he seems to spend his time going around healing the 'differently abled', encouraging everyone to pray, 'Our Father–Mother in heaven, blessed be your name. Your dominion come', and asking not for our daily bread, but 'our food for today'. Although how he manages to do even that is a mystery to me, since according to the *Guardian*, the Lord's Prayer was written by Henry VIII. Sins are no longer sins but wrong-doings. As for adultery, forget it, it's been abolished. You only have to be 'faithful'. Caesar is now just the emperor, which ruins all those good quotes. I mean, rendering unto the emperor somehow doesn't seem half as much fun as rendering unto Caesar. Crucifixion is also out, it's being nailed to a cross.

In some versions Christ no longer sits at the right hand of God but at the 'mighty hand' of Our Father–Mother, to avoid upsetting religiously challenged left-handed feminists, I assume. I once picked up some hip ad man's Bible which began, 'At the outset, God's agenda was basically to focus on his core deliverables, namely two leading edge products: a. Heaven and b. Earth. However, the Earth lacked an overall concept and had a low profile in terms of its audiences.' I put it down again very quickly.

Then there is the Klingon Bible. The Klingons might have been Captain Kirk's mortal enemies but they knew how to turn a phrase or two. Take the invitation to the biggest picnic of all time: 'We only have five loaves and two fishes.' In Klingon that comes out as *'vah Iwchab cha'ghargh wIghaj,'* which at least

sounds deep, serious and, obviously, sonorous.

But the most absurd Bible I've ever seen was the Ultimate Feminist's Bible, which kept referring to 'Our strong, mother God' and claimed that Christ was a woman who died in childbirth – what else could the water be that flowed from her side on the cross? – and that she was known to her friends as Mildred. Mildred! My God – sorry, Ma'am – can you imagine standing up in church on Sunday morning and singing 'Mildred the King', oops, I mean 'Mildred the Queen'?

My William Tyndale prize for the best translation I think I've ever come across, bearing in mind his dream to 'cause a boy that driveth the plough to know more of the scriptures', must go to the Black Bible Chronicles. I was wandering around some bookshops in Savannah, Georgia, when I found it. It kicks off with Genesis: 'The earth was a fashion misfit being so uncool and dark, but the spirit of the

Almighty came down real tough so that He simply said, "Lighten up."' From there on it's ploughboys to the scriptures the whole way. Take the Ten Commandments:

'I am the Almighty, your God, who brought you outta Egypt when things were tough. Don't put anyone else before Me.

'Don't make any carved objects or things that look like what is in Heaven or below. And don't bow down to these things like they are anything heavy. Not ever!

'You shouldn't dis the Almighty's name, using it in cuss words or rapping with one another. It ain't cool, and payback's a monster.

'After you've worked six days, give the seventh to the Almighty.

'You shouldn't be takin' nothin' from your homeboys.

'Give honor to your mom and dad, and you'll live a long time.

'Don't waste nobody.

'Don't mess around with someone else's ol' man or ol' lady.

'Don't go round telling lies on your homebuddies.

'Don't want what you can't have or what your homebuddy has. It ain't cool.'

Fantastic. You can practically hear the trumpets sounding and the heavenly choirs belting out another number.

The more I read the Bible, in whatever version, the more convinced I am that it was written by a bunch of townies. Although I once came across a church in Ghana which believed that God was actually a farmer. 'We are plants on his farm,' the minister told me. 'He is the farmer. He sowed the seeds. We are his crop.'

Take the walking through fields, eating the ears of wheat. Very picturesque. Very Sunday afternoon in the country. But what about the poor farmer? All that time sowing the corn, all that time looking after it. No help from the government. No subsidies. As soon as he even thinks of using any sprays or fungicides the Friends of the Old Testament Earth are down on him like a ton of bricks. Now, as if he hasn't got enough problems, this bunch of journalists starts walking through the middle – not round the edge, but right through the middle of his crop, helping themselves to whatever they want without so much as a by your leave or a telephone call to the press office of the National Union of Farmers.

Then, to add insult to injury, there are the Gaderene swine. It's all very well ordering devils out of people, but did they have to be sent into a herd of swine? The pig market is never good at the best of times, so to suddenly see your entire herd hurtling off the top of a cliff must be enough to turn any farmer vegetarian. And there's no mention of compensation, either.

And talking of compensation, what about the poor farmer who owned the field in which the old woman found the treasure? What I'd like to know is what she was doing trespassing in the first place, not to mention digging up the field without asking the owner's permission? And to then go and try to buy the field off him without telling him what she's found was grossly unfair. I'd be more than a touch upset if some little old lady persuaded me to sell her one of my fields only for me to discover later that she was really a scheming, two-timing treasure-hunter who had snatched a million from right under my nose.

The only reason for this anti attitude in the Bible that I can think of is that everybody blames a poor farmer for planting that damn apple tree in the first place.

And so, my life, evening came and morning and the second day passed already.

3. Lo, and so it came to pass on the third day that an Old Testament prophet, whose

face was covered with boils breaking forth into blains, chill and otherwise, said unto me, 'Hey, Barabbas. If you want to sin in Israel, Tel Aviv is about the only place you can go. Haifa works, Jerusalem prays. But Tel Aviv sins.'

Judging by the bits of the Bible I can remember, most Old Testament prophets seem to know quite a bit about sin, so I took him at his word. I went to Tel Aviv. But, checking out Dizengoff Street, where the action is supposed to be, the nearest I got to a golden calf was a poster for some kind of rodeo being put on by a bunch of kosher cowboys from the Golan Heights and their decidedly non-kosher cattle. I guess he must have been talking about sins like eating too much ice-cream, going overboard on the fried eggplant and coveting your neighbour's BMW.

Brash, cosmopolitan, reckless, abandoned, fashionable: Tel Aviv is none of these things. To give you some idea of how old-fashioned it is, let me tell you that it's the only place I've been in the world where dirty, worn-out, torn Levi's are actually cheaper than new ones. All the same, it's the nearest thing to excitement you'll find in Israel since Salome hung up her seven veils and no doubt went on to devote her life to looking after dumb animals.

'Tel' is supposed to be a mound or a hump over the top of some old building site. 'Aviv' means spring. Which just about sums it up. Tel Aviv is full of old people sitting around in coats and jackets going on about 'meat, meal, cakes of figs and bunches of raisins, and wine, and oil, and oxen and sheep abundantly', which makes you think it's spring. When, in reality, it's so hot that the mercury is about to burst through the top of the thermometer and spray everything in sight.

As for the town itself, it looks as though it was thrown together during a *barmitzvah* by a bunch of

New York dentists. Everything is neat and square and regular. It makes you think BC stands for Before Conran. What is not covered in a thick layer of plaque is hidden behind a dense mesh of iron railings. Then there is the occasional abscess, such as the weirdo Bauhaus buildings that look as though they were designed by Salvador Dali on an off day and built of cheap, low-grade wax which has begun to melt slowly in the Aviv sunshine. The beach front out towards Jaffa, where Jonah had a whale of a time and where St Peter lived in the house of Simon the Tanner, looks as though it has been given a cosmetic job by a bunch of Florida dentists. Huge sweeping hotels, patios, plazas, high-rise office blocks. A flash, modern opera house in the middle of a vast cultural complex, one of the most way-out in the world. And alongside it the feature that makes this Tel Aviv and not Florida: a Ministry of Defence head-quarters with so many aerials and dishes on the roof that they probably find it easier to call Mars than their own liddle ma's across the street.

The people have about them the look of yellow parchment that has been buried in a cave by the Dead Sea for over 2,000 years. Those who appear to have been buried for only 800 years are the teenagers.

The old dears with their heavily powdered noses sashaying around in their *shmattes* looked like great lumps of roast pork, if such a thing is possible. The blokes looked like victims of the Apocalypse. You think I'm kidding: it was three days before I realised that the hotel where I was staying was a heart-bypass hotel. Everybody there apart from me was on a free three-month holiday recovering from bypass operations. Not one of them looked as though they hadn't at some time or other pushed their hand under Abraham's thigh, man or woman. Apparently this is the least the government thinks it should do for anybody who has devoted his or her life to reducing unemployment in the food, healthcare and medical industry by stuffing himself non-stop with calf's-foot jelly, cold beetroot borscht and, of course, those cholesterol time bombs, *latkes*.

'The Kosher Nostra, that's what they call us,' one sad old *schmegegge* who had the air of a descendant of Judas Iscariot told me one evening while he was waiting in the bar for someone to buy him a drink. Which, of course, I did. Well, he had been there for three days. All the others simply told me that their sons were lawyers. I heard that the day before I got there, one woman had been running up and down the beach all morning shrieking at the top of her voice, 'Help! Help! My son – the one who's a lawyer – is drowning!' Conversation in the bar was not exactly what I expected. It was all 'I'm right,

you're wrong. You want me to apologise?'

'You know why so many Jewish husbands die before their wives?' the old man said to me.

I shook my head.

'Because they want to,' he said.

A vision of chicken livers and peroxide wafted by.

'You know why a Jewish wife does it with her eyes closed?'

Again I shook my head.

'Because she can't bear to see her husband enjoying himself.'

I broke all the rules in the hotel. I bought a second round of drinks. It was the nearest I came to Sodom and Gomorrah in the whole trip.

Jaffa, along the coast, is much more juicy, especially on Friday nights when the in crowd, all those without zimmer frames and who are determined to prove they don't live by bread alone, peel over there to eat the fat of the land and clog up their arteries on all the kosher and kosher-style food they can eat. Relaxed and peaceful and safe – here they take down all the shutters and barriers and barricades at least twenty minutes before they do in Tel Aviv – there are not even any hang-ups about serving pork and bacon – providing, of course, you order it as white steak and low cow. What with all the restaurants and shops and art galleries and artists' studios, it reminded me a bit of Piraeus. Or St Ives. Or anywhere that has lots of restaurants and shops and art galleries and artists' studios.

And so, my life, strolling around gorging myself on an enormous *falafel* I bought off a stall surrounded by Palestinian taxi-drivers, evening came and morning, and the third day passed.

4. And so it came to pass on the fourth day, I suddenly realised that the Jews really are a funny bunch. I don't mean *mensch* funny, I mean funny funny.

First, they're the most self-centred people in the world. An Old Testament prophet I met wandering around Jaffa early one morning told me this wasn't true. The Jews, he said, judged everything on the facts: whether they were good for them or whether they were bad for them.

They go on and on about what they call chutzpah, but look how they treated Moses – and he had God on his side. I don't think I've ever met any child of Abraham who wasn't *kvetching* or complaining about something. Like the young man who murders both his parents and then complains that he is an orphan.

Or the old lady in the house full of beautiful young girls when the Nazis burst in.

'Do anything you like with us,' say the young girls, 'But leave our granny alone.'

'Now, wait a minute,' she says. 'A pogrom is a pogrom.'

Or the actor's momma on hearing that her son has got

a part in a big Hollywood movie playing the husband: 'So why didn't you get a speaking part?'

In the old days they used to moan about one F-word after another: family, friends and philosophy of life. Today they're still moaning, even though they've got more than they have ever had before.

More traffic jams. Because they've all been out buying themselves brand-new BMWs and Mercedes and Volvos. The number of cars has doubled in Tel Aviv over the last ten years.

More and longer queues at the check-outs. Because they now have more shops and supermarkets selling more things than they've ever sold before.

More delays for flights taking off for foreign climes. Because more people can now afford more and longer holidays, especially to Antalya, a favourite spot in Turkey for Israelis.

Has it made them any happier? No way. They still complain about the kosher ice-cream made with margarine and eggs which they serve nowadays at *barmitzvahs* and Jewish weddings. About the matzo meal they use for *knedlach*, the dumplings that go in chicken soup. And about chopped liver. Everybody bewails the fact that nowadays nobody makes chopped liver the way Momma used to make chopped liver.

And they don't complain the way you or I complain: the slightest raise of an eyebrow, a quick, whispered comment, then back to the champagne. With them it's nuclear. It's as if they're not only still fighting the battles of the Bible but the wars of 1929, 1939–45, 1948, 1956, 1967, 1973 and all the others as well. They're so used to being aggressive it's as if they think any hint of politeness is a sign of weakness, and weakness means defeat.

Take something as simple as traditional Yiddish folk songs, which you would have thought would be one of the safest and most innocent matters on earth. The first time the ultras' very own ultra-ultra radio station played a Yiddish folk song (admittedly sung by a woman), there was practically a traditional Yiddish riot outside their front door. The ultras besieged the station, accusing them of pandering to the secular, giving in to the forces of evil and insisting that everybody had a religious duty not to listen to the station. The only way the radio people could stop the protest was by agreeing to play traditional Yiddish folk songs sung by women only during the day, when the men were out of the house studying or working.

In the factories the most peaceful people I think I met were the senior managers, who, at one time, were recognised throughout the world for the skill and sophistication and deadly accuracy of their defence equipment: the catapult. Now, as circumstances have changed, they have developed even faster and more deadly weapons: high-speed, supersonic, laser-guided catapults which use *knedlach* instead of stones. I saw companies making everything you can think of: optical-detection machines, computerised navigation devices, zinc air batteries, electric fuel, litter bins which can absorb the impact of a bomb explosion. Not to mention a million computer-aided production-engineering software products.

Everywhere the emphasis is on technology. In fact, to all intents and purposes, some areas are as hi-tech, if not more hi-tech, than Silicon Valley or Route 128 in Boston. The clever bits of Intel's 486 and Pentium chip were designed in Israel. The core circuiting in a string of mobile phones was developed in Tel Aviv. And tri-focal contact lenses, anti-virus software, small-scale satellite dishes, digital colour printing. But take care if you use an Israeli computer and do a spell-check: it still changes all the 'yous' into 'thous'.

Whether it's because so many Russians poured in after the Berlin Wall came down and Eastern Europe collapsed like a pack of Polish playing cards, I don't know. Whatever the reason, things have come a long way since the 1960s when, believe it or not, the biggest market the Israelis could find for their own specially designed and built car were camels. They just loved to get their teeth into all that fibreglass. Today the Israelis even export foie gras to France, jellyfish to Japan and make automatic lifts so that people living in high-rise apartments don't have to break the sabbath by pressing a button to get to the ground floor. I even met a flying rabbi who travels the world first class to check if the cattle being sent to Israel have been properly killed or not.

At the same time, a Jewish businessman is still a Jewish businessman. I went to one small hi-tech company just outside Tel Aviv where the employees showed me a letter they had just received from the owner. It said: 'Thank you for all your hard work during the year. I am pleased to enclose a cheque for US$5,000 as a sign of my appreciation. If you continue to work as hard next year then I will sign it.'

The kibbutz, however, has changed. In the old days a kibbutz was heaven on earth. Everybody worked for everybody else, even though, as one old kibbutz has-been told me, they all looked as if they drank vinegar for breakfast. Now nobody believes in Heaven, let alone Hell any more. The old kibbutz concept is gone. There was only one, I was told, which was still up and running, making money, and paying everyone exactly the same: the Kibbutz Yizreel in the Jezreel Valley. As for sharing everything, no way. Today everybody has their own house or flat, their own air-conditioning and their own videos. Children no longer sleep in vast dormitories away from their parents. They even have their own cars. There are also more single people living in kibbutzim than ever before. Except that now they're old, divorced and moaning about there no longer being any bonfires or club nights or even communal dining rooms, and all the other things they used to complain about having when they were young *kibbutzniks*.

Wherever you go and whoever you talk to, in offices, in factories or in kibbutzim – especially in kibbutzim – and whatever their titles or position, everyone acts and behaves as if they are in the same family: they hate each others' guts.

Listen to Moshe asking Ya'cot the time of day. You'd think they were starting the Six-Day War all over again.

Watch Yosef buying something from Avraham. It's almost as bad as watching one Israeli not buying something from another Israeli. Not only is Yosef, the old *meshugga*, convinced he's being cheated and sold a duff product at far too high a price, but Avraham, the *tsedrayter*, is convinced that Yosef, the *nebbish*, is deliberately not buying anything else just to annoy him.

Watch two old *toches-leckers*, Nissims and Rahamin, who look like a couple of retired Mossad agents, taking a *schlepp* down memory lane over their pickled cucumbers and boiled chicken legs. I was going to ask them if there was any connection between the famous Israeli shoot-out at Kampala and the fact that initially, when the European Jews launched their campaign for a homeland, they were looking at Uganda rather than at their present patch of dust. I chickened out. I could visualise them flicking a switch and turning their zimmer frames into flame-throwers to frazzle me to a cinder.

Watch, if you dare, any wife talking to any husband. It's the First World War, Second World War, the Vietnam War, and every other war rolled into one. One couple I met were Lamson and Daniela. Lamson was very nice, very pleasant, very civilised; Daniela was something else. One evening at the end of the meal, she suddenly let fly. 'Such a husband I have,' the old *farbisseneh* wailed at me. 'There was I waiting to marry him. All the family, everybody there. Then one of his friends' – she spat out the word – 'says to him: "Every minute you delay, 100 shekels I give you." Do you know what he did? This husband of mine?'

I shook my head nervously.

'A whole week, he keeps me waiting. A whole week!', she shrieked.

'Not long enough,' poor, battered, defenceless Lamson butted in. 'But at least it paid for the house and the car.'

One businessman from Manchester told me that years ago, when he first moved to Jerusalem, he was shocked by the way people spoke to each other. He used to keep reminding his children to say please and thank you, but they ignored him. 'You want us to look stupid or something?' they said.

As for the way the Israelis talk to the Palestinians, well, I know in Israel a bigot is someone who hasn't been mugged yet, but honestly, would you jump out of a cab because of a driver's accent?

I was with an Israeli businessman one morning at the Sheraton in Jerusalem. He wanted to go back towards Tel Aviv. A cab came up and we jumped in. The driver had no sooner said 'Bleeze' than – whoosh! – the guy was out of the door, shouting at the hotel doorman to get him a driver with a *kippa*, a skull cap. And he didn't say please, either.

Just happen to mention such an incident in passing to an Israeli, and he'll very politely and very courteously grab you by the lapels, throw you against a wall and holler in your face about constantly living under the threat of violence: never knowing, if you get on a bus, whether you'll get off it again; going to the pictures never knowing if you'll see the end of the film; walking down the street never knowing if you'll reach the end without somebody screaming 'God is Great!' and lunging at you with a knife.

'...or going to a mosque and never knowing if you'll finish your...' I added on one occasion. Which, of course, I shouldn't have done. Not that the guy particularly overreacted. It's just that I now know what it feels like to be an Arab thrown against a wall or a sheet of corrugated iron and frisked by an Israeli policeman.

Anyway, when we finally got a *kippa* – there are not many *kippa* taxi-drivers in Jerusalem – this Israeli guy went on and on about the dangers of Palestinian drivers. 'They

want to kill us. They have a chance, they kill us.'

Then he went on and on about how, when the *muezzins* climb to the top of their mosques to call the faithful to prayer, they are in fact doing no such thing. 'They are telling everybody where the next attack will be launched and to stay out of the way,' he said.

But of all the peoples, tribes and tongues of Israel, the worst, as always, are the most devout. And nobody – apart from an old Irishman I once met in Limerick, who told me he carried a card instructing that in no circumstances was he to be buried by a woman priest – is more devout than the ultra-Orthodox, the Hasidic Jews, the guys with the black coats, the black hats and the black beards, who know all the answers before you even ask the questions. They're unbelievable. If Abraham was to come back to earth, I reckon they'd brand him a liberal.

Watch them walking

down the street. It's as if the end of the world is coming and they just know they have got to get there in time to claim their seat in the front row.

The most horrifying thing of all is to see those black coats and black hats and black beards ranting and raving about McDonald's, even though they've gone McKosher.

'Worse than Hitler,' one of the black coats screamed at me. I thought perhaps he was joking. 'Such praise,' I began.

He went ballistic. 'Destroying the homeland. Contaminating the country. Eating people's hearts out. Making them jungle animals.' His ringlets were swinging around all over the place.

'But the stuff's kosher, isn't it?'

'Kosher it might be, but …' And he was off again. His ringlets now breaking the speed of sound. They mixed meat and milk: hamburger with a slice of cheese on top. They opened on the sabbath. And, worst of all, they were popular.

Once a tiny Yiddish-speaking group of Russian Jews, today the Hasidim – Hebrew not for hairy and dim, but for those who tremble in the fear of God – now account for over a third of the Jews in Jerusalem. They have taken over whole areas, like Mea Shearim and Geula, just north of Rehov Haneviim, the Street of the Prophets, and made them their own. Some of them are even pre-Holocaust and refuse to accept the existence of Israel at all. And with seven to ten children per family, they're growing fast. And determined to go on growing until the coming of the Messiah. One rabbi, I was told, preached tirelessly about people having children so that they could eventually gain power and bury the Arabs. He was known locally as 'the face that launched a thousand clips'. Already the Hasidim account for over half of all the children in the country under ten years old. I'm not saying that McDonald's' days are numbered, but I'd get that order in fast if I were you. And while you're at it I'll have a triple-chocolate milk shake as well. Thanks.

Yet the vast majority of Israel's 4 million inhabitants are calm, quiet, reasonable guys, who don't exactly claim to be infallible: it's just that they know they're 200 per cent right in everything they say or do. Well, fairly calm, fairly quiet and fairly reasonable until, of course, they are provoked. Then God help you.

However, the ultras have been making enormous strides. They practically control all the laws relating to marriage and divorce. In some parts of the country they've even joined hands with their arch-enemies, the Islamic fundamentalists, and formed local companies to introduce segregated buses. On one side of an opaque curtain sit the men, and on the other the women. And they're so strict about what you can and cannot do on the sabbath that I reckon if Abraham told them God had instructed him to kill his son on the sabbath they would object.

Killing a flea is out, going to the cinema is out, playing bridge is out. Eating yoghurt with a picture of a dinosaur on the lid is out. Getting a plumber, an electrician or even a gardener to do any work on the sabbath is out. Which, come to think of it, is pretty much the same whatever day of the week you're talking about anywhere in the world. Calling the fire brigade is also out. If your house catches fire you have to call the local rabbi first. He then has to check the Torah, study all the relevant references to fire engines working on the sabbath, call you back and let you know whether it's OK. By which time, of course, your house has completely burned down and the whole thing is academic anyhow. Killing a rat, however, is all right.

'They want to roll the

pavements up at six o'clock in the evening and stop everybody from having fun,' the Old Testament prophet I met back in Tel Aviv told me.

I was in Jerusalem once when over 150,000 of them marched down Bar-Ilan Street, one of the main roads running through north Jerusalem, demanding its closure on the sabbath, or *shabbat*, as they say. It was not a pretty sight. The thought did cross my mind that religion is show-business for ugly people.

'They close roads for shopping and for pubs and cafés. Why won't they close a road for prayer?' one of the ultras barked at me. Naturally, I agreed. Immediately.

Another black coat was more relaxed. Whether they closed the road or not wouldn't make any difference to them one way or the other, he said. 'Why?' I asked.

'Because we'll throw bricks at any car that comes along'.

One of these ultra-Orthodox holy men, a real *schlub* – I reckon when they circumcised him they threw away the wrong bit – told me that the Talmud gave him the right to kill Arabs. 'Page 58a, page 62b. If someone comes to kill you, arise, go quickly and kill him first. That's what it says.'

And so that's what he was doing. Every evening – apart from the sabbath, of course – he and a couple of like-minded devout men would put on their *kippas* and prayer shawls, pack a couple of Uzi machine-guns under their black coats and go out hunting down Arabs. Not to shake chickens over their heads, I can assure you.

He offered me a lift in his car. At least, I think it was a car: all I could see were stickers proclaiming, 'Israel is in danger. Don't betray it', 'Hebron. Once and Forever', 'You voted for Rabin. You got Arafat. What next?' and a million other slightly wet wishy-washy, liberal slogans. 'The Bible says if you say nothing you agree. This is my way of saying, I disagree,' said the *schlub*.

I agreed, or rather disagreed. Either way, I declined the lift. I didn't have a bullet-proof vest, or what they call a *tefillin*, leather straps decorated with lots of little boxes, each one containing a prayer, around my neck. One or the other guarantees your protection. Plus, of course, a sympathetic cop if something goes wrong. And to think of the fuss we make about masons and the police back home.

But in case I'm depressing you, let me tell you an interesting fact.

While I was in Israel a survey was published which revealed that 88 per cent of Israelis do not know the Ten Commandments. Two in five cannot name the five books of Moses, 13 per cent hadn't heard of Hitler, 22 per cent ditto Churchill, 46 per cent Stalin and 48 per cent Roosevelt, which is a bit of an insult when you think how much the Americans have done for Israel. Even more amazing was that 24 per cent hadn't heard of the Holocaust. But you can bet your life none of them were Hasidics.

And so evening came and morning, and the fourth day passed.

5. So it came to pass on the fifth day, I went to Jerusalem. There are two traditional ways of entering Jerusalem. The other way is on a number 18 bus from the Gonen Bus Station which, on two Sundays running before my first visit, had been blown up by Islamic suicide bombers. Every bus, incidentally, which has been blown up in Jerusalem since 1967 has come from the Gonen Bus Station, or the Cursed Station, as it is known locally. Which strikes me, but apparently not the Israelis, as somehow significant. I arrived the modern way: by taxi.

The first time I'd seen Jerusalem was from Mount

Nebo, where Moses in fact saw it for the last time. I was in Madaba, just outside Amman, Jordan, looking at the mosaics. I wanted to see what was left of the mosaic of a 1,500-year-old map of Palestine in St George's, the Greek Orthodox church in the centre of town. But I got there just at the start of their Sunday evening service and didn't get the chance. Instead I stayed on for the service, which was all heavy chanting and candles and lots of old men and women hobbling in and out.

Afterwards, as the sun was beginning to set and all the old men started trotting home on their donkeys, we climbed through the rich, red soil of Mount Nebo, which produces up to three crops a year. At the top, I got out of the car. There, glistening in the sunset, were the spires of Jerusalem. I closed my eyes to capture the moment. Then, suddenly, blaring across the hilltop I heard the lilting refrain of 'Paddy McGinty's Goat'. The driver had switched the car radio on. God knows why, but the local Jordanian radio station was having a season of Irish folk songs.

But actually being in Jerusalem, meeting and talking to people, buying people one drink after another, is an amazing experience. However, Finks ain't what it used to be – literally. Fink's, one of the great bars of the world, at the top end of Hisdarntt Street, seemed somehow to have lost its sparkle. Maybe it was the prices. Twice I had to rush back to see my friendly neighbourhood money-changer, Aladdin (honestly, that's his name) by Herod's Gate just to pay for one glass of champagne and one portion of Russian caviar.

And Café Atara, the famous art-deco coffee shop in Ben Yehuda Street, with its smoked-glass windows and rows of cream cakes – which boasted that it never closed during the 1948 and 1967 wars, when it was shelled by Arabs; nor in the 1970s, when a car bomb blew out the front window and killed the manager; nor in 1987, when a bomb was delivered to it in a cake tin – has closed. Where armies and bombs and terrorists failed over all those years, who finally succeeded? Pizza Hut, that's who. Say no more.

Yet the city itself is magical, partly because it nestles in the Judaean hills; partly because, in spite of its fast-growing population, somehow or other it has been able to avoid masses of high-rise buildings; but most of all, I think, because practically everything, every building you see, from your ordinary everyday house to your towering American University-style Great Synagogue is, by decree, built in what is known as Jerusalem white stone, which neither comes from Jerusalem – it comes from Hebron – nor is white. It's more a kind of pale honey colour. But in the fierce sun, it gives the whole place a kind of shimmering white

sheen. So which sensible, environmentally sensitive and aesthetically aware people made that decree? Are you ready? This will come as a shock to you. It was the British, in the 1920s. It's certainly paid off a million-fold, I can tell you.

And the other thing that struck me was how very little the Old City seemed to have changed over the years. I know that in reality it has all altered dramatically – even the meat in the butchers' shops must have been changed at least three or four times in the last 2,000 years – it's just that everything, including most of the people, still looks as though it could have been there since the year dot. Or, I suppose, strictly speaking, the year zero.

The surrounding wall is still there. Obviously it has been repaired and renewed in all kinds of places, but it's still there. The huge city gates are still there. Still choked with people, still bustling with pilgrims. Again, they've been rebuilt and redecorated and, in some cases, landscaped, but they're still there. Apart, that is, from the Golden Gate, which Christ entered on Palm Sunday. That is blocked up, with iron railings all round it and some dirty signs on top which I couldn't read, although my guess is that they say something like, 'Herod and Sons – Builders. Closed temporarily for repairs, Januarius AD35. A member of the Courteous Builders Programme.'

Inside, it is still, for a holy city, an unholy mess. A thousand tiny alleyways criss-cross each other, some straight and narrow, others twisting every which way. Some are long, steady slopes. Others have a thousand steps. Up and down. One seems to be Jerusalem's Butchers' Row. The whole alley is lined with butchers' stalls. There are lumps of meat, great huge carcasses and stacks of bones all over the place. Not to mention piles of insides all over the outsides. Another is

devoted to textiles and scarves and carpets, another to fruit and vegetables and every herb you can think of. And everywhere there are money-changers. In fact, judging by the comparison between the money-changers' mark-up and the prices the shopkeepers were charging on everything from a genuine Jerusalem T-shirt to a plastic crucifix, I reckon the money-changers have been cruelly slandered for too long. They deserve a new image immediately. It's the retailers who are making the fat profits.

This is not some hands-on folk museum with one hell of a theme. This remains a real-live, hustling, bustling, pushing and shoving quarter, home to 40,000 people and a *souk* or marketplace for practically the whole of Jerusalem. Early in the morning you can still see them collecting rubbish in wicker baskets lashed on either side of a donkey.

To millions and millions

of Jews, Muslims and Christians all over the world, Jerusalem is the holiest of holies. To Americans, however, the city has instead an enduring special significance all of its own: it is home to the largest shopping mall in the Middle East.

It is also, of course, the most divided city in the world. Which is crazy. To me a City of Peace should be a City of Peace, not a City of Pieces: a piece for the Jews, a piece for the Muslims, a piece for the Christians. And somehow, mysteriously, a piece for the Armenians, probably because they sound like Jews, look like Arabs and act like Christians. As a result each of the big three thinks that when the chips are down they'll be on the winning side, which is why they put up with it. On the other hand, it's great if you want an instant tour of the world's great religions.

For Matins, for example, I went to the Muslims. Well, to be accurate, pre-, pre-, pre-Matins, the Muslims

came to me. Just as the sun was rising I heard my first *muezzin* of the day who was, I am sure, despite what the ultras say, calling people to prayer.

Wandering through the Arab Quarter in the morning I saw fathers teaching their sons the facts of life. First sweep the area in front of the shop, then wash it down. Stack all the goodies way out front. Hustle everybody in sight. Offer them all a discount. Let the punter go away thinking he's beaten you down to the ground and got the biggest bargain of all time.

In the early-morning sunlight the Dome of the Rock is magnificent. Set in the middle of an enormous open plaza or courtyard, it glitters and sparkles. The amount of gold leaf on the dome itself is unbelievable. Not that anybody would admit it was gold. 'It is not gold. Only the knowledge of the right way is golden,' an old Arab prophet told me.

Neither could anybody

tell me how much it cost, only that it was paid for by King Hussein, whose father was assassinated in the mosque opposite in 1957. The mosaics all around the walls are in fantastic condition. If this is a holy shrine, then these guys know how to look after it, not like some people I could mention, who can't even agree on who keeps the key to the front door.

Inside, the decoration, too, is in superb condition, although you get the impression that it was designed by a Muslim scholar with a wicked sense of humour. Nothing is what it seems; everything is a clue to something else. This refers to that verse in the Koran. That to the other verse. And over there, hidden in that panel, is, would you believe, the Star of David. In the centre, behind a shaky wooden screen, is the top of the actual mountain where Abraham went to sacrifice his son; where David kept the Ark of the Covenant; where Solomon's

first temple and Herod's second stood and where Mohammed, in my eyes at least, proved himself one of the greatest men in history by insisting that there was no way he was going to ascend to Heaven unless he could take his horse, El Burak, with him. Which, of course, he did. All around the floor are hundreds of carpets, many of them threadbare, but at least that is proof of how often the Muslims get down on their knees.

'I live in the past. I know the prophets. I don't know my friends.' Yet another Muslim prophet looked up from his prayers. 'For fifteen years I have been seeing them every day. But do I know them? I don't even know their names.' He returned to the past.

Originally this was the place towards which all Muslims turned when they said their prayers. Now it's Mecca. If I was a Muslim I'd still want to face here.

Across the plaza, down some steps, is the Al-Aqsa

Mosque, which is much more workmanlike. Built on the site of Herod's great temple, before that, according to the Jews, it was the Great School of King Solomon and after that, according to the Christians, the Crusader Church of St Mary. It is long, about 400 feet, with six rows of columns running the length of it, some of them, the large marble ones, donated by Mussolini. Others are like the multi-coloured jobs you see in mosques in Spain. Everywhere, all over the floor, people are kneeling, bowing and even lying fully stretched out on the ground saying their prayers. I doubt whether I could do that. Not even at midnight mass at Christmas, although I've seen plenty of people try. I'm afraid I'm still a collar-and-tie man when it comes to going to church.

The feature which caught my attention, near the top of the building just past the column which still bears the mark left by the bullet that killed King Hussein's father in 1957, was a small showcase containing all the used CS gas canisters which the Israelis say were never thrown into the mosque.

Lauds I spent with a bunch of Roman Catholic Fijians in the Holy Sepulchre, which was most disconcerting. Not only did they come in their national costume, complete with hats piled one on top of the other which they kept on throughout the service, but when they started singing they made everything sound like some boating song. I half expected them to start sashaying around in their grass skirts.

As for the Holy Sepulchre, I can honestly say it strengthened my faith. Many was the time while wandering around it that I found myself raising my eyes to Heaven and calling on Jesus Christ by name. The place is a mess. The main door is covered in graffiti. All the walls are scarred and scratched and pitted and crumbling to pieces. There is mildew everywhere and centuries of dust on top of the mildew. Tiny side chapels lie empty and dark and unused. All the pictures are old and warped and wrinkly. There are piles of sand and bricks and breezeblocks in one corner, a stack of pews in another and three ancient Coptic priests fast asleep in a third. The Holy Sepulchre itself is held together by enormous iron girders which look like rejects from the Sydney Harbour bridge. Take one away and the whole thing would collapse. The fact it has survived so long can only be attributed to outside forces.

I'm not saying it should be dripping in gold, but damn it, Bateman's, Rudyard Kipling's house in Burwash, just down the road from me, has more care and attention - and cash - lavished on it than most of the churches in Jerusalem probably do. It's a blessing that it's not the original Church of the Holy Sepulchre, built by Constantine, which was double the size,

otherwise it would be in twice the mess today. This one was built by the Crusaders. To me it's a perfect example of what happens when a bunch of European nations try to co-operate without Britain at the heart of the project.

Bethlehem, meanwhile, is authentic. Very authentic. It is full of old cows pushing and shoving and barging around all over the place and sheep following their tour leaders. Standing around in the odd corner, refusing to budge, I spotted a couple of stubborn old mules and at least half a dozen asses making complete fools of themselves.

In Manger Square, a local shepherd told me, at midnight on Christmas Eve he looked up and saw on the roof of the church three robed figures walking slowly towards him.

'You don't mean...' I began.

'Israeli soldiers,' he continued. 'They were on all the rooftops all around us. But there was no trouble.

Why should there be trouble?'

As for gold, frankincense and myrrh, as far as I was concerned it was more gold, frankincense and blurr. Blurr because there was so much I wanted to see and so little time between meetings that I had to rush through everything so quickly. Frankincense was more Turkish cigarette smoke, because practically every Palestinian puffs away like mad. And the gold? That's all in the hands of the tour guides and shopkeepers, in particular the tour guides whose families are shopkeepers. The tour guide who latched on to me somewhere between the Holy Shepherd Store, the Bethlehem Star and the Paradise Hotel had just come back from three months in Europe visiting France, Belgium, the Netherlands and Britain. His family owned three of the shops along the back of Manger Square and a half-share in one on the edge of town. How did I know that?

Every time he told me something about the Church of the Nativity he told me where I could buy a replica of it.

'And here beneath altar is Cave of Nativity. You look. There is star on floor. My brother he sell you star. Mother-of-pearl. Very pretty, yes. We go now?'

'No, thank you.'

'He also sell Jesus doll. Very good. Yes? We go now?'

'No.'

'And this is Altar of Manger. My uncle, he sell baby manger. Olive wood, very pretty. With lights. I take you to his shop. We go now.'

'No.'

'Over there. Altar of Three Kings. My father, he sell three camels. Made of glass. Very good price. We visit his shop. Yes?'

'No.'

'Look down there. There is picture of angels. I have cousin, she make angels. Very nice dolls. With wings. Her shop is big shop, good prices. We see her now. She give us tea. Yes?'

'No.'

But, of course, in the end I went.

As it happened, the sister gave us wine, although mine tasted like the stuff they must have served at Cana before they hit the good stuff. Having promised to return to buy the shop, lock, stock and olive wood mangers, I escaped and slipped back by myself to the Church of the Nativity to try to soak up the atmosphere, which I did for about twenty-two seconds before I was kidnapped by another tour guide.

Built originally by Constantine the Great in AD325, it is far more impressive than the Church of the Holy Sepulchre and in a million times better condition. This, you feel, is what it's all about.

The tiny entrance door is a good idea. The books say this was designed to stop the Muslims riding their horses inside, but to me it not only gives you a sense of stooping as if to go into a cave, it also, once you're inside, somehow makes everything seem even grander and more impressive. The sanctuary is heavy Greek Orthodox. The four rows of huge, red sandstone columns running the length of the building makes it look solid, secure, everlasting. Under some of the old wooden floorboards you can see patches of mosaic, and here and there on the walls there are further traces of them.

I was about to go back down the steep marble steps to the crypt when this enormous American woman barged into me. 'We're in close proximity,' she drawled.

I nodded quietly, as is my wont in such circumstances. Then, talk of Three Ships Come Sailing By, she pushed me out of the way and clattered down the steps. A poor, downtrodden, pathetic man with her, whom I naturally assumed to be her husband, looked at me weakly and whispered, 'This is not conducive to how I had imagined it.'

Me neither, sunshine.

Who is to blame? An Essex girl. Not Queen Sharon, but Queen Helena, the last good, kind, devoted girl to be born in Colchester. In AD326 she identified the site of Golgotha, and from then on it was non-stop nag until she finally got her way and the first church was built on the site. Then came the Church of the Nativity. It helped, of course, that her son was Constantine the Great.

In the end, for me, the only good thing about the place was the fact there was no Bing Crosby and no Jingle Bells.

Prime and I was ready for the Copts, although the Copts were not ready for me. The little Church of St Helena was as deserted as Colchester on a wet Wednesday afternoon, which was a pity, because I'd been told there was usually an old Coptic monk there with a funny-looking hat, a great big white beard and a few words of English who tried to persuade anybody who went in there to climb down into some tiny hole in the ground. Depending on how nice you were to him, or how many candles you lit in the church, he either put the electric light on or let you slither down in the pitch black like some demented troglodite.

Terce I spent with the Abyssinians, as they still call themselves high in the beams of the Holy Sepulchre itself. To get to them I had to light a candle inside St Helena's, shake the priest by the hand and give him some money for the poor and needy Copts of Essex. He then opened the gate outside and there I was, actually on the roof of the Holy Sepulchre itself. And what's the first thing you see? A row of shacks which house a group of Abyssinian priests and their families who, in true Christian fashion, are not allowed inside the sepulchre itself. So instead they've set up home on the roof.

'Here we are nearer to God,' a great burly monk about the size of St Peter's in Rome boomed at me through an enormous black beard.

We walked across to the top of one of the smaller domes on the roof. 'Here,' he waved his arms around it, 'is where we celebrated Easter because they wouldn't let us in.'

Sext, I was with the Jews in the tiny synagogue on the way to the Wailing Wall. Now, I'm no expert on synagogues, although I shall never forget the first one I visited which was, I think, in Harrogate. We were all downstairs. Everybody had a *tallit*, a white prayer shawl, and a skull cap. One man had a top hat. All the women were upstairs. The service, I remember, lasted hours. There was lots of reading of the Torah as well as the Bible. The sermon was all about the dangers of extremism and the need to accept one another and live in peace and harmony together. I went to take out

my pen and an old Ministry of Defence security pass I had accidentally on purpose forgotten to hand in on which to make a note of what the preacher said and practically everybody went bananas. Or rather, pickled cucumbers. How was I to know that on the sabbath in Harrogate you're not even allowed to carry a pen and paper, let alone write down the words of a preacher pushing peace and harmony.

This time it was more relaxed. I didn't take out a pen and paper; I didn't even try to remember anything, in case that was wrong as well. All I can recall is that the make-it-yourself cardboard skull cap they gave me kept falling off.

After that it was down to the Wailing Wall with all the black coats and T-shirts proclaiming either, 'Don't worry. Be Jewish', or 'They don't pay you anything to be humble'. Although, I'll tell you now, if I was Jewish you wouldn't find me down there pushing little messages through the cracks. To me the Wailing Wall, the western side of Herod's temple – all that was left after the Romans destroyed the place in AD70, should be dark, sombre, mysterious. Instead it forms one side of a wide-open square and it's clean and bright and almost sparkling. The entire area looks as though it's been almost rebuilt by another bunch of New York dentists in that clean, open, fresh-air shopping-mall style you see in fancy US resorts. Give me the dark, mysterious old-fashioned synagogues, like Bevis Marks in the City of London, any time. The west wall on that is far more telling than any other western wall I know.

None was my turn with the Greek Orthodox which, I admit, I wasn't looking for-ward to as I'd left my sun-glasses behind. All that gilt and glass and mirror is, I find, a bit too much for my old eyes. I needn't have worried. No sooner had I got inside the chapel in the Holy Sepulchre than this old French woman came up to me and for some reason asked me if I was a priest. Why I should look like a Greek Orthodox priest I do not know. I'm not 6 feet 6 inches tall, I don't weigh 30 stone and I don't have an enormous black beard. She said she wanted to go to confession. I asked her, in my very bad French, if she was married. She said she was. I told her that in that case there was no way I could hear her confession and forgive her for all the unhappiness she had caused throughout her life. She grabbed my hand, squeezed it, thanked me very much and left. Which obviously proves it doesn't make a blind bit of difference what you say to a woman, she will always interpret it her own way.

Vespers just had to be with the Armenians. Of all the four quarters of the Old City, my favourite is the Armenian Quarter, and my favourite church is the Church of St James. To get to it you go down a stone passage, past a huge, polished beam which used to be thumped again and again to call the faithful to prayer in the days when bells were banned, and pull back a heavy leather curtain. Inside everything is dark and heavy and sombre, decorated with shadowy, mysterious paintings, lamps and candles. There are no pews, only carpets on the floor. Photography is banned, videos are banned, even crossing your ankles is banned. Three times I saw one old lady who might well have known Abraham as a boy approach some young American couple stretched out on the carpet and whack them with her walking stick, because not only were their ankles crossed, but they were sitting so close together they were actually touching each other. In the end they said something that I am sure was not very Christian, got up and stormed out. No doubt to some evangelical church somewhere.

The monks, dressed in black and gold with their pointed hoods, seem to pray all day long. At least, whenever I popped in, there they were chanting away in the gloom. This, to me, is the way to do it. If I ever jump ship I think I'll become an Armenian.

For Compline I got landed with a born-again fundamentalist from Portland, Oregon sitting at the outside bar of the American Colony Hotel, who somehow or other had got the idea that the King James Version was something to do with Billie Jean King and playing tennis.

In the end, to change the subject, I told him the only Jewish fundamentalist joke I know. The chief rabbi gets back from holiday and asks if there's any news. His assistant rabbi says, 'I've got good news and bad news.'

'So give me the good news,' he says. 'OK,' says the assistant rabbi. 'God called, but he said he'd call back tomorrow. The bad news? He was calling from Salt Lake City.'

The American guy didn't laugh either.

The only religion I didn't manage to take in were the Arab Christians who, I was informed, held their services in St George's Cathedral, the Church of England church just outside the Old City. When I got there I was told it was all off: there weren't enough of them left to make up a congregation.

And so evening came and morning and the fifth day passed.

6. Lo, and so it came to pass that on the sixth day I did the Via Dolorosa, the Stations of the Cross, the route taken by Christ on his way to Calvary and crucifixion. And I admit I cried. At first, I just had a lump in my throat. Then tears began to well up in my eyes. By the time I got to the Holy Sepulchre itself I was in full flood. Because the whole thing was so unbelievably – what's the word? – schmucky. If it's not schmucky it's something very like it.

Any Catholic church you go into anywhere in the world has its own Via Dolorosa, fourteen different pictures or panels commemorating the different events that befell Christ on his way to his death. So what is the first thing I discover when I get there? There is no such thing as the Via Dolorosa. Or, at least, historically there is not. The whole thing is based on hints, rumours and traditions. In fact, at one time there were almost as many different Via Dolorosas as there were Christian churches, one going this way, one another, with the Protestants for ever unable to make up their own mind which way they wanted to go.

The present Via Dolorosa turns out to be pretty much the invention of the Franciscans, way back in the fourteenth century, with one or two minor exceptions. Today we run it back to front, in the order in which the events took place. The Franciscans, maybe because they were Italian, who knows, ran it front to back, if you see what I mean, starting with the crucifixion and death of Christ and working back to the trial, like a series of flashbacks. Today we have fourteen stations, whereas the Franciscans had only ten. Which must be some form of ecclesiastical inflation, I suppose. Another 500 years and I guess there'll be eighteen. Either that or the Franciscans couldn't count as well forwards as they did backwards.

To many Catholics Making the Stations, as we say, ranks second or third after the Mass or after the Mass and the Rosary. Made either alone or in a packed, darkened church, it can be a moving experience. One priest I knew years ago, who used to be a missionary in China, was always in floods of tears by the time he got to the end of them. Everybody else in the church would be extra quiet and just shuffle off home rather than hanging

around outside chatting and gossiping about important ecclesiastical matters like Saturday's whist drive, next month's jumble sale and did you notice Mrs O' Donnell must be expecting – is it her fifth or sixth?

The real thing – or the supposedly real thing – I naturally assumed would be at least the same if not better. I was wrong.

The First Station, which recalls Christ being condemned to death by Pilate, is deep inside a Muslim complex incorporating a school, the El-Omariyeh College, a road, some shops and three churches. Originally the site of Herod's palace, it was also Pilate's official residence whenever he was in town. You cannot get into it. Which, you must admit, is one hell of a way, if you will excuse me, to start anything, let alone the Via Dolorosa. Your choice, therefore, is simple. You can stand outside and listen to the row coming from the school, dodge the kids throwing stones in the narrow cobblestone alley-ways, debate whether the trial took place in the open air or on a platform or relish the fact that after the way he treated the Holy Innocents, King Herod deserves a bunch of unruly schoolkids trampling over his palace until the end of time.

I did none of these. I popped back down the alleyway to St Anne's Church, which I reckon is probably the prettiest church in the whole of Jerusalem. Another old Crusader church, it has been everything in its time: the home of St Anne, the mother of Mary (funny, nobody ever mentions the father. Probably because it's impossible for a married man to be a saint); the site of the pool of Bethesda, where Christ upset the Jews by curing some disabled guy on the sabbath; a Muslim theological school and a rubbish dump. At one time the rubbish reached as high as the ceiling.

In 1856 the Turks gave the church to France in return for their help in the Crimea. The French, as they do, then handed it over to one of their religious orders, the Pères Blanc – not because they were dedicated to Jerusalem, or even good at clearing up other people's rubbish, but because they were devoted to doing good in Africa. The first thing they did was to dig up the pool next to the church, the scene of the miracles, and turn it into a garden.

Today, however, the church is very quiet, very pleasant, a genuine hide-away. So please don't tell anyone about it. If you wish, you can climb down into the crypt, which is said to be where the Virgin Mary was born.

Up the lane now, on the right-hand side, the Church of the Flagellation and the Church of the Condem-nation stand facing each other across a tiny court-yard. The Church of the Flagellation is one of those tiny, pretty, calm, almost severe little churches. Very light, very airy, the exact opposite of what, of course, it should be. The dome incorporates the Crown of Thorns. The windows show Christ being scourged, Pilate washing his hands and Barabbas being freed. The Church of the Condemnation, which is about the same size, is more ornate, has more statues and is perhaps more Italian. But take a look at the floor at the back – it's the actual road taken by Christ carrying his cross. Don't look too closely, though, otherwise you'll see, up against the far wall, carved into it the four-square symbol which proves that it originally came from a mosque, and that would spoil everything.

A Frenchwoman saw me studying it, came up, and in her best Joan of Arc manner, told me it was nothing of the sort. She said it was something to do with a game the Roman soldiers played with their prisoners. If the prisoner played the game and lost, he would be mercilessly abused and then crucified in the most savage and cruel way. If, however, he won he would be treated as their king and granted every possible wish until the time came for his crucifixion. He would still be crucified but, as far as was possible, without all the extreme agony and suffering. That's why, she said, Christ was dressed like a king by the Roman soldiers, given a crown, albeit one of thorns, and a reed as a sceptre, and why Simon of Cyrene was press-ganged into carrying the cross part of the way. Interesting, n'est ce pas?

Further along is the Ecce Homo arch and the Souvenir Collectors' Corner. Some people maintain that not only did Pilate not say *ecce homo*, or behold the man but that the arch did not even exist at the time. I don't believe them. I think they're just jealous that Pilate got all the best lines. Either he was a natural or Christopher Fry or Robert Bolt was hidden away somewhere in the background churning them out for him.

As for the Souvenir Collectors' Corner, nobody could possibly claim this didn't exist. On the contrary, it hits you between the eyes, especially upstairs on the second floor, where they have literally hundreds of genuine Russian icons for sale, some for as little as a few pounds, a few for well over £100,000.

As for the Third Station, where Christ stumbled and fell for the first time – well, it's best not to try to find it. If you do, you'll wish you hadn't. It's at the junction with El-Wad Road or alleyway. Turn right and you're heading out towards the Damascus Gate and Jerusalem proper; turn left and you're making your way deeper into the Old City and towards Calvary and the Holy Sepulchre. About ten paces on the left-hand side, up against the Armenian Catholic Patriarchate Mosque, is a pile of Coke tins, some black plastic bags, some rotting vegetables and a few cigarette boxes. That's it. And beware of little boys trying to pick your pockets.

The Fourth Station is where Christ met his mother. Right opposite the spot is the Fourth Station T-Shirt Shop. And of course, they're selling T-shirts bearing every possible variation on the 'So-and-so went to Jerusalem and all they brought me back was this lousy T-shirt' theme. I suppose we should be grateful that they are at least tasteful. They could be a thousand times worse.

The Fifth Station is where, for whatever reason, Simon got roped in to carry the cross. And no wonder: this is the start of a long, long climb up God knows how many steps inside one of those small, cramped, tight alleyways completely packed with people. Just looking at it made me feel weak. Today, of course, it's lined on either side with shops and art galleries and antiques and guys selling imitation everything under the sun.

The Sixth Station is where some woman called Veronica wiped the face of Christ with what is said to have been a silk veil. Go inside the church, which is run by Greek Catholics, and they'll pull the wool, if not a veil, over your eyes.

One old man told me that even although the Vatican claims it has the veil, in fact the Greek Orthodox monks have it hidden away in their secret museum in the Church of the Holy Sepulchre, together with this saint's finger and that saint's skull, which they only ever show to VIP visitors from Greece. Another old man maintained, equally vehemently, that that was nonsense: the monks had secretly smuggled the veil out of Jerusalem and, like most valuable foreign items, it was now being cared for and air-conditioned in Toronto, of all places.

As I left the church, a woman ran up to me. 'Come and visit my shop,' she pleaded. 'Good prices. You come.'

The Seventh Station commemorates the spot where Christ fell a second time. That's no surprise: it's right at the top of the long climb where the Via Dolorosa hits the main market street. Even today it's teeming with people, and you can imagine what it must have been like then. Just a few paces on, and in the first century you were through a gate, out of the city and in the countryside. Which is why some people maintain that the Church of the Holy Sepulchre does not really – oops, mind this bunch of Australians clod-hopping all over the place in their mountain boots – contain the Holy Sepulchre. The real Holy Sepulchre, they say, is outside the city walls.

The Eighth Station, where Christ met the women of Jerusalem, is the one everyone misses. You turn into the Sug Khan ez-Zeit Street and you are immediately tempted to carry on walking. Don't. Turn almost immediately right, up Aqabat-el-Khanqa Street, and there, just past the Greek Orthodox convent on the left, is a stone with a Latin cross on it. That's your Eighth Station, and the start of the - hell! Here come the Australians again - Christian Quarter. Now things get really - 'G'day, mate' - interesting. Some people claim - 'Know where I can get some water, mate?' - that the Greeks built churches over all the other stations. So it's not - 'No, that's no good. Anywhere else?' - possible to follow the route any more. Others say - 'Nah, she's only got big ones' - if the Via Dolorosa is all made up anyway, what difference does it make?

By the time you hit the Ninth Station, where Christ fell a third time, you're beginning to think they're right. You come back down Aqabat el-Khanqa Street with relief because it means escaping from those damned Aussies. Turn right back into Suq Khan ez-Zeit Street. A good way along you come across a shop proclaiming, perhaps ironically, 'Are you thirsty? Try our iced tea.'

Opposite is a slope. Take the slope and you slowly, amazingly, zigzag your way up on to the roof of the Church of the Holy Sepulchre itself. First, however, you pass Russian church buildings on your left, then some Coptic church buildings on your right, with 'Merry Christmas' scrawled in blue paint on the outside wall. Now take a left, then a right. Down a short alleyway and just outside the door of the Coptic Church, on the left, is a column marking the place where Christ fell for the third time. Immediately opposite is St Helena's and the missing Coptic monk.

Now to get to the Tenth Station, where Christ was stripped of his clothes, most people head back to Aqabat el-Khanqa Street and then follow it round to the entrance to the Holy Sepulchre Church. Don't - unless you want to try some of Mohammed's iced tea. Instead get the Abyssinians to let you on to the roof of the Holy Sepulchre so that you can make your way down inside. Once you reach the ground floor, you go up another flight of steps to what is either the Holy of Holies, the very top of the Hill of Calvary, or another giant historical Franciscan mistake.

Inside this tiny, heavily ornate chapel, with its life-sized icons and a million chandeliers and candles and scores of ashen, fragile Italian nuns is, on the floor on the right-hand side, a square and an oblong. The square is the Tenth Station. The oblong is the Eleventh Station, where Christ was nailed to the cross. When I went there a row of old Frenchwomen were resting their feet and complaining, '*Mon Dieu*, the heat.'

The Twelfth Station, where Christ died on the cross, is over there behind – God save us – that bunch of Americans, hissing and

sissing and shouting and flashing their cameras like a bunch of paparazzi. The hole where the cross went is just visible through a glass covering. And there, on either side, are two holes which are supposed to have contained the crosses where the thieves were crucified.

'Quick, quick. Another one of me like this,' some American woman resembling Shirley Maclaine's grandmother is screaming.

'Oh, come on, Alice. You've had enough. Let somebody else have a go.'

'No, no, just—'

'Jeez, Elmer. She's your wife, you talk to her.'

Elmer, who looks as though he's known her since before she was a virgin, does nothing but shrug his shoulders and try to disappear into the woodwork.

'Me? What can I do? I'm only...,' he mutters.

'OK. Now me.'

Through the scrum another American woman, all baseball cap, fluorescent green tracksuit, white trainers the size of moon-boots and sunglasses, arrives carrying some kind of lightweight cross on her shoulders. 'Hey, hold this thing for a minute will yah, honey?' She gestured towards me.

I put on my I'm-from-Planet-X-I-don't-know-what-the-hell-you're-talking-about look. There was just no way I was going to get involved with anything like that. In the end she gave it to one of the Greek Orthodox priests, who looked a bit like Salman Rushdie's younger brother.

'I wanna do my hair before I have my picture taken,' she giggled.

I tell you, I've seen Americans show more awe and respect, and even solemnity, traipsing around their own great holy of holies, that heart and soul of American culture, 'Grace-land', the home of Elvis Presley in Memphis, Tennessee. Where, incident-ally, it is absolutely, but absolutely, forbidden to take photographs. And no-body takes photographs.

On another occasion, I saw a tiny, fragile, Chinese-looking nun spend so much time on her knees kissing the spot where the cross had been that two awful American women grabbed her and pulled her away because she was holding up the queue. One was wearing a T-shirt that said, 'Keep the 7. Go to Heaven'. As they dumped the poor little nun on the bench by the stairs at the back of the chapel, the whole of Jerusalem could hear the other women saying to her, 'So where you goin' to after this, honey?'

The little nun merely raised her eyes to the sky, in exasperation, I'm sure.

'Oh, we're not goin' on the roof, honey lamb,' shrieked the American with the T-shirt. 'We're off to Cyprus. Now, you have yourself a good day.'

As I climbed back down the steps to the floor of the Holy Sepulchre, wondering whether I should turn

Buddhist, a young Arab boy ran up to me. 'Jesus, he not crucified here,' he said. 'He buried near Damascus Gate. In Garden Tomb. Quick, I take you now.'

At the bottom of the steps, almost in front of the main door, surrounded by an odd collection of battered candlesticks, is the stone upon which Christ's body was anointed. The Thirteenth Station.

Further along is a big queue to go down into the Fourteenth and final station, the Holy Sepulchre itself. There is always a long queue there. There's been one, as far as I can discover, since the year AD135, when the Emperor Hadrian first built a shrine to mark the spot. If you haven't got a couple of hundred years to spare, go round the back. There, inside a tiny chapel the size of a telephone box, a Coptic monk guards the top left-hand corner of the underground tomb. Wait 300 years to see the real thing, he seems to be saying, or come and have a quick look at the top left-hand corner in 2.5 seconds. Which, I'm afraid, is what I did. Because I knew that if I'd queued up I'd be thinking all kinds of unkind thoughts.

Like how come the Christians who are supposed to believe in Christ's birth, death and resurrection don't actually look after the place? The Church of the Holy Sepulchre is a disgrace. Then there's the way the Christians who are meant to be running the place behave towards each other. Here they are – Roman Catholic, Greek Orthodox, Armenians, Coptics, Syrians and Ethiopians – theoretically dedicated to God and their neighbour, and they can't even agree on who looks after the key of the front door. Instead it is held by the Joudehs and the Nusseibehs, two of the oldest Muslim families in Jerusalem. You can imagine how we'd be chortling away if the Muslims couldn't agree who kept the key of the Dome of the Rock and instead it was held by a vicar in Tunbridge Wells. It's a farce.

There's the story of the ladders as well. One day hundreds of years ago, or maybe it was only ten years ago, I was told, a workman repairing a window at the front of the church went off to lunch leaving his ladder propped up against the wall. For some reason or other he never returned. The ladder is still there today, because nobody can agree whose responsibility it is.

Then there's the way the Christians share out the holy places. I'm a Roman Catholic, so naturally I'm totally objective, rational and completely unbiased. In any case, in the interests of Christian unity and because of all the sensitivities involved, it would be wrong for me to take sides, so all I can say is, we should run the whole show. It's the only way things will get done properly. Take the Church of the Holy Sepul-

chre again. Now, I know all men are equal in the sight of God, but it seems to me at present that the Greek Orthodox are more equal than the rest of us. They're all over the place. They're even building a whole new gallery and chapel down from the roof of the church to make some more space, which is totally wrong.

As for the Old City itself, how come it's shared out almost equally between the Jews, the Muslims, the Christians and the Armenians? The Armenians only make up a tiny percentage of the Christian population of the world. So why have they got 25 per cent of the action? I know this is a delicate subject, and I may be upsetting many people, but everyone is entitled to his opinion. And as far as I'm concerned, anyone who disagrees with me that the objective, rational and completely unbiased thing to do is to give the Armenians a tiny percentage of the action and the lion's share to us is, as far as I'm concerned, three allelujahs short of a Messiah.

What do I mean, the lion's share? To Christians, Jerusalem is the most holy place in the world. So how come we've got to share any of it with the Jews and the Muslims in the first place?

The Jews have got Mount Sinai, where God came down to Moses (the Jews wouldn't spend the money to go and see God) and revealed the Torah. They've got the Red Sea and the desert. Does forty years following the pillar of fire by night count for nothing? They've got Hebron, the City of the Fathers, King David's first capital and the final resting place of the great patriarchs. Why do they want a share of Jerusalem as well? True, there is the Wailing Wall, but is that more important to them than Mount Sinai, where the whole thing began? There was all this fuss about them being exiled to Babylon, I know, but that's hardly a reason

for claiming Jerusalem as their holy of holies. What's more, they've had nothing to do with the city since they lost it to the Romans in – when was it? – AD70. In any case, some people might say that Jerusalem is the last place the Jews would want to be associated with. Not me, of course. I'm not like that.

It's the same with the Muslims. They've got Mecca and Medina: Mecca where Mohammed was born and Medina where he died. Jerusalem has only really been important to Islam since around 1187, when Saladin took it from the Crusaders. Up until then they were pretty relaxed about it. Some might say that Jerusalem is more of a political than religious symbol for them. But not me, of course. I'm not like that.

So, instead of queuing up for hours on end to see the actual sepulchre and thinking such unkind thoughts, I went back to the American Colony Club and had a good cry.

And so evening came and morning, and the sixth day passed.

7. And so it came to pass that on the seventh day, I realised it was time to go home, otherwise I'd be late for my next trip. I didn't take with me any traditional Israeli souvenirs, I'm pleased to say (most souvenirs of the Holy Land tend to be a sore head, a couple of cracked ribs and a stamp you don't want in your passport). In any case, whatever I take home for my wife from wherever she doesn't like: she was not keen on the voodoo dolls from Haiti, or the authentic wooden Burmese salt and pepper pots, or the genuine Inca key ring from Peru.

What I did take home, however, were some glorious memories. Of the Old City itself; of the poor Irish priest I kept seeing everywhere who, in the boiling heat, always wore an old black raincoat which he must have had since his ordination, if not before. Which could only mean that his knowledge of the Bible went as far as the story of Noah and the flood and no further. And, of course, that still, sombre, stirring view of the Mount of Olives, where one day in the dying sun, for a single moment, the world stood still as one man was laid to rest, a man who single-handedly so dramatically changed the lives of so many people and whose influence stretched across the face of the world: Robert Maxwell.

I'm not going to break any commandments to go back, but one day, if I can, I would like to spend Easter in Jerusalem.

And so evening came, and morning, and the seventh day passed. Already. Already.

GAZA CITY

I've just been to the most unbelievable airport in the world.

There were no problems getting in. No hold-ups on the access roads, no difficulties parking, no barriers, no no-go signs. No stroppy policemen, no kids trying to take your shoes off, no guys trying to grab your luggage. No queues for tickets. No mistakes on the tickets – not like in Yangon, where I was once given four separate tickets made out respectively to: Mr Peter Biddlecombe, Mr Please supply him, Mr One return ticket and Mr Yangon–Mandalay–Yangon.

There were no queues at check-in. No silly questions like 'Did you pack your own bag, sir?' I mean, who the hell do they think is going to pack my bag for me? My wife gave that up years ago. She also, incidentally, gave up unpacking my bag about the same time, which may or may not be significant. There were no long queues for security checks, no X-ray machines out of action, none of this searching your baggage for the sake of it. No hassles at Customs, no delays at Emigration, no crummy executive lounges full of icy women and warm beer. No rows about the exchange rate. No duty-free shops overflowing with the kind of things that, whatever you buy, your wife will complain about.

There was no showing your passport every two seconds for no apparent reason, no indecipherable announcements, no last-minute mad rushes for planes which were going to sit on the tarmac for two days while half a dozen people dithered about whether to change a lightbulb or not.

This is probably because there was no actual airport, either, but don't tell Yasser Arafat, because obviously he thinks there is. He's been going around bragging to the world and its mother that Palestine National Airlines is up and running; that there is a brand-new international airport just outside Gaza City; that the runway is 2,800 metres long and suitable for planes like the Airbus, the 737 and 757 but not the 747; that they are already running scheduled flights to Cairo, Amman and Larnaca, and are at any minute about to take on London, New York, Moscow and all points east of East Jerusalem; and that they can handle between 500,000 and 750,000 passengers a year.

Well, far be it from me to be the kid who declares that the president hasn't got a red and white checked table-cloth on his head, but I've been out there to see it. In the middle of nowhere, way out towards Egypt, surrounded by orange groves, past a Jewish settlement of around 4,000 people heavily guarded by Israeli soldiers. In the desert. All covered in sand. And you can take it from me, it ain't there. There's no such thing.

Not that I went all the way to Gaza City to see, or rather not see, an airport. I went there first of all to see if I could get in, and secondly, and more importantly, to see if I could get out. In between I also wanted to see – the Israelis will hate me for this – what the new Palestinian state was like. Not that I'm prejudiced: some of my best friends are Palestinians.

Getting in, I must tell you, is not the easiest thing in the world. Think of your brother-in-law's wallet. Multiply by a factor of 25 the length of time since he bought a round of drinks and you're beginning to get close. And the welcome you get when you finally get there is about as warm as an iced-up refrigerator. But if you're a masochist - I mean determined - the only way is by road from Israel, and Israeli drivers just do not want to go anywhere near it. In fact, Israelis generally are about as fond of the Palestinians as Herod was of first-born males. When the Israelis pulled out of Gaza after twenty-seven years it never made the front page of any of their newspapers. Which shows that it either wasn't as big a deal as we all thought, or they didn't want to make a fuss about it because they knew they would be back. Instead all the papers ran a big story about some young Mr Nobody who won an election in some trade-union organisation. Now does that suggest a central co-ordinating hand somewhere manipulating a totally free and independent press and telling them what to do? Of course not, how suspicious can you get? It was just a coincidence.

In the end, I managed to get to Gaza City only through pure luck. I picked up this taxi in Tel Aviv driven by an Israeli, and I was able to appeal to his better nature. In other words, I offered him way above the going rate. He immediately agreed, and off we went to the main check-point, Erez, about two hours out of town. But once we got to the border he refused to go any further. It was a U-turn, pedal to the floor, a cloud of dust and see you at the *barmitzvah*.

If you promise me you're not of a nervous disposition, I'll tell you what happened next. At the checkpoint, not at the *barmitzvah*. Even I'm too nervous to tell you what goes on at a *barmitzvah*. The checkpoint is not only the worst customs border in the world, it is also the first one I've ever come across designed by taxi-drivers. Quite apart from the chaos and the agonies and all the delays, it must be at least 100 miles, if not 200 miles long. Which means, of course, that the only way to get from one end to the other is by - you've guessed – taxi. The only good thing was that I didn't have to sleep all night curled up on the ground underneath a Land Rover in the middle of no-man's-land, as I did once trying to get into Algeria. Which, I suppose, puts paid to the chances of me ever going back to Algeria again.

The Palestinian police are not exactly in the Nelson Mandela league when it comes to forgiving and forgetting, but at least they're not prejudiced one way or the other. They treat everybody abominably. Put them alongside the Israeli military and it's not exactly fun, fun, fun. More like war, war, war. In fact, a few days before I got to the border there was practically a full-scale war between the two sides. Two people were killed and over 100 – policemen, workers, ordinary people trying to cross from one side to the other – were wounded, some seriously.

You can't take a taxi across the border, let alone your own car, unless you're on official government, inter-government or World Bank business. Or unless, like all the United Nations vehicles, you're desperately looking for a good restaurant. So, in the broiling heat, choking from the belching fumes of 1,000 lorries, you have to leave your vehicle at the so-called car park and walk 10 miles to the first of 1,000 checkpoints. You wave your passport at some soldier who can't see it because of the fumes. You only know he's waved you through because you're still alive and choking. At least, you think you're still alive: there is so much sulphur in the air you could be anywhere.

Next you walk another 50 miles to this upmarket cross between a Bedouin camp and a car-boot sale made up of containers which look as though they have fallen off the backs of lorries which died in the no-man's-land without ever catching a glimpse of their promised land. There are sheets of corrugated iron, plastic tablecloths and the craziest collection of chairs you've ever seen apart from those in the Great Mosque in Istanbul. But they're not for

sitting on: sit on them and you'll be there for ever. They
are there to torment you. Four of the containers are open.
Inside each is a battered table and about six more chairs.
On each one of these sits a soldier, barely able to stand
because of the bullet-proof jacket he's wearing, not to
mention the rifle he is casually waving around.

Years of experience dragging yourself around the world
tells you immediately what to do. You wait outside the
container with the longest queue. Because you instinctively know that the guys with the shortest queues are
either the slowest and most inefficient or the fastest and
the most efficient. Either way, it's not worth the risk. You'll
either be through in ten seconds flat or you'll be in jail for
the rest of your life.

So I joined the longest queue. Now, I'm not saying it was
vast, it's just that, for the first time in my life, I realised how
long Charlton Heston must have kept his hands in the air for
all the Jews to cross the Red Sea. And they didn't have to
worry about visas and passports and rubber stamps and
things. For the next two and a half weeks or thereabouts, as
I shuffled in the heat and fumes and dust and sulphur slowly
closer and closer to the head of the queue, I found I could
think of only one thing: how come, if it's so dangerous here
that all the soldiers are dripping with bullet-proof vests and
dirty great guns, am I just being left to stand like a lemon in
the open air with nothing to protect me from God knows
what but a reinforced cardboard British passport? I mean,
shouldn't it be the other way round? The soldiers are trained
for shooting and killing. We're not. They're all inside their
cosy little containers. We're not. They've got guns to protect
themselves. We haven't. No wonder more civilians are killed
in wars nowadays than soldiers. Yet here we are, all... The
door of one of the other cabins suddenly bursts open.
Through it comes this burly guy with a huge black beard,
screaming at the top of his voice.

'What's the matter with you? I'm a Palestinian! I've been detained by the Israelis three times. If you don't want me to come in, just tell me. I'll go back to Paris, to New York, to anywhere. But I tell you' – he started hammering on the sides of the cabin – 'I'm not going to put' – now he was surrounded by a group of soldiers 'put, put, put...'. And he was bundled back inside the cabin.

A bishop (or a monsignor, or perhaps even a cardinal, at any rate, somebody flashing a crimson front, a bald head and a cross) suddenly comes round the corner. Instinctively we all shuffle closer together. There's no way anyone is going to let him push in, bishop, monsignor, cardinal or whoever he is. He stands there, deciding which of the four queues to join. What was his infallible judgement? He joined ours, the longest. Which obviously proves something or other.

Two days later, I'm standing in front of the desk of this teenage soldier who quite clearly doesn't have any scruples. He is banging and crashing around and throwing his Kalashnikov all over the place. If the damn thing goes off, I'm thinking, I won't have any scruples, either. He grabs my passport. 'You from. . .' he mutters.

'Israel,' I say, giving him my British passport.

'Business? Tourist?'

'Business. Tourist,' I repeat. You can never be certain what's the right thing to say, especially with a Kalashnikov pointing directly at your valuables.

'You go to Gaza?'

Where the hell does he think I'm going? Paris? New York? Rome?'

'Yes, Gaza,' I reply weakly.

He then tries to write my name, my passport number and the inside measurement of my left leg on a loose, dirty bit of paper which you just know is never, ever going to see the light of day. I mean, let's be honest. If you're a terrorist, you're hardly likely to try to get into Palestine, are you? And especially not by the front door. In fact you could say that Palestine is the last country in the world which should worry about security, because if they don't know what's going on, we've all got problems. Finally he hands my passport back to me. He hasn't even bothered to stamp it.

Now the adventure continues. You get out of the container. Immediately you are rocked back on your heels by the heat and the fumes. Things are now so bad that you can't tell where the bishop, cardinal or whoever's shirt ends and his face begins. You feel that the next time he reads the Book of Exodus it will take on a whole new meaning for him. I head for the next scrabble of buildings shimmering like a mirage in the distance.

A taxi draws up. See, I told you the whole place was designed by taxi-drivers. 'For you, sir, I take you,' a bald-headed man with a greasy shirt and toothy grin hisses at me. I get in and he takes me for a ride. Yard for yard, minute for minute, it is the most expensive taxi journey I've ever had in my life. But what was I going to do? Die of the heat in the middle of no-man's-land and be pummelled into the dust by one container lorry after another? We'll see what you do if you ever have to take the decision.

As I climb out he waves his bald head at me. 'The other drivers,' he says, 'how much they charge you?'

'I haven't used any other driver. You're the only. . .' I begin to stammer defensively.

'No, no.' He pushes his head out of the car. 'To the border. Not here. To the border.'

'About three and a half shekels,' I say, knowing full well that it was about $103^1/_2$ shekels.

'Pah!' He spits on the sand. 'Thieves. I'll call the police. You stay. . .'

The taxi spun round on a shekel and he was off into the distance.

I turned, panting, and dragged myself the remaining 37¹/₄ miles to the final checkpoint. Another queue, more soldiers. But these ones looked as if they knew how to use their Kalashnikovs. More forms, more questions, and a new factor: long, hard, penetrating stares, as if they didn't believe a word I was saying. But at least it was something different. Then another long walk, another security check, and finally, welcome to the sovereign independent state of Palestine.

Which, of course, is no more real than the Palestine International Airport. All the Israelis have done with their land-for-peace programme is to give the Palestinians within the state of Israel what they call a Palestinian canton – the Gaza Strip, 150 square miles of nothing inhabited by 800,000 people, or rather, 70 per cent of it is. The Israelis control what's left: about fifteen tiny Jewish settlements of around 4,000 people, and, 60 miles away, Jericho, 25 square kilometres of flame trees, jasmine, palm trees, bougainvillaea and 21,000 people. They told them to be good boys and get on and run the place. Linking the two are four strictly defined road corridors. Which one is to be used is decided on a day-by-day basis. By the Israelis. Leaving one area, the Palestinians have to have their exit permits time-stamped. Entering another, they have to have them stamped again. Again by the Israelis. Which, to me, is super-clever Machiavellian politics.

Before, the Palestinians wanted their homeland – or wanted their homeland back, depending on which way you read the Balfour Declaration. To the Palestinians, of course, it was the work of the Devil himself, if not worse. Even today, over eighty years later, Balfour Declaration Day is still marked by strikes among Palestinians all over Israel. To me it was a Zion of the times: under pressure from a group of admittedly very powerful European Jews, who, after years on the move, decided they wanted to go home, Balfour caved in, completely ignoring the fact the Palestinians had been around a mere 3,000 years, and virtually promised to hand over the land they had dominated for longer than either the Christians or the Jews. Or, as Arthur Koestler wrote, 'One country solemnly promised to another the country of a third.' Or, to put it even less politely, one country promised to steal a country from another people and give it to someone else.

Now, I'm no expert on anything, as my wife keeps reminding me, but I seem to remember that Theodor Herizel, the founder of political Zionism, wasn't even particularly interested in Israel. He was quite happy to go to Uganda until some of his more influential followers talked him out of it. But talk to Israelis today, and even though they still light twelve torches around his grave and let off fireworks to mark the anniversary of his death, somehow they seem to have forgotten that little detail.

Not far behind Balfour on the Palestinian hate list comes not Mrs Thatcher, for a change, but the United Nations, which, of course, today comes not just occupying all the best seats in all the best restaurants in town but also bearing all kinds of gifts – aid, assistance, development and study tours around the world on all and every subject under the sun. But few forget that it was the UN, way back in November 1947, who decided to split the Palestinians' homeland into Jewish and Arab states. Jerusalem was to be an international city. The Jews, of course, agreed. Why wouldn't they? The Palestinians, of course, disagreed. The rest, as they say, is history, or rather, yesterday's headlines. The Israelis had all the problems, they say, of containing and controlling the Palestinians. Now they've given them back some of their own land, they are hailed as peacemakers. The Palestinians are trapped into accepting whatever land they are offered, because even though deep down they know it means finally accepting the fact they've lost the struggle against Zionism, there is no way they can turn down the offer of running their own show and, of course, being responsible for hunting down, controlling, or even eliminating their own gunmen.

To the Israelis, of course, the Palestinian state is not a state at all. It's merely a patch of dust run by the so-called Palestinian National Authority, which is totally under their thumb. They can close the borders at will. When I was there, for example, the border was, depending on who you talked to, closed, partially closed or strictly regulated. Either way, the Israelis were only letting through Palestinians who were over thirty years old, married and who had a job to go to in Israel. The Palestinians said that this was because, while the Israelis had given them a patch of dust to call their own, they wanted to make certain they didn't have the wherewithal, in other words the cash, to make it work. The Israelis said, 'My life, what do you expect? Two Palestinian suicide bombers have just killed fifty-nine of our people. What would you do in the circumstances?' Or words to that effect. Which presumably means that, in their eyes, any Palestinian under thirty, and unmarried, with no job to go to, is obviously a potential suicide bomber.

Whoever is right or wrong, the fact of the matter is that, with barely a trickle of Palestinians working in Israel, nobody is bringing home the bacon. If one is allowed to say that. One official in the Ministry of Finance in Gaza City told me that every day the border was either closed, partially closed or strictly regulated, Palestine was losing US$5 million. Which, of course, they could barely afford. Other officials have even more sinister theories. Another high-up in the ministry (I could tell he was high up – he could close the door to his office. He didn't, though. Closing it would have attracted too much attention, he said) was convinced it was all part of an elaborate game the Israelis were playing.

'Look,' he reasoned, 'the Israelis have got to pretend they want peace. They don't, but they've got to pretend they do. Because of the US, world opinion etc. etc. What they are doing, therefore, is giving us some land, making us responsible for it and making us responsible for policing it, because they know that whatever they give us, under whatever terms, we can't say no. But what they are not giving us is the opportunity to make it work. I mean' – he waved his arms across the window of his office – 'how can you build a country when you have no money in the bank and sixty per cent unemployment?'

He slumped back in his chair. 'In the old days the Israelis, whatever they said, needed us because we did all the run-of-the-mill jobs in Israel. We were the farm labourers, the builders, the decorators, the cleaners, the taxi-drivers. Now they are replacing us with Russians and Ukrainians and everybody else from Eastern Europe. They are even bringing in people from Sudan and Ethiopia. They say they are Jews. They might be Jews, I don't know. I don't care. But before they are Jews, they are cheap labour. They are doing the job we used to do and earning the money we used to earn.'

Whatever the subtleties, to the Palestinians in the street the patch of dust is Palestine, their homeland, somewhere they can call their own. Whatever the legalities, whatever the politics, whatever the Israelis say. As a result, they are busy rushing around doing all the things a sovereign independent state would do: flying their flag all over the place, issuing their own green and gold passports, scattering diplomats around the world, issuing licences and permits and number-plates for whatever they can think of, collecting VAT and income tax, setting up their own education and health services, issuing postage stamps. The day they issued their first postage stamp, I was told, Yasser

Arafat turned up to stick it on the first Palestinian envelope and put it into the first Palestinian postbox. But after he left they had to take it out of the Palestinian postbox, put it in another envelope and stick an Israeli stamp on it before bunging it back in the box again.

So what about Yasser Arafat? To the Israelis he is just the chairman of their artificial creation, the Palestine National Authority. To Yasser himself, he is simply, as his favourite radio station, the Voice of Palestine, hails him practically non-stop day and night, 'His Excellency, His Greatness, His Goodness, the Hero of all his Peoples, Our Hero, Our Leader, Our Protector sent by God to Earth to save his people'. No prizes for guessing why it's his favourite radio station.

I met one Palestinian businessman in a back-street bar in Gaza City who claimed he could read Yasser Arafat's moods by the way he folds the tablecloth over his head. If he folds it so that it comes over his right shoulder and his head looks like the shape of Palestine you see on a map, it means he's being presidential, a world statesman, a man of power. All you need to do is just call him Mr President. If he folds it so that it comes over his left shoulder, it means he's the party politician, the schemer, the manoeuvrer. You'd better call him His Greatness and His Goodness as well. If he folds it neither one way nor the other, call him everything you can think of, because it might just be one of those days. If he doesn't wear it at all, don't call him anything, just run for cover. To you and me, the top of his head might look like the Dome of the Rock in Jerusalem, but to insiders who know about this kind of thing, apparently it means you're on your way to Inner Mongolia as the first Palestinian plenipotentiary for the region. You have been warned.

One man who didn't read the signs too accurately was, I am pleased to say, a Frenchman, the chairman of one of their giant semi-state companies. Not only did he see His Excellency, His Greatness, His Goodness, the Hero of all his Peoples, Our Hero, Our Leader, Our Protector Sent by God to Earth to save his people, without his tablecloth, he went and blabbed to the French press afterwards about being kept waiting fifteen hours for an audience during which, he said, he was not only hugged by a sick and drugged old man but also kissed on the lips a number of times. The result? Oh joy of joys, they lost a whole string of contracts they had been working on for years to put in some basic infrastructure, if not actually to begin to modernise Gaza City.

Indeed, not to put too fine a point on it, Gaza City, not to mention the whole of the Gaza Strip, is 140 square miles of complete and utter disaster. There's no electricity, no water, no sewage system. There's hardly a building with the full complement of simple things like walls and ceilings and doors and windows. Even the Bank of Palestine looks as if it is more than a few tellers' windows short of Bank of England recognition. Which goes to prove either how many bricks and stones were thrown around during all the troubles, or that afterwards they couldn't be bothered to pick up all the free building materials in the streets and use them to repair their homes and shops and offices. You laugh? In the Netherlands I've been on trains full of Dutch football hooligans who take their own bricks and stones to throw at matches and go around collecting them up again afterwards so that they won't damage the environment.

What few roads there are are so full of pot-holes and cesspits that it's like driving through New York on a good day. To protect people from falling into them, most are lined with reel upon reel of barbed wire. Those which are not contain either wrecked cars, forming instant rough-and-ready car-repair workshops, or old men down on their hands and knees saying their prayers. Presumably praying that the car will have a few more days of life left in it. I can't imagine they are appealing for tickets to see the Egyptian belly dancer doing her stuff in a tent on Gaza Beach on Thursday nights, but you never know.

A new seaport, one of the first things the Palestinians built on their return, and which was supposed to establish Gaza as the number one Mediterranean gateway to the whole of the Arab hinterland, has already collapsed and been given an armed guard. Which, I was told, is unusual: in Palestine today most things are given an armed guard and *then* they collapse. The Palestinians say that the Israelis stopped the necessary quotas of cement from coming in, so obviously the port collapsed. The Israelis say that the necessary amount of cement didn't come in because, after all the essentials had been taken care of, there wasn't enough money left to pay for the damned stuff.

Again because of the Israeli blockade, there are hardly any jobs, apart from a bit of farming. Hence the Israeli jibe, 'There is nothing but vegetables in the Gaza Strip.' One morning, as I was coming out of the White House government building off Omar Mukhtar Street, built by Nasser when he was president of Egypt, one of the officials told me they had just advertised for a cleaner. Over 10,000 people applied, many of them doctors, lawyers and accountants.

There are some people, however, making money. The guys running the coffee bars, especially on Thursday nights, the eve of the Muslim sabbath, which seems to be the time everybody wants to get married. The old ladies in charge of the Donald Duck slides you see all over town. The manager of the new Summerland Leisure Complex which has sprung up opposite the Shati refugee camp. The guys behind the Regency Palace on the seafront, where everything is West, West, West. The food, the drinks, the music. Even the women, in their tight, fancy dresses who, by order of the management, have to be either your daughter, your niece or some other member of your family. But the real big hitters, I reckon, are the guys arranging meetings with Hamas guerillas, deadly rivals of His Excellency Yasser Arafat, His Greatness, His Goodness, the Hero of all His Peoples, Our Hero, Our Leader, Our Protector sent by God to Earth to save his people. I lost count of the number of people who sidled up to me in the street, in offices and even in government buildings and asked me if I wanted to meet a real, live Hamas guerilla. Prices ranged from US$50 way up to US$250. Guns and assorted weaponry was extra. But in the end, nothing came of it – not because I refused, but because as soon as the mysterious go-betweens realised that however much I might look like a smooth Italian television journalist, I wasn't one, they lost interest. And when they saw that I didn't have so much as an old-fashioned Box Brownie to record the event, that was it. They were off on their donkeys looking for other smooth international journalists to help.

Before he too did a Red Rum, one fixer I met, by the only set of traffic lights in the entire Gaza Strip, did tell me that the previous week he had arranged for a photographer from *Paris Match*, a lady, to take pictures of a whole bunch of guerillas. The problem was, she wanted them all wearing masks and carrying guns and ammunition, and there wasn't enough to go round. The only solution was to hire a bundle of guns from the Army for the afternoon. Which, of course, he did.

In spite of so much initiative, unemployment is still 50, 60, think-of-a-figure per cent. GNP per capita is £400, £390, £380 and falling rapidly – about 25 per cent of whatever it is comes from what few Palestinians have, or rather had, jobs. Except, of course, the donkeys. Most of them look as though they have been working practically non-stop since His Excellency Yasser Arafat, His Greatness, His Goodness, the Hero of all his Peoples, Our Hero, Our Leader, Our Protector sent by God to

Earth to save his people last had a clean shave. And I mean working. Some donkeys I saw were shifting by themselves whole loads that had arrived on the backs of huge Mercedes and Volvos and Iveco trucks.

And as if that were not enough, His Excellency Yasser Arafat, His Greatness, His Goodness, the Hero of all his Peoples etc. has decreed that there must be no booze, either. Although if you promise me that I will never, ever be on the receiving end of one of His Honour, His Great Excellency, Mr President's great slobbery kisses, I could be persuaded to divulge the name of the restaurant on the left-hand side three blocks down from the traffic lights which does a mean fruit punch.

In fact the city seems to be held together purely by all the President Yasser Arafat posters all over the place: President Yasser Arafat in his red tablecloth; President Yasser Arafat with, behind him, receding into the distance, the Dome of the Rock in Jerusalem; President Yasser Arafat in his immaculately pressed khakis and toothy grin; President Yasser Arafat kissing some poor guy to death. But, honestly, whatever the poster, they're all dreadful. I know it's probably treason to say so, but you have to admit that His Excellency, His Greatness, His Goodness, the Hero of all his Peoples, Our Hero, Our Leader, Our Protector sent by God to Earth to save his people is not, perhaps, the most beautiful of Allah's creatures at the best of times, and these posters make him look so bad you wouldn't be surprised if you learned they had been created by a Mossad double agent. In the dark, with one hand tied behind his back. The wrong hand. I don't know about spending money on big international airports that don't exist, but His Excellency, His Greatness, His Goodness etc. should get himself a decent portrait-painter. Somebody who can do him justice, like Francis Bacon. Or maybe Damien Hirst.

But if there is one thing you see even more of on the

streets of Gaza City than posters of His Excellency, His Greatness, His Goodness etc., it's policemen. All types of them. There are the blue-uniformed regular police in their battered Chevies, with their rusty old Kalashnikovs and old-fashioned walkie-talkies who, many people say, are the old khaki-clad Palestine Liberation Army. The number of shambling old policemen I saw who could hardly stand up made me wonder.

Then there is the General Security Force, the secret police, who are easy to spot because they are all tough-looking guys, neatly groomed, clean shoes, leaning against walls or walking aimlessly up and down. They are also the only guys who know where anything is. Believe me, whenever I got lost and I needed help, I always asked the nearest smart-looking guy. He always knew where I wanted to go better than I did myself. He also spoke immaculate English.

Next there is the Civil Defence Corps, which is called the Civil Defence Corps because there is no way the Israelis are going to let the Palestinians have a full-scale army of their own. There is no navy either, but that hasn't stopped them from having a coastal police force. However, seeing as it is based in Nablus, about 50 kilometres from the sea, I wouldn't worry about it too much.

The hardest hit Palestinians of all, I reckon, are, as always, the women. There is obviously such a desperate shortage of that dull, miserable, grey material they used as headscarves and to wrap around their faces that many of them are going around not only bareheaded but even walking side by side along the street with – oh, shock, horror – dirty great blokes with beards. A few, I couldn't help but notice, were even laughing and giggling, which must mean that all the men they go around with are their husbands.

Yet in spite of all the shortages and hardships and posters of His Excellency, His Greatness, His Goodness, the

Hero of all his Peoples, Our Hero, Our Leader, Our Protector sent by God to Earth to save his people, Palestinians are flocking back home from all over the world. From Tunis, from Amman, from Cairo. From Baghdad, Tripoli, Khartoum, even from San'a in Yemen. Policemen, deportees, bureaucrats, doctors, engineers, bankers, all of whom want to help establish and run their own country. So once they get going, they're going to roll. After all, these guys know how to run countries. Like the Lebanese, their elder brothers in terms of both making money and wielding power, they are already running plenty of other countries around the world, especially in the Gulf.

Talking of running countries, forget all this stuff about Palestine being a democracy. At the heart of the decision-making process is the sprawling civil administration compound, home to 7,000 civil servants, and the low, long, white-painted Presidency on the beach, protected by a couple of rolls of barbed wire, some iron gates and a single light armoured vehicle, which was originally going to be the Palestinian police headquarters, then the Palestinian Television Centre, before it was seized by His Excellency Yasser Arafat for his Presidency.

In the compound – where, incidentally, nobody had ever heard of PECDAR, the Palestine Economic Council for Development and Reconstruction, let alone could give me any information or details about it – the 7,000 civil servants toil long and hard to build their country, while in the Presidency, which has aerials on it the size of the Eiffel Tower, His Excellency Yasser Arafat, His Greatness, His Goodness, the Hero of all his Peoples, Our Hero, Our Leader, Our Protector sent by God to Earth to save his people goes around brilliantly doing what he is best at: creating even more chaos and confusion out of what is already a totally chaotic and confused situation by not only issuing non-stop a string of orders, edicts and decrees and countermanding them as soon as they are issued, but also by completely ignoring or flatly contradicting everything the civil servants come up with. While this is going on, of course, the rest of the country tries to survive as best it can.

In the so-called Ministry of Finance one old recently returned civil servant reminisced, with tears welling in his eyes, that twenty-seven years ago, when he had last been here, Gaza had been like England. The thud of leather on willow, old maids cycling to early-morning communion, green country lanes, beautiful houses, everything neat and tidy. Now, he said, it was a complete mess. I agreed – although I didn't know whether he was talking about Gaza or England. On the way out, I met the director of his department, another recent returnee, this time from the States. He told me in confidence that all the senior civil servants were complaining that His Excellency, His Greatness, His Goodness, the Hero of all his Peoples, Our Hero, Our Leader, Our Protector sent by God to Earth to save his people spent so much time travelling that on one or two recent occasions he had narrowly missed colliding with himself.

Yet things are happening. The big prison in the centre of town, the old British-built district headquarters, has been painted a gleaming, shining, white. Brand-new barbed wire has been positioned on top. The police headquarters you can hardly get into. I don't know about three o'clock in the morning, but it's certainly jam-packed all day long with BMWs and Mercedes and the big Peugeot 504s. All stolen, of course. Not by the police – that would be illegal. They've been stolen by other people and merely bought by the police in what is probably the second-most successful business set up and run by the Palestinians. I only discovered this when, early one morning, I was driving through Gaza City (in a battered old Peugeot, I hasten to add) and the driver suddenly swerved and pulled over on the side of the road. Not because he had spotted an Israeli car or truck - as Palestinians still instinctively do, even though they are the masters now in their own homeland, at least, in theory - but because he wanted to show me something.

'Quick! There,' he whispered, pointing to a row of BMWs and Mercedes lined up in the shade behind a crumbling brick building. 'Stolen cars.'

'So what building is that?' I asked.

'The police headquarters.'

'You mean they've caught the people responsible?'

'No.' He shook his head. 'They are for the police themselves. They have no cars. The only way they can get cars is from Israel. They must have stolen them last night and driven them across the border this morning.'

'Even though the border is closed?'

'Even though the border is closed.'

'But how come? I thought the Israelis...'

'Money.' His face creased up into a million different lines and wrinkles. 'Money.'

On the basis that no desperately poor country can possibly hope to survive without a string of luxury cars, somebody had obviously set up a Robin Hood business in BMWs and Mercedes and everything else between Israel and Gaza. Some people say it's your ordinary everyday wheeler-dealers, others that it's the Mafia - the Israeli Mafia. A few even say it's Hamas. In a whisper, of course, and very quickly. Whoever it is, somebody is lifting luxury cars from rich Israelis and virtually giving them to poor - well, not so rich - Palestinian policemen, politicians, civil servants and anybody else who can afford the price. New BMWs, for example, you can pick up for less than US$2,000. In cash, naturally. Mitsubishis are going for around US$1,500, depending on the colour, Volvos about the same. Mercedes, amazingly for only US$1,000. I thought this was because the logo looks a bit like the Star of David, but apparently it is because there are so many of them around they no longer have a rarity value.

And it's not just the police headquarters that is taking deliveries. The following day the Presidency, I noticed, was also jam-packed with BMWs and all kinds of other vehicles which do about $2^1/_2$ miles to the gallon, including the enormous armoured bullet-proof Mercedes which His Excellency Yasser Arafat, His Greatness, His Goodness, the Hero of all his Peoples, Our Hero, Our Leader, Our Protector sent by God to Earth to save his people used for protection when he first arrived to be welcomed as the great liberator of his people. Parked by the first of the security check-ins was another one of those light armoured gun carriages which had also clearly been lifted from somewhere. Probably from Lawrence of Arabia, judging by the condition it was in.

Apart from at the main government offices, you can see that some money from somewhere is being spent. Not on important things like luxury cars, but on frivolous things like floors being added to health clinics and surgeries. Youth clubs, I was told, have also suddenly found themselves in possession of all the sports equipment they require. An indoor sports stadium is under construction. Which again, a number of people whispered to me (it's amazing the amount of whispering that goes on in Palestine nowadays) was the work not of His Excellency Yasser Arafat, His Greatness, His Goodness, etc., but of his deadly rivals, Hamas. Why? Because they want everybody to see that they can deliver what Arafat can't. And also because it is a very clever way of softening up the market and recruiting new members to the cause.

One evening I was on my way to the Palestine Hotel,

which is along by the beach, when quite by chance, in the side streets behind the Islamic University – I could tell it was a university, because all the graffiti was pretty illegible – I stumbled across what I thought at first was a prayer meeting. Rows and rows of chairs were spread out across the middle of the street and all around them were bearded young men waving and jumping around and slapping each other on the hands and on the shoulders. Which, I guessed, might either be their traditional *dabka* dance or some preparations for the imminent death of any infidel who stumbled however innocently into their midst. Prayer mats were scattered around, and a few people, again mostly young men, were still sitting earnestly on some of them, deep in prayer. It turned out to be an Islamic rap concert organised by the local branch of Hamas.

One of the bearded young men who was waving and jumping about came up to me, gave me a bottle of sweet mango juice, which I noticed came from Egypt (it didn't seem to be the occasion to be seen to be drinking anything that came from America) and offered me a cigarette. They were Israelis.

'I thought you weren't allowed to smoke Israeli cigarettes,' I hollered above the noise.

'That was during the *intifada*,' he shouted back at me. 'It's all right now.' He waved a packet in front of me. 'Now we smoke these.' He pushed the packet in front of my nose. I could see they were Time cigarettes. 'Know why we smoke those?' He danced around. He punched each letter in turn. 'This Is My End,' he shrieked, and disappeared into the crowd.

Once I'd finished with the mango juice I did what everybody else did. I threw it on top of a pile of rubbish outside the nearest building. A little boy ran straight out of the door, grabbed it and ran straight back inside again. Within ten seconds it was probably full of petrol with a rag sticking out of the top. Old habits, I suppose, die hard.

What kind of swinging Islamic rap songs do they sing at concerts organised by the local branch of Hamas in the back streets of Gaza City? 'Our country is occupied. Our people are handcuffed. We will shed a waterfall of blood to be free.' Yes, well, the words might not be exactly, how should I put it, catchy, but the rhythm certainly was. Islamic rap, I was informed, was big business not only in Gaza but also in Israel itself, where apparently many Jewish families are innocently serenading each other behind locked doors with treacly lyrics such as, 'It doesn't matter how long the Israelis have trampled us in the dust, we will have our revenge.'

What's the top of the Paletinian pops? Some song called 'For a Peaceful Palestine Make Your Wife Wear the Veil', recorded by a group called the Martyrs. I dare you to ask your wife to buy it for you for your next birthday.

Jericho, the other bit of the empire run by His Excellency Yasser Arafat (His Greatness, His Goodness…) is completely different. The world's oldest town – it's been going for practically 3,000 years non-stop – is also the world's lowest town. Geographically, I mean, not morally or anything else. It is a staggering 400 metres below sea-level. The journey to Jericho from Jerusalem, which is about 800 metres above sea-level, not only sets the old ears popping, it also gets the perspiration flowing in bucketfuls. For you can generally reckon that it is always 10 degrees hotter there than it is in Jerusalem. How on earth all those guys had the energy to wade across the River Jordan, march on the city, blow their trumpets for seven days non-stop and sing all those songs, goodness only knows. The reason the Israelis gave for handing it to His Excellency Yasser Arafat was that it wouldn't take him seven days to destroy the place – he could do it in two or three.

Most people get there nowadays by taking the big, new

highway out of Jerusalem. I reached it by the small, old road through the mountains and across the desert, which was much more fun. Now, I'm not the world's greatest expert on deserts, although I've done a few in my time, but this one, I can tell you, is real desert: bleak, empty, desolate hills and valleys that go on for mile after mile after mile. It's also, as you would expect, very Biblical. You are constantly coming across Israeli patrols, huge Israeli trucks with trailers the size of landing strips moving enormous chunks of Israeli military hardware around, for peaceful purposes, naturally, and, of course, a million Israeli roadblocks. Dustbin roadblocks, dirty-great-chunks-of-concrete roadblocks, precarious-bits-of-wood roadblocks, single-lane roadblocks, double-lane roadblocks. Just-look-at-me-and-I'll-shoot roadblocks. Roadblocks with flags, roadblocks without flags. One day, if I live long enough, so help me, I shall write a thesis on the history and development of the Israeli roadblock and the Jewish problem.

You can also, if one of the roadblocks is not obscuring the view, see Bethany, Lazurus's home town, on the western slopes of the Mount of Olives, and the Inn of the good Samaritan, passing by on the other side of the road as everybody else does. I did suggest to the driver we broke down to see if anyone would stop and rescue us, put me up at the American Colony Hotel in Jerusalem for the rest of my life and pay all the bills without complaining, but he was against the idea. Probably because he was Palestinian, and he knew that the last thing a Palestinian would do would be stop his car on an empty road in the middle of nowhere with Israeli security forces wandering around all over the place. He wouldn't even take the turn off to Nebi Musa, where Moses is buried, nor the long,winding road down a steep canyon to St George's Monastery, which Elijah popped into on his way to the Sinai, so I suppose the least you could say was that he wasn't prejudiced. It was a pity, though, because the monastery actually claims to have the tomb of St George, and, given that everybody says he never existed, I was quite looking forward to seeing what he didn't look like.

Jericho, when we finally got there, was a revelation. It's a pretty little town, full of trees and fruit and lots of greenery. A bit tatty at the edges, although nowhere near as bad as Gaza City. In fact, compared to Gaza City it is paradise. They have electricity and running water. Indeed, for the last 7,000 years their running water has been gushing out of the Ein Sultan Spring nearby at the rate of 4,500 litres a minute. The houses have roofs and doors and windows. The shops have things to sell, including alcohol, which at first surprised me because I thought that like Gaza, it would be dry. I tasted their own local home-made beer made in the heart of the West Bank in a village called Delicious and it proved that the Palestinians are interested in brewing up more than conflicts and disagreements. It was fantastic. It probably explains why the only thing Jericho doesn't have is cars. It's the only place I've been in the Middle East which seems to rely practically solely on bicycles. But as they all call their bicycles their Mercedes, it doesn't seem to trouble them, and they can drink as much Delicious as they like.

To the Americans, of course, all of this is too modern and up to date, about 3,000 years ahead of the times. A bunch of them have moved into Jericho in the belief that it is the only place on earth where they can live the Old Testament life. They go around in long white cloaks. Some wear sackcloth. The children wear headdresses. They live in shacks and dilapidated old buildings that the Arabs wouldn't even keep their cattle in. But they're happy and it keeps them off the streets, so why not?

The Americans apart, the number-one attraction is the guest house, or rather mini-hotel, of His Excellency Yasser

Arafat, which is kept permanently ready in case he decides to pop in at a moment's notice. What was it before? A home for the handicapped. I'm not saying a word.

His Greatness, however, rarely does seem to drop in. Partly because, I was told, there's too much to do in Gaza City. Partly because of all the hassles involved driving or even flying to Jericho. But nobody seemed too worried one way or the other.

Very much the number-two attraction is the two-storey building which is home to the Voice of Palestine, the radio station that started all this stuff about His Greatness, His Goodness, the Hero of all his Peoples and all the rest of it. The trouble was nobody seemed to know where it was. Either that, or everybody I asked was a fully paid-up undercover member of Hamas. However, as you would expect, posters of His Greatness, His Goodness, the Hero of all his Peoples, Our Hero, Our Leader, Our Protector sent by God to Earth to save his people were everywhere. At a guess I would say that here they even outnumbered the policemen. I tried counting the ones on display around the tiny village square, but there were so many of them and it was so hot that I gave up and went and had another Delicious instead.

Afterwards, seeing as I was in the mood for ruins, I decided to take in Hisham's Palace on the outskirts of town, which dates back to the fifth century. Started but never finished, presumably because of an Israeli blockade, it covers maybe 4 acres and is all properly excavated and laid out. One day you can see it becoming quite a tourist attraction. I'd certainly go there again.

Seeking refreshment I plunged into a tiny, dark shop which seemed to be run by a little girl who couldn't have been more than eight or nine years old. But she handled everything. She knew all the prices, brought the drinks to the table, served them, collected the money and gave me the change as if for all the world she was running the Ritz and I was one of the regulars, which obviously meant that even at that age she'd been trained as a Mossad agent.

I reckon Jericho of all places should give into temptation and start blowing its own trumpets. It's a wonderful little place to visit. It has all the history and more that any town could wish for. It has plenty of places to see. On top of that, visitors would help bring in some desperately needed revenue. Unfortunately, at present it has only one Temptation Café and thirty-eight hotel rooms, most of which are occupied pretty much all the time. By cockroaches.

Getting into Jericho might have been difficult but getting out should have been easy enough, even if Goliath didn't manage it because of some kid and a catapult. But of course it wasn't. My Palestinian driver started getting all temperamental. I wanted to visit the most tempting place on earth: the Mount of Temptation, where Christ was tempted twice by the Devil, but no sooner had we got out of town than he decided he was going to lead me not into Temptation, the Mount of. Something, he said, to do with the heat, the air-conditioning going on the blink and the monks in the monastery on the site being against visitors. Which I didn't believe for one second. I reckon he wanted to get back to his Israeli girlfriends in Jerusalem who, he told me, were all over sixty. So I must report, the only place in the world where nobody could possibly feel guilty about being tempted was the one place in the world where I never even got the chance.

In getting out of the Gaza Strip, however, I was sorely tempted many times. To doubt, to despair, and to little things like suicide, murder and mass murder. And even the greatest curse of all: promising to go back and visit them again some time in the future. It is not just a question of all the nonsense the Palestinians put you through before you can get out, it is also the very real threat that at any time the Israelis could close the borders and – zap! – you could be trapped for ever with His Excellency, His Greatness, His Goodness... And when they close the border, they close the border: there ain't nothin' nobody can do about it. At best you could be out again in a couple of weeks; at worst you could end up like His Excellency, His Greatness, His Goodness, growing a beard and spending the rest of your life going around slobbering all over everybody. It is not a pleasant thought, I can tell you. And even if the border is open you could make it and then, taking your very last step on Gaza soil, be killed in the crossfire between Israeli and Palestinian troops. It's happened before, and it will probably happen again.

However, I was, you'll be sorry to hear, lucky. I got to the first checkpoint. The guy manning it looked as though he had just wandered in from one of the Bedouin camps up in the hills. He had a greasy white crocheted skullcap on his head and was playing with his beads. I didn't know whether to interrupt him. In the end, on the basis that discretion is the better part of valour (in other words, he had the gun and I didn't), I waited. And waited and waited and waited until he must have prayed for not only his wives and mothers-in-law and fathers-in-law and seventy-three cousins twice removed but for every Bearded One in the world. Finally, he looked up.

'I am normally man,' he said. Which, in the circumstances, I wasn't going to argue with. 'I say my prayers.'

I smiled weakly. He waved his gun at me. I turned towards the— Gee whizz. A dirty great truck skidded to a halt right beside me. It was so close that had I been breathing out at the time I'd have been a dead man. 'Many, many, many borders,' the driver spat at me between his broken teeth. 'Many, many, many polices.'

I stared at him.

'You get in,' he beamed at me.

As there were no taxis to be seen I climbed in. The alternative was a 6-mile walk to the next checkpoint.

No sooner had I climbed in than he was telling me that he used to own a Mercedes and showing me photographs of it, the way people show you photographs of their wives. Providing they died young. Nobody ever shows you photographs of their wives if they die old. He even showed me the key, which he had sellotaped to one of the photographs, the way people used to sellotape locks of their loved one's hair to their photographs. But on the plus side I was through the Bedouin camp in a flash. Well, a Palestinian flash, which is about twenty-seven minutes. This was partly because this time the soldier could actually write, although he did have trouble finding where to put down my name, age, distinguishing characteristics and passport number on the grubby bit of paper in front of him.

Finally, the last of the 1,000 checkpoints. Only 10 more – cough, cough – miles to go. Still the lorries are belching out their fumes in the broiling heat. Still the trucks are queuing up. Still the... Wait a minute! The Israeli soldiers just on the other side of the border. They seem to be... It looks as though... They can't be, not now. Please not now. Please. Please. I run and leap and skid and stagger.

I'm through. I'm back. I'm in...

Zap. The Israelis close the border. Again.

RIYADH

Hell, I feel awful. I've got this thick head. My eyes feel like sandpaper. My mouth is like the bottom of a birdcage. What's more, I've just caught myself pacing up and down the hotel room trying to work out an easy way to get at the cooling fluid in the fridge. The reason I'm reduced to this pathetic, embarrassing and totally humiliating condition is simple. It's been exactly twenty-seven hours and seventeen and a quarter minutes – no, I tell a lie, it's been exactly thirty-one hours and seventeen and a quarter minutes, I forgot the time difference – since I've had a drink. A real drink, I mean. Not this melon frappé stuff I've been forcing down me for the last twenty-nine hours and seventeen and a quarter minutes.

Saudi Arabia, let me tell you, is not my kind of country. Neither is it my liver's kind of country. However, so that there can be no possible misunderstanding, I would like to say straight away that, by the Grace of Allah, although I am not a Muslim, I respect the Muslim faith, every Muslim that has ever lived, and all those who sail in her. As far as I'm concerned, even though the Americans dismiss Saudi Arabia as a 'camel-oriented country' (this is no joke – I saw it in an economic report in the US Embassy), I fully support the Saudis, everything they think, everything they say and everything they do.

Good. Now that's out of the way – you can never be too

sure, you know, when you're dealing with the Saudis – I'll tell you what I really think about the country. I think it's about as exciting as a plastic cup of lukewarm orange juice.

Scenery? Sure, it's got scenery. It's got desert, about 2 million square miles of the stuff. About half of that is the so-called Empty Quarter, the Rub' Al-Khali, which Thesiger keeps on about. So-called because, thanks to Thesiger and his going around reciting whole passages of the Koran from memory and discussing Ethelred the Unready with a Ma'dan sheikh, it's now crawling with German, French and American tourists, all sitting comfortably in their huge air-conditioned, luxury Mercedes trucks wearing their whoopy-do look-at-me-I'm-an-explorer jackets and waving their towels all over the place. Not even the Bedouin, I was told, want to go there any more. Not because of the tourists, but because of Thesiger. They're frightened that if he sees them he'll latch on to them again, and this time they won't be able to get away so soon.

As for the rest of the country, it's about as many laughs as a Baptist church summer fair. Providing you can get in in the first place, of course. Because you can't just turn up unannounced. You must be invited by somebody in the country. How do you do that if you don't know anybody there? Simple. You get hold of some Saudi company's name, address, telephone and fax number, lean on somebody with a PC and make up a letter-heading for the firm yourself, print it out, crumple it up, type yourself an invitation on it (remembering to include lots of spelling mistakes and bad grammar) and, by the beard of Allah, you're in.

Next you've got to survive the flight. If you think flying into Helsinki is heavy, you should try flying into Riyadh or Jeddah. It's like a rugby club Christmas outing. Everybody is trying to sink as much booze as they can to last them at least two weeks, if not three. A guy from Lancashire who was sitting next to me on one flight was drinking whisky topped up with Drambuie practically non-stop the whole way. Those afraid that they won't be able to sink enough are trying to hide the miniatures wherever they can. And every Saudi woman on the plane is clambering out of her Versace and Armani and Gap and Women's History Network T-shirt or whatever and pulling black robes and veils all over herself.

Watching the passengers disembark must be like watching the arrival of the walking wounded. People are slipping down the steps, slapping each other on the back, shouting and hollering and wandering around all over the airport. Getting past Customs and Immigration takes about as long as it takes to get from London to Saudi in the first place. A word of caution, therefore, if you feel that in spite of everything your life is still worth living. I'm not talking about trying to smuggle in booze inside your toothpaste tube or in a colostomy bag strapped around your body. I'm talking serious stuff. Forget the Marks & Spencer blazer or that cheap Prince of Wales lightweight check thing they do. As soon as they see that they'll take you apart. You might even get the rubber-glove job. Why? Think about it for a moment.

Also be careful how you fill in the forms. Now normally, I admit I'm the last person to take forms seriously. Usually, whenever I fill in an immigration form and they want to know my profession, I put down 'housewife'. Not once have I been stopped, I promise you. But Saudi is different. In Saudi they read everything. The first time I went there I was standing behind some guy who was taking ages to get through. Again and again the immigration man gave him a form to fill in. Again and again he tore it up and gave him a new one. Again and again he filled it in. Again and again the immigration official ripped it up.

Now, you know how reluctant I am to interfere in anything that doesn't concern me, but this was taking hours and I had things to do. Gingerly, I stepped past the red line and asked nervously if there was anything I could do to help. Immediately the immigration official gave me the guy's form. In the time it takes to behead an old man for stealing a loaf of bread, I spotted the problem. There, in the box marked 'Religion', he had written 'Jewish'. In a flash, I grabbed my pen and added 'Christian'. The immigration official snatched back the form, stamped it a million times and we were all through in about ten minutes. You'd have thought the Jewish guy would have been grateful. Instead he went bananas. There was no such thing, he said, as 'Jewish Christian'.

'I know,' I kept telling him. 'I know that. You know that. The immigration guy knows that. But this is Saudi. OK?'

He still wasn't satisfied. He wanted to go back to the guy, would you believe, and explain that it was all a mistake. Next time, I promise, I'll keep quiet.

Now Customs. I've been through a million customs checks in my life, but a Saudi customs check is the only one of its kind in the world. In Lagos, Kinshasa, half of Africa, you know they're only giving you aggro because they are looking for some readies. In Saudi they are doing it because they believe in it. As a result, whether you like it or not, you must open your suitcase and stand there like a schoolboy waiting to have his satchel searched by his mother after he's been away at weekend camp for the first time in his life.

We all know the rules. No alcohol, no drugs, no jazzy magazines. No nothing that looks like it could cause the slightest offence. The guy goes through my suitcase. Clean. He searches my briefcase. Clean. He then wants to look at the bundle of papers and magazines I'm carrying under my arm. I hand them over to him. He lays them out on the bench and starts flicking through them. As I'm busy repacking all my stuff as best I can, I swear on the Koran, he's suddenly screaming and shouting and yelling, 'Obscene!', 'Perfidious!' or something or other. 'A crime against the holy religion of Islam.' I should be thrown in jail and left to rot. I look up as casually as one can in the circumstances. I'm surrounded by policemen. Everybody is staring at me. My sad, pathetic, miserable life begins to flash before me like a grainy old silent movie. What filthy, salacious publication does he push in front of my face? The *Daily Telegraph* I picked up on the plane on the way out. What filthy, salacious photograph has sent him nuclear? Some picture of Princess Di coming out of some nightclub, or perhaps it was a hospital, late at night. It was difficult to tell which by the way she was dressed or, as the customs officer obviously thought, undressed.

All the same I was lucky. I got off with a yellow card. The guy behind me had a couple of boring company videos in his suitcase all about the thrills and excitement of water pumps. The customs men arrested him on the spot, took him into police custody and kept him at the airport until a couple of state high censors had arrived to examine them, frame by frame. He was there practically two days before they finally realised the films were nothing but boring company videos about the thrills and excitement of water pumps.

A whole bunch of Pakistanis, fellow Muslims, don't forget, were getting it a million times worse. They were literally being taken apart, bit by bit. One young guy had a box of brand-new tennis balls. Every one of them they split open. Most of them were carrying bags of fresh fruit of one kind or another. Every single fruit the officials cut up. One poor old man, practically stark naked and as thin as a rake, was carrying a bundle of rags. Every one of them they tore to shreds. They said they were looking for drugs. Pakistan is a major supplier, and if they were going to keep Saudi free of drugs they must do everything they could to stop them coming in.

'But the old man?' I said to one policeman who was looking on.

'Why not?' he said briskly. 'He is the kind of person the drugs organisations would use. We have to do it. We have no other way.'

So now you're in at last, what's the second most important thing you should do as soon as you arrive? Plug yourself into the black market, where a bottle of Johnnie Walker Black Label will cost you as little as US$175 a bottle. Unless, of course, you can talk your way into a different embassy reception every lunchtime and every evening every day of the week or, alternatively, unless you're prepared to drag yourself from one shop to another buying tiny quantities of grape juice, sugar and baker's yeast in each so as not to arouse suspicion, take them home and, deep in the cellar under cover of darkness, brew up some sludge of which you have to knock back at least 3 gallons before you can convince yourself it even begins to taste anything like wine. Taste another half a glass after that and you're dead. If you're really desperate you could do as some Saudis do and make a poor man's *arak*: mix some sweet water with glue, cover the top of the glass to keep the fumes in, then suck it slowly through a straw. A rich man's *arak*? Sweet water with a dash of petroleum jelly. Stir strongly. Say your prayers and prepare to die. It is, I'm told, a killer, but that doesn't stop people from drinking it.

Drinking and driving, as a result, is totally unheard of. First, because if you're forced to drink your own home-made sludge, you're not capable of moving afterwards, let alone driving. Second, because if you are able to find the real stuff and you're stopped, the police will do everything they can to look the other way.

'How do you mean, look the other way?' I asked one particularly jolly expat one evening as we were drinking what was allegedly orange juice in this secret little hide-away I was taken to three streets down from that big building opposite the water tower. For the faint-livered, I can tell you, it was not.

'H'easy,' he said knocking back another one. 'They giff yoo thees freafaleezer. You fat your h-hands hall haround hit. Lika dith.' He bunched both his hands up to his chin. 'You thlow thlike f-mad. F-but, thnot thinto thee bag.' He blew like mad through theese hands, I mean, his hands.

'Thay thlook that thee . . .' A deep breath. Another one of those orange juices. '. . . Thee bag. Thnothin. They thlet thee go. They not thwant throblems.'

As he finished, another equally jolly expat came up to me and told me not to listen to a word he said. It was all a lot of silly expat nonsense. He was just a troublemaker. The Saudi police were very strict. They did stop expats if they thought they had been drinking, and they did give them a breathalyser test. The trouble was that in order to enforce their own strict controls on booze, they had developed a technique for using the bag to make certain they got a far more accurate assessment of how much alcohol anybody had consumed.

'How do you mean?' I wondered, 'Computers? Read-outs? That kind of thing?'

'Even worse,' he said slugging back an orange juice. 'They give you the breathalyser. They make certain you blow through it. Then, to check how much alcohol you've had' – another slug of orange juice – 'they snip the end of the breathalyser and smell your breath coming out the other end. If they can't smell any alcohol, they let you go.'

Oh, sorry, I forgot. The most important thing everybody should do as soon as they arrive? Arrange to leave.

The other thing you have to get used to is prayer times.

Five times a day everybody says their prayers. Around about 4.15 in the morning, 12.30, 4 pm, 7 pm and 8.20 pm, depending on the sun and whatever time it says in the newspapers and on television. In offices and factories work stops and people shuffle across to the company mosque. Forget the Gideon Bible: in every hotel room in the country, there is a prayer mat and a sign pointing you in the right direction. Towards Mecca, that is. In shops and restaurants woe betide you if one of the Mutawa, the religious police, spots you not saying your prayers. They will rap sharply on the window with their long wooden sticks. Not only is this the quickest way I know of getting indigestion, but you could end up either being detained for an hour or two, or worse still being arrested and sent to jail. Innocent or not, nobody will believe you. What the religious police say is gospel, if you see what I mean.

One Muslim I met, told me he had been stopped and arrested many times for not saying his prayers. But so far he had escaped going to jail.

'What, you mean you er, er, cough, cough?' I said.

'No,' he said. 'Every time they stop me, I tell them it's the first time. They can't remember me. We all look the same.'

There is no entertainment. No theatres, no cinemas, not even any churches. They're all forbidden. So there's no way you can even slip away to a Mothers' Union whist drive, let alone a Young Wives' bring-and-buy sale. One poor Filipino was caught a few weeks before my first trip arranging a mass for his fellow countrymen. He was arrested by the police and sentenced to 2,000 lashes, which are apparently being administered fifty at a time at two-week intervals. Oh, Torquemada. Thou shouldst be living at this hour. All the same, in the best traditions of the Counter-reformation, I did discover where mass was being said regularly on a Saturday night. But I'm only prepared to reveal it on receipt of a signed photograph of one of the English martyrs.

About the only form of entertainment I could discover was trying to work out why various photographs in the newspaper had been censored and who had the agency for thick black felt-tip pens, because they were obviously making a fortune.

Princess Di. Sure, I can understand why. Photographs of the occasional ankle, well, maybe. Photographs of various women politicians showing a leg? Depends. Practically life-sized photographs of certain women members of the House of Commons? Almost certainly, yes. Indeed I'd happily pay for the felt-tip pens myself.

But why did the censor do nothing about the reports and photographs of the Porn Hot d'Or Awards at Cannes or a detailed report of another bonkbuster novel about the House of Commons when he completely obliterated Vivien Leigh from the poster of *Gone With the Wind*?

The trouble is, after a while you find you're not reading the newspapers at all. Instead you're spending all your time looking for what's been censored and trying to work out why. That's what Saudi Arabia does to you.

Failing that, the only other ways of enjoying yourself are driving up and down the Corniche looking at all the crazy way-out foreign sculptures, which can only be the product of diseased drug-ridden cultures; sitting on a mat by the side of your car, making tea on a Bunsen burner and watching the tide go in or out; observing a gang of workmen lazily polishing the marble pavements outside any one of a thousand swish, upmarket super-luxury shopping malls; or stuffing yourself in snack bars and coffee shops on circular toasted sandwiches with two perfectly circular fried eggs sitting on top of them, staring at you straight in the eye, which, for some reason, they call Croque Mesdames.

The less financially sophisticated tell me they spend their spare time counting the number of empty buildings being put up everywhere and calculating how much they represent in terms of laundered money from one deal or another being pumped back into the system. But I wouldn't know anything about that kind of thing. As for the non-financially sophisticated, you'll find them hanging around outside the ladies' section of the Riyadh Bank in El Khayyat.

Oh yes, and talking of entertainment there are no women. Anywhere. No secretaries in any of the offices, so busy chatting all day on the telephone that they haven't got any time to make a cup of coffee. No chambermaids in any of the hotels going through your baggage. No nice, polite young ladies hanging around hotel lobbies pushing various services of one kind or another. The only places I came across any women were inevitably the so-called cocktail lounges in the hotels. Except there the women were Shirley Temples (passion fruit, pineapple, a dash of grenadine, topped up with lemonade), Hot Marys (tomato juice, a drop of lemon, Tabasco and Lea & Perrins with a dash of celery salt) and a Cinderella, which I'm sure was orange squash mixed with tap water and served in an old boot, only to be recommended after midnight. If you're desperate. I tried a Paradise instead (orange, grapefruit and Grenadine). Which definitely wasn't.

Now and then you do see these huge black mobile bin-liners waddling down the street. Of course, it would be more than my life is worth to have tried to investigate what was hidden beneath the bin-liner, or *abbaya*, to give it its correct technical name, but I was told on good authority that more often than not they contain a Saudi secret policeman. So if you're not careful they could give you a severe case of the Arabian frights, as opposed to the Arabian nights. I was led to believe that now and then they might even contain a real, live woman. However, I suspect that they have all secretly left the country and are living it up with a bunch of playboys in Marbella or Florida or the south of France, or anywhere but Saudi. The way to tell which is which is, of course, the walk. The great, big, heavy loping gait is a woman. Tiny little mincing steps is a secret policeman.

Not being exactly an expert on women's clothing, I am pleased to pass on, out of academic interest only, the information imparted by a certain lonely little *habibty* with a tiny pair of smouldering almond eyes, a ton of gold on her wrists and an American accent whom I just happened to bump into late one evening while she was spending her Arabian nights wandering forlornly around the El Khayyat shopping centre. Her name I cannot reveal for the sake of my health – even five lashes could do me untold damage. She said that the big black bin-liner is like a choir robe, and that it is usually worn at least three sizes too big. To fix the length, there are a string of tiny bows. To tie it around the head there are still more tiny bows. Over the face goes the veil. On top of that goes the face mask, which is fastened at the back with, would you believe, a bit of Velcro. Over the face mask goes a flap which hides the face completely. In spite of all this, however, she assured me that if the occasion arises, anyone can be out of them and doing their duty in a split second. What type of occasion? Why, when, for example, a secret policeman suddenly spots a subversive Filipino with a prayer book and decides to give chase. What were you thinking of?

Not that I'm against any of these things. In fact, in many ways I think I am more of a Muslin than many Muslims. Not, I hasten to add, that I want four wives. One mother-in-law is more than enough, thank you. But as far as everything else is concerned, I wouldn't knock it.

Alcohol, I think, is wrong. It is the thief, as Shakespeare said somewhere or other, who slips between your lips and steals away your brains. Bars are unlicensed hotbeds of gossip and intrigue where, when you think about it, all you do is buy other people drinks and they never buy you one back. Theatres and cinemas are nothing but avenues for peddling silly stories and stupid ideas. Censorship I can support 100 per cent. Especially if it means banning every single travel book apart from mine. Praying four or five times a day is not a problem, and praying just before your plane takes off is, I think, a brilliant idea. In many ways, on many of the flights I travel on, it's about your only chance of landing at the other end. If I lived in Saudi, my only problem would be limiting it to just five times a day, but presumably one would adjust. As for the way the Saudis treat women, I admit I'm no expert – there are only two occasions on which I don't understand women: before marriage and after marriage – but I completely agree that they should be banned from driving. Look at all the rows and problems it would avoid. No spats about teaching them to drive. No arguments about whose turn is it to use the car. No heart-attacks whey they signal left and turn right. And none of those niggling little discussions you have when you discover that your wife has just driven your brand-new Jag the length of the M4 at 120mph with the handbrake still on. The Saudis, I think, are to be commended for their courage. Long may it continue. But don't, whatever you do, tell the wife I said that, or I'll never hear the end of it. Similarly the veil. I think that's a fantastic idea. There are many women I know who would benefit enormously from having to wear a veil, preferably the one that goes right down to their ankles or, rather, below their ankles.

Only one thing puzzles me: the way the Saudis insist that a woman's place is in the home. I always thought a woman's place was shopping at Harvey Nicks, doing lunch over half a lettuce leaf at San Lorenzo's with a bunch of other bulimaniacs and then heading to the fourth floor at

Fortnum & Mason for a cup of the old lapsang souchong. But if that's what the Saudis say, I'll go along with it. I mean, Saudi wives get up early to get your breakfast. No moaning, no complaining, no slamming the doors until they drop off their hinges. They only speak when they are spoken to. No hollering, no shouting, no screaming. No more vegetarian food. And they do everything they're told. No going on about what their mother would say. No headaches.

Heaven!

And I'd also go along with the *thobe*, the long, sparkling white nightshirt the men wear. Not to mention the *ghuttra*, the headdress. Can you imagine all the fuss and bother it saves? All the agony spent looking for suits, all the rows with the wife because she doesn't like the colour and, in any case, it makes you look too old. All the fuss wondering whether to wear the white tie with the purple splodge, the red tie with the mauve star or the old Royal Bank of Scotland tie you were given twenty years ago on a freebie visit to Edinburgh. Not, of course, that Tie Rack would agree.

Indeed, I was told by an impeccable source who knows all about this kind of thing that in Jeddah the expensive Japanese versions of the nightshirt are currently selling like hot cakes. To women. After thousands of years they've just realised that if they wear the veil, they can't go out, go to restaurants, hang around with the fellas or even walk down the street with their boyfriend or, if they're desperate, their husband. But if they wear the *thobe* and headdress they're immediately free. They can go everywhere and do practically everything. They can even walk through the middle of town, giggling and laughing and holding hands with their boyfriends or lovers. Because in Saudi, with its strict moral, virtually police-state codes on practically everything, there is nothing wrong with two men in their *thobes* and headdresses walking through the middle of town, giggling and laughing and holding hands.

What does give me a bit of a problem, however, is the only form of entertainment the Saudis allow: public executions.

Now, I know all the arguments. Saudi is the safest country in the world, murders are rare, there are few burglaries. Even when some prince moved out of his hotel apartment and the staff found seventy-five cases of Johnnie Walker Black Label left behind, they didn't take them. They kept them under lock and key until he came back to reclaim them. Women and young girls can walk the streets late at night – or they could if they were allowed to. Drugs are nowhere near the problem they are anywhere else in the world. And you don't get kids running up to you all the time as you do in other countries wearing T-shirts saying, 'God and Allah help me. I am deaf and dumb', and then because they don't think you've given them enough money, chasing you down the street shouting and screaming and heaping every curse imaginable upon your infidel head.

But somehow it still seems wrong. What am I saying, seems wrong? It *is* wrong. Go and visit any of the big mosques anywhere in the country and you'll see what an ordeal executions are for the spectators. Outside in the car park you'll find a large, low platform. That's where the deed is done. After prayers most Fridays, Mondays and sometimes even Wednesdays. Men and women are brought out, blindfolded, with their hands tied behind their backs, everybody shouts 'Allahu Akbar' and zonk, that's it. The heads are then collected, together with the bodies, taken to the nearest hospital and stitched back on again – something to do with a man or woman having to be buried whole unless their crime is so bad that they don't even deserve that. In that instance, even today, the heads are stuck up on a post or stick and propped up outside the mosque for the whole world to see.

On the other hand, in Texas, where they also execute people most days of the week, all they do is throw a wreath over the fuse box and go off for a hamburger.

Up until a few years ago, I was told, women were still being stoned to death for certain crimes. One Saudi businessman I met who claimed to be a liberal told me that afterwards the bodies were barely recognisable, they had been so badly smashed up.

'Would you have thrown stones?' I asked him.

'Why not?' he said quite briskly, in a no-nonsense fashion which I must admit amazed me. 'If they do wrong, they must take the punishment.'

'And what about lashing somebody?'

'Of course. They do wrong, they must be punished.'

'But isn't it cruel?'

'What they do is cruel. They do wrong, they must be punished.'

Then he broke into a grin. 'You know French fries?' he asked.

'Sure.'

'You know what we call people Americans kill in electric chair?'

'Eh?'

'American fries.'

Obviously Saudi liberals are those who believe that before having your head cut off you should be allowed to kneel on a cushion.

In spite of all this, or maybe because of all this, the Saudis don't seem to have any problems persuading people to accept their way of life. The country is crawling with expats who, no matter where they come from, admit that they are there for one of three reasons: money, money or money. I met Indians living 200 to a building who told me they could make more in five years in Saudi than they could in a lifetime in Madras or Bangalore or even Bombay. Brits, Germans, Italians, even Americans (who, incidentally are known locally as Septics - septic tank, Yank. So much for Saudi gratitude for helping them with the Gulf War) reckon it's the best place in the world for saving money. Because there is absolutely nothing to spend it on.

On top of that the cost of living is practically nil. There is no income tax. Petrol costs nothing. Not that there is anywhere to go. If you're desperate to go somewhere there is always Bahrain or Dubai or Kuwait. Fly out on a Thursday to avoid the Muslim weekend, and return early on the Monday morning. If you are lucky you won't be sober again until it's time to fly out again the next Thursday.

As for the odd one or two parts of Jeddah beyond the expat compounds, the place is, well, interesting. Traditionally the jumping-off point for the two holy cities, Mecca, where Mohammed was born around 570, and Medina, where he died in 632, it has always been a wheeling-and-dealing and trading centre. Fifty years ago it was virtually nothing. It covered barely half a square mile and was home to around 40,000 people huddled in scruffy old buildings made of Red Sea coral and sand and held together with wooden rafters and prayer.

Today it has advanced enormously. It covers over 500 square miles, has more than 2 million inhabitants, is one of the major ports in the Arab world, handles over 80 per cent of the business for the whole of the country, is virtually the gateway to the kingdom and at festival time is full of Bengali children who have been deliberately crippled by their parents the better to beg from the pilgrims. The first time I saw them I didn't believe it. Just as the first time I saw the enormous money-making operations that go on behind the festivals I didn't believe them, either. These children, generally from West Bengal, mostly girls aged five, six or seven and known as 'disco' girls, are sold first by their parents for as little as 3,000 rupees, or literally a couple of cents, to a so-called disco agent. The disco agent then sends them to Jeddah and on to Mecca to beg twice a day during the pilgrimage season. What money they make the agent keeps, apart from the bare minimum he gives them to keep heart and soul together. After all, there's no point giving them too much, because nobody is going to feel sorry for a well-fed crippled beggar.

The official money-making machine is equally ruthless and equally efficient. Huge international exhibitions are organised before the season even begins, promoting one pilgrimage service after another in order to help local businessmen make a good profit out of the millions of pilgrims pouring in from all over the world, and since the collapse of the Berlin Wall, from all over the CIS countries as well. Which must mean at least another 50 million people. Everything is on show, from silver pilgrimage key rings and handicrafts through scale models of Mecca and Medina to computer software programs of the event. Total expenditure is currently running at around a staggering US$5 billion a year. Within two years, and with the right marketing, I was told, it could be as high as $10 billion.

Riyadh, by comparison, is a big disappointment as far as capital cities go. I mean, here we have the capital city of probably the richest country the world has ever known, and it looks a mess. Admittedly there is the occasional spectacular building, such as the Ministry of the Interior or the Ministry of Petroleum, which appear to have been based on designs rejected by President Mitterrand because they weren't exciting enough for Paris, as well as all the royal palaces, the size of football stadiums, clustered together where the big six-lane highway to Jeddah suddenly judders to a stop in some mudbank. Apart from these, however, it is nothing but squalid, US-style suburban sprawl with mosques scattered around all over the place. Even then it's not your quality sprawl. There are great patches of nothing everywhere. On a visit to the Second Industrial City at the southern end of the city, where I was visiting companies, I turned a corner and was surrounded by a flock of scrawny sheep sniffing around for bits of grass. Another day, to the west of Riyadh, I was bombing back to the hotel to get my daily fix of Saudi champagne (apple juice, mineral water and a sprig of mint) when I spotted this enormous domed building in the middle of nowhere. Inside, I was told, there were nearly 300 rooms, not to mention a huge debating chamber. The man on the door told me it was Saudi's new Parliament. But I might have imagined the whole thing. Too much Saudi champagne does things to you.

In Damman I wanted to visit the big, sprawling University of Petroleum and Minerals because, in the good old days, I'd been involved in supplying them with some enormous bits of equipment. At the time everybody was buying everything, companies included. They were just firing off purchase orders by telex – you remember telexes? – to firms all over the world. Not just small orders, big stuff as well. You know how suspicious we are in the UK. Nobody believed the telexes, they just didn't think business came through the door as easily as that. So, for one reason or another, I got the job of chaser-upper for a string of Saudi companies and other government institutions. In other words, all I had to do was contact various British companies which had been sent a telex and tell them, that yes, the telex was for real, yes, it was true, they did want to buy. And yes there were no problems about the money.

Was it easy? Was it hell. The vast majority of British companies did not believe me, either, and were not prepared to ship the goods even though they had been ordered and guaranteed by every official bit of paper you can think of. It was out of this world. But eventually I got through to them, eventually they believed me and eventually we started shipping out the goods. And I'm talking about furnishing complete laboratories, building lecture theatres and even designing and installing wind tunnels. Well, I say designing and installing wind tunnels. One Christmas Day, in the middle of lunch, the phone rang. It was Adli.

'The wind tunnel,' he said. 'You remember the wind tunnel?'

Remember the wind tunnel? How could I ever forget the wind tunnel?

'Well, they've just realised it's too big for the laboratory. They can't get it in. Can you ring round and get some quotes for building a new laboratory?'

Well, you can imagine what you-know-who said. But I rang round, got some general quotes and rang him back. He said he would come back to me, but he never did. It was the last I heard from him. My chaser-upper days were over. But I always wondered what happened to the wind tunnel and whether they had had to rebuild the laboratory or not. I still don't know. By the time I got to the university I reckon I was suffering from acute withdrawal symptoms. At the airport, I remember breaking out in a cold sweat. When I got to the hotel I was shaking all over. I can just about remember going to the big Chamber of Commerce building with some Egyptian taxi-driver who couldn't read Arabic, couldn't speak a word of English and then afterwards couldn't find the university. And I can also vaguely remember somewhere in the background somebody singing, 'Lonely is the Night' and somebody else offering me a Saudi wife.

'You want Saudi wife, sir? Muslim, good girl. Sixteen to

eighteen. For you, sir, 100,000 ryals. No? You want better? I give you Saudi wife. Good girl, Muslim, very young. Good family. 200,000 ryals. Yes? I make arrangements.'

And that's it.

On the other hand, you can't help but like the Saudis, although now and then, when we're shaking hands, I will admit I feel that... Call me suspicious, if you must, but I feel that they are maybe holding on to my hand perhaps just a fraction of a second longer than is strictly necessary with the normal mechanical English handshake. And, oh my dear, when they then put their other hand on top of mine as well... It is quite difficult, though, to actually find any Saudis. Most of the country is made up of Indians, Pakistanis, Bangladeshis, Filipinos, Malaysians, Somalians, Sudanese, British, French, Germans, Italians, Dutch and, of course, the Septics, or rather Americans.

In the old days it was simple. You only had to go into any nightclub, bar, casino or luxury hotel anywhere in the world and there you would find all the Saudi Arabians you would wish to meet. Today it's not so easy. The rich Saudis have bought up all the decent nightclubs, bars, casinos and luxury hotels in the world and have virtually made it as difficult to get into them as, say, we have made it for Saudis to get into Britain. If you have the money it's possible: all you have to do is catch them in the odd few minutes they're in the office between arriving late, shuffling off to say their prayers, wandering up and down holding hands with their friends and leaving early to tank themselves up on milk before hitting the evening's embassy cocktail-party circuit. Not that I'm saying they're lazy, but during one trip there was great rejoicing and breaking open of home-made dandelion wine bottles among the expat community when the Saudis announced they had just signed a multimillion dollar contract with the Australians to supply them with sand.

As for spotting a Saudi in a factory, you've got about as much hope as catching a glimpse of an ankle on Riyadh High Street in the middle of Ramadan. While every other visiting businessman spends his time topping up his tan around the hotel swimming pool, and no doubt, dreaming of ankles, if nothing else, I'm dragging myself up and down one industrial estate after another. And some of these industrial estates, I can tell you, are enormous. I've been to factories employing ten, twenty, fifty people as well as those employing as many as 600, 700, even 1,000, and I have yet to come across one single Saudi. They're all run by Indians or Bangladeshis or Sudanese, or even Brits, which, I suppose, proves they might be sheikhers. But they're definitely not movers.

Not that Saudi companies haven't tried to take on Saudis. The manager of one company, a Scotsman, told me that for all the usual reasons a few years ago he had been forced to employ a young Saudi without any qualifications whatsoever on a salary of over US$5,000 a month gross when he could have got a qualified Bangladeshi for less than US$500 a month. Did he regret his decision? No, he said, because he felt it had been a privilege to know a Saudi who not only had 253 aunts but who was also so unfortunate that they died one by one, day after day, for a whole year before he managed to find the time to come to the office and even begin thinking about doing any work. And when he did eventually turn up, he still didn't do any work. During my last trip to the country I spotted an advertisement in the local *Arab News* which said: 'Wanted. Non-smoking executive assistant. Aged 30–35.' It gave the name of the personnel manager, obviously a Saudi, and his telephone number, with the instruction: 'Must be telephoned between 5 and 5.15 pm only.' See what I mean?

The situation will have to change, if only because, since half the population is under sixteen, there are going to be an awful lot of Saudis looking for jobs in the near future. The trouble is that most of them, about 99.9 per cent, want to work for – correction, have jobs with – the government or any one of a thousand state companies or organisations, where, if they went to a different auntie's funeral every day of the year for five years, nobody would notice. The remainder, who are so highly trained they have to hire some poor Bangladeshi to hang their paper qualifications on the wall, expect to waltz straight into a job as a director, if not a managing director, not because of their knowledge, skills, competence and experience, but simply because somebody in their family knows somebody in somebody else's. And we're not talking small numbers. Latest government figures, which were no doubt prepared hurriedly between funerals, estimate that there must at the moment be more than 350,000 young Saudis looking for a job.

How they're going to solve the problem, Allah only knows. Sure, the government is going to have to insist on what they call greater Saudi-isation. That will mop up a few. But the more graduates are churned out, the more jobs are being replaced all the time by computers.

The other problem, of course, is that Saudis, generally speaking, are not really businessmen. Because they are so, so, other-worldly. Perhaps for no other reason than to prove that our Christian God has a glorious sense of humour, while we've been promised that perhaps one day, if we behave ourselves we'll inherit the Earth, he has actually already given the greatest Muslim nation on Earth practically everything below it. Or, at least, everything worthwhile below it. The result is that the Saudis don't really have to worry about doing business. They own 25 per cent of the world's known oil reserves. Or rather, the Saudi royal family owns 25 per cent of the world's known oil reserves. But, seeing as there are 20,000 members of the royal family and they are growing at the rate of thirty male members a month, and that each in turn has a string of dependents, it's as near as damn it the whole country. In any case, the place is run as if it's their own private family firm anyway. Consequently, few Saudis if any know what it's like being an ordinary businessman like you or me, lying awake at night wondering what you can do because you're down to your last US$1 million.

Trying to talk business to a Saudi is, therefore, a bit like trying to explain to your wife that she can't have that coat or that car or that six-week trip looking at the dolphins in Antarctic because you haven't got the readies. She just looks at you and carries on regardless. The Saudis are the same. They just don't understand what the real world is about.

Look at the mess they're in at the moment. They hit the big time in the 1970s with the oil boom. Suddenly everybody was worth billions. Well, maybe not the guy who sleeps with the goats, but more or less everybody who could afford a *thobe*, let alone a *ghuttra*, was worth so much they didn't have any money problems. In fact, most of them gave up the whole idea of working altogether. Things steadied down a bit in the 1980s, but only a little. Still the vast majority of Saudis had nothing to do all day but to keep reinsuring the bank where they kept their money for ever-increasing amounts. Then came the Gulf War. Contrary to the official line, things suddenly boomed again. They made even more millions. Come the late 1990s, with the slow-down in the price of oil, this time they have really hit problems. The same ones we all have: too many bills, not enough coming in, and no money in the bank. But of course, in their case it was on a massive scale, which was something they could not even begin to understand. To them money was something everybody else worried about. It didn't concern them. Mind you, they still owned a mere 25 per cent of the world's oil reserves, and they were still the West's favourite Middle East oil-producer – the Gulf War proved that beyond any possible doubt. They still made the world go round. Wealthy Saudis had over £200 billion stashed away in banks around the world. Prince Abdul Aziz alone had £70 million given to him as a present by his father, King Fahd, when he was just twelve years old, not to mention the exclusive right to market a million barrels of oil a day. Being forced to cut back and balance their books was something they just didn't comprehend.

So they carried on regardless. It was as if they were in a beautiful, non-alcoholic haze, if anything non-alcoholic can be beautiful. They heard the words, they understood everything apart from the bit between 'Well, Mr Minister,' and 'So I trust we'll see some action.' But they just didn't think it could conceivably apply to them.

Just as in the old days they couldn't spend any money, today they can't save any money. The result is that the whole country is being slowly squeezed for cash. Many government departments as well as many of the big state enterprises just don't have anything left to pay their staff, let alone their suppliers. Consequently many small and medium-sized companies don't have any cash to pay their own staff or their suppliers. In some companies I visited, the ordinary Indian and Bangladeshi workers told me that not only had they not been paid for months, but their wages and salaries had been halved as well.

Some residential areas of Riyadh, I discovered, had also gone without water in the heat of the summer. And in Saudi, don't forget, bathing in iced champagne is not an option. Well, not outside some of the big palaces. Some companies I visited told me they had been forced to bring in as many as fifty tankers of water a day for weeks on end just to keep going. Power cuts have become more common, and many offices I visited were without air-conditioning. They said it was because they had voluntarily turned it off to help conserve energy supplies, but I could tell what was really going on.

Yet your ordinary Saudi is still continuing to spend, spend, spend an estimated US$7 billion a year on this and that. Walk roung the shopping malls in Jeddah or Riyadh. They are still crammed with bin-liners and young men in their traditional long white dresses hugging and kissing and holding hands. Around US$4,000 on a mere afternoon's shopping spree, I gather, is nothing. And that's not including tips of US$1,000 or more.

The roads, or rather the ten-lane motorways circling Riyadh and Jeddah are still choked with traffic, because if there is one thing the Saudis love more than anything it is curvy models with their tops down. In other words, fast cars. I reckon they see their entire lives as but a brief journey from Jags to riches. And by riches, I mean your Lotus Esprit V8, your Aston Martin DB7, your Porsche 911, your McLaren F1LM, your Ferrari F50 and, of course, any Lambo going. Especially the latest, the Diablo VT, which is the one reason, I'm told, for regretting not being born a Saudi. Although why, I don't know. People tell me it's impossible to get into, impossible to see out of, impossible to drive, but it's heaven.

The Saudis are into cars practically from the moment they are born, and they go in for all the wild, way-out accessories as well. Everything from anti-bacterial steering wheels and adjustable airbag deployment systems which can tell the difference between a grown man and an empty bottle of Johnnie Walker to special infrared vision-enhancement systems for avoiding camels when crossing the desert at night. Or more likely the police.

One evening, for some reason I cannot now remember I was with one Saudi who was a few gears short of a gearbox. He told me the integrated dictation device he had in his car was so complicated that he didn't even know how to turn it on. We left his office. Vroom. Suddenly we were bombing through downtown Riyadh at the speed of light and – wazzat! – the Ministry of Petroleum was nothing but a blue blur. Vroom. Around the roundabout we hurtled. Vroom. Down on to the motorway we rocketed. I was beginning to feel like a crash-test dummy. OK, a bit more like a crash-test dummy than usual. Then, suddenly, this guy practically stood the car on its bonnet as we skidded to a halt. Standing on the edge of the pavement was this sweet, innocent little girl with a shawl around her head.

'OK,' he said to her, 'get in.'

'No!' she cried.

'I'll give you some sweets,' he smiled.

'No!' she screamed.

'I'll give you some money as well,' he purred.

'*No!*' she yelled at the top of her voice.

As you can imagine, by now I was wondering whether I should do something. Then I hear this kid whining: 'Look, Daddy, if you want to buy a silly old Jaguar, that's your problem. But don't expect me to drive in it. I only want to drive in the Ferrari. That's fun.' Which, I suppose, is the way Saudi children keep their parents up to the marque.

Later a number of expats told me I was lucky it was a Jag, that he was driving in town and that he actually stopped to pick up his daughter. Every other Saudi they'd ever come across drove at top speed, parked at top speed, even turned off the engine at top speed. And as for brakes, what the hell are brakes? Speed limits they treat the same as commissions on arms deals: they don't believe there should be any restrictions. I reckon that in the Koran it must say something about it being forbidden to give hand signals or to drive at less than whatever the speedometer says when the needle hits the red patch. And I'm not just talking about your average middle-aged Saudi swinger, either. I'm talking all ages, literally.

Way out near Saudi City on the outskirts of Jeddah is one of the country's top schools, the Eton, people said, of Saudi Arabia. The day after the examination results were announced, some fantastic souped-up 2-ton, V8-engined, 381hp 6-litre Mercedes Benz SL500 driven by an eleven-year-old with all his mates in the back, obviously celebrating Daddy's little present for passing his exams, came hurtling down Abdulla al Kahyl Street at 1,000mph, braked sharply and smashed straight into the thick steel railings outside an office building. Everybody in the street rushed out and did the first thing anybody would do in the circumstances. They rang the police. Not the ordinary police, the special black-uniformed police. Within seconds they were on the spot. The kids they rushed to hospital, the car they removed immediately. The owner of the building was there and then given a fat cheque, told to get the railings replaced *tout de suite* and to forget that the incident ever took place.

You think that's crazy? Apparently the latest thing for young Saudis to do, in the absence of anything else of interest, is to hit the desert in two souped-up rocket-propelled sportscars, drive them side by side at a million miles an hour and then clamber out of the window of one car and in through the window of the other. The first car they then allow to smash itself to pieces in the middle of nowhere.

But my favourite Saudi Carmageddon story is one I heard one evening from a young sheikh, another torque of the town, who kept on about how too much driving had given him some kind of toenail fungal disease. Anyway, he said that one of his friends, another turbo-charged sheikh in some other part of the country, was hurtling across the desert one evening in his Lambo, obviously under the affluence, when he suddenly came off the road, careered across the sand and crashed into a gulley. He was found by a rescue crew sitting by the car wailing at the top of his voice, 'My Lambo! My Lambo!'

One of the crew realised that he had a hand missing. He says to him, 'You're hand is missing.'

The Sheikh looked down at the stump and immediately began crying, 'My Rolex! My Rolex!'

True or not, to me that's Saudi Arabia.

By the time I got back to Gatwick, having felt rough for the whole trip, I'd lost so much weight that my suit looked the size of a Bedouin tent. When I got home and took a shower, I had to walk around to get wet. All the same, I suppose it was cheaper than going to some health farm and gagging on muesli for a week. It was also probably more enjoyable, even though I managed to escape being lashed, and certainly a darned sight cheaper. But those melon frappés: I shall live with that taste for ever.

KUWAIT CITY

You'd never think there had been a war. I mean, all those Scud missiles, all those bombs, all those journalists rushing around all over the place. All that devastation. All that damage. Streets piled high with rubbish and dead bodies. No water, no electricity, no food. Rats everywhere. And then the oil wells: over 700 of them deliberately set on fire. Blackening the sky by day, lighting it up by night, pouring 11 million gallons of crude into the Gulf. One of the worst man-made environmental disasters of all time.

Experts said it would take decades to put everything right, yet here we are today, only a few years after Kuwait Radio went off the air on 2 August 1990 with the words, 'Arab brothers, Muslims, hurry to our aid' and they've practically rebuilt Kuwait City. The historic old Sief Palace on the waterfront, which goes all the way back to the 1880s, has been reconstructed with the aid, would you believe, of old books found in Maidenhead Public Library. Not, I suppose, that the Emir could care tuppence about that. To the north and west they've built a brand-new government complex covering over 75 acres, complete with all the fancy canopies and arcades and courtyards and *darwazas* and *roushanas* – entrances and niches to you and me – you can imagine. It's like 1,001 Arabian Nights meets 1,001 tons of red tape. Running the length of the whole thing, deep underground, is over 1 kilometre of secret passages. Not for your Scheherazades to scamper backwards and forwards plying their wares, but to protect politicians and civil servants from the harsh environment outside. Whether it's the political environment or the economic environment or just the sizzling heat of the midday sun I have no idea. All I know is that they've been built and they're there.

The Sheraton, too, is back in business and looking smarter than ever, although perhaps more municipal-swimming-pool smart than Topkapi Palace smart. All the other hotels badly hit by the Iraqi bombing have also been remodelled, rebuilt and refurbished. The Bayan Palace, home of a million international conventions, is once again doing what it does so superbly: boring delegates to kingdom come. The telecommunications tower is buzzing, the first, fifth and sixth ring roads are flowing with glistening new BMWs, Mercedes – even the occasional Rolls-Royce – and echoing anew to crunching gears, squealing tyres and anguished calls from mobile telephones for a new Lambo. Not that you would ever be involved in an accident with another car: the roads are so fantastic and the traffic so light that you stand more chance of a camel crashing into your car than another driver. They've even built a brand new 'Liberation Tower', 40 metres higher than the Eiffel Tower, not to mention a string of memorial plaques and statues all over town.

All the banks – which now outnumber mosques by about fifty to one, the proof of a truly Muslim nation – are open and doing business again around the world. The stock exchange, with its new computerised trading system, is humming – with rumours. A huge new £700 million sewage- and water-treatment plant is doing whatever sewage- and water-treatment plants do. Whether this is more important to the health and wellbeing of the country than the stock exchange I wouldn't know, but if you think about it, there are bound to be many similarities between the two. Goodness me, even the chorus line for the next local production of *The Mikado* is now complete, although they are still looking for tenors. If you're interested call 5339810 or 3727622 for details.

One morning I had the shock of my life. For a split second I thought the fruit juice had finally destroyed my liver. I was driving past the glistening white National Assembly building. The roof sweeps up in all directions and it looks like... No, it doesn't. Yes it does. Impossible: the Sydney Opera House? This, I discovered later, is not surprising given that it was designed – I think that's the right word – by the same Danish pastry. It was obviously a shrewd move by some clever Kuwaiti Machiavellian brain somewhere because, just as the Sydney Opera House is too small to stage most operas, the National Assembly is too small to hold national assemblies, and thus the power remains firmly in the grip of the same small ruling elite.

Be that as it may, the people who own 10 per cent of the world's oil reserves and who are the biggest couch potatoes on earth are back in the same boring old routine: oil. Once more they are pumping it out at the rate of 2 million barrels a day, and more. They have upgraded their refineries, a new world-class petrochemical complex is on stream, and by the year 2000 they plan to be producing 3 million barrels a day and to have oil revenue coming out of their ears.

So once again times are good – very, very good. There is still no income tax, still no charge for filling your swimming pool. Electricity, water and telephone charges remain nominal and petrol still, as you would expect, costs next to nothing. So do customs duties. The customs duty on a Mercedes, for example, is a mere 4 per cent. All the expensive stores have been refilled to overflowing with Versace and Armani. The only thing that forces the doors closed in the evenings is all the money they have taken during the day. The ordinary shops and *souks* - my favourite is the Abdulla Taki Center up towards the big Kuwaiti Tower - are crammed as full as they were before with all the basic necessities of life: Rolex watches, jewellery, hand-made leather everything and, for some reason, American mattresses.

And, of course, the backbone of the economy, all the big guys, including the Emir, the crown prince, every single member of the royal family and the entire Cabinet, who all felt the best way they could serve their country during the war was by fleeing to expensive luxury hotels around the world and following the reports on CNN, have come home. Thankfully they are once again doing what they're good at: spending money on all the things they're not allowed to not spend their money on, if you see what I mean, secure in the knowledge that if it happens again all they have to do is pick up the phone and the world will come galloping to their aid, while they are, of course, going hell for leather in the opposite direction. Not many countries have such a cast-iron, bomb-proof, invasion-proof guarantee.

But start making calls, moving around and checking out the place and you'll see the Kuwait behind the façade. One morning early I was on my way to the Shuwaikh Industrial Area. We took a turn along Arabia Gulf Road. On the left was an enormous burned-out shell which in Britain would have been an exhibition centre but in Kuwait was probably a pied-à-terre for some sheikh or other.

'What's that?'

'Saddam Hussein,' the driver said. 'Crazy man. Minister's home. They torch it.'

Further down what looked like the wrecked hull of a fair-sized passenger ship.

'Saddam Hussein,' the driver said again. 'Crazy man. It was hotel. They torch it also.'

It was the same in town. The police station has still not been repaired. Lack of funds, I was told. But I don't believe that. It stands in such a prominent position that it makes an ideal reminder of a Muslim's love of his fellow Muslim. But the thing that amazed me more than anything else was the National Museum and the planetarium. I knew the Iraqis attacked defenceless women and children, but I never realised they also attacked defenceless museums and planetaria as well. The Kuwaitis seem to be keeping it the way it is, no doubt as a National Museum of Atrocities of Saddam Hussein.

Here nothing has changed since the day the Iraqis moved out. There's rubbish and rubble everywhere. Where ceilings have collapsed on the floor, they're still on the floor. Where showcases have melted in the heat, they still lie spread out in solid pools. Everywhere there is dust and ashes and inches-deep soot. In the planetarium the seating has all gone to the stars, but in the centre the twisted, burned-out skeleton of the projector remains like some piece of modern sculpture. 'What they could take, they took. What they couldn't take, they destroyed,' one of the planetarium staff told me.

Another said he had stayed in Kuwait the whole time the Iraqis were there. 'The soldiers, they take everything we have. They take toys from the children. They take the taps and the water heater and even the tiles from the bathroom. They also take trees and shrubs from the garden. It is unbelievable.'

The psychological damage and the financial damage are there, too, but you have to look for it. First, the psychological damage. No doubt about it, on a national level the Kuwaitis were knocked every which way. That their Muslim brothers could do such a thing to them is something they'll never ever get over. That the West came to their aid so quickly and so decisively is something they will always be grateful for. But deep down, oh, how they wish they didn't have to rely on the US, Europe and the other thirty countries which eventually liberated them. On a personal level, I heard one story after another of appalling horror and incredible bravery. Of brother turning against brother. Of how people lived for months on end on roofs, in attics and even in the sewers. As for the financial damage, I'm afraid I'm not going to lose any sleep on their behalf.

Are they determined it will never happen again? One evening at a reception I met a US brigade commander, built like an ox, who told me he had a team of US army advisers with him from Georgia. They were trying, he said, 'to lick the Kuwaiti army into shape'.

'You going to do it?' I wondered.

'Nope,' he said. 'Not a hope in hell. They're just not the fightin' type.'

'So what happens if there's another war?'

'We'll be right back.'

Which probably accounts for the boom in sales of bricks and cement – after, of course, Lambos, high fashion and jewellery. In spite of everything, the Kuwaitis have not forgotten the war. They're all building false walls and rooms in their homes and basements where they can stash any valuables and stockpile food and drink and things like torches and batteries in case it should happen again.

So last time, when the war was finally over, being Muslims and against all forms of booze, how on earth did they celebrate? 'Not a single sheep was safe that night,' a Kuwaiti bank manager told me.

The mind boggles.

Kuwait, which has a population of around 1.5 million, is about the size of a US$100 bill. Not that your average Kuwaiti would know what a $100 bill was, never having had to deal in such small sums of money. Unlike many Arab countries which demand letters of invitation, sponsors, three signed copies of the Emir's photograph and a bottle of whisky (the bottle of whisky is for the guy in the visa office – such is life) before they let you in, getting into Kuwait is easy. As the Iraqis discovered. The plane lands. Within minutes we're through Immigration. Within seconds we're through Customs. Outside the car is waiting, and in twenty minutes I'm in the centre of downtown Kuwait City. The first thing that strikes me is that it is more relaxed than in Saudi. Far more relaxed. At the hotel, the traditional Arab welcoming cup of coffee is served perhaps a trifle later, maybe because Article 2 of their constitution says that Islam is only 'a main' source of legislation, although inevitably there are growing demands from the fundamentalists to make Islam the sole basis of the law.

Dresses are not so long. The occasional glimpse of ankle, it seems, is not so shocking. Nor is the occasional glimpse of jewellery. And there doesn't seem to be any limit to the amount of perfume that can be used. That's the men I'm talking about: as far as women are concerned, they're exactly the same as any women anywhere in the world. They can do whatever they want to do and there is apparently nothing on earth anybody can do to stop them. Some women, of course, are veiled from top to toe; others are skipping around in either Armani or jeans and T-shirts. Trouble is, all those skipping around in Armani and jeans and T-shirts should, I reckon, be veiled from top to toe and those veiled from top to toe should be skipping around in Armani and jeans and T-shirts. But that's life. Or women. Or, I suppose, both. Not that I would dare to criticise any woman anywhere in the world, let alone a Kuwaiti woman. I haven't forgotten the things they did to the Iraqi soldiers during the war when many of the men were too frightened to even watch CNN from the safety of their penthouse apartments – in New York, Los Angeles, Marbella, Monte Carlo or Vienna.

You see women working in offices and driving cars as well as serving in shops and restaurants. Western, or rather Eastern, women. From Hong Kong, Taiwan, Thailand, South Korea, the Philippines. What's more some of them have got l-l-legs. Or, at least, legs that go up to their k-k-knees or even, in some cases, Allah preserve me, to just above the knee. Men don't have the same freedom. They can work anywhere except in the real centres of power and influence: ladies' hairdressers. It's against the law, even if they look like Warren Beatty. The Ministry of Islamic Affairs says it is forbidden by the Koran for a man to touch any woman who is not his wife or a close friend. But I can guess the real reason. The Kuwaitis have given women the vote, so we all know what's going to happen next. They will change the law so that men can work in ladies' hairdressers, providing, of course, that they look like Warren Beatty.

The calls to prayer still croak and crackle from every mosque five times a day, although maybe not with the same insistency and the same quality of reproduction as in Saudi. People still flock to say their prayers, although maybe not with the same determination and maybe not in the same numbers. But not everything closes down. Some shops stay open, even some offices. And I can't remember seeing any of the dreaded religious police you see all over Saudi banging on shop windows to remind you to say your prayers. They're still just as strict on the booze, but at least when they give you a bucket of some enormous mango and mineral water sludge which looks like liquefied Colman's mustard, they don't say, 'Enjoy.'

Not that they make it simple for you. One afternoon I met an African businessman at a restaurant rather surprisingly decorated with English hunting prints. I ordered my usual bucket of sludge; he wanted a glass of milk. It blew the system. They didn't know whether they could serve a glass of milk. They didn't know how much to give him. They didn't know what to charge him. You'd have thought he was insisting on a bottle of Black Label. In the end, I ordered five cups of tea, he drank all the milk and I drank all the tea. It wasn't what I wanted, but it solved the problem. By the end of my trip they had got to me. I had had so much mango, strawberry and every other kind of juice that in desperation – and I'm ashamed to admit this – I was actually drinking water. I can tell you, when I finally got back to civilisation it took a lot of champagne to cleanse my system.

The problem of censorship they seem to have solved in a novel way. Instead of employing vast hordes of censors to check every single page of every single publication that comes into the country, as they do in Saudi, the Kuwaitis simply give everybody so many names that by the time the newspapers have printed two or three of them there's no space left for any criticism, let alone any salacious photographs. Fred Smith, for example, becomes something like His Highness Sheikh Zayed Khalifa bin Kuwait Town Council al Hamden bin Mubarak Obeid Abdullah al Fred Smith. You can imagine how much space is left for photographs on page three by the time you've listed everyone invited to celebrate the fifty-sixth birthday of Major-General Sheikh al Wathba on the Metropolitan Line Saeed bin Zayed Saif Ahmed bin Everything Else.

Yet in spite of all these revolutionary developments, Kuwait is still not exactly a bundle of infidel fun. Stretch pants are against the law. There's not a single disco in the whole country. There are no forests or rivers or mountains, either, come to think of it. In fact, at one time it looked as though there wasn't going to be any Kuwait at

all. Pop concerts are forbidden, Barbie dolls are banned
and so is Popeye, because he keeps chasing Olive Oyl. It's
also illegal to own fewer than five cars, to fire bullets in
the air after a wedding – people think it's the Iraqis coming
back, and besides, it interferes with planes flying overhead
– or to spend less than twenty hours a day engaged in
traditional *diwaniyas*, which means occupying all the best
seats in all the best hotels chatting away with your mates
over first tea, then coffee, then, if the wives are playing up
and complaining again, another cup of tea.

If you're in the hotel or restaurant business it's forbidden not to play 'Scheherazade' non-stop twenty-four
hours a day. How King Shahriyar could have put up with
the real Scheherazade rabbiting on night after night, I
don't know. Just one night would exhaust me. Unless, of
course, it's better in the original. I remember once years
ago, when I was doing some research into something or
other, I tried to plough through one of the translations by
Sir Richard Burton. I got as far as some king being 'betided
with sore cark and care and chagrin exceeding' and gave
up. If I couldn't understand what that was, how was I
going to understand what was going on the other 1,000
nights?

Finally, it is also absolutely forbidden under everything
they can throw at you in the Koran to turn up on time for
anyone or anything. There are so many stories about
Kuwaitis and their time-keeping that if I started telling you
them all now you'd be late for Christmas, I mean Ramadan.
My favourite, though, concerns the British ambassador
himself, who one day turned up on the dot at the Ministry
of Foreign Affairs for a meeting with the minister. He
waited and waited. The officials kept assuring him that the
minister was sorry for the delay and he would see him in
a minute. After two and a half hours the ambassador gave
up. He went back to his office, switched on the midday

news, and hey presto, there was the minister – in London at a conference.

One of the world's major financial centres, Kuwait City is crammed with enormous towering banks and office blocks. At least, in the centre it is. Yet it is still a desert town. One minute you can be sitting on the twenty-second floor of a Kuwaiti bank that could swallow practically every building society in Britain before breakfast, and the next, just across the road, you're wandering around in the sand and dust looking for your driver, who's obviously disappeared into a *souk* for a little bit of hubble-bubble or whatever. One minute you can be chatting to a Kuwaiti and the next minute – or rather, for the rest of the day – you are talking to expats. They're all over the place: from India (mostly from Kerala State), from the Philippines, from Hong Kong, Korea, Thailand, from all over Europe. Even from the US, although not very many of them, which is surprising. I suppose the US packed so many of their citizens into Saudi to make certain they got more than their fair share of the thank-you contracts that were going after the Gulf War that there weren't many left to push into Kuwait. Indeed, Kuwaitis are a minority in their own country – expats make up more than half the population, although the Indian guy from Bangalore in the Kuwait Statistics Office was reluctant to admit this. He was also reluctant to admit that all the Palestinians, Jordanians and Lebanese have gone, largely because they were considered to be on the wrong side. Taking over from them, he told me, were the Bidoons, Arab refugees who now make up the bulk of not only the police force but the military as well, even though they are not entitled to Kuwaiti citizenship.

Whatever their nationality, or lack of nationality, everybody speaks English. Well, I say English: what I mean is everybody speaks some kind of English. In practice it's usually the same ten or twelve standard phrases. Every morning I was there, I would drag my aching, world-weary body across the hotel reception. As I reached the revolving door, I would close my eyes, hold my throbbing head in my hands and take a deep breath. Through the door, my stomach would churn, my limbs would feel heavy and the sunlight would melt the back of my eyes. This is what lack of alcohol does to me.

Every day there was a different taxi-driver.

'Hey. Moh. Howareyahdoin?' I would mumble.

'Saddam Hussein. Him bad man,' the driver would always reply, wherever he came from.

'Listen. I'd like to go to. . .' And I'd name the office I was visiting.

Delicately, he would help me into the car. 'He come here. I go. Very quickly.'

I'd settle in the back seat and rest my head against the window. 'You know the way, OK?'

'He destroy everything.'

With an enormous roar of the engine, we'd shoot away.

'Not the long way round via Bangkok, like the guy did yesterday.'

'Him bad.'

'The short way.'

'Him come again. I go. Zoom.'

We swing into the awful roar of traffic.

'Just up the street. Second on the left.'

'You American? I charge you US$120. OK? We go?'

'No. Me Chinese.'

'You Chinese?' I get that long, hard stare. 'OK. You Chinese. I charge US$20. We go?'

It always works.

There are so few Arabs in Kuwait that whenever I go there I take the opportunity to try to brush up my Arabic. That way, if I actually pluck up courage to say something in Arabic and it's wrong, the chances are nobody will notice the difference and I won't be sentenced to seventy-five lashes and forced to read two chapters of Bruce Chatwin. If you say something in Arabic in an Arabic-speaking country and it's not right the whole Muslim world knows about it. Not that I know much Arabic, apart from the usual, '*Mahaba habbiti*', which I first picked up years ago from a Jordanian scrap-metal merchant who was as far removed from your traditional image of a scrap-metal merchant as an evening in Kuwait City is from enjoying yourself.

He was a Palestinian, and had originally made his fortune, he told me, as a result of the Six-Day 'Yom Kippur' War way back in 1967. When the Israelis backed off, he stepped in. A few dollars here and a few dollars there, he said, and he got into the desert and stripped clean all the planes and tanks and guns that had been left behind.

'First of all everybody wanted spare parts. We took all the spare parts we could get. We also took everything that hadn't been used: guns, ammunition, everything. Then we took whatever valuables we could find. Money, documents, cables, electrical gear, anything we could sell.'

'But surely you couldn't just walk in and start taking what you want.'

Well, I didn't think you could, although I suppose everything is possible. Especially in the Middle East.

'I knew one of the generals very well,' he grinned. 'We are brothers. He gives me permission, I do work for him, he is very happy.'

I first met this guy in London. He was staying at the Churchill Hotel. After that, I ran into him a number of times in different parts of the world – Ethiopia, Namibia, the Baltics. Whenever I saw him, whether it was in an office, a bank, a restaurant or an hotel, he always happened to be accompanied by a niece, a different one every time, all of whom happened to be nurses at St Thomas's Hospital in London. Funny that.

I've never forgotten the first lesson he taught me about dealing with the Arabs.

'It's all right to make noises while you eat,' he told me over lunch one day at the Churchill. 'Providing they're the right kind of noises.'

'What kind of noises are they?'

The niece with him that day prompted some suggestions from him.

'Wives keeping well?' she grinned icily at him.

'Grunt,' he replied.

'And all the children?'

'Grunt. Burp.'

'If, of course, you remember them all.'

'Grunt.'

Then came the crash course. Arabs are very polite, very hospitable, very courteous people. When you first meet they'll shake hands with you, maybe even kiss you. Maybe even kiss you and hold hands with you. Unless, of course, you waggle your finger at them, in which case they'll chop off your arm without a second thought. Inquire about their wife or wives, and Allah knows what they'll chop off.

If it's morning, say '*Sabaah al-khair.*' If it's afternoon or any other time of day, '*As-salaam alaykum.*' Which roughly translated means: 'Did you say five per cent of fifty per cent? I always get so confused.'

Then there was the usual. Don't flash the soles of your shoes at anyone. Don't scratch your chin. Always eat, drink and offer the cigars round with the right hand. Drink as much as you like, but never more than your host. Not even if you're just back from a swing through the Middle East, you're in Paris and there's three bottles of Krug open on the table in front of you.

Never admire anything. It forces your host to give it to

you. Unless, of course, it's his favourite Ferrari or Lambo. Then you can admire it until kingdom come without any danger of him giving it to you. If you go visiting, take a present like a Jag or a Rolls-Royce or a numbered bank account in Vienna. If somebody else is there, don't worry – not even if it's your arch-competitor. The Arabs are great ones for partying. If one person is invited, everybody is invited. Especially if it's going to help send little Mohammed to Eton. To buy the place.

Useful phrases for such occasions are: *'Kayf haalak?'* (Why the hell didn't you tell me this schmuck was going to be here?) *'All-humdoolillah.'* (How the hell should I know? He just turned up out of the blue.) *'Inshallah.'* (So what are we going to do now?) *'Inshallah.'* (Come and see me later. We'll sort it out between us.) *'Maa as-salaama.'* (Wait a minute – is that a pigskin briefcase he's got?)

If it's a meal, leave after the coffee. Well, you might as well. There ain't goin' be nuttin' else. If it's not a meal, leave immediately. That way you can get back to the hotel, work out whether your prices are cheaper than the other guy's and fax them back. Alternatively you might prefer a more creative approach. Leave before your competitor, go back to your hotel and send the Arab a copy of *The Satanic Verses* – with your rival's business card.

In Kuwait I kept expecting to bump into this Palestinian guy and another one of his nieces at a bank or visiting an oil well. But no luck. Which either means he's retired, worth millions, had one heart attack too many or was at the time hurtling across the desert like a Scud missile collecting more scrap. Instead, one afternoon in the gloriously seedy, typically Arab Carlton Hotel around the corner from the Sheraton, I came across another Palestinian who was posing as an Egyptian. He too was making certain Kuwaiti generals very happy, but he was more upmarket than my friend. He was interested only in hi-tech scrap – PCBs, computers, computer systems and the fancy stuff that goes into today's weapons.

'Today, there is so much more to do,' he laughed. 'We have computers and PCBs; we also have lasers, laser systems. There are big markets for them. It is good business. Very good business.' Kalashnikovs, live hand-grenades, tanks, all kinds of guns, Iraqi military vehicles, many of which are apparently still buried under the sand and marked with red flags to warn people to stay clear: he dismissed all of them. 'Old-fashioned,' he said. 'No market. No money.'

Furthermore, the business was too competitive. 'Every-body is doing it. There is not enough to go round.' Business, he meant. Not nurses from St Thomas's Hospital. There seems to be an everlasting supply of nurses from St Thomas's Hospital.

He also offered what I can only describe as an interest-ing view of the Gulf War. 'Saddam Hussein,' he said, taking a big draw on his cigar and looking me straight in the eye, 'was' – he paused and looked around him – 'a CIA agent.'

Surprised? I nearly dropped my glass of orange juice.

'Look at the facts,' he said, jabbing his cigar into a tin ashtray on the table between us. 'He did a lot for America. He united them behind their president, gave them a sense of purpose, gave their defence industries a boost and enabled their military to play games and test their weapons and procedures against a real live enemy. And to get the whole thing paid for by everybody else. The fact the Americans killed more people on their own side than Iraq's was, obviously, part of the deal.'

'Yes, sure. But he did invade Kuwait.'

'Sure. And Kuwait is a non-democratic country. Who'd have thought the US would ever go to war to help a non-democratic country?'

'But doesn't that prove that he can't be a CIA agent?'

'Not at all. It just proves how out of touch the CIA is with the rest of the US government, which was, you must admit, not the first time and will not be the last time.'

'Yes, but—'

'And the final argument. Are you ready?'

I nod my head. 'And the final argument: why haven't the Americans tried to assassinate...'

'Oh, come off it.'

'Wait a minute.' He waved his hands at me. 'Are you trying to tell me that if the Americans, the greatest nation on earth, wanted to assassinate him they couldn't?'

'Yes. Well, it is...'

'Look what they did to Noriega. Against all international laws and conventions they airlifted him out of Panama, brought him to Miami and made him stand trial. Are you telling me that if the Americans really wanted to get Hussein they couldn't get him out?'

'Yes, but...'

'The reason they don't is that they're frightened of what he would say. They can't afford the risk.'

'Oh, come on. You can't...'

'And the other thing he did was hand the Americans the rich Jordanian market. The Americans knew the Jordanians could never make up their mind which side to support. They knew this would give them the excuse to slap an embargo on them.'

'But how does that help the Americans? I don't...'

'You don't understand. I tell you how it helps the Americans.' He lit another massive cigar. 'The Americans knew if there was an embargo, they would be the ones to enforce the embargo. So what did they do? They stopped every other country breaking the embargo and then when the embargo relaxed they delayed every other ship from getting through apart from US ships. The result? American goods got through. Everybody else's were delayed. What did it do?' He thumped the table. 'I'll tell you what it did. It made the Jordanians order American, because that way they knew the goods would get through and not be delayed for weeks on end.'

He put his cigar down in the ashtray. 'Am I right?' he asked. 'Am I right?'

'You're right,' I said. Not because I agreed with him, but because too much orange juice was beginning to affect the poor old brain.

But if the idea of Saddam Hussein being a CIA agent is absurd, so is the idea of Kuwait nowadays calling itself Free Kuwait. Because free it most definitely is not. Everything costs an arm and two legs. Especially the hotels. Don't get me wrong, I don't want to go to war about it. But Expensive Kuwait or even Very, Very Expensive Kuwait would be nearer the truth.

DOHA

Typical. It's my centenary. My 100th country, that is, not my 100th birthday. And where am I to celebrate this momentous landmark? I'm stuck on a 4,250-square-mile patch of dust between Saudi Arabia and Iran where, over the years, many people have either forecast I would end up or promised to put me. In the gutter. Or Qatar, as for some reason they insist on spelling it, probably as a result of the number of Americans they've allowed in to start preparing for the next Gulf War.

Admittedly petrol is around 50p a gallon. There is no income tax. Health, education and local phone calls are free. Electricity is free. There's free land for building a home of your own and even free trees and plants and shrubs to plant in the garden as well. Not to mention free grass seed. On top of that they somehow manage to be friends with Iran, Iraq, Israel, the United States and British ministers of defence, who keep dropping in trying to sell them guns and tanks and jet fighters. Which, bearing in mind there are only 400,000 people in the whole place, is a bit like trying to arm the residents of Camden High Street as distinct from the whole borough.

Oh, I nearly forgot to mention that, thanks to an accident of geology over 600 million years ago over which they had no influence whatsoever, today Qatar is also the second-richest country in the world: US$3 million of oil money a day, yes a day, is pouring into the coffers to be shared among just 100,000 Qataris. I say 100,000: that includes Iranian Qataris, Saudi Qataris, and Qataris who've married Bangladeshis, Indians or whoever. There are probably only around 60,000 pure, genuine 100 per cent Qataris left to share the spoils, which is not bad when you think they all started off as a bunch of slaves 100 to 200 years ago.

What's more, things are destined to get better and better every year. Because not only have they got oil coming out of their *dishdashes*, but they will very shortly also have gas pumping out as well. Lots of it. Just off the coast they've discovered the world's largest single reservoir of natural gas, more than in the entire United States, including Alaska. And they've got enough of the stuff to last them 200 years. In other words, a shore investment.

On top of that, as each year goes by there are fewer and fewer of them. At present there are supposed to be around 1,971 men to every Qatari woman, which, you must admit, is a bit of a problem. To make matters worse most Qatari women, if you ever catch a glimpse of what is hidden away behind their black robes and veils and masks, all seem to look like Saddam Hussein's grandmother, complete with moustache. I suppose that is not surprising: they're taken care of, so why should they worry? They've got their house (paid for by the government), their garden (paid for by the government) and a car of their own (paid for by the government). Their fathers are happy, having made a profit by offloading them on to some poor unsuspecting innocent. If their husband ditches them for someone else he's still got to give them a house, a garden and a car. All they can do is sit in front of the television all day long watching old movies, eating chocolates and getting even fatter.

There are, of course, exceptions, and the exception

during my trip was the talk of the *souks*. A young Qatari girl had become too friendly and chatty with the boys on the school bus, so her father insisted that instead the family's long-serving, devoted, trusted, reliable, hard-working chauffeur drove her to school. You've got it. She ran off with the chauffeur.

Whatever you may think, to me the whole place is a miracle, because it proves once and for all that there is a worse place on earth than Auckland, New Zealand. Unless, I suppose, you're a long-serving, devoted, trusted, reliable, hard-working Pakistani chauffeur, in which case it obviously has its attractions. There are no bars, no clubs, no real alcohol – not even in the secret expat bars in various hotels. There's no sheikh, rattle, let alone roll. The only entertainment is being stopped by the police. They've already got so much money that I kept wondering how much they were going to give me as a bribe to drive recklessly along the Corniche at 37mph just so that they could have a bit of excitement.

As for tourist attractions, well, it's hot. About gas mark 73, or fifty-five minutes in a microwave oven. Doha, the capital, is about the size of a village. Well, all right then, a big village. The bay is quite nice. Nothing spectacular, mind you. The West Bay, the upmarket sector, is a laugh – especially watching the Qataris trying not to notice the new Israeli Embassy which has just opened for business. So is visiting the Commercial Department of our glorious British Embassy in the super, grand, luxury Toyota Building. Oh yes, and there's the post office, the most modern electronic post office in the world. Which is presumably why it looks like a series of fancy letterboxes piled haphazardly on top of one another.

The National Museum is unique. It's the only building in town still with its own original natural air-conditioning system. It also boasts the very first Qatari dhow to be fitted with an outside motor. Upstairs in the oil section a whole load of felspar rocks and clays are on display under the very helpful descriptions, 'Some kinds of Felspar' and 'Some kinds of Clays', which I thought if nothing else showed how deeply interested and seriously committed they are to the source of their untold wealth. It's enough to make you go to the 'Simple Life Before Oil' section and cry into their bleeding cups.

If scenery is your thing, there's plenty of that. There are the machine-guns looking down at you from the roof of the army headquarters next door to the Emir's palace, not to mention secret cameras everywhere. There are local handicraft stalls where you can while away a couple of days watching people spinning camel hair to make genuine Bedouin tea towels. If you prefer more dangerous pursuits, you can watch twenty-six Bangladeshis cleaning a single manhole cover outside the local court or try to perfect your Qatari social graces by practising the sophisticated art of wiggling the coffee cup. This is what you have to do if you want to stop them from drowning you in the 2 million barrels a day they produce of the thick, deep yellow, sandy-coloured high-octane sludge they call cardamom coffee.

Local food? Well, there's a new Thai restaurant on the C ring road near the Ramada traffic junction. Even though there are over thirty-six different kinds of fish in the Gulf, nobody has actually got around to opening a traditional Qatari restaurant serving traditional Qatari food. Probably because there isn't any. And even if there was, no Qatari would know how to prepare it, cook it, serve it or even charge for it. Putting it in the bank, Dogger or otherwise, and watching it pile up is, however, something they are past masters at.

Even the good old tried and tested traditional ways of passing a few hours elsewhere in the Middle East are out of the question There are no traditional Hasu coffee pots to watch boil. There aren't any daily beheadings to go and see. They normally take place only on Tuesdays, but even then there are not so many of them since the Qataris decided in their infinite wisdom and mercy that nobody should any longer be beheaded twice for the same offence. They've cut back on the number of secret police-men hovering around hotel lobbies and the amount of telephone-tapping that used to go on, so there is no point in trying to spot your minder so that you can sidle up to him and offer him an illicit drink. Neither is there anything to be gained from going from one public telephone box to another in the hotel lobby making mysterious calls to government departments.

The final straw is that they've just abolished press censorship. This is a great pity, because before you could always rely on spending at least an hour every morning poring over the newspapers, holding them up to the light to try to find out why the censors had obliterated various photographs under a thick film of black ink.

Wrapping-paper censorship, however, continues. One morning as I sat in the hotel coffee shop weeping into my third orange juice, I was joined by a Brit who told me he had been happily doing business with Qatar for ages until, all of a sudden the previous year, his shipments started being delayed and then confiscated by the police. He checked all the documentation and everything was in order. He asked his agent to get on to the police, but they wouldn't talk to him. Then, quite by chance, he discovered the reason. In order to save money, his dispatch department had started wrapping everything in old newspapers instead of brown paper. And which newspapers did they use? Why, the *Sun*, the *Mirror* and the *Sunday Sport*, of course. Immediately he put a stop to this practice deliveries resumed.

So you can see why I don't rate Qatar as one of the fun

spots of the globe. 'The most boring place in the world,' a
Dutchman told me as for the fifty-ninth time the same
morning we inspected the flowers alongside the edge of
the road thriving on recycled sewage. 'I tellyah, buddy, it's
the Aberdeen of the Gulf,' an American oilman kept
shouting at me across the hotel dining room whenever I
saw him. Which of the two comments is the more
insulting I don't know. More insulting, that is, to Auckland,
whose claim to the title disputed by the Dutchman I've
always fought to defend to the last yawn. Even on a
weekday when the sun is shining.

To protect businessmen from ending up in the gutter, I
mean Qatar, I reckon countries should be given health
warnings. How many countries can you think of that
could be labelled 'Free from artificial colours, flavours and
preservatives'?   Perhaps   Bermuda?   The   Bahamas?
Myanmar? Then there are those that should be marked
'Keep out of the reach of children'. Amsterdam? Hamburg?
Bangkok? Budleigh Salterton after ten o'clock on Saturday
night in the summer (you mean you haven't heard)? As for
those that should carry the instruction 'Do not exceed the
stated dose', I'm afraid I haven't got time to list them. Doha,
though, is simple. It should be labelled, 'Doha is no Do-ha-
ha. It's more Do-nothing-ha-ha'. To tell you the truth there
was so much do-nothing-ha-ha to do by lunchtime on my
second day that I was ready to throw myself in the river.
Unfortunately there are no rivers anywhere in Qatar. The
alternative was to wander down to the gold market and
sell my duty-free bottle of Scotch for more than the price
of a couple of kilos of the yellow stuff. Even though the
previous evening I'd been told to be very, very careful: just
giving a bottle of whisky as a present to a Qatari in the
privacy of his own palace was dangerous.

'It's very difficult,' a typical British expat told me.
'Especially at birthdays, what, or if they're taking

examinations. They often ask me if I can give them a jolly old bottle. But I always say no. It's not worth the risk, either for them or for me.' But I was so desperate that it seemed worth the risk. If I got caught, I could end up by being arrested and sentenced to fifty strokes of the cane. However, I was told by one who knows about these things, since they are administered by a policeman who has to keep a copy of the Koran tucked under his whipping arm, it's not that bad. In any case, if I was arrested and sentenced to fifty strokes I could whip round afterwards and sell my story to the *Daily Mail* for £11,000, appear on the David Frost programme wearing a 'Black and Blue is Beautiful' T-shirt for £2,500 and write a book about my experiences making, say, another £10,000, which is not bad money for a night out, whichever way you look at it. If I didn't get caught, however, I would have wasted all that time and effort for nothing. And I wouldn't have the bottle of whisky any longer.

All in all, being in Do-nothing-ha-ha makes you wonder whether it's worth dragging yourself round the world in order to try to make ends meet. All that time traipsing around Africa, crossing deserts, sloping around malarial swamps and drinking champagne that has not been properly chilled. All those years travelling all over Eastern Europe on ramshackle Russian trains in which even the cockroaches refuse to buy return tickets. All that time struggling to survive in the old Yugoslavia on nothing but McDonald's and the best Iranian caviar. And, of course, the final straw: all those jokes when you finally get back home about it being all right for some, having a good holiday and enjoying yourself.

When you think about it, it's crazy, isn't it? Turning up at airports at the last possible minute because of meetings at the office and driving round and round the airport trying to find somewhere to leave the car. NCP, I reckon, means

No Convenient Parking. The constant baggage checks, the rows about hand luggage. Everybody else, it seems, can take six or seven trunks on the damn plane. Me, I carry dental floss in my pocket and I get bounced.

And all the inane announcements. 'If anyone needs special assistance in boarding will they please come forward now.' I need special assistance. I'm bombed out of my mind, I haven't slept for a week, and I'm suffering from post-AGM depression. Do I get special assistance? Not on your life. Some old lady, however, gets special assistance even though she can walk just as easily as I can. To add insult to injury, it's her one and only flight with the airline in 100 years, whereas I've flown with them a million times.

'Passengers with young families please board now through Door A.' I know one guy who always goes to Door A. 'Excuse me, sir,' bawls a failed sergeant major in a skirt. 'But you can't go through yet. You haven't got a young family.'

'Yes I have,' he says. 'But I left them at home.'

Then there's all the nonsense on the plane. 'Good morning, ladies and gentlemen. Welcome aboard this flight to Boulogne ... er, I mean Bologna.'

'Will you please pop your little tables away?'

'Excuse me, coffee for anyone, at all?'

'Has anyone found Irving's ring in the toilet?'

'I need your front alignment adjustment,' one of those bossy American stewardesses barked at me once. Front alignment adjustment? What the hell is front alignment adjustment? It turned out to be something to do with the seat. At least, I think it was.

And if inane announcements are bad in English, they are four or even five times worse in four or even five different languages. Some flights I've taken in the Far East come up with so many announcements in so many foreign languages that they're at it practically non-stop from the moment the team of yaks drags the plane on to the runway until it bellyflops at the other end and screeches to a halt just in front of yet another awful corrugated-iron shed.

And there are the passengers to contend with as well. The howling kids, the fat ladies who somehow seem to ooze over the top of their armrests and gradually take over the two seats on either side of them as well, the non-stop moaners.

I once sat next to a middle-aged couple off for the holiday of a lifetime in darkest Lithuania.

'Have you got your glasses?'

'Yes, dear.'

'No, they're not your glasses. You want your other glasses.'

'Yes, dear.'

'You've left them on the dressing table.'

'Yes, dear.'

'You've got your own socks, you don't want to wear those.'

'No, dear.'

'Give them back. Tell them you don't want them.'

'Yes, dear.'

'Don't put your dirty knife there. Put it back in the plastic bag.'

'Yes, dear.'

'Did you take your tablets?'

'Yes, dear.'

Then, talk about a coach outing, the wife took out of her shopping bag a flask, a pile of sandwiches in a poly-thene bag and the pair of them proceeded to munch their way through them all the way to Vilnius.

Which brings me, unfortunately, to airline meals. The reason they close the curtains between first class and economy is that they're so ashamed of the so-called expensive food and booze they're doling out to the high-rollers for all the extra money they've paid and don't want us sensible guys at the back to see it. Think about it. If they were proud of it, they'd leave the curtains open so that we'd all be so jealous that next time we'd all want to fly first class as well.

Not that the food at the back is much better. Many's the meal I've tried to force down that has smelled like something found inside one of Tutankhamun's bandages. I should think the face tissues would taste better. Not that there's any point complaining. Once, many moons ago, I dared to point out to an air stewardess that whatever it was she had just given me to eat was practically over-flowing.

'Of course it's watery,' she said. 'It's fish, isn't it?'

And what about all that *Boy's Own* bravado? 'No worry folks,' says the pilot. 'Plenty of experience landing these suckers at night in a Force Eleven gale in the South China Sea. Rain, heavy seas, everything they could throw at us. So hold tight, here we go.'

And that was coming into Birmingham. Birmingham, England.

Whenever I say anything about hotels, I'm always accused of nit-picking. But believe me, in many of the hotels I'm forced to stay at that's exactly what I'm doing all night. That and trying to open the door of my room with one of those electronic keys. Do I drop it in the slot and open the door? Or do I wait for the light to come on? Or do I wait for the light to come on and then flash on and off three times? Then do I take it out straight away? Or do I open the door and then take it out? Will someone tell me what's wrong with an ordinary key?

Next you've got to try to remember which way those flipping new-fangled taps work. Is it to the left or the right? Is it backwards or forwards? Is it up or down? If I want hot, do I turn half left, three-quarters forwards and two and seven-eight inches down? Or do I... Hell. Why can't you just turn the thing on and off?

Then the final ordeal. You land back at Gatwick in the middle of the night and some jolly-hockey-sticks games mistress comes bouncing up to you waving one of those travellers' surveys in the air and shrieking, 'Are you a Virgin person?' I might not be a Virgin person, but I invariably come home a different person than the one I was when I left.

Having suffered all that and more, much more, you'd have thought I could have celebrated my 100th in, say, Venice or Salzburg or Rheims or Cracow. Or maybe somewhere on the Italian lakes. Or wandering around Dublin or Boston or Budapest, or knocking back the Cuba Libres in Havana. Or looking around the churches in Quito or the mosques in Bukhara. Or listening to Vespers in the Church of St James, the Armenian church in the Old City of Jerusalem. Or even going out for a ride, galloping across the fields on Old Herbie.

So why Qatar? Admittedly, it's the traditional home of the Three Wise Men, but don't forget, even they didn't rush home. They put off their return for as long as possible by taking the long way back. It's amazing that, with all the money that has poured into the place over the years, it has remained so boring for so long. For generations there was virtually nothing to do apart from to drink red tea and go pearl-fishing. In the absence of any other diversions so many people went in for pearl-fishing that Qatar became virtually the world centre for it. At the turn of the century more than 10,000 men, virtually the entire male population, were pearl-fishers. Their dhows, which Marco Polo said could never withstand the sea, were all over the Gulf. Qatari fishermen and fisherboys risked life and limb and jellyfish attacks to find and bring back not only the finest pearls but all their arms and legs as well. The reason *The Pearl Fishers* is set in Sri Lanka and not in Do-nothing-ha-ha is, I reckon, that Andrew Lloyd-Webber, or whoever it was who wrote it, dropped in one day and, after taking in a couple of traditional Qatari bars of traditional Qatari music played on their traditional Qatari *rebabas*, the traditional Qatari one-string violin, got so Bizet that he fell fast asleep.

The Japanese, having got the idea from *The Pearl Fishers*, then moved in and destroyed the whole business, just as they have destroyed so many other businesses all over the world, by coming up with something better: the cheap cultured pearl. Suddenly there was no need for Qataris to risk their lives and limbs to find pearls which women in jewellers' shops all over the world could grandly dismiss as 'too yellow', having 'not enough shadow', or 'Oh no, no, no, darling. Just look at it. It's white.'

Even around forty years ago, therefore, Doha was still your typical desert outpost: a fort, a collection of dilapidated buildings, a couple of palm trees, donkeys ambling up and down, the odd camel. And at night packs of wild dogs ranging all over the place. As for the Qataris themselves, they take very seriously their government's warning that it will not accept any negligence, neither will it forgive any misconduct or misuse of authority. 'Those who do good will be rewarded and those who do bad will be punished,' it says.

So, in case anything they do might be construed as negligence, misconduct or misuse of their authority, they just sit around all day bored out of their tiny minds while the Indians and the Iranians and the Bangladeshis and the Pakistanis and the Filipinos and whoever else get on and run the country. The Qataris wouldn't dream of plugging a television set into the wall, let along fitting the plug, although they say it's because they are the masters of the house and they must not let Qatari women see them doing the work of tradesmen.

Then, of course, they discovered oil and now gas. From being the tiniest and most desolate and most under-developed of all the Arab states, suddenly they became the tiniest, the most desolate, the most underdeveloped and the richest of all the Arab states. As a result today the place is full of those Indians and Iranians and Bangla-deshis and Pakistanis and Filipinos and two guys from the Sudan. Practically the only people it is not full of are the British, which is probably not surprising, seeing as we've quit the place not once but twice. The first time was in 1940, when, I suppose, there were one or two other things going on that needed attention. After the war, though, we virtually owned the place - the oil industry, the gas industry, even the little shop by the third palm tree on the right by the bus station. It was all ours.

So what happened? Just as things were beginning to take shape, just when the good times were around the corner, we gave up. With our glorious knack of doing the wrong thing at the wrong time, the then state-owned British Petroleum walked away and handed the whole country, lock, stock and 378,000 barrels a day, to the Japanese, the French, the Italians and even the Danes. So today, even though the Qataris are nice and friendly and polite to us, the Qatari armed forces now carry out their military exercises with the French, businessmen study industrial development with the Germans and whenever a British minister is in town a change of government is deliberately arranged so that there is nobody around to meet him. They also insist that expats have a Qatari driving licence. Why? Because once, when the head of police was in London, he got nabbed for parking. None of our friendly bobbies, the so-called envy of the world, believed him when he told them who he was, so as soon as he got back home he decreed that everybody had to take a Qatari driving test and have a Qatari licence.

The Qataris, not surprisingly, live to the grand old average age of seventy-six while the rest of us, if we're lucky, die at sixty-two, the world average. I say the grand old average age of seventy-six, but it's difficult to be precise. Early one morning as I was getting in some practice at killing time watching the grass grow outside the hotel, I met an old man who looked as though he'd been around to look after the camels when the Three Kings finally got home.

'How old am I?' he asked me.

'Um, about thirty-nine,' I mumbled diplomatically.

'About thirty-nine?' he exploded in mock anger. 'I am twenty-three! Before my father died I said to him, how old am I? He said, twenty-three. All my life I never contradict what my father tells me.'

In any hotel – the Ramada, the Sheraton Gulf, or the Sheraton Doha, which looks like a pyramid designed by a committee – there they were, lolling about in the lobbies all day long with their feet up, playing with their prayer beads and picking their toes. Which always strikes me as doubly insulting – not just to Allah, but to the rest of us as well. I mean, how many times have we been lectured about not being discourteous to Arabs by showing them the soles of our feet and waving at them with our left hands, yet there they are, sprawled out over public seats in a public place, gouging great lumps of sand out of their toenails and picking away at their big toes with of all things, their right hands. And if they're not doing that they are lounging around the coffee shop or even the restaurant, toying with their red lentil soup while in the background a tiny Filipino pianist is belting out 'Around the World in Eighty days' for about the 300th time. And wherever they are and whatever they're doing, they will invariably be going on about some recent visit to Las Vegas, where they lost 'US$80,000, $90,000, or $100,000 on the tables in one evening', because it was something to do.

You think that's crazy? The present ruler, Sheikh Khalifah bin Hamad al Thani, is so worried that he might get bored that he is not content to potter around in one luxury royal yacht. He's ordered no fewer than three to be built specially for him, the biggest around 300 feet long, about the same size as our battered old Royal Yacht *Britannia*, presumably on the basis that if he gets fed up with one he can always trip off to the next one.

But there are exceptions. The really dashing, adventurous types now and then drag themselves down to their nearest government office, wave their I'm-a-100-per-cent-Qatari identity card at the poor, overworked, underpaid Bangladeshi clerk behind the desk, and tell him they need some money for a new car or a new house or a new anything and they've got it. Not in cash, because that would show up as cash and upset all the government's national income statistics. Instead they get vouchers to redeem the goods. Others, the truly reckless types, demand four visas so that they can bring in a cook, a housekeeper and two gardeners. They get them, no questions asked. Then it's another slow amble down to the marketplace, where they sell them at 2,000,000 ryals a piece to some desperate expat. For all that he gets 8,000,000 ryals for an hour's work. Around US$2,000 – about what your average Qatari would expect for just thinking of doing something, rather than actually doing it. Then, six months later, it's the same thing again. I suppose it makes a change from counting your oil wells. Would the poor, overworked, underpaid Bangladeshi clerk ever tell? What do you think? Don't for one moment, by the way, think these wild, reckless Qataris are stupid. They're not. They do all this while chewing tobacco at the same time.

Qatari civil servants might turn up in the office in time for tea but do they do any work? All I can say it that, with all the time and money in the world, Qatar is the only country I know that hasn't got time to provide half the information they are supposed to supply to the International Monetary Fund. Look at the IMF statistics on the country. Whole sections, such as government finance, international reserves, the average number of cups of thick, soupy, cinnamon coffee drunk by civil servants per day are either blank or grossly underestimated. Their figure of 6.7 million is more likely to be 12 or maybe even 14 million. Cups of thick, soupy, cinnamon coffee, I mean. Per day.

As for Qatari businessmen, they don't even have to bother to play golf and lose to their clients to make another fortune. All they do is take enormous full-page, full-colour advertisements in all the local newspapers congratulating the government on whatever they happen to be doing at that moment and all the government business they want just rolls in. The really successful ones who get all the big contracts are those who, day after day, say things like, 'We wish the country every success and continued progress under the wise leadership of HH the Emir.'

The other reason they're able to do so little work and make so much money is that they never pay their bills. Or if they do, they pay them so late that everybody has forgotten they ever billed them in the first place. This applies to the US$12 billion man himself, the Emir, who one year, just by stopping signing cheques – he signs all cheques over US$50,000 himself – swung the national deficit from US$525 billion to a surplus of US$100 million, and at the same time brought inflation down from a staggering 35 per cent to a more acceptable 7 per cent. Which is good news when you're a country, but absolutely disastrous when you're an individual.

On one swing through Do-nothing-ha-ha I met a British businessman who had not only been forced to sell his house back home in Reading but had lost over £20,000 on top of that because one Qatari businessman didn't pay his bills. They started out as the best of friends – holidays together in Spain, lunches and dinners, visits to each other's homes, that kind of thing. Amazingly, they were still the best of friends afterwards. I couldn't believe what I was hearing. 'But this guy owes you money! It's because of him, you've had to sell your home. It's because of him you lost all that cash.'

'Yes, but he's so friendly, so pleasant.'

'But you've lost...'

It was the usual story. A smart Arab wheeler-dealer, lots of money, picks up innocent Englishman. Promises him that if they work together they can make millions. English-man falls for it. Friendly Arab places bigger and bigger orders with innocent English businessman. Innocent English businessman buys with his own money and rebills. Bills always paid on time. Then comes the big one. Innocent English businessman buys and delivers. Smart, friendly Arab refuses to pay. Innocent English business-man up the Swannee but still his best friend.

The other easy way the Qataris have developed for making money, maybe a lot of money, for one short, sharp, burst of activity is selling their daughters. In Qatar daughters are virtually treated as a commodity, which is more than you can say of some countries. Prices run approximately thus:

For an average girl: US$70,000.

For a bit of class: US$100,000, maybe $150,000.

For something with access to the royal family: anything upwards of US$250,000.

Providing, of course, that the long-serving, devoted,

trusted, reliable, hard-working Pakistani chauffeur hasn't got to them first. Which, a number of Qataris told me over endless cups of cinnamon coffee, is becoming more and more of a problem and is therefore forcing them to keep their daughters at home even more securely under lock and veil.

Sons, quite rightly, can do whatever they want. Which is why today you can forget falcons, hunting and endurance riding across the Qatari desert with Fergie – indeed, anything to do with Fergie no doubt involves a great deal of endurance. The most popular sport in the country now is smashing brand-new Range Rovers to bits. This is not a difficult sport to master. First, take a long flat stretch of desert. Second, slap an enormous sand dune at the end of it, ideally one like those in the south of the country which weave backwards and forwards sometimes three or four times. Third, drive like hell down the long flat stretch of desert, hit the sand dune at a million miles an hour and shoot straight up it. The trickiest part is, just as you get to the top, you need to swing right – sharp right, it's an Arab country, don't forget, and everything is done with the right hand. Then simply zoom back down again without rolling over and killing yourself or any of the crowd of spectators who are actually standing at the very top of the sand dune looking down on the cars racing like mad towards them. The winner is whoever smashes the Range Rover into the most pieces in the shortest possible time or kills the fewest spectators.

When I was first privileged to watch this highly sophisti-cated traditional Qatari national event the joint winners were two young men in separate immaculate Range Rovers. How young? Fourteen. Yes, fourteen years old. What's a smashed-up Range Rover between father and son? It takes something marginally more important than a car to cause Qatari families to fall out. Something like US$12 billion.

The father of the present Emir lifted US$12 billion from number one bank account of the Diwan, or ruling family, at the National Bank of Qatar and tucked it up safe and sound in secret accounts in Geneva, Zurich, Monaco and London. Son finds out. While Dad is in Switzerland, resting no doubt, from the stress of the thought of how he was going to spend all that money, he stages a coup and takes over the running of the shop.

Father rouses himself from his exertions to protest. From the day he himself deposed his uncle, who also happened to be resting in Switzerland at the time, he never drew a salary, let alone expenses. He built the place up; without him nothing would have happened. Besides, as good old Louis XIV used to say, tossing a curl over his left ear, 'L'état c'est moi.' Which, roughly translated, means, 'If I want to put my hand in le till, there ain't nothing you or anyone can do about it.' In any case, nobody can steal their own money.

Not so, said the son. Le père was not l'état. L'état was something different. He should never have taken the money, and would he now please return it immediately or the son would sue and expose to the world one of the great and glorious Arab traditions of preaching Sharia law in public, ignoring it in private, helping yourself from the coffers and then pretending that what you stole really belonged to you in the first place. Besides, $12 billion was one hell of a lot of money to take, and without it even Qatar was having big, big, financial problems. And what was this computer disk we found, quite by chance, in an hotel in Bahrain containing some stuff about a counter coup with the Saudis and hiding bazookas and Kalashnikovs and rocket-propelled grenade-launchers and heavy machine-guns in and around Doha?

Upon which le père promptly surrendered, blamed the banks, as anybody would do in the circumstances, and said he would return all but a billion – after all, he wasn't getting any younger and like everybody else he wanted to put something by for his old age. Not to mention his French bodyguards.

This, of course, was immediately hailed as a victory by everyone: the father, the son and every brother, sister, aunt and uncle of every ruler in the Middle East who, by ancient Arab tradition, it is said, pockets 25 per cent of their country's annual oil revenues. The only people who were unhappy were the banks. They immediately ran around saying it wasn't US$12 billion after all, it was only $3 billion. Which is about par for the course. I've only got about 3s 6d in my bank account and still they can't get it right. Just think of the mistakes they can make with US$12 billion.

Was your average Qatari lounging in his Mercedes 600 interested in what was going on? Was he taking sides? Was he gossiping about it with his friends while they – flick – were cleaning their toes – flick – curled up on all those sofas in the hotels? No way. I went all over what there was of Do-nothing-ha-ha. I visited various offices, ministries, hotels, restaurants. Not a word. I went to see one very smooth, very elegant old Qatari in his home just outside the city. The whole place was air-conditioned, but the doors were wide open.

'I like to feel the cool desert air,' he smiled. Did I say anything? What do you think?

To try to understand the underlying reason for their attitude, I decided to take a look at the cause of the problem: the oil and gas operations at Umm Sa'id, about half an hour south of Doha. By Mercedes, of course. These developments are huge, Huge, HUGE. So huge, I was told, that they can actually be seen from outer space. Umm Sa'id, originally an oil-sodden patch of dust, shipped its first oil supplies in 1952. At the time there were hardly any roads. The airport was a single landing strip with a one-roomed hut. The Emir's palace was only half built. Come 1957 the palace was finished, a mosque had appeared and Qatar was boasting the most modern hospital in the Middle East.

After that things just took off. Today, Umm Sa'id is one of the largest on and offshore oil developments in the world. There are also vast cement plants, flour mills, fertiliser operations and steel mills and everything else you would expect to support such a huge operation: a golf course, a sailing club, a cinema that doesn't work and intense security. I wanted to visit some of the factories but the Pakistani security police wouldn't let me in. They said they wanted to see letters of invitation, a bunch of special code numbers, my passport and the name and telephone number of my dentist.

I did what anyone would do in the circumstances. I backed up to the Al Shallah Restaurant just off the main highway, which is more of a transport café than a restaurant, dropped an Egyptian lorry-driver a couple of dollars and returned with him in his truck. He kept telling me, 'Saddam Hussein, he like English in old times.' Whether he was trying to say that Saddam Hussein admired Henry VIII, Elizabeth I, Cromwell, Judge Jeffreys and all the others, or that Saddam Hussein admired the way English people generally behaved twenty or thirty years ago I couldn't establish. What I did discover, however, was that nobody was interested in the ruling family now. Nobody mentioned it, and when I did, nobody seemed to know what I was talking about. Which, I admit, is not an unusual position for me to be in.

But what I discovered at their other huge, huge, EVEN HUGER development, Ras Laffan, the world's biggest liquefied natural gas plant, I'm not sure. There I was, standing by the side of a long four-lane highway leading into the site. In front of me was the coast, the sea, and far out to sea, the gas rigs themselves. All around me was nothing but desert. Stony desert, not your nice sandy, sand-dune, let's-go-and-smash-up-a-couple-of-Range-Rovers desert. In the far distance there was a herd of camels ambling slowly towards me. It was boiling hot, so hot I could see the heat shimmering all around me. I turned around to see two London buses hurtling towards me.

I must admit, for a split second I thought they were a mirage. But as they roared right past me without stopping I realised they were quite genuine. In fact I could see on the side of one of them a poster saying, I kid you not, 'London: £22 return'.

Assuming that everything else I saw was as real as the two London buses, all I can say is that, even though I can't find Ras Laffan on my London Transport route map, it must be one of the biggest construction projects ever. It's not just the world's biggest liquefied natural gas plant, it's also the world's largest port-construction project, one of the world's largest dredging operations, one of the world's largest breakwater operations and undoubtedly the biggest thing ever attempted in the history of the world without the aid of alcohol. Indeed, it's also going to be the scene of the world's biggest non-alcoholic opening cere- mony, so if you're thinking of trying to gatecrash, don't bother. You'd have more fun tasting the home-made wine at the Young Wives' summer fête.

Wherever we went my Mercedes driver, when he wasn't telling me the story of his life – 'Yes, sir. I'm qualified water engineer. From Sri Lanka, sir. Tamil Tigers, they ruin everything, sir. I have to leave, sir, because I need money. My wife, sir, and my daughters, sir, they are still in Sri Lanka. I go back to see them once a year, sir. Life is very, very different, sir' – was telling me how the place had changed. 'Ten years ago, sir, no road here. Just desert. Five years they start looking. Just a track across desert. Now big roads, sir. Big, very big project, sir. Everything change, sir. Everything different. Nobody else, however, wanted to say a word. About the project, about how much money Qatar was putting into it, about how much they were having to raise. About who else was investing in it. And especially about Bank Account Number 1.

On the return journey, having told me the story of his life and the history of Qatar, the driver tried a different approach. He kept on and on about how the most important thing for a Muslim was prayer. But when we got back to the hotel and instead of paying him I offered to pray for him, he turned quite Tamil Tiger.

That apart, the only exciting thing that happened to me in Qatar was the leaving of it. When I checked in at Gulf Air on the way out I told the Indian guy at the check-in, who looked and acted as though he'd flown with Bomber Command during the last war, that Qatar was my 100th country and he promptly upgraded me to Falcon Class. But for some reason or other he made my ticket out to Mr Patel, so I wasn't allowed to celebrate my 100th in my own name.

But wait a minute. Didn't I stop off once in Kampala for the afternoon to meet a Mr Patel? Yes, I did. Thank goodness for that. This wasn't my 100th after all. Qatar, and especially Do-nothing-ha-ha, is no place to celebrate anything.

MUSCAT

Well, all I can say is I hope Thesiger is pleased with himself.

Before he went off on his little trek across the Empty Quarter, the dreaded Rub Al Khali desert, one of the most arid regions of the world, Oman, the second largest gulf state after Saudi Arabia, was the desert kingdom to end all desert kingdoms. In the north they grew dates, about 100 varieties of them. In the south they grew frankincense trees and supplied, among others, the Three Wise Men and the Queen of Sheba. In between, the odd one or two Bedouin prayed for rain. But since he started churning out book after book about his trip, oh man, oh man, the whole country has become a pantomime. Oh yes it has.

So much so that the fellas have ditched the usual white cotton *thawb*, the black *bisht* and the white headdress you see all over the Middle East. Instead they're running around in *dishdashes* in a mass of bright colours: violet, apricot, even pink, with black or cinnamon-coloured cloaks usually embroidered with gold and that funny-shaped *tarboosh* or turban on their heads. When I was there the in colour was mauve.

For women, the difference is even more dramatic. Not for them black veils and masks and dresses. They wear long, flowing robes of reds and oranges and purples. Many of them still wear the veil, but somehow they seem to throw it casually around their face like a designer accessory. The whole place, as a result, looks like something out of Ali Baba and the Forty Thieves. Oh yes it does.

You think I'm kidding? OK, so who's the most important person in Omani history? Sinbad the Sailor. Oh yes he is.

Thanks to Thesiger, present-day Oman, if anything, is more of an Empty Quarter pantomime than the Empty Quarter itself ever was: empty of history, empty of culture, empty of atmosphere and most noticeably empty of that wonderful silence of the desert. They've already got Wilfred Thesiger books everywhere. It won't be long before they have the *Wilfred Thesiger Desert Cook Book* – 'First catch your camel' – Wilfred Thesiger key rings and even, I suppose, Wilfred Thesiger prayer mats. The ultimate, of course, would be Wilfred Thesiger meets Sinbad the Sailor. To the sound of Omani drums playing 'The Dunes of Glory'.

Before – I'm speaking as an old Sahara hand, although I'm afraid I've only crossed it two and a half times – the desert was the desert. It was vast, empty, totally silent. Now it's simply somewhere to go to do what the Australians call Wadi-bashing. The whole area not just the fantastic sand dunes of Al Shaft, has been shafted by Land Rovers, Land Cruisers and every type of off-road 4×4 you can think of, including something called a Hummer, which was apparently the second-most popular thing with the military during the Gulf War. The first was giving interviews to CNN. I'm no expert, but to me it looks like an economy-version Land Rover put together by a bunch of Russians with the aid of instructions in Braille on a Friday afternoon after being told they were about to be privatised. What's more, or rather what's worse, it can do even more than all the other off-road 4×4s can do. It can climb sand dunes and mountains no other 4×4 can climb. It can then skid down them like no other 4×4 can. It can also drive for days on end in 2 feet of water and generally destroy the environment like no other 4×4 can. If you don't want to go wadi-bashing, don't worry, you can always go sand-skiing – providing, of course, you haven't forgotten your chillproof underwear. And if you fancy a break, there are signs all over the place saying, 'Natural Picnic Spot 2kms'.

Before, if you were trekking across the desert and you came across a large brown Bedouin tent with camels and goats around it, you would automatically be welcomed into the *majlis*, or reception room, invited to pull up a cushion and there for hours on end you would chat away and drink tea with the fellas while the women bustled around making certain everything was in order. After-wards, as a sign of gratitude you would be expected to wipe your hands on the flaps of the tent. Today the only Bedouin tents you see in Oman are invariably full of tourists trying to enjoy a so-called authentic taste of Oman. An authentic taste of Oman? The tents are practically smothered in mosquito nets. If you stand up you get caught in an electric flying insect-killer. If you take one step to either side you risk tripping over any number of ultrasound rodent- and bird-deterrents. So numerous have they become and so successful are they at killing rodents and birds, I reckon it won't be long before the white storks give up coming all the way from Eastern Europe to Oman for the winter. With no rodents or birds around, they might just as well save themselves the effort. If you get up to wipe your hands on the flaps of the tent, a thousand old men in Sinbad the Sailor suits will leap at you from nowhere with tiny scented towels neatly wrapped in polythene. When I got up to wipe my hands, admittedly within seconds of arriving, I was firmly told that a belly dancer had been laid on, which I suppose was bound to happen sooner or later, and, hands still unwiped, I was ushered back into my place.

As for the traditional Bedouin welcome of a bowl of

dates and a flask of *kahwa*, forget it. Nowadays it's more likely to be a Mongolian barbecue, if you're lucky. If you're unlucky you could end up in a McDonald's or even in a genuine, authentic, 100 per cent Omani Wild West restaurant where you can 'hang out in the saloon or grab a table and git yourselves some Wild West cookin' straight from the Sizzlin' Grill' or the '01' Ranch menu'. Go on a Friday night and you can 'Eat as much as you like. Five free drinks.' Go on a couples night and 'Ladies can drink as much as they can. Choice of set menus and surprises.' Allah help me. I'd take the goatskin water bottle any time.

And what about the *khanjar*, the glittering dagger the Omanis always used to wear? They've been reduced at best to a fashion accessory to mix and match with the fancy coloured cloaks and *dishdashes* and at worst to a mindless souvenir to give someone back home who is going to thank you profusely and then throw it in a drawer and forget all about it. Pre-Thesiger, everybody made them: the ordinary everyday kind with the wide hilt; the more upmarket *sayyidi* with the narrow handle which was either completely covered with silver or silver thread, and the top-of-the-range *zari*, covered with gold and gold thread. Now, not only is the *khanjar* a dying instrument, its production is also a dying craft. In the whole Sharquiya region, for example, I could only find one Omani making the real thing. Well, I say making. What he was doing was getting other people to make the bits and pieces and simply assembling them. Plenty of others were making cheap imitations using ivory, rhinoceros horn, marble, sandalwood and even, horror of horrors, female goatskin, which, as everybody knows, is nowhere near as tough and strong and long-lasting as male goatskin. See what useful bits of information you pick up crossing the Sahara. The situation is now so bad that the government has set up various centres and associations all over the country to teach people the skills and crafts they have practised for generations: not just *khanjar*-making, but weaving, pottery, basket-making, cushion-making, wood-carving and jewellery-making as well.

Pre-Thesiger, dhows ploughed backwards and forwards all over the Gulf as well as to India, China and even Africa. Now they've been replaced by noisy fibreglass motor-boats, not to mention what they call 'tube' and 'banana' rides, aquabikes and funny-looking things called knee-boards. The long, sandy beaches, the lagoons and coral reefs and rocky islands, the deep fjords in Musandam at the very top of the country on the Straits of Hormuz now echo to the sound of divers giving each other 'buddy checks' and practising their 'buddy breathing exercises'. Personally, I can't wait for the day they do their buddy disappearing act. The only dhows you're likely to see nowadays in Oman are in the middle of roundabouts, where they have been reduced to mere focal points. Meanwhile the fishermen who have been fishing along the coast and around the Gulf for nearly 5,000 years are now being sent back to school to learn how to fish. And who is teaching them? South Koreans.

Gone also are most of the old *souks* with their narrow lanes and tiny shops selling everything from rose petals to herbal medicines. In their place are enormous, brassy, US-style shopping centres featuring Sinbad's Adventure Play-grounds complete with dodgems and bouncy castles and every type of fast-food you can imagine. Ugh.

As for actually meeting a poor 'generous, courageous, hardy, patient and good-humoured Bedouin', whose noble qualities Thesiger said he had never seen anywhere else in the world, your only chance is to go on one of their 'Meet a Family of Bedouin' desert safaris, which come complete with barbecue and your own personal souvenir photograph of the occasion. All the rich, generous, courageous, hardy, patient and good-humoured Bedouins have taken their nobility, Allah help them, off to the UK to have it knocked out of them. If they are young they're thrown into godforsaken boarding schools in the middle of nowhere, like the present ruler, Sultan Qaboos bin Said. He was sent to some small private school in, of all places, Bury St Edmunds. From there he scaled the academic heights to that pinnacle of learning, Sandhurst. After that there was no stopping him. He became an adjutant with the Scottish Rifles, the Cameroonians. Fully trained and equipped for the modern world, he then got a job where he could use his education and his experience to the utmost. He became a local-government officer in Bedford. It was all downhill from there. After all, Bedford has a population of over 2 million. Oman's is only around 1.1 million. He went home to a warm welcome from his father, the old sultan, who promptly locked him up in his palace in Salalah, way down in the south of the country, where, for six years, he had a hot, sweaty, sticky time with 150 concubines. Hot, sweaty and sticky because of the weather. Salalah, the second-largest city in the country, is known for its monsoons. It's about the only part of the region that gets them. The concubines were not for him – he was given his own personal cook and teacher and forced to study Islamic law and theology – but no doubt his experience of British public schools stood him in good stead.

As for the generous, courageous, hardy, patient and good-humoured Bedouin who are lucky enough not to have been sent to English boarding schools, the nearest they get to the desert nowadays is when some yahoo is looking for a guide to take him to the best stretch of sand on which he can wreck his brand new 4×4.

Strangely, even though Thesiger banged on about the generous, patient, etc. etc., he actually preferred to spend his time with Walis. In other words, the imams, the guys who tell the sheikhs what to do. There's still plenty of them around, except that now they're wearing Hawaiian shirts, bawling into mobile phones and going on about how authentic everything is.

It's not difficult to see the impact Thesiger has had on the country itself. Take Nazwa, the former capital, for example. For over 1,000 years it remained virtually unchanged. It was the main town of the *al joof*, the interior of the country, and for centuries the traditional seat of the Al Yarubi dynasty. It was a key stopover for the caravans plying copper and frankincense backwards and forwards across Thesiger's impassable Empty Quarter to Saudi Arabia, Yemen and even to Iraq. It was also one of the first towns to receive messengers from the Prophet Mohammed, Peace be upon Him.

Way back in the 1750s, however, I'm sure the first imam of the Al Yarubi dynasty foresaw the arrival of Thesiger, and didn't even want him there for the traditional Arab three and a third days (three and a third days not because that was about as much as they could stand of anybody's company, but because that was the length of time they reckoned it took for food to go in one end and out the other). That, I reckon, is why he ordered the construction of a fort to keep at bay the foreigners who he knew would one day eventually destroy the place. Today, if you can get close enough for the tourists crawling all over it, you can see everything they did to try to keep him out: the huge battlements, the enormous round tower, the gun emplacements, the solid doors, the muzzle-loaded guns, leather belts full of bullets made by their own hands should their curved silver *khanjars* fail, even the cauldrons of burning oil they were prepared to throw on top of him if he got anywhere near the gates themselves. I even spotted in one of the tiny downstairs rooms a mincer made by Spong and Co. Ltd, England. What exactly they were going to use that for nobody could tell me, but the very sight of it brought tears to my eyes. In case the fort alone would not be enough to stop him, they even set up a system to send messengers throughout the country to warn everybody that Thesiger was coming.

But it was all in vain. He got in.

Inside the fort you can see what life was like pre-Thesiger. Apart from all the rebuilding, which has practically changed the shape of the thing. Apart from all the electric lighting and other mod cons. And apart from all the modern furnishings.

Drive into Nazwa today, through the gateway with statues of horses on either side, and it blows your mind. There's a Pizza Hut, a Butchery shop, a Modern Oman bakery, a Snow White Laundry, a big industrial estate, hot-air balloon rides, a thousand antique shops, posters saying 'Opening Soon. Fish Shop' and a huge sign outside a sports stadium saying 'Youth Complex', which comes as no surprise to me in Oman, or any other country, for that matter.

In the centre, facing the fort, is a massive car park, about the size of a football pitch. It is always full, especially on Fridays. For not only is the place full of tourists, but all the locals go there as well for the weekly market. So if you're not careful you're as likely to find an old goat in the back seat of your car as your mother-in-law. Alongside it are a string of specialised markets, all in their own Sinbad-the-Sailor-style buildings: a spice market, a date market, a goat market, a vegetable market selling potatoes from Syria, apples from Iran and oranges from Brazil, and another market which was either selling flies or fish, I couldn't make out which. Further along are your traditional Arab shops. I could tell they were traditional Arab shops because there were no flies on them. One was holding a 'food stuff sale'. Another was running an 'already made dress sale'. There were shops selling exercise books from Indonesia, postcards from Taiwan, cans of a strange-tasting malt drink made from barley harvested in Oman itself and guns and daggers, which the shopkeeper assured me had been made specifically to be used against Thesiger.

Head out of Nazwa for Muscat, the capital, and you will see signs of Thesigerisation wherever you go. Practically every fort you pass has been rebuilt, restyled, modernised and whitewashed. Which is a bit disconcerting: most of the secret panels and passages have gone and there is little evidence of the prisons and torture chambers of old.

Take the Jabrin fort, for example. It is in a superb position – for the tour guides – sitting all by itself in the middle of a flat level plain. They can spot a tourist a million miles away. Inside, next door to his bedroom, is the upstairs stable where the Sultan used to keep his horse though the ramp has gone. If the poor old horse came back today he'd have about three flights of stairs to climb before he could get to his room.

Bahla, which is surrounded by an 11-kilometre wall, is not so much a fort as a fortified city. Once famous for witchcraft and black magic, today it is the pottery centre of Oman. Wherever you look there are lumps of clay, potters' wheels, enormous rough-and-ready kilns and, no doubt hidden away in the shadows, young girls called Anna dreaming of freedom and life in the big city.

Barkat Moos, a tiny village which for thousands of years did nothing but grow bananas is now on the tourist map too. Huge sections of the country are criss-crossed by ancient, intricate networks of underground water channels, known as *falaj,* a trick the Omanis picked up from the Persians 2,000 years ago. Poor old Barkat Moos is unfortunate enough not only to have its own intricate network of underground water channels, but to be sufficiently north of Nazwa to be what they call a 'comfort stop' as well.

However, Al Hamra, the starting point for Jebel Shams, which is the Arab answer to the Grand Canyon, is just off the beaten track. For me the best part of going there is standing by the old fort overlooking the town. From here you see a pretty little oasis town – tiny little streets, neat little houses, the occasional satellite dish.

As for mountains, I've seen mountains in my time, the Hajar Mountains are fantastic, completely different from anything you see anywhere else in the Gulf (well, maybe with the exception of the eastern part of the Emirates, where the mountains gradually come to a halt and disappear). Here they're like enormous cliffs that suddenly drop sheer to the ground. They are also a mass of different colours: dark grey, light grey, dark red, copper, blue. I'm no geologist, but you can see why they are being mined for everything they've got: oil and gas, of course, but also ochre, manganese, chromate, copper, sardoine, jasper, cornelian and aventurine. Stone tablets have been found which show that 4,000 years ago they were mining copper in Oman, which is no surprise.

Drive through Jabal Akhdar, the great green mountain, along the Sumail and Halfein valleys, turn right and you hit Ibra on the edge of the vast, barren plains of the Sharqiyah, where every Wednesday they have a market for women only. No, not that kind of market for women only, a market run by women for women. Which is about the nearest you'll come to Women's Lib in the whole of the Middle East. Come eight o'clock in the morning the men shuffle out of the market square with their loved ones, their goats and their camels, and in come the women, bedecked in their colourful robes and belts and jewellery and their *birkas*, or leather face masks, to hustle and sell jewellery and make-up and dress material and plastic buckets to other women bedecked in colourful robes and belts and jewellery and *birkas*, or leather face masks. But enough of such serious business.

Turn left and you'll hit Sohar, the so-called home of the

most famous Omani of all times and in its day one of the greatest trading cities in the world. Good old Al Muqaddasi, a famous Arab traveller of the tenth century, called it 'the hallway to China, the storehouse of the east'. It also handled all Oman's huge exports – witness the stone tablets. Today its only claim to fame is that it is the home of the Sinbad Wondercentre Fun City. Whatever you do, don't stop here.

Keep straight on and you'll come to my favourite town of all: Bidbid. Now, if that's not the ideal location for the Omani stock exchange, I don't know what is. Just behind the fancy bus stop, I would suggest, right next to the general store. I'm thinking of buying the site as soon as I get my next dividend cheque. Bidbid is, appropriately enough, where I learned the secrets of an ancient stock exchange tradition: drinking coffee. Nowadays, of course, it's drinking champagne. To get an Omani caffeine jag – eat your heart out, Seattle – you need one part cardamom to nine parts coffee, preferably coffea arabica from Ethiopia. You make it in a *medlah* or *dallah*, stirring it with a *yad*, preferably not behaving badly, and ladle it out with a *mishaseh* into tiny handle-less cups. They recommend that you drink it with dates. But I still prefer drinking champagne.

To make the best coffee – listen carefully, I got this from the experts – you should keep your raw coffee beans in a small leather bag in an old iron chest at the back of your tent. The longer you keep them, the better. To crush them you need a brass mortar and a heavy pestle. Every third stroke of the pestle, you should bang the side of the mortar. This has got nothing to do with making coffee: it's to tell all your neighbours you're about to brew up and if they want to come and join you they can. Watch out, though, exactly how you bang the mortar. Bang it one way and you're telling your mates you're a good guy and they could be in for some laughs; bang it another way and you're telling them to watch out for a government official, a taxman or, worse still, that Thesiger is in the area. Having completed your Omani morse code, roast your beans over the fire in a long-handled frying pan. Once roasted, they are ready for the *medlah*. Roasting and grinding the beans first before you boil them is better than roasting and grinding them and storing them for a million years. And apparently, lots of little cups of coffee are better for you than one big one. With or without a cigarette.

What does it taste like? Well, to look at, as I've said, it is like a thick, heavy, sandy sludge. The taste is ... well, interesting. Depending on how much cardamom you put in. Too much and it tastes like thick, heavy, sandy sludge. Too little and it's about right. Back home, if we don't want any more coffee we shake our heads from side to side. In Oman they shake the cup from side to side.

But does it enable you to get the max out of your camel? Gee whizz, I should say so. I've seen guys have two tiny cups of the stuff and they're hollering and shouting louder than if they had downed a whole pint of Nicaraguan Nuevo Segovia. The camels don't know what's hit them. They're leaving skid marks all over the desert. As for having one for the road, it's more of a killer than a bottle of Scotch or a Colombian cappuccino (a real Colombian cappuccino, if you see what I mean). In fact, some people maintain that Omani coffee was the world's first neutron bomb: it killed all the people but left the buildngs intact. Which is why today the population is next to nothing and the whole place is buried in sand.

I certainly needed a couple of dozen little cups of the stuff to set me up before I hit the sickly-sweet capital, Muscat de Beaume de Venise, or Magan, as it was originally called, because of all the rich copper deposits in the area. If, on your way back to the hotel after a particularly busy working lunch, the hills around you seem to be alive with lots of little men, don't worry. It's nothing to do with the alcohol, lack of or otherwise. It's caused by the copper in the soil. At least, that's my excuse.

Thirty years ago Muscat was nothing but a shanty town on a beach surrounded by a mud-brick wall with a rough-and-ready Emir's palace. There was no gas, no electricity (except in the Emir's palace, of course) and no running water. There were three primary schools and only one hospital, run by an American missionary group. Cars were banned, smoking was forbidden, newspapers were not allowed. Even wearing sunglasses was against the law. Playing musical instruments was a heinous offence. Anyone caught with even a traditional musical instrument would be brought before the courts, the instrument would be burned and the owner thrown in jail. Everybody had to be back in town by sunset, when they locked the massive wood and iron gates. If you were out, you stayed out until they were opened again the following morning at sunrise. The only proper road in the country ran just 17 kilometres from Muscat to the old Bait al Falaj Airport, or rather landing strip, where, when the Emir was bored, he would go hunting. Not for animals, for passengers. Apparently he enjoyed nothing better than lurking in the shadows taking pot-shots at people as they got off the odd plane that dropped in from time to time. For, not surprisingly, all foreigners were barred as well. Some people claim that the reason he was so fond of taking pot-shots at people arriving at the airport was that he was convinced that one day, by the law of averages, he would get Thesiger.

Gradually, however, as Thesiger grew older and more feeble and less likely to come back, the old Emir relaxed. And we all know what happens in the Gulf states whenever an old emir relaxes: the son puts the knife in. In this case, however, it was with the help of the British. A bunch of SAS guys burst into the old Emir's palace at Salalah one night and overpowered his slaves and bodyguards. The old Sultan drew his revolver, but he got it all wrong. Instead of shooting the SAS he shot himself. In the foot. Literally. The son ordered his men, all Omanis, to arrest him but Father put his other foot down. He said he wanted to be arrested by the British. Obviously he was nervous at the thought of the traditional Arab reception the Omanis were preparing for him, remembering all those years he had kept them in abject poverty while all around them the Middle East was booming. Eventually, as in all good coups, a compromise was agreed. He was arrested by the Omanis and then promptly handed over to the British, who saw him on his way to exile. In the Dorchester in London.

The son then had to send out for a tiny 1-kilowatt radio so that he could announce to a country without radios that he had taken over and that 'a new dawn will rise on Oman, a new dawn which will give its people a new life and a new hope for the future'. Which sounds to me suspiciously like an extract from one of the Queen's Christmas broadcasts. I suppose it shows that at least one person in Britain used to listen to her Christmas message.

Ex-Bury St Edmunds public schoolboy, ex-Sandhurst cadet, ex-Bedford local government officer Sultan Qaboos then set about modernising the country so that it could stand proudly alongside the rest of the world. First, he dropped the idea of having everyone address him as 'His Highness', as his father had done. Instead he insisted that people called him 'His Majesty'. Then he married a wife with no name – the official announcement, published a week after the ceremony took place, referred merely to a 'respected daugher of Sayyid Tariq bin Taimour of the royal family'. A few years later he then divorced the wife with no name, who had no children with no names either. She is now believed to be living in London at an address which nobody knows. His next big decision was to introduce five minutes of Western classical music on television every evening before the news.

At the same time, even though Oman is not one of the richest of the Gulf states – poor dears, they've only got about 1 per cent of all Arab oil supplies, enough to last a measly twenty years – he also set about building schools, healthcare centres, hospitals – there is even one at Haima in the middle of the desert especially for the Bedouins – and, of course, roads. He encouraged rapid, massive development, but whatever was built, he insisted, Prince Charles-style, should be in keeping with traditional Arab architecture, right down to the size and shape of the windows, the type of galleries, the shape of the fountains, the tiles and even the wall decorations. And I don't just mean towers and office blocks, but bus stops and telephone boxes as well. The result is that the entire country seems to have been designed by Beau Geste on a day off from you know what.

The Omanis, of course, say that this is to safeguard the environment, conserve their culture, protect their heritage and ensure that throughout the country there is a unity and harmony of architecture. Others, late at night over surreptitious large Scotches, away from the cameras and microphones, say it is the most fantastic way in history of maintaining a construction closed shop. Only Omani builders know how to build Omani-style.

But whatever anyone says, the Omanis love their Bury St Edmunds-educated, Sandhurst-trained Bedford local government officer. To them he is more important than God. They never refer to him as anything other than the full 'His Majesty'. They never, ever say 'him' or 'his' or 'the leader' or even the almighty, all-powerful or all-gracious. It is always 'His Majesty'. On one trip I came across a stroppy Australian girl who was working for the Emir as some kind of secretary. She went on and on about His Majesty said this, His Majesty said that, His Majesty did this, His

Majesty did that. His Majesty got up in the morning and put His Majesty's socks on and went down to His Majesty's kitchen to have His Majesty's breakfast.

I asked her what all this 'His Majesty' bit was for. Had the Emir banned the use of the personal pronoun, or was it some kind of innate Australian respect for royalty? Did she go bananas! I was being disrespectful to His Majesty. His Majesty had not banned His Majesty pronouns. It was just that one should show respect to His Majesty for all His Majesty had done since His Majesty had been in His Majesty power. If one lived in His Majesty's country one should show His Majesty respect for His Majesty, all His Majesty's rules, all His Majesty standards and all His Majesty traditions. She then reported me for being disrespectful to His Majesty. The laugh was, I discovered later, she was breaking every rule in His Majesty's book. She was living with some member of His Majesty's royal family, which is definitely not His Majesty done in His Majesty's country.

Old Gulf hands – British, of course – smile at all this 'His Majesty' business, twirl their moustaches and tell you that Oman is more British than any of the other Gulf states. Not so. It's clean, it's neat, it's tidy, there's no litter and no rubbish stacked outside people's houses. There are no broken-down cars in the street. What's more His Majesty reportedly drives His Majesty's BMW around the streets of Muscat late at night, talking to ordinary people to find out what they really think. He also retains a British sense of fair play picked up in his formative years, so much so that clubs and associations are banned on the basis that whenever two or three people gather together they will probably moan about Thesiger. Receptions, however, are allowed in moderation. But again because of his British sense of fair play, they treat everybody the same. Each embassy, for example, is permitted to hold only one reception a year: whether you are tiny little Qatar next door, with barely 60,000 genuine 100 per cent pure Qataris, or India, with 900 million people and over 300 different languages.

That apart, if His Majesty will excuse me, Muscat is spectacular. A spectacular backdrop to a spectacular production. Of *Sinbad the Sailor*, what else? Everywhere, thanks to their building policy, there are traditional Arabic domes and traditional Arabic arches and traditional Arabic carved wooden balconies and traditional Arabic stained-glass windows and magnificent traditional Arabic gardens with grey-green Arabic date palms, pink and purple Arabic petunias, thousands of Arabic shrubs and a million miles of lush, Arabic manicured green, green lawns.

Towering over the tiny bay, surrounded on three sides by mountains, is a huge Arabic white frankincense-burner and, incidentally, a kids' playground complete with dodgems, slides, bouncy castles and racetrack. Go there at dusk to watch the sunset and you can just about see it through the fumes pumped out by the popcorn machines. Either it's that or the frankincense-burner has sprung a leak.

Out on either side of the bay are two old forts, Jalali and Mirani. Jalali was built by the Omanis but modified by the Portuguese shortly after they captured Muscat in 1506. Mirani was built by the Portuguese to back up Jalali. So secure were they that the Omanis only managed to get them out because, in 1646, Britain, perfidious as ever, decided to turn against its oldest ally and throw its weight instead behind Imam Nasir al Yarubi, a member of one of the oldest tribes in the country and the leading anti-colonialist of the day. It worked: within three years the Omanis had reconquered the forts and the rest of the country and begun a centuries-long love-in with Britain.

Overlooking the whole bay is His Majesty's palace, or rather, one of His Majesty's six palaces. Come, come, that's not extravagant. His Majesty has only one personal airport, two royal yachts (one sail, one power), one support ship, a mere 750 horses, a more than economic £5 million manor house at Henley-on-Thames and an estimated 2.5 million CDs and cassettes of classical music. This palace looks like a row of huge upturned blue and yellow trumpets with a slab of white gold on top. All terribly over-the-top Ottoman. I assume it is meant to symbolise his love of music – he flew the entire BBC Philharmonic Orchestra to Muscat by private jet at a cost of £500,000 to play a series of concerts to mark his twenty-fifth anniversary in power – and his love of traditional Arab architecture. Surrounding it are masses of trees and flowers and unseen security equipment.

In the old days when the Brits virtually ran the place, the British Embassy stood right next door to the old royal palace. Not any more. In order to persuade the Brits to move out, the Omanis gave the ambassador the opportunity to choose wherever he wanted to live in the whole country. He chose a site miles away, far up in the hills overlooking an enormous yachting marina which can handle up to 400 yachts and cruisers and what have you at a time. Now the Japanese are the Omanis' major trading partner.

Surrounding His Majesty's royal palace today are government buildings, either lovingly restored old ones or beautiful new sandstone ones. There is also the Al Khur Mosque, His Majesty's mosque, or rather, one of His Majesty's mosques. A word of advice. If you're going to have a look around, go at night time. Like most things, Muscat looks better at night. Somehow the floodlights bring out the colours, the definition and the detail far more than natural light. In the morning, particularly the early morning, all you ever see are imperfections. But then, you don't need me to tell you that.

Muscat is not just Muscat. It is also the Al-Bustan Hotel which, with its massive ten-storey-high beautifully decorated octagonal atrium, is about as big as Muscat itself. It must be one of the greatest hotels in the world.

Then there are Matrah and Ruwi and Qurum and Al Khuwair, all rolled into one. Matrah, set on an equally magnificent bay with mountains on just one side, is the old business centre. Thirty years ago tiny boats would be pulled up on the sand and goods would be unloaded and strapped on to the backs of donkeys. The donkeys would then carry them up to the *souk*. At times the sea would wash across the beach and flood the whole area. Now the whole bay is virtually one huge port. Dredgers, cargo ships, even liners now dock there and instead of donkeys there are huge container lorries. When I was there they were unloading a cargo boat full of live sheep. The main *souk*, however, is still there – just as busy, just as over-crowded as ever. Alley Number 1 is the antique dealers' *souk*. Alley Number 2 is the jewellers' *souk*. Alley Number 3 is the Versace-comes-to-the-Middle East fashion *souk*. Alley Number 4 is the spices and perfume *souk*.

Ruwi is the new town, full of banks and insurance companies and hotels and luxury restaurants. But – Milton Keynes eat your heart out – it's not just any old new town. It's beautifully designed and immaculately laid out. On one side, the highway takes you out to the airport; on the other side it leads to Wadi Al Kabir.

Qurum is where you drag yourself from your luxury office to your even more luxury home, where at dusk you wander along the beach with its barbecues shaped like logs and its litter bins shaped like fish, and where you watch the fishermen come in to the sound of a million kids shrieking in the Jurassic Arcade at the Araimi Centre, with its 55,000 video-game machines, including, of course, its very own Jurassic Park simulator.

Al Khuwair is great fun. This is where you try to spot the difference between the ministries and the ministers' homes. I'll give you a clue: the ministers' homes are always bigger. Indeed, one minister's home is so big it practically covers the whole district. To be fair, though, it does include his own personal mosque, his own personal zoo and a house so vast that nobody has yet been able to count all the rooms in it. It is also where you play Guess the Embassy. As Muscat has expanded and developed, so the government has been trying to concentrate all the embassies in a single area. The trouble is, this being Oman, and the Omanis going in for fancy modern Arabic-style buildings, each embassy tries to outdo the other. First on the block is the British Embassy, which resembles a Richard Rogers sketch for something else. Next comes the US Embassy, a poor relative of Fort Knox. The Jordanian Embassy looks like a trial run for Petra. The Iranian Embassy is terribly Persian. But funnily enough, unlike all the other embassies, it has no security checks and devices. I wonder why. The Egyptian Embassy should have been in the shape of a pyramid, but it isn't. The Abu Dhabi Embassy is nothing but flowing arches, the Saudi Embassy is like a fort, the Qatar Embassy a mosque. The Kuwaiti Embassy is stout and solid and sturdy and impregnable. Finally, the last one, the French Embassy (obviously, the French will count the other way and say it is the first) is a mass of pillars with a funny-looking dome on top. Perhaps there is a much deeper meaning to it than my little Anglo-Saxon brain can fathom.

At the end of the street are most of the Omani ministries. My favourite is the one that looks like a telephone. This is the Ministry of Fisheries. Presumably its shape is intended to represent the number of times the Omanis call Brussels to complain about the amount of illegal fishing being carried out in Omani waters by Spanish fishermen. In the centre of all the ministries is, would you believe, an ice-skating rink. Obviously this is where the Omanis, who are just as friendly with the Americans as they are with the Iranians and Iraqis and the Israelis, perfect their skills at skating on thin ice.

To add to the atmosphere, wherever you look, whether it's above Muscat City itself, or Matrah or Ruwi or Qurum or Al Khuwair, you are guaranteed to catch a glimpse, up in the crags peering down at you, of the rare Arabian oryx. Replicas of, made of fibreglass. Maybe that's what helped Muscat come first, ahead of sixty different countries, in some worldwide beautiful-city competition. The biggest *souk* in Muscat, one of the biggest in the Middle East, was so pleased and honoured that to celebrate they stuck a dirty great fibreglass lump of traditional Bedouin jewellery on top of their main entrance. I thought that was unfair. If anything they should have stuck three dirty great fibreglass lumps of traditional Bedouin jewellery on top of their main entrance: one for Muscat City, one for Matrah and one for Russi, Qurum and Al Khuwair. Which would have been one in the eye for Thesiger.

You think I'm being hard on the old boy? Let me tell you, he agrees with me. For years after his trek across the Empty Quarter he refused to go back to Oman because, he said, he dreaded the changes and the disintregration of society that had taken place. Of course, he tried to blame it on the oil companies, but we all know they're not the culprits. The oil companies have created the wealth which has enabled His Majesty to build all those schools and hospitals and health centres and things that he despises. It's Thesiger, though, who created the tourists, which are a million times worse.

It doesn't make sense to me, but then, maybe I don't understand his 'life-long craving for barbaric splendour, for savagery and colour and the throb of drums'. Oh man. Give me the simple life any day.

ABU DHABI

'So how much is that?'
  'What do you think?'
  'No idea. I don't know anything about this stuff.'
  'Guess.'
  'US$45,000? $100,000? I don't know.'
  'A million dollars.'
  'A m-m-million dollars?'
Unbelievable. Sure, there was a lot of work in it. All those fiddly bits and diamonds, and I suppose the chains were gold as well. But a million dollars!
  'Would you like to see it?'
  'Er, no thank you. Just looking.'
  'I can show it to you. No problem.'
  'No thanks. There's no need...'
  'We have lots of them. They're very popular.'
Very popular? It looked like the kind of chain the Lord High Aztec Mayor of California would wear. All pink and feathery and... yuk.
  'So how many of these do you sell a day or a week?'
  'About five or six.'
  'You mean a day or a week?'
  'A week. About five a week.'
  'But who to?'
  'To the sheikhs. They come in here with their wives.

They look around, they decide what they want to buy,
they buy.'

'How much do they spend?'

'Usually about a million dollars.'

'A time!'

'A time.'

'How do they pay?'

'Cash. They have a great big bag, a holdall. They pay you
from the bag.'

'In *cash?*'

'Always cash.'

For days my driver had been on at me about visiting the
gold *souks*, the shopping malls and even the hole in the
wall round the corner from the hotel from which they
sold sweets and chocolates and newspapers. Anywhere, in
fact, where one of his cousins from Kerala was working.
From Kerala, not from India. That's what they all tell you.

But shopping is not my hammer. Much as I hate
boasting, I must tell you that I'm the only person in the
world who's been to Abu Dhabi, Dubai, Sharjah, Ajman,
Umm al Qaywayn – I couldn't make Ra's al Khaymah or Al
Fujayrah, the other two emirates – and not brought back a
single thing, either from the *souks* or from duty-free.
Everybody else I know goes bananas about it. They're no
sooner taking off from Heathrow than they're binding on
about the *souk* in Sharjah, which everybody calls The
Train because it looks like a series of railway carriages
parked on either side of a platform.

'Fourteen carpets I've already bought from the *souk*
there. Best prices in the world,' a poor, bedraggled middle-
aged businessman told me on the flight over. Another Brit I
bumped into, or rather, staggered into, in the flashy-looking
yacht club in Dubai kept on about teddy bears. How he'd
bought a teddy bear for his daughter when she was three.
How he bought her a teddy bear every year for Christmas.

How now she was twenty-seven and married he had started every Christmas buying teddy bears for his grandson, and the best place for buying teddy bears in the whole wide world was Dubai Duty Free. How, by the time his grandson had a grandson, they would have the biggest damn collection of whatever he was on about in the world.

One morning I did have a few minutes to spare. I was on my way back from the Hyatt Regency, a funny pyramid-shaped hotel in Dubai way out by what's known locally as Russian Beach, because it's been practically taken over by Russians chasing the good life. The whole area is full of Russian hotels, Russian restaurants, Russian clubs, Russian girls – and Russian dead bodies washed up on the beach nearly every morning. I didn't feel like going Russian so when the driver began his customary entreaties I gave in.

He had taken me to this run-of-the-mill jeweller's shop – well, kiosk really – in the old gold *souk*, one of thousands dripping with rings and bracelets and necklaces. You know the kind of thing.

'Some sheikhs come in maybe two, maybe three times a month.'

'And spend a million each time?'

'Why not? They have the money.'

'But it's crazy. All that money.'

'Better they spend it with me than with somebody else.'

The place was empty. It was Diwali, the Hindu Festival of Light, which meant that all the Indians in town were working harder than ever while everybody else took the day off to celebrate on their behalf. The jeweller, the big guy, who must have been about seventy or even eighty, with a big bald head and huge stomach, offered me a handful of some strange-looking Indian nuts. They didn't exactly make me look forward to the next traditional Indian festival. They were as tough as the Stock Exchange Yellow

Book used to be. It probably explained why the place was empty: nobody wanted to risk breaking their teeth on his nuts. Whatever the case, he was in a chatty mood.

'Business is booming, then.'

'Could be better.'

'Could be better? You must be worth millions!'

'Can't complain,' he smiled a weak smile, 'Have another nut.'

This is what the gold business is like in Dubai. One small shop the size of half a dozen phone boxes. Turnover, say, US$25 million, maybe US$50 million, a year. Overheads next to nothing. And there are literally hundreds of them, some bigger, but not much bigger, many even smaller, full to overflowing with gold rings, gold necklaces and gold everything. Inside each one a big guy walks up and down, usually an Indian. Around him a couple of thousand sales assistants crammed behind tiny counters. Yet none of the Indians ever wear any jewellery; at least, none of those I saw ever wore any. They always looked as though they had left their rickshaws parked round the corner and were trying to get their breath back before starting on the fourth shift of the day. As for the Indians I met around town, they always looked more like dishevelled civil servants or university professors or doctors. And none of them wore any jewellery, either.

'So what's the profit then on a million-dollar necklace?'

He didn't tell me, of course. But he told me about the business. To the punters it's fashion, extravagance and trying to avoid a row with the wife because come Sunday morning you're off on this fantastic – sorry, I mean boring – six-week swing through South America that's just come up. To the trade, it's a commodity just like lead or pork bellies. It's for trading, not buying and selling. The shopkeeper, or rather, *souk*-keeper, doesn't buy the gold from the wholesaler. He gets it free in return for paying an agreed deposit, say US$1 million. Whenever he sells anything he calls the wholesaler and pays out of the US$1 million deposit that day's price for that day's sale. If the price is lower than when he bought the gold, he makes money. If it isn't, he doesn't. But whether it is or it isn't, or whether he does or he doesn't, he has still covered his costs, so he's happy. The reason why they reckon their prices are so competitive is that the success of the whole thing depends on sales. If the price of gold falls, sales increase and the retailer maintains his margin and makes a higher profit. If the price of gold increases, sales still increase, the retailer still maintains his margin and still makes a higher profit.

'Turnover. That's the only way we can survive. That's why we need sales all the time. We wouldn't get sales unless we guaranteed quality and good prices.'

'But don't you play the gold market as well?'

'Some people do,' he grinned. 'Go into their back office about four o'clock in the afternoon when New York opens, and they are all on their mobile phones, wheeling and dealing. But not me. I'm a poor man.'

'So how much are they playing with? One million, ten million?'

'About US$25 million dollars, on average. I know many people who have at least US$25 million.'

'Gee, that's big money.'

'Oh no.' He grinned even more widely. 'That's only in their trading accounts. They really have much, much more than that to play with.'

So how big is the gold business in Dubai and the Emirates as a whole? Work it out for yourself. Say there are 500 gold shops in Dubai and the rest of the Emirates. Each shop is turning over around US$10 million a year. That's $5 billion a year which, you must admit, is worth a few bags of decent nuts. On top of that there's the gold-bullion market as well.

But that is not to say that when you are out there buying gold you're buying pure gold. You are also buying a thousand different alloys and additives as well. I know, I've watched them at it. I've been to millions of precious-metal plants all over the place and seen what they can do with a single gold ingot. It's unbelievable.

'If you're going to buy gold, buy gold. Always buy twenty-two-carat. Most Europeans buy eighteen because they like the colour. That's silly, it's not worth the money. Never buy twenty-four – it's too soft. Not practicable.'

So how do you know it's 22-carat? The answer, in Dubai, is that you don't. There's no hallmarking system, no government assaying system, just the reputation of the Indian shopkeeper himself. If he say it's 22 carats, it's 22 carats. Not like in India or wherever, where 22-carat gold is likely to be 19 or even less.

'So is that all you have to look for?'

'You've also got to check the quality. You mustn't pay super-extra prices if you're buying extra or even three-quarter extra jewellery.'

'Super extra' means lovingly crafted, hand-made jewellery created using diamonds and other precious stones cut and polished by thousands of starving, slave-like little boys in western India who, because of the appalling conditions they are kept in, will probably be dead by the time they're twenty or thirty. 'Extra' means not so much love, but still made by hand using diamonds and other precious stones cut and polished by thousands of starving, slave-like little boys in western India who, because of the appalling conditions they are kept in, will probably be merely half blind and suffering from lung disease by the time they're twenty or thirty. Three-quarter extra and half extra mean it's made by machine. Ordinary means I'll need some more newspapers – the papier mâché has gone all wobbly. A machine-made thing, I mean chain, the kind you buy your wife, costs around a dollar. A lovingly crafted handmade chain for you-know-who – don't worry, I can be discreet – could cost anything between US$10 and $10,000.

'I know I shouldn't say this, but if you're buying a machine-made piece, buy a Singapore machine-made piece. There's less mark-up on it than on an Emirates-made piece. They're very good value.'

'But how do you know that what you're buying is good value? How do you know what you're paying for?'

One typical know-all English guy I ran into one evening at the bar at the hotel – blazer, old-school tie, suede shoes – told me he was the world's greatest expert on buying gold. 'Check the gold price. Once you know the gold price, it's easy. You haggle on the mark-up. There's no way you'll catch me paying the fifty, sixty or even eighty per cent mark up,' he said.

What he didn't take into account in all his calculations was that the Indians buy gold in what they call 'tolas', some Indian gold measurement, while everyone else buys in kilo bars. Neither did he seem to know that in London the price is quoted in dollars to the ounce, whereas in Dubai it is quoted in dollars to the gramme.

'But do you want to know my best advice?' the poor, struggling Indian jeweller said to me as I went to leave, empty-handed, of course.

'Sure.'

'Don't buy gold at all. As an investment it, how you say, sucks. The price of gold today is less than it was three years ago. That's not what I call a good investment.'

'Not even for the sheikhs?'

'Not even for the sheikhs.'

The Emirates – Abu Dhabi, Dubai, Sharjah, Ajman, Umm al Qaywayn, Ra's al Khaymah and Al Fujayrah – the United

Arab Emirates, to give them their full title, is really nothing but an air-brushed multicoloured dream world where waiters can pick up a US$5,200 tip for serving a US$3 bottle of mineral water, where penguins waddle around in the middle of the desert (well, in the aquarium in Al Ayn, Abu Dhabi's second-largest city down near the Omani border, to be precise), and, incidentally, the home of the only camel market left in the country. And the government will actually pay you to marry a local girl, which says a lot for the local girls. It is also the kind of place where you have no problems with the currency. Everything costs a million dollars, or multiples of a million dollars. A new factory making giant pressure vessels to ship back to the UK: US$200 million. A new gas plant: US$300 million. Expanding the airport: US$400 million. Building some big resort development: US$500 million. A cup of coffee: US$1 million (no, I'm just kidding, that's only half a million, but you get the idea).

Smoking – including hookah-smoking – is banned in restaurants and public places. Give a girl a lift in your car and that's fifteen days in jail and your car confiscated. Give her a kiss in the back seat it's a month. Say something less than respectful about the Prophet and you hit the jackpot: six years in jail followed by deportation.

To most people, however, Abu Dhabi, which is about twice the size of Belgium with a population of just 800,000, equals oil. Around 2 million barrels of the stuff a day, 100 million barrels of reserves. About 10 per cent of the world's total and (hang on, there's more to come) gas reserves of practically 6 trillion cubic metres, about 5 per cent of the world's gas reserves. Which make Abu Dhabi bigger in terms of financial power than the rest of the emirates put together.

Forty years ago it was nothing but an empty beach, a couple of dhows, half a row of *burasti* huts, a large white fort and – cue music – a spring of sweet water. Today it prides itself on being a city of mosques. There are around 400 or them already and new ones are being built and opened every day. Very soon they'll be opening the grandaddy of them all, a mosque the size of ten football fields featuring inside a chandelier the size of a seven-storey building. It is also, but don't tell them I said this, a sprawling city of tree-lined streets, lush, green parks, fountains, free healthcare, free education, air-conditioning and skyscrapers. Not your tiny, sedate back-street skyscrapers, your real Manhattan skyscrapers. And not just one or two: there are streets and streets and streets of them.

I have to warn you that, in their own polite, courteous, Arabic way, they are sick to death of the story of how one day 200 years ago a bunch of guys led by a certain Bani Yas Bedouin – take a bow, Bani – stumbled across the spring while out hunting, saw a gazelle drinking from it and promptly called the place 'Homeland of the Gazelle', which, in Arabic, is of course Abu Dhabi. Had it been a warthog or a rat, I shudder to think what the place would be called today. Probably New York. Or Much Itchin in the Crotch. Or, worse still, Auckland. I also shudder to think of what's going to happen to me if the Emir ever hears of my little joke.

But forget the mosques, the skyscrapers, the spring of fresh water and forget, if you can, all that oil: Abu Dhabi is all about duty-free shopping. Now, as I've said, I'm no expert on shopping, but I'm told it has won more awards for duty-free shopping than I've drunk bottles of sixty-year-old McCallan's. Cigarettes, cigars, booze, perfume, jewellery, watches, videos, music centres, golf clubs, ties, shirts, socks – apparently you can buy them all at Abu Dhabi Duty Free cheaper than anywhere else in the cosmos. Whether it's true or not, don't ask me. All I know is that for a good few months, because of the exchange rate I was buying Scotch at Heathrow with deutschmarks and getting back in change more sterling than the deutschmarks were worth – plus a free bottle of Scotch. So apart from the fact that Abu Dhabi Duty Free looks like the inside of a magic mushroom, it seems pretty much the same as any other duty-free to me – somewhere to be avoided unless you're determined to take back for your wife something else she won't like. Like a bottle of perfume I saw in duty-free in Seoul called 'Sting'. Underneath it said 'Great Future'. I did once see something I thought she might possibly like in the duty-free at Heathrow: a magnum of Château Margaux which, of course, I could share. The price worked out at a mere £850 a glass.

Yet since I was in Abu Dhabi I thought I should give it a try. I went up to the counter selling watches. The girl gave me the hard sell straight away. Within seconds all the surfaces were covered in every kind of watch you can imagine. I picked up one that was so encrusted with gold and jewels I could hardly lift it. The girl was completely unfazed by it all. 'You can tell the time,' she pointed out helpfully, 'just by looking at the hands.' Wow. Such technology.

In the end I did buy a present for the wife. I was strolling past the fountain pens when I saw this sign saying, 'Cross. Since 1846.' That's it, I thought: the perfect gift. And what was she when I gave it to her? You don't need me to tell you that.

Unfortunately, Abu Dhabi is where I went horse-racing. I say unfortunately, because my big ambition or at least my big horse-racing ambition, was to go racing at the equestrian holy of holies: the fantastic Nad al Sheba Racecourse built, for Allah knows how much money, by Sheikh Maktoum bin Rashid al Maktoum – the Crown Prince of Dubai, the defence minister of the whole of the Emirates and more important, the biggest racehorse-owner in the world – at the bottom of his garden just outside Dubai City on the edge of the desert.

Now, I admit I'm not the greatest horse expert in the world. My wife goes on and on about how I can't even muck out the stables properly. But then, she also claims that I don't know how to throw a stick for the dog, either. Animals I tend to like in inverse proportion to the number of legs they've got. Anything with 100 or over is way, way, way out. Twelve is way, way out. Eight is way out. But anything with four legs that is sleek, beautiful with soft, brown eyes and goes like a bomb is for me. So I'm a horsaholic. Believe me, if you've never had 17 hands between your legs, you haven't lived. If I had my time over again, the neighs would have it. I'd stick with horses, any type of horse. I'd go hunting all week, eventing at weekends and team-chasing in between, with maybe a spot of polo afterwards. I'm not proud, I'd mount anything.

Yet as far as racing is concerned I don't follow the horses like some people do. I'm afraid I haven't got a brown trilby, let alone a checked suit and a pair of binoculars. But I do watch the *Morning Line* on Channel 4 on Saturday mornings whenever I get the chance and, like the day Kennedy died, I can remember what I was doing the day Frankie Dettori went through the card at Ascot and produced seven winners in a row. And whenever I get the chance I like to go racing. I've been to all the major fun spots of the world: Plumpton, Lingfield, Ostend, a field just outside Ballynacally in County Clare in Ireland. I was at a meeting there once years ago when an announcement came over the loudspeaker: 'Will all fallen women please report immediately to the doctor.' On a Sunday morning I've even ended up on a patch of dust outside Dakar in Senegal.

I've even had a go myself. Well, with a name like Biddlecombe, what do you expect? Admittedly, it was on the old Lewes Racecourse on the South Downs.

Admittedly, the racecourse was closed. But I was on Old Lad, or Ditton Lad, to give him his old racing name, my best friend in the whole world. He doesn't moan. He's never irritable or bad-tempered. He never goes on at me because my tie doesn't match my shirt, I've got the wrong shoes on or I've had too much to drink. He might not, I grant you, figure in the lists of the world's greatest racehorses, but that's the fault of the people compiling the lists, not his. As far as I'm concerned he was pure magic or, as an old Irish farmer told me once, 'Sure and he's the best thing any man could hope to throw his leg over.' We went everywhere: across the fields, through the woods, down on to the beach, all the way along the top of the South Downs. He was fantastic. I'd be proud to polish his hooves any day. In fact I wouldn't mind being buried next to Old Lad. Providing I'm dead, of course.

I'm not the greatest rider, or the most stylish rider, either. To get most horses going I stand up in the stirrups, wave my arms in the air and shout 'Geronimo!' It might not be Pony Club rules, but it works. Not with Lad, though. Most horses have three speeds: walk, trot and canter. Lad's were: fast, very fast and whaaaaaa! But he was sensible as well. Some horses are just racing machines. Not him. You could actually feel him thinking. Many's the time we were out in the fields or woods swinging in and out under the trees and I would put my head down, close my eyes and just let him get on with it. Not once did he let me down. Well, he had far more experience galloping on four legs than I had.

I shall never forget the moment I took him out of the horsebox at Lewes. Normally I've only got to pull on my boots and pick up my whip and that gets them going, but not Lad. He knew he was at a racecourse, albeit an old racecourse well past its prime, but that didn't make any difference to him. Immediately he was 6 inches off the ground, 20 feet tall. Every nerve in his body was tingling with excitement. I clambered aboard. It was like sitting on top of a ton of dynamite primed to go off at the slightest tremor. Blink your eyes too quickly and you could be in the horses' equivalent of heaven. I swung him towards the track. He was now 6 feet off the ground and 200 feet tall. Run round the world and be back in time for lunch? No problem. He could do anything.

There were only three other horses going round the track with us, all young, highly trained Arab racers. But Old Lad knew he could beat the lot of them, even on three legs. We walked down the track to the starting point. I say walked – we soared down the track to the starting point. Old Lad was ready to explode. The veins in his neck were throbbing. Sweat up? He was beginning to boil over. The excitement was almost too much for him.

Then we were... Wheeeee! Mach 1, Mach 1.5, Mach 2, whatever. We were doing 1,000, 2,000mph. Head down, hooves thundering like mad. Everything around me was a blur. Arkle? Red Rum? Desert Orchid? They were nothing. This was the National, the Cheltenham Gold Cup and Sheikh Mohammed's US$4 million Dubai World Cup duel in the desert between Cigar and Soul of the Matter and L'Carrière all rolled into one. At first – well, all right, for half a second, I was thinking, I shouldn't be doing this. I shouldn't be doing... I shouldn't be... The rest of the time it was wow-ee.

When we set off we were way out in front, zooming like mad around the course. Lad was flying like an angel on ten legs. Then the others caught up. I can just about remember us all hitting the winning line at about the same time. It was fantastic. It took me about two weeks to get my breath back.

To you it might be nothing, but I don't care. To me it was racing.

Ten, fifteen years ago when I was bombing around

Lewes racecourse, racing didn't exist in the Emirates. Or rather, horse-racing didn't. Camel-racing was pretty popular. The only racetrack in the whole of the Emirates was in Umm al Qaywayn, the smallest of all the emirates, way out on the Gulf coast. The only professionals were an Irish jockey and an English trainer, and consequently race meetings were few and far between. If you went horse racing you went by invitation.

Around 1984-5 things started to canter. By this time there were racecourses in Sharjah, about half an hour from Dubai, and in Ajman, on the camel track. But there were no stables. Horses had to be tied up under trees before they raced. If they wanted a drink, water had to be carried in by hand and sloshed into great oil barrels for them. In 1986, however, they started galloping like mad. Sheikh Maktoum decided to build Nad al Sheba behind his palace, just down the road from the sprawling 10-kilometre camel racetrack. He commissioned some consultants and he told them to copy Newbury Racecourse in England, one of his favourite courses in the world. He virtually gave them a blank cheque. But the first year, instead of race meetings they were seriously thinking of holding swimming galas: there was a freak winter and the whole place was underwater.

The course finally opened in February 1992. Unfortunately, this clashed with Ramadan, and racing is banned during Ramadan. So they launched floodlit racing after sundown, which for some reason doesn't seem to be covered by the Koran. But they learned their lesson. When they decided to build their next racecourse they called in the army to do it. It took them two months and they've never had any problems with flooding.

The main grandstand at Nad al Sheba is spectacular. It looks like a cross between a traditional Bedouin tent and the Sydney Opera House. The racetrack itself is minutely manicured. To the left is a golf course, modelled on some famous Scottish course, which I could see was in full swing: all the little golf carts were racing backwards and forwards through the little tunnel under the racetrack to get to the course. But golf is not important. What is important is that this was the hindquarters, I mean the headquarters, of the worldwide Maktoum spare-no-expense horse-racing empire, which is run by a thirty-year-old former Dubai policeman.

Here, the kind of place horses dream of, they turn out winner after winner after winner. Their best horses they fly back from frosty Newmarket and foggy Lambourn to winter in their non-stop 25-degree or thereabouts temperatures and, like all holidaymakers, to have their fill of wild oats – about 10 or 15 pounds a day if they're in training; anything between 15 and 20 if they're in peak condition. Although I suppose anything getting that amount of wild oats a day would be bound to be in peak condition. So while you and I are freezing to death pacing up and down a deserted railway station in a desperate bid to earn some money to lose on them, they are luxuriating in their summer coats in non-stop sunshine.

Also at their disposal is a high-tech five-star hospital for horses the like of which the world has never seen. From the outside it looks more like one of those exclusive upmarket country clubs you come across in California or even Florida. Inside it's packed with every sophisticated latest electronic this and that you can or cannot imagine. Including good drains. It is staffed by the world's leading experts in arthoscopy, laparoscopy, endoscopy and every other scopy you can think of. The operating theatre, which is a million times better than many operating theatres for mere humans, even has its own fresh-air supply – we don't want to risk any nasty desert germs affecting the horses – and large-screen televisions so that people can watch the operations taking place. The sick bays are made up with only the finest shavings made from logs specially flown in. The hay comes from Washington in the States, the feed from Australia. The nuts are made at the hospital itself in a feed mill designed for the purpose.

Unfortunately, when I got to the racecourse it was closed. I had the place to myself. Well, I say to myself: there was a solitary security man fast asleep under an umbrella by the entrance. I wandered along the empty stands and strolled over to the fence by the finishing line. Nobody around. As for the course itself, it was immaculate, but, again, deserted. No trilbies, no Burberries, no winter warmers. Not that, I hasten to say, I went to Dubai to go horse-racing. I had to go there in any case, and I thought that if, by chance, it just happened to coincide with one of their race meetings, I might be able to pop in for a few seconds. Just for a quick look, you understand. But I got the dates wrong. Actually, that's not true: the travel agents got the dates wrong. But I can't blame them or I'll suddenly find I'm flying all over the world to the wrong places on the wrong flights at the wrong prices.

So in the end I went racing in Abu Dhabi, and I'm ashamed to say that I lost half a million dollars. It was at the enormous, sprawling equestrian club on the edge of town, just round the corner from the royal palace.

The weather was fantastic: warm, a slight breeze, perfect conditions for racing, or at least, for watching the racing. The whole place was floodlit, the grass was beautifully green and smooth and the club was packed, the grandstand full to overflowing. There were crowds in front of the grandstand, crowds around the saddling enclosure, crowds lining the rails. And the colours were spectacular: blue, greens, mauves, purples, violets, crimsons, pinks – a thousand times more colourful than Gold Cup Day or

Ascot, or even our local point-to-point at Heathfield. But they were all being worn by men: there were no fillies in sight. Not the kind of fillies you see at Gold Cup Day or Ascot or the local point-to-point at Heathfield, anyway. It was a male-only occasion.

I know you're going to find this hard to believe, but I didn't see one brown trilby, which I suppose means that the Abu Dhabi Equestrian Club is not bound by Jockey Club rules. They did not seem to know the rules concerning the use of the whip at any rate. Instead the place was a mass of *dishdashes* and cloaks and white scarves and turbans and fancy embroidered skull caps and *ghuttras*, which are what the Arabs wear on their heads, with a twisted black *agal* to keep it in place. Some men had pure blue silk scarves wrapped around their heads and shoulders. Others had white headdresses that were so enormous I wondered whether, when they were unwound at night, they doubled as hammocks for sleeping in. Without the ladies, of course, there was no schmaltz. No picnics in the car park in the pouring rain, no waterlogged prawn balls, no fuss and bother because some silly hat the size of the Eiffel Tower kept collapsing and blocking the entrance to the Members' Enclosure. Just pure, wonderful, glorious racing.

The other thing that was unusual was that, unlike other meetings I've been to, I can actually remember the last race. Because it was dry. No champagne, no large brandies, not even a single half-pint of warm bitter. There was no betting either. I remember an old Irishman once telling me that racing without bookmakers was like 'Cinderella without the ugly sisters', but it was something, I admit, I could live with – especially since at the last point-to-point I'd been to I got stuck with this guy who had more tips than a packet of Benson & Hedges, and every one of them was wrong. Not that I gamble. I only gambled once in my life. Never again. Even so, winning and not being able to celebrate by spending your winnings on at least one glass of champagne – what am I saying, one glass? I mean one bottle – somehow didn't seem right.

Well, I say there was no betting. In fact, it was a bit like in China, where horse-racing is officially banned, betting is illegal and the only way you can make money is to win a prize for guessing the winner. Because gambling is forbidden by the Koran, in Abù Dhabi they have this strange kind of bingo-card system of not gambling. You have to guess the first, second, third and fourth of every race. Get all four right and you win 20,000 dirhams, the equivalent of US$5,750. If you also happen to guess the first in every race on the card you get the jackpot: 100,000 dirhams (US$28,000). The problem is, you have to place your bets, oops, I mean make your selection at the very start of the meeting, before the first race and before you even see the horses. The only thing you've got to go on is the form, what you've read somewhere else, what you've been told, officially or unofficially, and whether a *muezzin* crossed the road in front of you on your way to the mosque that morning. Well, my father would never place a bet if a nun crossed the road in front of him while he was on the way to the barber's shop to place a bet in the days before there were betting shops. The other snag is that if a horse doesn't run it's just your bad luck.

Everybody I spoke to agreed it was unfair, but they also agreed there was nothing they could do about it. 'How can we complain when everything is free?' a Sudanese in huge white flowing robes asked me as we leaned against the rails of the saddling enclosure waiting to see the first batch of horses trotting out. 'It's free to get in. It's free to take part. There's no charge for the card. Everybody is given the chance to guess the winners and win the main prize. So how can we complain that we're being unfairly treated?'

One advantage of not gambling is that you don't have Big Mac wandering up and down bawling at you when he is the one waving his hands and doing silly things at the camera. That apart, it was pure Arab racing. Half the horses came from England, Ireland, France, Germany and Scandinavia. Most of the jockeys were either British or Irish or French. The commentary was in English. Or rather, Irish.

Because we couldn't actually bet any money, a few of us gambled Mickey Mouse-style – a couple of Sudanese guys, a man from Senegal, an old boy from Pakistan who seemed to be wearing sky-blue pyjamas with a red tea towel on his head, and me. We bet each other $10, $20, $50 and even as much as $100,000 that our respective horses would win. And who won the first race? You've got it. After that, of course, I was in. I was the big horse expert. None of the other horses I backed came anywhere, they were all Bismarcks, but it didn't seem to make any difference. There I was, arguing about whether Akbar was a better five-year-old than Al Tareer, whether Malesh could beat Izentespeshal and what it was like there on 29 April 1995, when Lester Piggott rode his last professional race.

One guy in a pair of salmon-pink pyjamas seemed to know his Arab horses inside out. He could tell you all about their breeding. Chndakar, voted the best five-year-old bay for the previous season, was out of Dormane and Malika Fontenay. So was Darike, the best four-year-old bay. The best four-year-old grey, however, was out of Blaise and Sarava Du...

Quick. The second race. We all ran over to the saddling enclosure. I picked number 2. Everybody else chose numbers 1, 3, 4, 5, 6, 7, 8 and even number 9, who kept swinging round across the grass in the centre and put up a big fight when the jockey finally got on him. Now back to the rail. They all flew past to the starting gate. Number 2 looked fantastic. Number 9 was still acting the fool. Into the starting gate they went. They're OFF.

Number 9 won and number 2 came last.

Another chap, this one wearing a fabulous rose creation, seemed to know everything about the history of Arab horses. Apparently, Mohammed, peace be upon him, said that when God decided to create the horse he told the Wind of the South that he wanted to make something that would be prestigious to anyone who was loyal to it, a disgrace to anyone who was against it and a charm to anyone who obeyed it. Arabian horses, however, have nothing whatsoever to do with Islam. Their bloodlines can be traced back easily to pre-Islamic times. Salmon-pink pyjamas nodded vigorously in agreement.

Race number 3. Into the saddling enclosure they come. There are three beautiful greys. I bet the Senegalese guy US$10,000 that number 4 will win. He stamps up and down screaming with laughter. Number 6, he says, US$20,000 to win. Others agree with him. The bets range from $5,000 to $50,000. Out they go, down the track. Number 6 refuses to go into the starting gate. They try pushing him in. No good. They blindfold him. He starts rearing and bucking. The jockey practically falls off. Then, all of a sudden, he's in and they're off and number 6 is like greased lightning. By the time they turn the far corner he's way out in front and past the winning post in a flash. The Senegalese guy is telling everyone he's now over a quarter of a million dollars in the black.

Back at the saddling enclosure an elderly Lebanese tells me that his wife lives in England and breeds Arab horses somewhere in Surrey. Someone else, I think he was from Tunisia, told me he knew a Brazilian who owned over 1,000 Arab horses. As for the best Arabs in the world, everybody said the British-bred horses were the best. After them came Sweden. France they didn't like. They went on and on about how the French had diluted the line by cross-breeding with other horses for speed. And the Americans? They hated them. 'Don't talk to me about Americans,' spat the Lebanese guy. 'They make agreements. They break agreements. They promise not to do this, then they do it. Animals, that's what they are. Animals. You can't trust them.' The Americans, he said, had had so many warnings and broken so many agreements that they were now planning to throw them out of the big prestigious World Arab Horse Organisation.

Somebody mentioned saddles. The best saddles in the world were made in England. Again, I thought they were kidding me. Not at all, said one gorgeous yellow extravaganza. He always bought his saddles from someone in Walsall. Someone else said he always bought his from Gidden's in the Burlington Arcade in Piccadilly. As for saddles made in France, Australia and the despised United States, they were all rubbish. It was the same with everything from vets to farriers to jockeys. As for the greatest jockey of all time, there was no doubt in anyone's mind: Lester Piggott. 'He's been here often,' Sky-Blue Pyjamas told me. 'I was photographed with him. I still have the photo.'

And so the evening went on. From the saddling enclosure to the rail. Everybody straining for the off, the wild, hilarious cheering as the horses turned the corner and made for the winning post. By the end of the evening I reckon I'd met every colour and shade of the rainbow. I knew more about Arab horses than anyone else in the world. And – this is going to shock you – I was stone-cold sober. OK, so I'd lost over half a million dollars, or at least, that's what the Senegalese guy claimed. But it hadn't cost me a penny.

If Abu Dhabi is the city of mosques, then Dubai is the city of Muslim fundamentalism: the fundamental right of

Muslims to encourage non-Muslims to have fun, fun, fun.

A hot, dusty, barren desert town it is not. It's a super, modern city with more skyscrapers to the square inch than camels. It's clean, safe, sensible; Islam with an American accent, a Harvard degree and homes all over the world. The electricity works, the supermarkets are full to overflowing. The hospitals are so clean and modern you feel guilty that they've gone to all that effort and you haven't even got a headache. And there is every kind of sports facility you can imagine. Those you can't imagine are forbidden by the Koran anyway.

The most relaxed and friendly city in the Gulf, Dubai is fundamentally the only fundamentalist free zone in the whole region. Twenty years ago, when they started selling aviation fuel at rock-bottom prices, it was nothing but a cheap middle-of-the-night pitstop for flights to and from the Far East. Now, because they've only got twenty years' supply of oil left and, poor dears, they can see poverty staring them in the face, they decided that, instead of putting all their eggs in one barrel, they had the fundamental right to become another Hong Kong or Singapore – and judging by what they've done so far, I reckon it won't be long before they make it.

Dubai is really Dubai and Dirah. Dubai to the west, Dirah to the east. Between the two of them is Al Khor, the creek which flows in from the Gulf. They decided it was too much of a mouthful to call the combined city Dubai and Dirah, so they opted for Dubai, presumably because they felt that Dirah wasn't exactly an appropriate name for an international trading centre.

They realised that they couldn't become another Hong Kong or Singapore by themselves. There are only a few hundred thousand of them. They needed people. OK, they said, bring in the people. As a result, Dubai today is 80 per cent foreign. All the banks and insurance companies are run by Europeans; so, too, are most of the big companies. The leisure sector, hotels, restaurants and bars are managed by Asians, mostly from Kerala as opposed to India, of course, and Sri Lankans and Filipinos. Indeed, some hotels are known as Sri Lankan or Filipino hotels or whatever. Shops are usually run by guys – and girls – from Hong Kong, Taiwan and Singapore. Most middle managers are Egyptians, Syrians and, again, Indians. Accountants are generally Asians from Uganda or Kenya. The dirty work is all done by Bangladeshis, as usual. Oh yes, of course, the oil industry: that's run by the guys with big hats and loud voices from I forget where.

To encourage so many people to come from so many places, Dubai guaranteed everyone their fundamental rights: to work like hell, make all the money they could and to keep the lot. In Dubai there's no such thing as taxes. You can import and export whatever you like. You can wear what you like (providing, of course, you don't go too far and mix blues and greens together. Women, please note). You can worship whoever or whatever you like wherever you want. Unlike other Gulf states, Dubai is full to overflowing with churches and temples and Hindu burial grounds. And finally, praise be to Allah, you can drink whatever you like, wherever and practically whenever you like. As long as you know the right people. Indeed, in Dubai not only can you drink all the Johnny Walker Black Label and Gintonic you like, you can even get bombed out of your mind during Ramadan.

But above all, Dubai believes in everyone's inalienable fundamental right to bore themselves out of their tiny minds by playing whatever sport they fancy. Swimming, surfing, sailing, water-skiing, deep-sea fishing, scuba-diving, powerboat-racing, catamaran-chasing, ice-skating – some hotels even have their own private ice rinks. Snooker, rugby, something called sand-skiing, windsurfing, archery, clay pigeon-shooting, even bird-watching – they have laid on 370 different species for you to ogle. Tennis you can play until your arm drops off, golf until you've lost your balls on courses planted with genuine Bermuda grass and computer-controlled pop-up sprinklers to keep it looking green the whole year round. Some of the golf courses used to have their own flamingos as well, but sadly they've all been killed, apparently, by the local Arabs practising their swings. If none of these appeal to you there are the traditional Arab pastimes such as hair-dancing, hand-painting, buying luxury hotels or, if you're really desperate, you could, I suppose, watch other people watching other people play volleyball.

Dubai is determined to bore as many people as it can from around the world as well, which is why today it is the venue for an increasing number of international sporting events. There's the Dubai Tennis Open; the Dubai Duty Free Snooker Classic, the largest snooker championship outside the UK; the Dubai Desert Golf Classic; the Dubai World Championship Powerboat Grand Prix and so on and so on. They even qualified for the Cricket World Cup and are desperate to join the long list of countries who have beaten us at the game we play best.

As a result of the efforts to cater for the crowds flocking to such events, the whole place is a perpetual building site. Everywhere you look there are new hotels and apartment blocks and conference centres and exhibition halls going up. And not just ordinary hotels and apartment blocks and conference centres and exhibition halls – the Dubai Airshow, for example, is already bigger than the Paris Airshow – but enormous, spectacular, stunning new landmark hotels and apartment blocks and conference centres and exhibition halls. Take Chicago Beach, which they are putting together on a man-made island south of Dubai. Designed in the shape of a spinnaker sail spread across a mast, it is going to be one of the tallest hotels in the world. Alongside it, they're building another hotel, twenty-six storeys high, in the shape of a wave. As if that's not enough they're also planning a two-storey conference centre: the ground floor seating 1,200 delegates, the first floor 450, in the shape of – guess what? – a boat, not to mention marinas, sports centres, swimming pools, a thousand restaurants, a couple of hundred tennis courts and I forget how many golf courses.

And shops. They might not have any theatres or concert halls or art galleries or museums (apart from the one in the old fort, which is supposed to give you a comprehensive picture of the country's history but completely fails to mention the Arab horse) but have they got shops. There are millions of them, and all of them completely tax-free. Land at the airport and you are immediately assailed by shops, shops and still more shops. The biggest, most modern and most luxurious duty-free shopping complex in the world, it has over 500 staff who are all guaranteed to be serving somebody else when you want to ask them anything and over fifty check-outs which are always full when you want to buy a little something quickly for yourself, like a Porsche or a Ferrari.

Dubai really ought to be called Dusell. They sell everything you can imagine cheaper than anywhere else in the world. The reason the Russians, for example, make for Dubai, not to mention the guys from Uzbekistan, Kazakhstan and all the other stans, is television sets. One Russian couple I met, both built like huge bright red Russian tanks, with gold-rimmed glasses, gold chains round their necks, gold bracelets round their wrists, gold-plated pens in their shirt pockets and enormous gold rings on nearly every finger, told me they were there to go 'roast-beef shopping'. As they grinned they each revealed a set of gold teeth.

In the mornings they went shopping, in the evenings they went shopping. The rest of the day they stretched out on the beach. After two weeks they went home with two television sets each. The money they made selling the television sets not only paid for the trip but enabled them to live off roast beef until they came again six months later. According to the Russian couple, Al Maktoum Street is the place to go if you want watches. Satwa and Karama are the areas for clothes. Al Fahidi Street and Al Nasr Square are the places for anything electronic. For computers, though, try the area between the Falcon roundabout - so called because of the falcon sitting in the middle of it - and the Ramada roundabout, which, confusingly, doesn't have a Ramada in the centre of it.

Then there are the shopping centres. Dubai is probably the only place in the Middle East which has more shopping centres than mosques. There's the al Ghuraiv Centre, the Bur Juman Centre, the Al Manal Centre, the Markaz Al Jumeirah, the Magrudy Centre, the Al Mulla Plaza, the al Dhiyafa Centre and the Hamarain Centre. Each one more modern, more luxurious, more expensive and more boring than the last. On top of that there are a million *souks*: the famous gold *souk*, reputedly the best place in the world for gold; the spice *souk*, which is ditto for spices; the fish *souk* ditto for fish.

The shops are open day and night, well, until around 11 pm at any rate, so there's no excuse. If you want to spend, they're there, ready and willing to help you. Not that nobody cares about the shopkeepers and shop assistants working all the hours Allah sends: in Dubai, as you would expect, they're very conscious and solicitous towards all the people from all over the world who have left their families and homes in order to help them become another Hong Kong or Singapore, especially in the summer months, when the temperatures begin to soar and you begin to feel like you're taking a sauna in a Chinese laundry. The government has decreed that the moment it hits 50 degrees Celsius – which, let me tell you, is hot, hot, hot – everyone must stop work. However, I was told more than once, even in the severest summer heat the mercury in the official government thermometer somehow or other keeps banging away at the 49.9-degree mark without ever managing to break through it, even though everybody else's are showing 52, 53 and even 55 degrees.

So popular is shopping in Dubai that they now organise special shopping weeks to bring in even more visitors. During one six-week bonanza they pulled in over 1.5 million shopaholics from around the world and generated way over US$700 million in sales. Thank Allah I avoided that. And to add a little bit of excitement they organised a raffle for the happy shoppers. The prize was forty-nine gold bars, worth in excess of US$80 million. Which, you must admit, makes our Christmas raffles for a turkey and a bottle of port look a touch stingy.

What amazed me was the complete lack of security. No locked doors, no guards, no video cameras – not even in the jewellery shops, which must have millions of dollars' worth of goods on show. Not that crime doesn't exist in Dubai. It's just that there's less of it than practically anywhere else in the world. However, over a couple of large Johnnie Walkers in the Forte Grand by the airport, I was told by a bunch of expats that white-collar, or, I suppose, white-*dishdash* crime is becoming more and more of a problem. So is the way that they deal with it.

The general manager of one of the big hotels, the expats said, was thrown in prison for something he didn't do. 'He was put in jail for embezzlement,' one of them whispered. 'But he didn't do it. I know he didn't do it. Everybody knows he didn't do it. Even the police know he didn't do it. It's just the way they do things here.'

'So who did it?' I asked very softly.

'His deputy. He confessed and all. But he's still around. The police haven't touched him.'

'But that's crazy!'

'You try telling them. They're not interested. They say the general manager is responsible and he must take the blame.'

'So how long is he in jail for?'

'Nobody knows.'

'Hasn't he been tried?'

'No.'

'So how long has he been there now?'

'Ten months already.'

'How much longer will he be in jail?'

'Nobody knows.'

'That's the way,' they all chimed in, 'they do things here.'

They went on to tell me another horror story about one of their chums, a Brit. His driver, a Bangladeshi, knocked down a local Arab girl. She later died in hospital. But the driver wasn't jailed, the Brit was. Because he owned the car.

'But that's crazy,' I began. 'That's like saying—'

'Shhhhhh!' they all shivered, picking up newspapers and slipping back into their chairs. 'That's how they do things here. Throw you in jail first, then ask questions. And the jails are not very pleasant, either, I can tell you.'

'But I haven't seen anything about them in the papers. I mean, haven't there been protests, letters to Amnesty and all that stuff,' I whispered.

'You won't, either. That's not,' they all chorused silently, 'the way they do things here.'

The stories began to flow.

'There was another Brit, who designed and built golf courses. He was in partnership with a sheikh. They built lots of golf courses here, all over the Emirates. The Sheikh then discovered he was being charged double for everything he bought. He told the man. The man said he was sorry and the Sheikh let him off.'

'How much we talking about? Five, ten, fifteen million?' You see, I'm already beginning to think like an Arab.

'No,' they said. 'One hundred and twenty nine million dollars.'

'GEE WHIZZ! Sorry – I mean, "Gee whizz".'

'The man then set up in competition with the sheikh. They both quoted for building a golf course in America. The man won, and the sheikh was hopping mad.'

'I don't blame him.'

'He then insisted that the man paid him back everything he owed. Everything, all US$129 million.'

'Did he?'

'No, of course not. He didn't have the money. But it broke him. Last I heard he was back working on building sites again.'

Much as I enjoy listening to the gossip, for me the best part of Dubai is wandering up and down the creek, shaped like a scimitar plunged deep into the heart of the town, and seeing how America's favourite country in the Gulf is routinely flouting its wishes as regards doing business with Iran. This is real Conrad country. The whole length of it is lined with dhows, two, three, four abreast, still built the traditional way by hand and eye without any of your modern blueprints or fancy computer-aided designs, still captained by mysterious one-eyed *nakhodas*, still sailed by tiny, wiry, barefoot Kashmiris, Goans and Bengalis and still scouring the Gulf, sailing across to India and all the way down to East Africa and, of course, over to Iran.

You've only got to go a couple of hundred yards to see for yourself what's going there. Electric fans from China, spices from India, babies' milk from Holland, rice from

Pakistan. All kinds of canned fruit from Italy. Frankincense from the Sudan. Stacks of broken cardboard boxes containing nails made next door in Oman. Soap, vegetable oil, paint, aluminium kettles, fridges, enormous coils of plastic cable, wire fencing. What do they want wire fencing for? Then, for all the world to see, there are huge piles of Pepsi, great lumps of oil-drilling equipment, towers of Caterpillar earth-moving equipment, a mountain of General Motors spare parts and, most important and profitable of all, heaps of genuine authentic American jeans. All with stickers on for Iran. Or even Iraq.

At the Saudi Chamber of Commerce one official told me in a matter-of-fact way that maybe US$1 billion worth of goods were being shipped out every year by the dhows. Another went further still. He said that of everything imported into Dubai, 50, 60 maybe even 70 per cent was re-exported to Iran and Iraq, and some more through Iran to all the old Soviet republics in central Asia.

'So how much of that is American?'

'Shhh.' He put his fingers to his lips.

The problem – well, to the Americans it's a problem; to Dubai, it's an opportunity – is, of course, that out of a total population in Dubai of 420,000, around 70,000 are Iranian and another 70,000 of Iranian origin, so there's no way they can stop it. Iraq, of course, is just business – to the tune of US$200 million a year, some say. Another problem, I'm sure, is that in spite of President Clinton slapping or threatening to slap over sixty unilateral sanctions on thirty-five countries in his first term of office alone, in this case those great believers and arch-advocates of free trade would rather look the other way and stay friends with Dubai than make an issue out of it, lose and risk not being able to play on all those golf courses again.

The other thing I like doing in Dubai is going camel-racing, strictly speaking dromedary-racing, although nobody seems to be interested in speaking strictly. It isn't the same as horse-racing, or better still steeplechasing, but you either like it or hump it. There isn't that buzz and that excitement; there isn't much cheering and screaming, even when the camels turn the final corner into the straight. And there definitely isn't any hugging and kissing and drinking champagne when the winner pads past the winning post by a very, very long neck. And afterwards it is a bit of a shock to see the jockeys walking hand in hand with the owners through the car park back to their 4x4s. Not quite the kind of thing that goes on at Heathfield point-to-point, I must say. On the other hand, it doesn't cost me anything to get in, I don't spend a penny on booze, I don't lose a fortune and it doesn't take three hours to get out of the car park, even if there is nothing but roadworks, diversions and a million traffic cones outside.

The first time I went I was with a retired Bangladeshi police inspector. At least I think he was retired. He kept telling me that he had a lot of money in Bangladesh but had decided to come to Dubai because he liked the weather and the people. 'Very nice weather, sir. Very nice people, sir,' he kept saying.

We'd been to Nad al Sheba, the proper racecourse. As we swung out he turned left and started to head back to the skyscrapers of Dubai City. On the right was an enormous expanse of desert. In the centre there seemed to be a collection of houses, but as we drove along I could see that they were not houses. They looked more like warehouses. All around them were trucks loaded with enormous bales of hay. Then, just as the road signs changed from 'Reduce Speed – Bumps Ahead' to 'Reduce Speed – Humps Ahead', I spotted them, coming out of the desert. First, one, then two, then a collection of four or five. Then more: another three roped together, one on its own, a whole huddle of five or six, one trotting along in front looking long past his race-by-date and the rest bunched up behind. Some looked white and sleek, others were brown and patchy. Some had filthy blankets tied around them. One sported a red and white checked tablecloth and another had what looked like a white sheet wrapped around him.

Camel-racing is, in fact, big, big business. Bigger than the horse-racing business. Some people own thousands of camels: Sheikh Mohammed is said to own 6,000. The good ones, which cost around £10,000, are fed on specially imported milk from dairy cows to keep them in peak condition. Once on a swing through Togo, my favourite country in West Africa, the local newspapers had been full of stories about a camel being sold for what they described as the '*coquette somme*' of US$134,366, all because it could cover 5 kilometres in eight minutes sixteen seconds. Another had been sold for US$154,200. The really good ones, however, can go for as much as US$2 million.

Equally, there's also plenty of money to be made out of camels, providing you've got the right ones, of course. A week-long camel race meeting, for example, can carry prize money of over US$3 million, far, far more than you'd get horse-racing.

On top of the camels I could now see tiny little jockeys. 'Bangladeshis, sir,' the police inspector, retired, said. 'Children, sir. They're only five or six, not much more. They're very small, sir, ideal for jockey. But they don't last long, sir. Maybe, four, five, six years. That's all, sir.' He leaned across the steering wheel towards me. 'After that, sir, they say they are finished. Never grow any bigger. Problems with back. But life very good for them now, sir. They earn 1,000 dirhams a month. Very good money, sir. Plus food. Plus clothing. Plus accommodation. Plus everything, sir.'

We followed an Arab in a Range Rover, with a falcon perched on the seat next to him, swung off the road on to the sand and headed to where all the camels were coming from. It was the racetrack. Or rather, the grandstand of the racetrack. We parked by the equivalent of the saddling enclosure, a patch of sand where a thousand camels were sitting, chewing the cud, spitting and drooling over each other and generally discussing tactics. Guarding them was half a regiment of what looked like military police: all about 6 foot, red berets, smartly turned out and heavily armed. Some poor young guy went to take a photograph of one of the camels and was jumped on and dragged off for, I suppose, a spot of dissuasion. An elderly Arab in an extra-white *dishdash* with a somewhat bouffant headdress intervened and everybody ended up shaking hands and laughing. But the guy still didn't get his picture of the camels.

The grandstand wasn't exactly grand, but at least, I didn't have to stand. The centre section, with its rows of deep leather armchairs and series of huge televisions housed in giant wooden boxes, was obviously the VIP box. Either side were five or six rows of blue plastic strips for the punters. Not that there were many of us, apart, that is, from all the military, who were all over the elderly Arab, lining the back of the whole grandstand and practically sitting next to everybody in it.

'He must be sheikh,' my own personal one-man Bangladeshi police protection squad whispered. 'Sheikhs very important, sir. Need lot of protection.' The sheikh, I discovered later, was the minister for foreign affairs and, even more important, chairman of the Emirates Camel Racing Federation.

A whole mass, and I mean mass, of camels and men and little boys and military suddenly came bursting through a gate on to the racetrack. It looked like a cross between a riot and a street party. As one, they turned left towards the winning post and rolled along towards it and beyond it, wheeled through another gate on to an inner track, past a rickety old starting gate about three storeys high, and then, before I realised what was happening, they were off. No line-up, no chats with the starter. Nobody getting tangled in the wire. Twenty, maybe thirty camels were now heading off into the unknown with their miniature jockeys already belting hell out of them. There are obviously no rules about the use of the whip when it comes to camel-racing.

At first it looked crazy. Camels are not the most attractive-looking creatures at the best of times, and racing, they lope rather than gallop, like giant tortoises who've been scared out of their shells. The jockeys looked ridiculous as well. They were so tiny in comparison with such large animals and sat so far back that they appeared to be attached by Velcro and seemed likely to fall off at any second. But gradually, I admit, I was won over. Even so, there were no bars to go to, no bookies to chat up and the commentary sounded like Peter O'Sullevan on speed. The only thing to do was to watch the race on television.

Already the leaders seemed to be way out in front, maybe 20 or 30 yards or, I suppose, 10 lengths from the others. Their initial burst seemed to have slowed down to a cross between a vigorous walk and a fast trot. Most of them had their necks sticking out. One had his neck stretched right back, as if he was staring up at the stars; another was looking around all over the place. But all of them were still being whipped and thrashed by their minuscule jockeys. The commentator was by now working himself into a lather of sweat, although how he could distinguish between one camel and another and remember all the jockeys' names beats me.

'Very nice drivers, sir,' said my Bangladeshi expert.

All of a sudden what looked like a young camel broke away from the pack at the back. Out he came into the middle of the track, galloping, or rather lolloping, like mad.

How much the jockey had to do with it, I have no idea. All he seemed to be doing was sitting there bouncing up and down and whacking the thing for all he was worth. Gradually it started catching up with the leaders. People began shouting at their television screens. The commentator kept shouting what sounded like 'Thimon! Thimon!' Closer and closer it came to the front. The little jockey was now shooting up and down crazily. If he had been hanging on with the help of an enormous pad of Velcro, it was now wearing decidedly thin. Now it was in the lead. The minister was clapping his hands and laughing, the soldiers were throwing their berets in the air and a couple of old Arabs in front of me started slapping each other on the back and doing a little jig around the television set. Another old man at the end of the row knelt down and started wailing away at his prayers.

'Very, very good driver, sir,' said my expert.

Way out to the left, we could just about see the television vans and the coaches shadowing the race. The screen showed some of the other camels fighting back, but in vain. The young camel was too good for them. He was way out in front and increasing his... yes, there he was. I could actually see him. He looked miles ahead of the others. As he passed the winning post everybody was on their feet, clapping and cheering him. His time was 8 minutes 39.04 seconds. I couldn't see what the tiny jockey was doing. I hoped he wasn't attempting a Frankie Dettori: throwing himself off the top of the camel would probably break every bone in his body.

I can't remember when the second and third came in, but it was a long, long time afterwards, and the rest of the field were later still. In fact, I doubt that the last one has made it yet.

There being no winners' enclosure as well as no bar in which to celebrate or winnings to collect, we were immediately into the next race. Another scrum came bundling through the gates, along the track, over to the starting gate and were off. Again a small group broke away, but this time they stayed there for the length of the race. The commentator packed up halfway through because he had nothing to say. The sheikh went inside the grandstand, obviously to discuss foreign affairs, and the military started getting all efficient again. The old man at the end of the row stopped saying his prayers.

I won't say it was the most exciting afternoon of my life. But it was fun. And I didn't get the hump. Well, I had to say that, didn't I?

Now a warning. Before reading on - I hope you will - you must adjust your sense of priorities even further, otherwise you might do yourself a mischief. OK, are you ready?

How much would you pay for a bird? Yes, a bird, with feathers.

a) US$1,000   b) US$100,000   c) US$1,000,000.

If you bought a bird, how would you bring it home?

a) In a cage   b) In a special box   c) In your private plane.

If you bought a bird and you brought it home, how would you look after it?

a) By feeding it steak   b) By taking it to the local vet   c) By building a special hospital equipped with a staff of sixteen international experts and paying them each over US$20,000. In cash. Every month.

The answers? I'll tell you. I was in another one of the seven emirates, Sharjah, so called because compared to Dubai everything is so unbelievably cheap that people go around all day asking each other, 'How much they Sharjah for that?'

Originally the poor relation, it is catching up fast. Well, I say it's catching up fast: at eight o'clock in the morning it's about twenty minutes east of Dubai; at four o'clock in the evening it's about two days away because all eight lanes on the motorway linking the two cities are blocked solid. While Dubai is full to overflowing and building like crazy, Sharjah still has plenty of room and is building slowly. Whereas Dubai is relaxed and free and easy, enjoys the good life and pretty much allows you to do whatever you want to do so long as you're discreet and don't get caught, Sharjah is restrained, self-controlled and strictly Muslim. So strict that some of the French perfume on sale in the shops had to be relabelled, I was told, Muslim Dior as opposed to Christian Dior. On top of that they've banned the booze. Half the world says it's because Saudi Arabia gave them the money to build a big new mosque on condition that they banned alcohol. The other half say it's because the local sheikh was sick to death of people being killed on his roads because of drink-driving and just woke up one morning, decided enough was enough and banned it there and then.

So, while people go to Dubai for fun, fun, fun and, in the Russians' case, funski, funski, funski, people usually go to Sharjah late at night to sleep. Most people who work in Dubai, as opposed to just hanging round being an expat, actually live in Sharjah, because it's much, much easier to find somewhere to live, and much, much, much cheaper.

During one trip I had just had a meeting with a couple of Indian businessmen who wanted to talk about building a car plant in the Netherlands. (Don't worry, every Indian businessman wants to build a car plant in the Netherlands.) We finished early so I took a quick look at the fish market down by the port and tried once again to brush up my recognition skills, as the Americans say. Not of the fish, of the people.

That guy over there with the pants and the long shirt is

a Pakistani. Probably from Peshawar, where the train runs across the airport runway. The man who looks like a Pakistani but has a full beard is an Iranian. The two with immaculate white *dishdashes* and red and white tea towels on their heads are easy: they're Saudis. That tiny little man pulling the car who looks about 110 is obviously a Bangladeshi. The Bangladeshis, wherever they are in the world, always get the lousy jobs. The man with the two-tone shirt, tie, smart suit and fancy shoes is an Indian.

Now, of course, I'm late for my next meeting. No problem: the driver says he knows a short cut. We swing out of the car park, zoom up the road and practically do a Steve McQueen 90-degree turn between two enormous office blocks. A left, a right, past a huge floral display proclaiming 'Smile in Sharjah'. A bit further on we go over the biggest speed bump in the world. It's about 2 feet high. Alongside it, stretched out on the grass, a bunch of Arab women are sunbathing – with their long, black robes and masks on, of course. Two lefts. Suddenly the road disappears and we are on sand. Not your beach sand, but solid, compact sand which is deeply pitted and rutted. Around another corner, past the only bit of graffiti I've ever seen in the Emirates – it said: 'The life is a game' – into an open bombsite-type area and... wait a minute. What's that? A large wire cage, and sitting inside it on long, low perches, a dozen, maybe two dozen, falcons. Well, what would you do? Go to the meeting or get out and have a look?

I went through the door by the cage. A young man was standing inside in front of a mirror propped up on a brick, having a shave. He seemed pleased to see me, which was unusual in itself. He took me into a kind of rough-and-ready courtyard full of rubbish. It couldn't have been bigger than our kitchen at home, I think – it's been a long time since I've been in it, thank God. On each side was a door. Through one I could see canvas matting on the floor and a pile of old cushions around the walls: traditional Arab housing modern-style. Through the other was another collection of falcons, all of them hooded, all sitting on long, low wooden perches.

These birds, he told me, were worth anything from US$10,000 to US$50,000 each. Yes, each. They came from Pakistan, Iran, even Uzbekistan. He knew people who went out into the mountains and caught them with huge fishing nets. They then passed from one dealer to another until they reached him. He had to do this, he explained, because, he was pleased to say, the sheikhs had declared the Emirates a conservation area and banned people from catching falcons there. The result, of course, was that prices were soaring, he was making more money and falcons had now become even more of a status symbol and so even more people wanted them.

Most of the falcons he got, he said, he sold on to either to other dealers or to customers of his own all over the Gulf states. Only the day before he had sold one, called something like Wocheri Gara, a one-year-old, to a Saudi for US$36,000. What was the Saudi going to do with it, I asked. Go hunting?

'No,' he grinned. 'Sell it to a sheikh for US$100,000.'

If one bird cost US$36,000, how much were they all worth?

He laughed. Well, say each bird on average was worth, what, US$10,000, that meant that together they were worth US$300,000, $400,000 or maybe even $500,000. So here he was living in, let's be honest, a shack, with, I would guess, the very basic facilities, if that, with US$500,000 worth of feathers around him.

How did he keep them fit? Again he grinned. Hamburgers. Meat. Bread. But no fish.

If I wanted to see the real dealers, the professionals, I should go and see Mr Siddiq in the bird market at the back of the cattle market. Which, of course, I did, because I knew that when I eventually turned up late for my meeting, the Arab businessman I was seeing would still be unfailingly polite and hospitable. Either that or he wouldn't have bothered to turn up himself. Unfair, I know, but I was interested in falcons. Many's the time back home I've been to country shows and stood watching falcon displays for hours on end. Once I was seriously thinking of getting one myself. It was only going to cost me £1,000 and I thought it would be great fun to go out riding at weekends with a falcon sitting there contentedly on my arm. But the wife, of course, said no, as in NO. Like she says NO to everything. Something to do with not liking the idea of throwing live day-old chicks into the air for the falcon's lunch. But then again, she is a vegetarian.

Mr Siddiq, when I finally found him, up and down some more narrow streets, across some more wide, open patches, was in his shop at the back of the market. His falcons were obviously more upmarket. They all looked much sleeker and slimmer, their feathers smoother. They were also more expensive: US$50,000, US$65,000, one was even US$100,000.

While we were talking a very nice, pleasant man came up to us, black beard, the traditional *dishdash*, the red and white tablecloth on his head. He told me he was the official falcon-buyer for one of the big sheikhs. So how much did they pay for falcons, I wondered. What was the top price?

'Three million dirhams,' he said. About US$1,000,000. What did I tell you? The official currency unit for the Emirates.

How could a falcon be worth so much money? It wasn't, he explained. It was because the sheikh wanted it and was prepared to pay a million dollars. So did he get his money back? The sheikh, it seemed, was not interested in money.

It was having a better, more expensive falcon than the other sheikhs that interested him.

'Yes, I know.' I persisted. 'But did he get his money back?'

That enigmatic smile. The sheikhs, said the falcon-buyer, did not gamble because it was forbidden by the Koran, but when they went hunting they had competitions to see whose falcon would come back quickest from a longer distance than anybody else's. The quicker the bird came back and the further the distance, the more it increased in price. If the sheikh then decided to sell the bird he would make more money. In the old days, because sound travelled so far in the desert, they trained the falcons to respond to their voices. Now they didn't even bother to do that. They simply trained them to respond to the horns on their Range Rovers and Land Cruisers.

'You mean they go hunting and never leave their cars?'

He grinned.

Now we were joined by a big, jolly fat man with a thick, bushy moustache sporting a light violet *dishdash*. He was the market's number one falcon-dealer. Did I want to buy a falcon?

'No,' I admitted. 'Just looking...'

'I'll show you a good falcon,' he said, and promptly disappeared. The keeper of the sheikh's falcons told me that the Emir of Abu Dhabi was a falcon man. He had over sixty prize birds which he kept at Al Kazanah just outside the town of Abu Dhabi in a specially constructed compound, attended day and night by a full-time staff of sixteen doctors and surgeons, including two Americans trained specifically to look after them. Their monthly salaries plus villas plus cars came to 150,000 dirhams – US$50,000. Each. The whole shooting-match probably cost him around US$6 million a year. Plus, of course, the cost of the falcons themselves.

The number one falcon-dealer reappeared. Sitting on his

arm was a falcon. It was a year old, he said, and came from Uzbekistan. The distance from the tip of its shoulders to the end of its tail was exactly 18 inches, the perfect length for a prize falcon. Its chest measurement was also 18 inches, again, perfect for a prize falcon.

'Here,' he said, handing me a tough, reinforced leather sleeve to put on my arm. The falcon clambered on to it. It sat there, as good as the purest Dubai gold, and let me stroke its feathers and tickle its claws. It had a nice temperament, the dealer continued. If I kept it with me all the time, sat it on the back of the seat next to me when I went driving then put it on a chair at home in the evenings, within a week it would recognise my voice. It would be mine.

How could I get it home? Already I could see myself, falcon on one arm, riding through the village early on Saturday mornings to spend a day out hunting. No problem, he'd get me the necessary papers and put it in a box. All I had to do was take it with me.

Oh, hell. Of course, the wife. You know how she goes on about falcons, hunting, those day-old chicks… But I was beginning to waiver. I asked him what was the most expensive falcon he had ever sold.

'One million dollars. It came from Siberia. It had a lot of white on the chest. There was also a lot of white on its back.'

No, I'm sorry, I thought. Much as I'd like to take a falcon home with me, I'd better stick to the usual present for the wife: nothing. 'So this falcon worth a million dollars. How did the sheikh bring it home?' I asked.

'He sent his private plane, of course. How else do you bring home a falcon worth one million dollars?' How else indeed? How silly of me to ask. This was, after all, the Emirates.

MANDALAY

Poor old Kippers. The sun must have got to him, or something, because his Road to Mandalay was nothing like my road to Mandalay, or Manders, as an old Burma Star veteran I met on the plane to Bagan kept calling it. As we were flying Air Myanmar, one of the most dangerous airlines in the world – the Foreign Office advises you not even to walk under the wing of one of their planes on the tarmac in case something drops off – I didn't want to get into an argument about the respective merits of Mandalay, Manders or even Mandy, in case we didn't have time to finish it.

'... *the temple-bells they say:*

'*Come you back, you British soldier, come you back to Mandalay.*'

Not as far as I'm concerned, they didn't. I went all over Mandalay, one-time legendary city of kings and now home to the country's holiest monks, most skilled craftsmen and finest curries. I visited every temple they've got, not to mention all the shrines, *zedis*, *payas*, monasteries and Chinese take-aways as well, and the first thing that struck me was how few temple bells there were, with the honourable exception, of course, of the world's biggest uncracked bell in Mingun, just north of the town. Gongs, drums, sticks and lumps of metal hanging from bits of string, there's millions of them, but not one of them sounded as if it was saying anything like 'Come you back, you British soldier, come you back to Mandalay.' If anything, they were saying, 'Please to pay, you foreign tourist, please to pay US dollars.'

'Where the flyin' fishes play.'

Is this guy crazy? Flyin' fishes? A good couple of miles from the Irrawaddy, now the Ayeyarwardy River, with temperatures up around 90 degrees and climbing, if there were any fish in Mandalay the last thing they would be doing is flyin', let alone playin'. And I know nothing about fish.

' 'Er petticoat was yaller an 'er little cap was green,

'An' 'er name was Supi-yaw-lat-jes' the same as Theebaw's Queen,

'An' I seed her first a-smokin' of a whackin' white cheroot.

'An' wastin' Christian kisses on a 'eathen idol's foot.'

Petticoat? Cap? A-smokin', I mean smoking, whackin' white cheroots? Christian kisses? No wonder he can't speak properly. He's either flipped his képi, bombed out on Mandalay rum or he's suffering from an acute attack of DTs – Damn the Tourists. Now, again, I'm no expert on *bamahsan chin*, Burmese customs, etiquette and manners, but I've never, ever seen a Burmese woman wearing a little green cap let alone smokin', I mean smoking, a dirty great white cheroot. As for petticoats under sarongs, I'm afraid my research has not extended quite far enough in that direction, but I'm working on it. And the Christian kisses? No way. Anybody, even your typical American tourist, knows that the Burmese, good Buddhists that they are, believe in discretion, reserve and modesty above all things. Some believe that even to touch a woman is to be defiled. You would no more see a young Buddhist girl kissing the foot of the Buddha than you would flyin' fish a-playin' in the streets of downtown Mandalay.

Most roads I've been up and down in my life have been

littered with rubbish, but I don't reckon I've ever come across any road as full of it as old Kipper's Road to Mandalay. I bet you my paperback edition of *Puck of Pook's Hill* to a grilled flyin' fish that he never even crossed the road to Mandalay, let alone travelled the length of it. Otherwise he wouldn't have come up with so much tosh, unless, of course, he couldn't find anything to rhyme with Kyauktawgyi, Serkyathiha or Shwe in Bin Kyaung.

Had he really known his Burma, of course, he wouldn't have written about Mandalay in the first place. He'd have written about Pagan, or Bagan, as they call it today. It's older, more steeped in the past and boasts far, far more pagodas than Mandalay. Originally there were over 5,000 of them. Nowadays, what with the ravages of time and tourism, they're down to a mere 2,000, of which 300 have been restored and are more or less in working order, including my favourite, the Ananda, with its four huge standing Buddhas. But I suppose he didn't like the idea because it wasn't Christian. On top of that, he probably couldn't find a rhyme for it, either, apart from Fagin. Which again isn't exactly Christian, is it?

Travel the road now and you can see how the Burmese not only have it ruddy 'ard but are being Kiplinged to death as well. The land either side might be just as clean and green as Kippers said - it was about the only thing he got right - but you can't help but notice how it is paved with nothing but bad intentions and horrifying conditions.

The farmers working all day every day in the paddy fields that stretch as far as the eye can see have to sell more than half their crops to the government, even though the government only pays them around 60 per cent of the market price. The women repairing the road from dawn to dusk are either rounded up from nearby villages and given the choice between volunteering and being fined or worse, or they are just clapped in leg irons and marched off under armed guards to whichever part of the road needs repairing. I say repairing: all they do all day is push rocks into the oozing red mud with their bare hands. The mud, I'm sure, is red because of the amount of blood that goes into it from the huge cuts and weals and lacerations on their hands.

'Every family is told they must send one person. The men, they work in the fields, so the women go,' a French businessman I met in the Swan Hotel in Mandalay told me. 'If they refuse they are arrested for being anti-government.'

'What if they're pregnant?'

'Doesn't matter, they still go.'

The young men and boys you see keeping up the non-stop supply of rocks work all day in the nearby limestone quarries for around – are you ready? 50 cents a day. But don't worry, for that money they don't have to sift and carry and load up the lorries themselves – that's done by their mothers and grandmothers and little sisters. For even less.

The markets you see along the roadside are nothing like the markets in China, Vietnam or any other non-Tiger economy in south-east Asia. They are tiny and insignificant and seem to sell nothing but rice, dried fish, some funny fly-blown meat, ghastly-looking fish paste, chillies, peppers, barbecued chicken's heads on dirty wooden sticks and bundles of *thanaka* wood, which women all over the country grind into a yellow paste to smear over their faces as make-up. Until I realised this, I thought they were all suffering from jaundice or something. It was, I can tell you, quite a relief. I stopped at one stall and the guy tried to sell me some opium weights. I ask you, what could I possibly want with opium weights?

As for the traffic along the road, it's unbelievable. Ox carts, pony carts, horse-drawn tongas, bicycles, rickshaws, jeeps, ancient Chevy buses, old – God help them – British cars. All straining like mad at every set of traffic lights you come across, watching the seconds-by-second countdown to zero which flashes up alongside first the red light and then the green one.

As for Mandalay itself, with its low-rent bargain-basement Raj era atmosphere, it looks as though it has been reincarnated at least seven times, and a little bit of each reincarnation has been left behind. The result is a glorious biryani of Indian, Chinese, Nepalese, Arab, Victorian, Japanese and English home counties. Not from the years when the British were around – most of that legacy was totally obliterated long ago – but from the new upmarket totally out-of-place Western-style housing estates, complete with wide, clean Western-style streets, trees and even lighting, which are springing up on the outskirts. Not to mention all the Western-style super-markets and Western-style hotels which, for some reason I cannot fathom, in temperatures way up in the 90s and with the surface of the road actually bubbling under your feet, insist on wishing you a 'warm welcome' and boasting that the speciality of the house is 'London fish 'n' chips'. Note the Kippers spelling. It's about the extent of the influence he's had on the place.

But ignore all that and it is still gloriously Mandalay. It has wide, dusty streets choked with traffic. It has thou-sands of battered rickshaws that are dangerous even to look at. It has millions of bicycles careering around all over the place because everybody tries to ride them with only one hand on the handlebars and the other clutching an umbrella to keep off the sun. It has pavements full of sewing-machines whizzing around so fast that little boys have to keep throwing buckets of water over them to stop them from bursting into flames. It has thousands of mysterious tiny back streets. It has still more women working on building sites, carrying enormous bags of cement on their heads and shoulders and more young boys, hurling bricks, barehanded, one by one from street level up three or four storeys to the bricklayers all day long. It has great gaping holes in the ground revealing what passes, or rather does not pass, as sewage. And it has stalls and shops and markets everywhere which seem to be full of nothing but cheap Chinese goods, fake US-labelled jeans, strange-looking medicines, individual corn-plasters, all kinds of foodstuffs, bicycle tyres, umbrellas, drugs and computers – yes, computers. Everybody everywhere now sells computers, fridges and pirated compact discs, ranging from Michael Jackson to names I've never heard of, for just US$3 each.

Even the entrance to the only fire station in the centre of town is so blocked with street stalls selling VCRs and televisions and satellite dishes and tape decks and CD-Roms that if there was an emergency, by the time they got a path cleared and the fire engine out, whatever was on fire would have burned down. Come to think of it, that's probably what happened to Mandalay Fort. An enormous walled palace about the size of the Hidden City in Beijing, and completely surrounded by a huge moat, slap bang in the centre of town, the fort caught fire during fierce fighting between retreating Japanese and advancing British and Indian troops in 1945. Nobody was able to get to it in time and it just burned to the ground.

I even discovered a gem market hidden away on the edge of town where you can take your chances and buy piles of stones, uncut, which is far better and much more sensible than buying them when you're half cut or even bombed out of your mind. To me one uncut stone looks pretty much like any other, but judging by the expensive suits, gold watches and thick wadges of dollars people were passing backwards and forwards, they must have been the real thing. I think.

But whatever the marketplace in whichever part of the

country you visit, practically everything on sale, I was told, is made in Guangdong Province in China then shipped to Lashio, the big Burma–China trading centre near the border. From there it is trucked down to Mandalay and on to Yangon and all points north, east, south and west. In the opposite direction go all Burma's rattan furniture, timber and gems. What influence the Chinese couldn't acquire by financing years of undercover activities, not to mention the Burmese Communist Party, it seems they are now gaining through trade.

Like Mandalay, the country itself is also at a crossroads. Left is where they've been before: protests, violence, turmoil, mass killings, assassinations, stagnation. For the best part of thirty years it was in the iron grip of General Ne Win, one of your old-school military dictators. While he got richer and richer the country sank first to socialism, then to bankruptcy and now to international pariah status. What should be one of the richest countries in south-east Asia is now one of the ten poorest in the world. A cross between Mao Zedong, Joe Stalin and Mrs Thatcher, the general is, I reckon, the most superstitious person on earth. One day he suddenly abolished the country's entire decimal currency system and replaced it with new units of 45 and 90 kyat, because he realised that not only were they divisible by nine, his lucky number, but you could add them up and they would still be divisible by nine. Another day he woke up and decreed that all traffic throughout the country should drive on the right-hand side of the road instead of the left because one of his astrologers told him that the right was always better than the left in everything. You can laugh, but with or without the help of his magic charts, he's survived a long time. He was there when, within weeks of Pearl Harbor, the Japanese marched in and set up the Burma National Army with him as chief of staff. He was there when, towards the end of the war, Burma rapidly changed sides and backed the British. He was around when an eager, passionate thirty-two-year-old advocate of democracy called Aung San and six of his assistants were assassinated. Six plus one equals seven – an unlucky number. Where exactly he was standing at the time nobody has ever been able to establish conclusively, although most people reckon it was somewhat closer than nine paces.

In 1962 (1+6+2=9) he seized power, abolished Parliament, set up his own Revolutionary Council, announced Burma was going socialist and nationalised everything in sight. The results were dramatic. Everything immediately started going downhill, fast, and so it has continued.

In 1981 (1+9–1=9; 8+1=9) he retired, though nobody believes that even today. At over ninety years of age (9+0=9), having had nine wives, he spends his time at home in Malik Street in Myangon Township in Yangon – having nine boiled eggs for breakfast, nine prawn curries for lunch and nine London fish 'n' chips for dinner, washed down with nine bottles of champagne – or out playing golf with nine partners. On the full eighteen-hole (9×2) course, naturally.

Where was he when his three (3×3=9) successors took control? Where was he when the present bunch, General Saw Maung and the ludicrously named State Law and Order Restoration Council, came to power? Again, the feeling is not more than nine paces away, manipulating, pulling the strings, all nine of them. At least, that's what the fortune-tellers say in the back streets of Mandalay.

Like the traffic, right is obviously also the direction being taken by the bunch of generals who are at present running the place as a military dictatorship. There are politically motivated arrests and detention, forced labour, torture, summary and arbitrary executions, and secret police all over the place. One Western diplomat told me he believed that as many as one in ten Burmese were working for the secret service. Even tour guides are forbidden to talk about the government and have to sign bits of paper agreeing not to do so. They are also at the mercy of a string of undercover agents and informers. One wrong word and zap! anything can happen. Like having to show Americans around.

But in their own eyes, of course, they're not right wing and oppressive, just as Burma is no longer Burma. Instead they call it Myanmar as in Me and ma piano, which is the Myanmar for Mayanmar, just as France is the French for France, if you see what I mean. Not that I'm against countries or even cities changing their names. Upper Volta did it. One day it was Upper Volta, the next it was Burkina Faso. Similarly Côte d'Ivoire. One day it was the Ivory Coast and overnight it became Côte d'Ivoire. The trouble is the wrong places change their name. The States is the worst. There are Bastards all over the place, not to mention Japs and Squaws. But not much Sex, although Montana, amazingly enough, has not only a Sex Peak but a Sex Peak Lookout as well.

The other totally unjust, outrageous and oppressive thing the military have done, apart from improve the roads, splash some paint on the odd public building and tear down the odd rat-infested hotel and replace it with a swish modern one, is to ban Pepsi Cola. Myanmar is the only country in the world where you can only get Coca-Cola, which is just as well, because it's about the only thing I know that cleans the glasses after you've been hitting their local Mandalay rum.

If the generals are obsessed with going as far right as they can go, the ordinary man in a pagoda seems more than content to take the straight and narrow road, because that way lies Nibbana, the local Buddhist equivalent of Nirvana. Which, to those in the know, is Thervada Buddhism as opposed to the Mahayana Buddhism you find in China, Vietnam and among the Chinese in Singapore, Hong Kong and Taiwan. Tantric Buddhism you find in Tibet and Nepal; Zen Buddhism is all the rage in Japan, as well as among followers of the New Kadampa Tradition, not to mention the bunch up in Cumbria who keep criticising the Dalai Lama and accusing him of religious intolerance and hypocrisy and the I-might-not-go-to-pagodas-but-I-know-what-I-believe-in-Buddhism they go on about in San Fran. But of course, you know that already. Either way, the straight and narrow road is a dream world of golden spires, white pagodas, misty lakes, fresh grasshoppers for lunch, unlimited supplies of Coca-Cola, the smack of leather on willow and old maids cycling along country lanes on the way to early-morning... oh no, that's a different kind of Nibbana, although to be fair, it was the Nibbana of a certain Burma policeman: George Orwell.

The problem, as always, is how to get there. Some say Mrs Aung San Suu Kyi knows how to get there, especially her friends, members of the Nobel Peace Prize Committee and the crowds who fill the pavement outside her home at 54 University Avenue at 4 pm precisely every Saturday when she climbs on a table by the front gate and offers them the promised land.

Others are more cynical. 'How can she say she was severely shocked by the assassination of her father and that it had such a profound effect on her that she decided to devote her life to democracy and introducing a lasting democratic ideal to Myanmar when she was only two years old when he was killed?' another French business-man, obviously a Cartesian, asked me.

A German businessman I met wondered how she could believe so strongly and firmly in principles and justice and honouring commitments when she had virtually given up her family in England to devote herself to her campaign for democracy. A British diplomat, however, told me he was very impressed by her. She was, he said, like Edward Heath in his heyday. She walked like a young girl, talked like an old woman and smelled like a flower.

Before I went to Burma, I mean Myanmar, all the experts I met in London kept telling me I would have great difficulty finding her. Spies and secret-service agents were everywhere. Drivers would refuse to go there. Nobody would admit she even existed. Nonsense. I picked up a cab in the centre of town and told the driver to follow the billboards proclaiming, in English and Myanmar:

'Oppose those relying on external elements, acting as stooges, holding negative views.

'Oppose those trying to jeopardise stability of the State and progress of the Nation.

'Oppose foreign nations interfering in internal affairs of the State.

'Crush all internal and external destructive elements as the common enemy.'

Within ten minutes we were there. What's more, every time we passed a poster the driver turned to me and grinned, 'General's desires, not people's desires. General's desires, not people's desires.' So much for the experts. But having been there, all I can say is that the mess her house and gardens are in makes you wonder how efficiently she would run the country. And she has yet to come up with a magic nine-point plan, apart from being kind to elephants. I mean, doesn't she know anything about what makes Burma, I mean Myanmar, tick?

Maybe it's because of Mrs Suu Kyi, not to mention the UN Commission on Human Rights, Amnesty International and the *Guardian*, that Myanmar is one of the few countries left in the world which is not overrun with tourists. What tourists there are seem to be French, not because, I suspect, they particularly like the place, although they would obviously go for the fresh grass-hoppers, but because being French, they take a perverse delight in going to all the places they shouldn't go to. Like Iran, Libya, Iraq, Cuba and Blenheim Palace. Or perhaps they just like the idea of visiting a country where they worship a god, or rather goddess, called Lady Bandy Legs.

Talking of bandy legs, the whole country seems to be suffused in an all-pervading Buddhist atmosphere. Most men spend part of their lives as Buddhist monks. Every-body donates a part of what little income they have to their local temple, and I don't mean the odd few pennies in the plate on high days and holidays, I mean serious money. And everybody wants to be smothered in nats. Not nits, which makes a change. Do something good and the *nats*, or spirits, will write it down in their little gold-leaf books. Do something wrong and down it will go in one of their dogskin books, and before you know what's happened you'll be living in Florida – or at least, you'll be in Florida. On top of that they're kind to elephants. Some people say they care more for their elephants than their wives, but as most of those who say this are wives, nobody takes much notice – it's the kind of thing wives say all over the world.

The fact remains that the Burmese elephant is not only the most sensible and intelligent elephant in the world, he is also the easiest to train. Not like the African elephant, who is thick and completely impossible. About the only thing he is good at, I was told, is putting his trunk into other people's pockets. But as the guy who told me that was with the World Bank and had spent most of his life trying to sort out Nigeria, he might have been slightly prejudiced. Most of the heavy work carried out in Burma's huge teak forests, the largest in the world, is carried out by elephants, some owned, reared and trained by the government, others by private contractors who hire them out like contractors hire out tractors and combine harvesters at home.

Burma is the one country where there is no question about who's boss. The women, their beautiful enigmatic smiles hidden beneath that ghastly chalky yellow mud, smoke dirty great cigars, not just after a decent meal but all day long, while the men wear dresses, or *longyis*. As far as the generals running the show are concerned, on the odd occasion they pluck up courage to appear in public they are invariably festooned with so many medals that you can't tell whether they've got a *longyi* on underneath or not. For all I know they might not feel the need for any protection, although if I were them I wouldn't risk it. Then there is this whole thing about adjusting it and retying it all the time. It still, I'm afraid, makes me nervous when I see these guys suddenly throw their *longyi* wide open, shuffle it around a bit and then gently retie it again. At first I didn't realise that it was a giant tube of material and they were safely inside it however much they jiggled it around. But even now I know how it works, I still can't get used to it.

Would I ever wear one myself? No way. I know less than nothing about fashion – which is why, whenever I go, people come up to me in the street, press 50p or a couple of bottletops into my hand and tell me to get myself a cup of tea – so I would never be able to decide which style suited me best: the swish, elegant, expensive cotton materials or the darker, dirtier, greasy alternative with what look like patches of something or other in all the wrong places. Then there is the length. On the ankle? Above the ankle? On the calf? Or, if I wanted to be really daring, on the knee? Which, I suppose, would be a shorty-*longyi*. Colour would be another problem. Red? Blue? Green? Purple? Plain? Check? In the end, for a super-control freak like me, I suppose it would have to be grey,

to fit in with the rest of my somewhat limited wardrobe.
And where would I tie the knot? In the centre? To the left?
To the right? Slightly loose and sagging? Medium? As tight
as hell? Finally, the most important question of all: what do
you do with your valuables?

Deep down, I suppose the real reason I like Myanmar is
not because of the *longyis*, shorties or whatever, but
because of the pagodas. If you think the place is crawling
with soldiers you haven't seen the pagodas. There's even
more of them: in high streets, back streets, up on the top of
mountains, down the end of dirty alleyways. Set in the
middle of magnificent gardens. Trapped inside a huddle of
filthy shacks. Go anywhere, and there's a pagoda. Their
principle, I'm sure, is if it doesn't move, slap a pagoda on
top of it. Or even if it only moves a bit: there's even a tiny
7.3-metre high pagoda on top of an enormous rock which
is itself balanced precariously on the edge of a sheer drop
at the top of Kyaikto Mountain. How come it's never fallen
over? Because inside the pagoda, just, just, just maintaining
the balance is a hair of the head of the Buddha. Well, that's
what they told me. And in strict, military-run pariah
nations where one in ten of the population is working for
the secret police, I always believe what people tell me.

I reckon I am to pagodas what John Betjeman was to
parish churches. So, if you're sitting comfortably, lotus
position, of course, I'll begin. A pagoda is not really a
pagoda at all, that's only what we call it. But as we still
insist on calling Myanmar Burma, that's hardly here nor
there. A pagoda, if we're going to be strictly boring, or
rather Burmese, is a *paya*. As in 'Why the hell do I have to
paya through the nose for everything I look at in this
damn country?'

There are two kinds of *payas*: a *zedi* and a *pahto*. A *zedi*
looks like a bell. It's usually rock solid and contains bits
and pieces of the Buddha himself - his teeth, his hair or

whatever – or, since there are not enough bits of teeth or lumps of hair or whatever to go round, the rate they are building these things, it can be practically any holy this or that providing it's been blessed by a holy man or *sayadaw* (as in 'Saya daw I have to really take my shoes and socks off to go into this place?'). Some unkind people have suggested that it is shaped like a bell because there's no way the Lord Buddha's teeth and hair and whatever have survived 2,500 years so someone must have dropped a clanger somewhere. But I wouldn't say that, especially in a strictly military-run etc. etc. A *pahto*, as in 'Hell, has pa too got to take his socks off? He hasn't taken them off for the last fifty years,' is really a square or rectangular-shaped building or shrine or temple, somewhere to go when you're wandering around a *zedi* and it starts pouring with rain yet again. But if all that's too complicated just call them pagodas, I mean *payas*. Hell, call them whatever you like.

Now, don't get me wrong. Just because I reckon I've visited every single one of the 2,567,923 pagodas in Myanmar – they have more pagodas per reincarnated bare foot of population than anywhere else on earth – it doesn't make me a pagoda freak. It's simply that I can tell the difference between a *keinnayi* and a *keinnaya*. Which is just as well, because one's male and the other's female.

I've also done the pagodas in China, Taiwan, Thailand, Cambodia, Laos and Vietnam, but as far as Myanmar is concerned, here are my top nine Burma star pagodas. Nine, because it's a lucky number. Don't you remember anything? In any case, everybody else does top tens, so let's be different.

OK, the number one star slot is not old Kipper's Moulmein Pagoda lookin' lazy at the sea, but the big daddy of them all, the Schwedagon Pagoda, which also happens to be the most sacred of all Burma's shrines and the only one to boast an escalator as well. But that's not the reason for it being my number one. It's my number one because it's not really a *paya* or a pagoda at all. It's a glorious mishmash of hundreds, maybe even thousands of pagodas of all shapes and sizes, all clustered together on top of Singuttara Hill in the centre of Yangon. Imagine a Buddhist theme park in, say, Hawaii thrown together by a failed Italian wedding-cake designer hooked on marijuana and practically smothered in millions of tiny Christmas lights, and you're almost there. Some are deep and serious and heavily reverential; others are chocolate-boxy. A few, I will admit, are a bit tacky and embarrassing. But there are so many of so many different styles that it's almost got to be one of the wonders of the world. And I'm not saying that because I want to take tea with Mrs Aung San Suu Kyi or to get a medal from one of the generals.

To get to the Schwedagon Pagoda you can either climb a million steps, go by lift or take the escalator, which was built by prison gangs. But far from being the easiest and quickest route to the top the escalator is often, I was told, the slowest and most dangerous because so many local people are not used to it. So apart from getting on and off it, they have problems in the middle as well. They lose their balance, fall and slip or, frightened to step off at the end, backtrack and jam the whole thing up. Before you know it all these calm, inscrutable Buddhists are flopping around all over the place trying either to surrender themselves to the next life or to get the hell off the thing as quickly as possible.

Naturally, I opted to take the steps. The thought of wandering through the monasteries or monk houses at the foot of the hill and then slowly climbing past the shops and stalls selling all kinds of Buddhist religious nick-nacks seemed somehow appropriate. Then I was instructed: 'Footwearing Prohibited', and since footwearing included shoes and socks, I quickly changed my mind and decided on the lift. Once inside it, however, I began to have second thoughts. It was dark and the floor was as tacky as hell. It was also one of the most ancient and temperamental lifts I've ever travelled in. The only way the self-appointed driver could get it to work was by continually slamming the gates and rushing to the handle at the other end and jiggling it furiously up and down for all he was worth. Eventually, probably with the aid of a couple of hundred mantras, we were up and away.

When I stepped out into the open at the top I must admit I experienced one of the greatest religious sensations I think I've experienced in the whole of my life. The marble paving stones were – youch – so hot on my soft little lilywhite feet that for about thirty-five minutes I was dancing around like a howling dervish amid all the devout Buddhists before I could even attempt to walk. Well, you might be used to frolicking around barefoot, but I'm not. I'm a boring old businessman, don't forget, with a thing about grey *longyis*.

Once I had acclimatised and got used to the inscrutable, imperturbable Buddhists staring at my white feet, I was able to take in the view. It was spectacular. Not as spectacular, I admit, as the size and condition of the colonial-style British Embassy compound in downtown Yangon, where they still serve Madeira and sing 'Mad Dogs and Englishmen', but it was certainly the most dazzling collection of pagodas I've ever seen, and I've seen enough to last me through this life and about another four reincarnations.

I'd been expecting an open courtyard and in the centre a single striking pagoda, but they were all over the place, thousands of them. It was breathtaking. I stopped and stared, stunned. This is obviously what Orwell must have been feeling when he kept on about his Burmese daze.

All around me people were bowing to the ground and

worshipping their Buddhas. Like the way the Tories used to worship Mrs Thatcher all those years ago. Others were sitting intently in their lotus positions. Young people were strolling around, businessmen carrying their briefcases and umbrellas were tripping barefoot from one pagoda to another. Young girls were doing what young girls do all over the world: huddling together and giggling. Kids, inevitably, were crawling around everywhere howling and screaming.

In front of me was the main pagoda, the Golden Dagon. It was unbelievable: the height, the size, the gold leaf. You couldn't help but be dazzled by it. Especially in the early evening as opposed to first thing in the morning. But then, most things look spectacular in the early evening as opposed to first thing in the morning. To Kippers it was a 'golden mystery' and a 'beautiful winking wonder'. But he was obviously as familiar with it as he was with the Road to Mandalay. I thought I could detect traces of the Schwedagon Pagoda between Wetkyi-in and Nyaung U near Bagan, the home of one of four surviving teeth of the Lord Buddha, but as I say, I'm not an expert like Kippers. I've only been there and seen it.

Some people say it's over 2,500 years old. Others say that bits of it might be, but most of it goes back only as far as the eighteenth century. Either way, everybody agrees it was built to house just eight hairs of the head of Prince Siddhartha, who gave them to a couple of brothers from Yangon who happened to be in India doing a spot of wheeling and dealing just when he attained his Buddhahood. Why eight hairs and not nine, and why he gave them to them and not to somebody else, I have no idea. One old monk told me that it was in payment for some cakes, but I don't believe that. Nobody exchanges cakes for hair. You normally get them both together: you buy a cake and inside it you find at least eight, nine, ten or maybe even more bits of hair and things all mashed up together, at least you do if the cakes I had in the famous tea shops of Mandalay are anything to go by. Maybe Prince Siddhartha just went around handing out eight hairs of his head to all and sundry. If so, it would certainly explain why he was bald from such an early age. And it must have been a darn sight cheaper than buying everybody a round of drinks.

On the other hand, maybe the two brothers were peddling some kind of prehistoric hair-remover and the Buddha gave them the eight hairs to prove that the damn stuff didn't work and demanded his money back. Whatever the reason, they kept the eight hairs, rushed back to their King in Myanmar and sold him the idea of putting them in a gold casket in a gold chamber with a huge gold slab on top and building this enormous pagoda on top of the whole thing as well. Which suggests that, in addition to trading, the two of them dabbled in a little bit of property-development as well. For my part, I'm grateful the good Prince Siddhartha only gave them eight of the hairs of his head. If he had given them anything else, I shudder to think how much land the brothers would have had to have bought up and how big the pagoda would have needed to have been.

As for all the gilding, Queen Shihsawbu is supposed to have started the craze a few hundred years back by offering her own weight in gold. Not to be outdone, her son-in-law Dhammazedi, either out of respect for his mother-in-law, which I admit is unlikely, or perhaps because he wanted to soften her up before breaking it to her that he didn't want to spend yet another Christmas with the family, went a stage further and offered four times his weight, plus the equivalent of his wife's, in gold to further gild the thing. Which tells you that either he was very thin or his mother-in-law was very fat. What the history books say, I don't care. I know what I believe.

Now the design. Unless you're planning to take a GCSE in pagodas, forget all this stuff about *pyisayans* and *khaunglaungs* and Baung Yits, not to mention Kya-Lans, Hngnet-Pyaw-Bus, Htis, Hugetmanas and the Seinbus, even though they are decorated with a mere 1,485 gold and silver bells, 5,440 diamonds and 1,431 other precious stones. First, there is the lower, base section, which is really a whole series of terraces – in other words, the plinth. This, I reckon, must be about 20 feet high. All over it on all the different terraces or steps are other pagodas: large ones facing north, south, east and west; medium-sized ones on the four corners of the plinth itself, and around forty to fifty even smaller ones all around them. On top of the plinth sits what looks like an enormous gold hand bell. Look at it closely: the bottom section is octagonal, but as it rises it slowly, slowly becomes circular. Clever guys, these Buddhist architects. Finally, there are all the fiddly bits: the lotus petals, what's known as the banana bud and on top of that the *hti*, the cone, the jewelled vane and, on the very top, the diamond orb.

Honestly, you could stare at it all day long and there would always be something different to see. There would also be a million different things to watch going on all around it. Young men on their knees bowing low to the ground. Girls kind of semi-squatting and doing the same. Old men and women, many of them nothing but skin and bone, stretched out on the ground itself, some on carpets, some of their own little pallet boards. Businessmen standing in silence for five, ten, fifteen minutes. A young man in white shirt, tie and trousers is sitting on the ground in the lotus position, eyes closed, oblivious to everything and everyone. 'He comes every day,' a young monk told me. 'He stays like that for an hour. He should be monk, not me.'

More old women are huddled over tiny bamboo cages full of sparrows. Release a sparrow, they say, and the higher it flies, the near it gets to Heaven and the more Brownie points you pick up from the Lord Buddha. And, of course there are the monks. Young monks in their bright red robes, older monks in their darker robes, walking from pagoda to pagoda, kneeling down in front of the Buddha, sitting still, contemplating, whispering advice to people. There's even the occasional lady monk.

You see the same devotion in, say, the Mahamuni Pagoda, the other big, big pagoda just south-west of Mandalay. Originally built over 200 years ago, this is another Buddhist theme park with huge temples and art galleries and museums everywhere. One is given over to Buddhism around the world and, curiously, dates all its exhibits BC and AD. In the centre of the complex is the shrine itself, a 15-foot-high bronze image of the Buddha completely covered in gold leaf. So precious and so sacred is it that only men are allowed to go anywhere near it. Women, like footwear, are not permitted. Get up early enough in the morning and you will see a team of men cleaning its teeth and giving it a wash and brush up, although not too much of a wash and brush up because of all that gold leaf. The reason it's not my number one star pagoda is not because it is not impressive, or because it gets so crowded. It's because I still can't get over seeing so many people outside the temple watching the ceremonies on video and bowing down and worshipping the television screens.

Having studied the great Schwedagon Pagoda I now did what every honest, devout, God-fearing Buddhist does. I adjusted my lucky Buddhist amulet and started following all the splayed feet and stubby upturned toes around it in a clockwise direction. Walk around it anticlockwise and you're not only a wicked Buddhist, you're also going to get trampled on by the crowd coming in the opposite direction.

Around the base of the main pagoda are hundreds of shrines, the most important being shrines for each day of the week. If you were born on a Tuesday, you head for the Tuesday shrine, and so on. I've got no idea which day I was born on so I kept walking. So how do you know which shrine is your day? Easy. The Monday shrine has a tiger, the Tuesday shrine a lion. Wednesday is an elephant either with or without tusks, depending on whether you were born in the morning or the afternoon/evening. Thursday is a rat. OK, OK, that, I suppose, must be the day on which I was born. Friday is a guinea pig, Saturday a dragon, Sunday a garuda. Goodness me, don't you know anything?

I particularly liked the Reclining Buddha in the Prayer Hall with the Dr Spock ears, who looked as though he was lying down after a particularly good lunch, and the little brass Buddha sitting all by himself under a banyan tree grown from a cutting from the very banyan tree under which Buddha himself sat one day. Well, that's what they told me. And in a strict, military-run etc. etc.

Temples have cats, and the pagoda cats are all over the place, doing all the things cats do. Sleeping on benches in the sun, scratching away at the back of a Buddha. Crawling out from under a pile of candles or incense sticks. Not like the cats up in Nga Phe Kyaung, an old wooden monastery built over a lake in Ywama in the far north-east of the country. There the monks have taught their cats to leap through a series of hoops, which must mean that either the monks have plenty of time on their hands or the cats are reincarnated politicians.

There were also plenty of pagoda dogs hanging around, sniffing whatever caught their fancy, settling down and falling asleep in the sunshine. When I say hanging around,

I mean hanging around. Most of them had all manner of things hanging from all kinds of places, which put me off the whole idea of reincarnation. It's all very well to come back as a 17-hand hunter, going hunting four days a week, being loved, cherished and spoiled the whole of your life. Fabulous. But come back as a pagoda dog? No, thank you.

What struck me most was that the pagoda was not just a Sunday-morning affair but a vital, integral part of everyone's lives. Maybe it's easy to be a Buddhist. Maybe it's easy to be a Buddhist when everybody around you is a Buddhist. Maybe it's because there's no footwearing – perhaps taking your shoes and socks off somehow makes you feel and act and behave differently. Perhaps we should try it ourselves one Sunday morning and see if it makes any difference.

Number two star pagoda has got to be the Kuthodaw Paya in Mandalay. It is also known as the Maha Lawka Marazein Paya, which means beware the postcard-seller. She's the deadliest creature known to man. I was there around the 10th of the Waning of the 2nd Waso, 1358 ME, in other words last Tuesday week, and I promise you, you won't get out of there without buying at least a dozen postcards you don't want and you don't need for friends you're not going to send them to. You have been warned.

Similar to the Schwedagon Pagoda, this is not so much a pagoda as the biggest book in the world. The Tripitaka, every single one of the holy books of Buddhism, have been carved on to no fewer than 729 huge marble slabs. Each marble slab has been put inside its own individual pagoda and then all 729 of them have been arranged, row after row after row after row, around a single central pagoda. To read the lot of them once took a team of 2,500 monks working in relay almost six months, but they did it, which is probably more than they would have managed if they were trying to plough through a Jeffery Archer. The sheer size and scale of the thing is unbelievable. And I've never come across any book that has been stuck on a shelf for so long – apart, that is, from some of mine in that sophisticated centre of learning and culture, Auckland, New Zealand.

Walking up and down all these rows is a bit like wandering up and down one of those old Italian cemeteries full of glorious crumbling wedding cakes. Three things occurred to me. First, if I was to carry on visiting pagodas like this I was going to end up with first-degree burns on the soles of my feet. Second, how come the Buddhists came up with the idea and not the Christians? After all, the Christian religion is based on a couple of stone tablets, so it would make sense if somebody put the Bible on to a couple of thousand stone slabs as well. Third, when is that old man going to stop banging that lump of metal hanging from the roof of the big central pagoda and singing and chanting away like mad? Maybe that's why it took all those monks so long to read the Tripitaka: they couldn't concentrate for all the noise going on around them.

The pagoda right next door, the Sandomani, is the cheap, paperback edition, so to speak. This, too, has hundreds and hundreds of stone slabs, here with commentaries on the holy books inscribed on them. Again, they are each in their own tiny pagodas, lined up in rows around a central pagoda. But somehow the Sandomani doesn't make the same impact. The buildings are a bit tattier, the paint is peeling off many of the little pagodas, and their postcard-seller is nothing like the Kuthodaw postcard-seller.

My number three pagoda is the Atumashi Kyaung, also in Mandalay. After all, Mandalay, once the capital, is still the religious and cultural centre of the country. They even speak better Burmese there than they do in Yangon, or so

I'm told. There are not many wooden pagodas in Myanmar, but as far as I'm concerned the Atumashi Kyaung takes the golden tooth, even though, strictly speaking, it's a monk house, as they say, with a pagoda inside, as opposed to a pagoda pagoda, if you see what I mean.

The Shwe in Bin, another monastery, I mean monk house, with a pagoda inside, just across town, is smaller, darker and more ramshackle. Otherwise it might have got the nomination. It also has some interesting cartoons of the British, complete with képis and riding boots, in Burma in the old days, although what they are doing in a monk's house I have no idea. Perhaps they are used as a warning to the young monks to meditate properly, lest they come back as Englishmen.

Both are fascinating, built entirely of wood and on stilts. You have to clamber along shaky bridges to reach them. Both have rough-and-ready planks of wood for a floor, which is a bit unnerving, especially if the soles of your feet are red raw from visiting so many other pagodas. It is obvious that both are also working monk houses – not because of the timeless reverence and devotion pervading the whole building, nor the continual prayer and chanting of the monks, but because the monks' washing is hanging up all over the place. Furthermore, there are monks sprawled across the floor of the pagodas themselves without so much as a sermon going on in the background. Which I must say amazed me. I always thought monks had to sleep on their right side, just like the reclining Buddhas in Yangon and Bagan, or even the one in Myinkaba, come to think of it. Not wrapped round benches clutching on to their *kammawas*, or with their feet halfway up a sacred pillar.

The Atumashi Kyaung pagoda is more elaborate, with more decoration and gilt. I also liked it because, again unusually for a pagoda pagoda, there are lots of photographs displayed of famous monks who have visited the pagoda, and some of their own monks as well as pictures of the monastery itself, which helped put everything into context.

Pagoda number four is a problem. At first I thought it would have to be the Shwemyethman Pagoda of the Buddha with the Golden Spectacles, which is way out of Yangon in the middle of nowhere, put there by a man whose wife's sight was restored as a result, he claimed, of the Buddha. Which makes me grateful that his wife only had problems with her sight, otherwise I dread to think what type of Buddha he might have put there. Then I remembered the tiny pagoda on 76th Street in Mandalay, by the old fort, and the tiny one hidden away in a collection of little shacks opposite the medical school in Yangon. There's nothing grand about them – they are obviously parish church as opposed to cathedral pagodas, although the one in Mandalay is in beautiful condition: clean, sparkling, glistening in the sun. But to me their lack of grandeur was what was interesting about them. It proves that Buddhism is a genuine, everyday faith which appeals to people across the board. It also shows the almost total grip that Buddhism has on its followers.

Then I thought about the little shrine and pagoda at Eindawya near the big Zegyo Market, which looks like a prototype for the first moon-based pagoda. It's all bluey-white and made out of what seems to be a mass of misshapen moon rocks.

But on reflection, I think I'm going to plump for the tiny floating pagoda on the edge of Lake Kandawgyi. Called the Shiukobomoque, or something like that – no Westerner had ever been there before, according to a passing monk, so they had never had to write the name down in English – it's about the size of a four-man dinner table. In the centre is a profoundly uneasy Buddha who appears to be having problems sitting on the water. Whether he'd have problems walking on it is, of course, another matter.

Pagoda number five is easy. It's the Sule Pagoda, right slap bang in the centre of Yangon. Why? Because it sits in the middle of the roundabout at the junction of Sule Pagoda Road, which I suppose is obvious, and Maha-bandoola Street. It stands over 45 metres high, and some people say it is over 2,000 years old, which I doubt, because they didn't have roundabouts 2,000 years ago. There is even a mini cable car to carry flowers and other offerings halfway up the pagoda itself: a neat, clever hi-tech way of getting your gifts closer to Buddha. All around it are other tiny pagodas, including one outside which a brisk no-nonsense soldier-type in T-shirt and *longyi* kept banging a drum, chanting, bowing to all and sundry and accepting offerings of fruit all day long.

Incidentally, just by where you collect your shoes and socks and cross over the bridge to get back to the traffic and the real world, you'll find one of the best of the black-market money-changers in town. Officially the exchange rate is about 6 kyats to the US dollar. He was giving me 120, which you must admit is one hell of an incentive to go on a pagoda crawl. But, perish the thought, that's not of course my reason for nominating this pagoda number six. However, I must say that I was a touch more generous when it came to stuffing notes into the collecting boxes.

Pagoda number seven star should be the fantastic Ananda Pagoda in Bagan. It out-wedding-cakes anything you could imagine. It's enormous, beautifully decorated and probably the best-preserved pagoda in the area. The trouble is, to make room for the tourists visiting Bagan, the government has been going around uprooting people and destroying their houses. Suddenly, in the middle of the night, one whole village was literally ordered to leave there and then, marched 5 miles down the road and just dumped in a peanut field in the middle of nowhere. Bearing that in mind, there's no way I could possibly vote for a Bagan pagoda because that would look like a justification of the government's actions, and there's no way I'm having anything to do with that. So instead I'm going for the famous Reclining Buddha propped up on an elbow with an oh-so-sweet come-hither smile playing on his lips, who lives in a pagoda the size of an aircraft hangar on the outskirts of Yangon. It is almost as long as the Shwethalyaung Reclining Buddha in Bagan, but not quite. What put me off it originally was the way great flocks of birds kept flying in and out of his nostrils. There was I at Stage Four of Buddha's famous Eightfold Path to Enlightenment and zoom! out flies this ugly great crow and – thud! – I am back at st-st-stage W-W-One again: the Rightness of Speech. It just doesn't do anything for the concentration.

I mentioned this later to one of the monks living in the row of houses opposite. He became very agitated and wanted to know whether the birds were flying out of the right nostril or the left. Out of the right nostril was OK. Out of the left nostril meant the Buddha was having problems with his *ida* nerve channel, which runs along the spine. If it was blocked – or, to use a technical Buddhist term, bunged up – it could make him restless and irritable. Which could cause all kinds of trouble. For the Buddha or for me, he wouldn't say.

We then got into one of those tense how-many-angels-on-a-pin-type arguments: when is reclining reclining and not stretched out falling asleep? Once again the monk grew agitated. Some people, he said, maintained that the Shinbinthalyaung Reclining Buddha up in Bagan was not reclining but actually stretched out on his right side. If this was true, it meant it was a dying Buddha, which was a whole new bag of tricks.

And I'm afraid I don't quite go with the story about My Lord Buddha's feet. There is the poor Lord Buddha, tramping the highways and byways being a friend to all and handing out teeth and clumps of hair to everybody he meets. Yet his feet are in nothing like the state mine are in, and I only spent a couple of days traipsing barefoot around pagodas. The toes are long and slender, the nails beautifully manicured in a touching shade of pink. And the soles of his feet have no blisters, no calluses, no corns, no scratches, no bruises, no nothing. Except exactly 108 beautiful marks and symbols that are, I suppose, the soul of Buddhism.

Number eight are all the other pagodas I've missed out, because I don't want to upset anybody. Especially in a strict etc. etc. etc. Well, when I say all the others, I mean all the others apart from the ones in Bagan. I know your average tourist is happy to see beautiful old buildings levelled to the ground and people moved out of their homes just to make way for a car park so that it takes them only two and three-quarter minutes to walk to their luxury air-conditioned coach instead of three and half, but I'm not. Which is why I don't believe in tourism. I only travel, don't forget, because I'm forced to do so in order to make a living.

Finally – a quick roll on the pagoda drums – the award for pagoda number nine goes to General Ne Win's pagoda. Because he is General Ne Win, because nine is his lucky number and because I just love the idea of a politician having his own pagoda. It's as if he's saying, 'I know I fouled up and ruined everything in this world, but maybe if I build a pagoda or a temple, or a church, it'll give me a bit of influence in the next.'

As for the pagoda itself, it's superb, because it is so appropriate. Like all politicians, it fails to live up to expectations. Officially called the Maha Wizaya Pagoda it's opposite the southern entrance to our number one star choice, the great Schwedagon *paya*. It was only built in 1980, to mark the unification of Theravada Buddhism. The King of Nepal threw in some relics, the government of Myanmar provided the land and the people – inevitably – stumped up the money. And, no doubt, the hard work. From the design point of view it's OK, nothing spectacular. What makes it outstanding is that when they came to build it our General Ne Win insisted on adding on two more storeys to make it higher than the sacred Schwedagon Pagoda. Isn't that just typical?

Maybe old Kippers could have written a poem about it. It's got all the ingredients: funny words, impossible rhymes, and, of course, the ultimate. He could have composed the poem without ever having to go and look at the place.

LA PAZ

So there I was, 12,000 feet up in La Paz in the middle of the Andes, doing what I do best: having a drink in the Pig and Whistle, the local English pub and expat hang-out.

One of the guys I was with - blue blazer, slacks, Guards tie, moustache - was telling some long involved story about an Irish cocktail being a pint of Guinness with a potato in it.

Then - *schrack!* Gunfire.

So? Gunfire's gunfire. It happens all the time when you're doing your bit, travelling the world trying to help the balance of payments. Especially in countries famous for student protests and riots and insurrections. We had another round. Well, why not? I'm halfway through my pint when - *schrack!* - more gunfire. This time it sounds ... The door bursts open. An elderly civil-servant type, wearing an old-fashioned sports jacket and a somewhat distinctive pair of brown trousers, rushes up to the bar.

'What would you like, sir?' says the barman briskly.

'A Scotch,' he pants.

'Anything with it, sir?'

'Another Scotch, you bloody fool. The army are out there. They're heading this—'

Now I can hear people outside running and screaming. Then, suddenly, nothing. Total silence. We finish our beer. I'm just ordering another round when suddenly, yaaaahhhh! My eyes are streaming, my nose is running, my stomach is burning and heaving. The bar is full of tear gas. A canister has gone off just outside the door. The barmen, choking and retching, are rushing around lighting candles - apparently an open flame helps to burn away the gas. Everybody is heaving and panting and retching and choking. The only thing I can compare it to is the sudden sensation you get when you take that first gulp of Beaujolais Nouveau in an off season.

I'd read about tear gas many times, of course, but I'd never experienced it. That's nothing new: I've read about a lot of things many times and never experienced them. But I can now see its usefulness. It's immediate. Within seconds it totally incapacitates you, burning your eyes and searing your insides so that you can hardly breathe. In some people it causes temporary blindness or second-degree burns. It can even damage your lungs permanently. What's more it lingers. You're still coughing and spluttering and choking for maybe thirty minutes afterwards. It stays in the atmosphere for hours and on your clothes for days on end. Sometimes it even lasts until you get back to the office, as proof - yaaaaaragh! - that overseas travel - yaaaaaragh! - is not all expensive bars and restaurants. Not that anyone believes you, naturally.

When I finally got home from La Paz I was spitting up blood all over the carpet for a good half an hour before my wife said a word. Finally:

'So what's wrong with you then? Drinking too much again. Serves you right.'

'Actually, it's - yaaaaaragh!'

'Well, don't expect any sympathy from me. It's your own fault. If you insist on going to these—'

'CS gas. I was - *yaaaaaragh!*'

'A fine story. More like too much cheap whisky, if you ask me.'

Even when I collapsed, choking, in a heap on the floor, it didn't make any difference.

'Mind the dog's blanket. I washed it last week. I don't want to have to do it all over again.'

By now I was tearing at the floorboards.

'Typical. I get a cold and I have to get on with it. You get a little cough, and just look at the fuss you make.'

Then the drawbridge came down, the shutters slammed shut and she refused to talk to me for a week. Because, she said, I had been drinking too much.

So what can you do to protect yourself against such uncontrolled, hysterical behaviour? (Tear gas, I mean, not your wife). The answer is nothing. A handkerchief up against your face is worse than useless. It just means that if your photograph ends up on the front page of the overseas edition of the *Daily Telegraph*, nobody will recognise you. Which might or might not be a bad thing. A wet scarf? Not worth the bother. What's more, you'll probably end up by getting a rash and being unable to shave for a week. The police sometimes use lighted flares to disperse the gas immediately in front of them, but that's hardly practical, is it? I mean, you can hardly walk around town all week, going to meetings and wining and dining the usual bigwigs, with a bundle of flares under your arm, just in case. The only sensible thing to do, therefore, is not go there in the first place. Go to St Lucia instead. Any other suggestions, however, would be gratefully received, written on the back of a gas mask and sent to the Pig and Whistle, La Paz.

On the other hand, one of the best possible places to be trapped during a tear-gas attack has to be in a British expat pub. Because, in true British fashion – cough, cough, heave, spit – we carried on regardless – yaaaarrragh! Unlike in Moscow, where if anyone throws a petrol bomb into a bar, there's an almighty rush to drink it.

'I say, old man. Three more - cough, splutter, heave - of the local, please.'

'No, no. It's my - retch - turn. You bought the - sneeze, heave, splutter - last one.'

'Yes, but this is a - retch, heave - special occasion.'

'Well, if you insist. But just this - YAAAARRRRGGGGHHHH once. Next time it's ...'

The barman, who looks as though he would be more at home on the outside throwing in, plops our drinks down on the bar muttering about what I swear sounded like 'Betty Swallocks', which just shows you the difficulty some people have picking up even the simplest English phrases. Then, thud, another canister lands outside the door. Everyone immediately starts heaving and retching and squirming three times as badly as we're engulfed by yet another wave of gas. This is about par for the course for an army which must be modelling itself on the French: they've never won a war in the whole of their glorious history.

The effect the gas has on you is unbelievable. It feels like hot, sulphurous sandpaper scraping the inside of your lungs. Your eyes are streaming, your face is red raw, you are choking for breath. But every breath you take makes it a million times worse. Like the way you feel after the second gulp of Beaujolais Nouveau in an off season.

Now there is more gunfire. I'm no expert, but it sounds like rifles. Suddenly, in the distance, there is an explosion. Then silence. We look at each other through streaming eyes and the haze of the gas. Everyone has a handkerchief or a serviette or a towel up to their face. Everybody is still heaving and retching and choking. Then, of course, the jokes begin. Mine first. 'I would say that was Tiananmen Square - cough, cough, splutter, yaaaacht - 1989,' I say, sniffing the air. 'Left-hand side.'

'Really? I would have - cough, cough, splutter - said the ri—, rii—, rrriyaaahhhttt-hand side,' counters a major-in-the-pay-corps type propped up against the bar beside me.

'On the other, cough, hand it could have been Trafalgar Square. CND marches, 19— yaaaaragh!' says a weird-looking new-age drop-out slumped in a chair by the window.

'Touch of Northern Ireland – fyaaahhh – I would have said,' offers a defence-attaché type further along the bar.

The conversation turns to where the stuff is made.

'Can't be made in India. No whiff of fyaaahhh curry,' says the major.

'Maybe France. French are good at this fyaaaggghhht kind of thing, although they never, never, never fyalk about it, of course,' says the defence attaché.

'No, not France. No garlic.'

I won't tell you who said that.

'Like shingles, old chap,' came a voice oak-aged by too much cheap South American claret. 'Always hits you when you least expect it. And when it hits you, oh boy does it hit you, what?'

'The only good thing about it,' added the clipped tones of another defence-attaché type 'is that you can't smell the cordite in the air.'

As it turned out, the gas was made by some company in Pennsylvania. After everything had died down I went outside and picked up all the empty canisters I could find, took them back to the hotel and sold them off to people who had bolted themselves in their rooms at the first rumour of soldiers in the street so that when they got home they could regale everybody with tales of their heroic adventures in the front line. Well, what would you have done? Given them away?

Now there was the sound of sirens. 'What's that? The police?'

'No. Ambulances.'

'Don't be daft. They won't bother with ambulances. Not for these b-b-bastyaaaghts.'

'My mum's still got her old gas mask from the war. Why don't I get her to send it out to you?'

'No, don't bother. He's already got his gas mask on. You can take it off, now, it's all over.'

'Gas masks are no good. Not your ordinary gas – cough – mask. It'll get through that. No problem.'

'I had a dog once. The postman came to deliver some letters and she ran up to h-h-him barking. Do you know what he did? Fyaaaggghhh! He maced her. Just like that. Dog was blind for nearly two hours.'

'OK. My round. What are you going to...?'

By now the gunfire was continuous. There was also the rat-tat of what could have been machine-gun fire. People outside were screaming, horns were blaring, dogs were barking.

Someone opened the door of the pub.

'Don't do that. What the...'

'No, it's better outside.'

'Yes, that's true.'

The sirens sounded as if they were coming closer. Then they sounded as if they were going away again. More gunfire. More screams.

'Shouldn't we try to get back to the hotel?'

'Are you crazy? You don't know what it's like out there.'

'I'm staying put. Best place to be if there's any trouble. In a pub. What?'

'Yeah, that's right. Let's have another drink. What you gonna have?'

'Same again, squire.'

'The things we do for British exports.'

'Wait a minute, is that chanting I can hear?'

We all strained like mad, listening.

'You're right. It is.'

'You think they're winning? You think they're going to beat the...?'

'Listen, shouldn't we get out of here? I mean, anything could happen.'

'You want to go out there, you go out there. Me. I'm staying put. Here we're safe. Out there, who knows?'

'Yeah, you're right.'

'My turn. What you going to have? Same again? OK.'

'Betty Swallocks. Betty Swallocks. Betty Swallocks.'

Yurgaahhhh. More – cough, choke, spit, retch – tear gas.

There was no way anybody could do any business for the rest of the trip. The students and the police and the military were fighting each other all over the place. Nobody was in their office; nobody was even on the streets apart from the students, the police and a few battle-hardened military. And everywhere, wherever two or three ex-pats gathered together, wheezing away like old bicycle pumps, there were the same old jokes.

At the hotel: 'Is tear gas extra or is it included in the price?'

In the bars: 'Well, at least it added some flavour to the local beer.'

In the offices: 'Of course I don't know if it is tear gas-proof. But I'll take it out with me this evening and find out.'

At the Café Montmartre: 'If I collapse, will you promise not to give me mouth-to-mouth resuscitation? I haven't had the jabs and I've got a wife and family back home.'

My lasting memory of the incident is of a director of a big British bank, who spent practically the whole time he was in La Paz hiding under the bed in his room. One morning he was forced to venture out for an important meeting at the Ministry of Finance. There had just been another riot and there was still tear gas in the air. He caught the slightest whiff of it. His eyes streamed and he coughed and spluttered and rubbed his eyes so much that suddenly we all realised that his deep tan didn't come from water-skiing in the Bahamas but out of a bottle. And the more his eyes streamed, the more he rubbed his face, the more his heavy suntan became a swirling, ugly mess, like the bottom of a cesspit or a particularly virulent piece of contemporary art. What they thought of him when he turned up at the Ministry of Finance I have no idea, because unfortunately, I never saw him again. Sorry, I mean fortunately, I never saw him again.

If the tear gas didn't provide enough excitement there were plenty of other problems to worry about in La Paz. The attitude and the lack of oxygen, for example. There is just not enough of the stuff to go around. As a result the air is as thin as the new ideas file for next year's corporate plan. This causes all kinds of problems from the moment you arrive, or rather, from the moment before you arrive. The air is so thin that planes have difficulty coming in to land. There is so little to support them that once they're over the airport they tend to drop right out of the sky - thud! - straight on to the runway. And when they take off it takes them ages to get off the ground. Then, when they're finally up, you can almost feel them clawing at what air there is in order to get fully airborne.

Then there is smoking and drinking. Not especially because they're bad for your own health, but because they're bad for everybody else's health as well. There are no sprinkler systems in any of the hotels or offices - there is not enough oxygen in the atmosphere to operate them - so if you smoke and fall asleep the whole place could go up. Hit the booze as soon as you arrive, and your white corpuscles will think it's party time and you'll be on the floor within ten minutes, if you're lucky. The reason drinking is bad for other people's health is that obviously they'll rush to catch you, and because of the sudden exertion, have a heart attack themselves and collapse on top of you. Even if the other guy doesn't die of his heart attack you'll die from suffocation. The lack of oxygen can cause all kinds of other personal problems as well, from minor irritations, like not being able to breathe, to really serious things like losing money. The worst trouble I had was trying to get to sleep at night. I've never stayed in any hotel where there was so much puffing and panting going on.

To help you deal with the altitude, the locals recommend *maté de coca*, which is a poor man's cup of weak tea. Except the tea is coca, the thing that puts the kick into cocaine. They say it's non-addictive, harmless and the only way to adjust quickly and easily. All I can say is, I'll stick to my usual. Each cup was supposed to contain three or four leaves about the size of a postage stamp. I was drinking the stuff with three or four hundred leaves in it, and it still didn't make any difference to me. Bring even a teaspoon of it back to Heathrow, however, and before your suitcase hits the tarmac it's the hand on your shoulder, the rubber glove and six months in Wormwood Scrubs. Which might not be as bad as it sounds, because by the time you're released your suitcase will just about be coming up on the baggage reclaim. If you're lucky.

One guy I know, a real expert on Latin America – he speaks Latin like a native – has big, big problems with the altitude. As soon as he hits La Paz he practically keels over. He's reeling around all over the place, gasping like a fish. His eyes are rolling, his face ashen. It's as if he's got permanent jet lag. He is frightened to take the coca tea in case, he says, it gets into his blood and he becomes a raving drug-addict and all his teeth drop out. He's tried whisky instead, but, of course, the sudden intake of alcohol makes him much worse. He also tried, he told me, something he hadn't done since his youth: a non-stop regime of cold baths, on the basis that they would build up his red corpuscles. Which is not what I thought cold baths were meant to achieve, but then, I must have different problems from him. In the end he found the only solution was to take his own oxygen supply with him. So today, in addition to his Vitamin C tablets and his anti-diarrhoea tablets and his malaria tablets, he won't go anywhere without his own personal canister of fresh oxygen. Unfortunately this means his suitcase is so heavy that whenever he picks it up he gets out of breath and has to have a quick shot. As a result, by the time he arrives in La Paz the canister is invariably almost empty.

Another guy I know, one of your typical golf-mad Americans with a 1 or 2 handicap, had an even worse experience. The lack of oxygen cost him a fortune. On his first trip to La Paz, he brought his golf clubs with him and challenged the locals to a game. He insisted on everyone placing enormous bets all round, so confident was he that he was going to wipe the floor – or, rather, the green – with them and clean up. He'd forgotten about the thin air. He overshot every hole by a mile and ended up practically buying the golf club.

I was lucky. I didn't have any of these problems. To tell you the truth, on my first trip I didn't even realise the lack of oxygen could wreak this kind of havoc until I noticed that, whenever I rushed past any fat old woman with a black bowler hat, a mouthful of rotten teeth and a vivid fluorescent pink sweater, sitting on the pavement huddled in blankets with six babies strapped to her back, I would catch my breath and my heart would begin to flutter. I tried cold baths for about three days, but they didn't help – not that they had ever helped much in the past. Then, just as I was beginning to get seriously worried, it suddenly clicked. Of course – the lack of oxygen. There could be no other possible reason. Thank goodness.

On the other hand, the thin air makes La Paz a civil servant's dream come true. Everything is oh-so-slow and determined. Nobody exerts themselves, nobody rushes around or tries to do anything quickly. If the phone rings it takes three minutes for anyone to answer it. Ask somebody the way and it would be quicker to fly back to London to get a guidebook than to wait for them to tell you. Order a glass of wine in a bar (apart, of course, from in the Pig and Whistle), and you'll die of thirst, if not from tear gas, by the time it arrives. Everybody ambles along in first gear. Try to operate in second, let alone third, and you risk a heart attack, or worse, a three-page memo warning you that you might lose one of your grades, a gold star or even your government-issue plastic briefcase. In triplicate. Come to think of it, it's not unlike Liverpool. I remember one day checking in at Liverpool Airport and the young guy behind the counter just stood there staring at me for three minutes. At last he said, 'Sorry about that. I just had to take a deep breath. I needed it after the rush.' The rush? He'd just checked in two people in ten minutes.

Visiting businessmen find it hard to adjust. It's probably the only place in the world where you don't see export managers rushing straight to the nearest bar as soon as they arrive. They walk there slowly instead. Government officials, however, take to it like ducks to water. This, of course, is something the Bolivians have not been slow to take advantage of. If they want you to agree a contract, sign a deal or lend them some money, they deliberately leave everything to the last moment. Then they telephone you and tell you you must be with them in five minutes. By the time you have rushed across town, climbed the 527 steps outside the office and laboured up three flights of stairs, you haven't got any breath left to object to whatever conditions they want to attach to the deal.

'Delivery, pant-pant, by next Tuesday? No p-problem. Painted pant-pant in sky-b-b-b-blue pant-pant pink? Whatever you pant-pant say. Wrapped in y-y-yellow ribbons?

It'll pant-pant be a pant p-pleasure,' you say as you fall off the chair and spreadeagle across the office floor. Why else have they put all the boardrooms and big government conference rooms on the twenty-seventh, twenty-eighth or twenty-ninth floor of whatever building you go in?

You think I'm kidding? Listen. The government wants to privatise – or capitalise, as they call it – all their aged, loss-making industries. So, like every other government in the world which wants to offload its deadbeats on to a bunch of innocent, dewy-eyed foreign investors, it builds a lavish information centre and multimedia presentation unit stocked to the roof with champagne. But where is the Bolivian privatisation centre? On the twentieth storey of a towering government office block, that's where. As if that's not bad enough, you have to climb 703 steps up from the pavement even to get to the front door of the building. By the time you reach the office, believe me, you haven't any breath left to resist whatever they throw at you. I know – I've been there and done it. And I've still got a couple of million white corpuscles to prove it. In fact the only reason I'm not today the proud owner of a string of municipal waste dumps in Cochabamba is that the phone happened to ring at the crucial moment and the deputy assistant undersecretary had to rush, or rather amble, off and exchange memos with some assistant deputy undersecretary.

As for La Paz itself, the setting, as you would probably expect, is literally breathtaking, if not truly spectacular. It may not be as beautiful as, say, Cape Town, but it is certainly the equal of San Francisco. Imagine one of those black bowler hats turned upside down inside some enormous mountain valley. All around it are snow-capped mountain peaks. Just below the rim, high up on one side, is Vino Tinto, a huddle of jerry-built shacks. Deep inside the bowler is La Paz proper, named after the battle which gave Bolivia their independence from Spain in 1824.

Running practically the length of the city is a single street, the Prado, down which, in the 1860s, a British ambassador was once led sitting back-to-front on a donkey, having been forced to drink a whole barrel of chocolate, because he dared to criticise the local *chica*, some part-fermented wine. When news of this reached Queen Victoria she was not amused. She called immediately for a map of South America, found Bolivia on it – oh, those glorious days when Britain ruled the world – drew a thick, black mark through the middle of it and declared that it no longer existed. Today it's in pretty much the same condition as the British Empire: virtually non-existent. Everything is falling to pieces or just crumbling gently into the dust.

The main section of the Prado has some smart buildings: lots of banks and government offices. On either side of this, however, to all intents and purposes you're in mediaeval Spain. A vast, tortuous mish-mash of tiny twisting streets, like Avila or Toledo, or maybe Córdoba, but without the whitewash, once grand, elegant squares and once glorious churches. The noise is deafening. Broken-down old cars without any brakes chug along. Police cars and huge, rusty, 2,000-year-old army trucks cough and groan all over the place. Sirens scream. Guns go off round every corner. Bombs explode in the distance. Pavements are choked with stalls and benches and those fat old ladies with bowler hats selling everything from gnarled and twisted potatoes that look like diseased appendixes to diseased appendixes from some animal or other that look like gnarled and twisted potatoes.

Strolling down the pavement is impossible. You have to take great loping steps to avoid treading on people or knocking over piles of maize patties or *chicharron* or lumps of pork crackling. All along the edge of the pavement *cholitas* are selling fruit and vegetables, ponchos, colonial silver, alpaca sweaters, *charanges*, armadillo hides and genuine Inca key rings. A must for every family. Outside every office there are small groups of Bolivians in tight fancy suits with big scarlet fingernails. The women, though, wear either bowler hats or Versace. There doesn't seem to be anything in between.

You can also see everywhere the legacies of the other major influence on Bolivian life: an Argentinian-born doctor called Ernesto Che Guevara who, with his artificially created receding hairline (a Cuban barber plucked out the hairs one by one to make him look older and more serious) criss-crossed the country again and again by motorbike, trying to ferment what he called 'a second Vietnam' until he was ambushed by US-trained Bolivian troops in the jungle and gunned down. His hands were immediately chopped off and sent back to La Paz to be checked for fingerprints and his body was quickly buried underneath a runway under construction near Vallegrande. The university in the centre of town, for example, boasts the most enormous mural you've ever seen of good old Che – apart, obviously, from the one you used to have in pride of place on the wall of your squat when you were a revolutionary Marxist proud to be at the behest of the 'bestial howlings of the triumphant proletariat'. Of course, that was before Daddy landed you that job in the City where you now regularly clean up a million or even more at Christmas. And that's just the bonuses. Inside, I discovered that the students are still revolting. Six-year degree courses on subjects like Che Guevara and the Art of Motorcycle Maintenance, Che Guevara and the Art of Airport Construction and Che Guevara and the Art of Lobbing Tear-Gas Grenades Back at the Police, they easily spin out to twelve years or more. And they're actually allowed to choose their own teachers. If the teachers should insist on anything as revolutionary as doing any work, they can also get rid of them. Examinations, they maintain, don't count. Hardly anyone passes them, anyway. Yet still they complain and riot and arrange for me to be choked with tear gas.

But funnily enough, the one thing you don't see anywhere in Bolivia is Bolivian pipe bands, and the one thing you don't hear is Bolivian pipe bands playing the Flight of the flipping Condor. Obviously this is because they are all playing everywhere else in the world. In Covent Garden, in the big underpass in Bratislava, at the Central Station in Warsaw, all over the south of France, in Marbella – wherever you go nowadays you can't escape them. Presumably the theory is that even if all you can do is blow a pipe or bang a drum, at least you can do something to make some money, so you might as well get out there and earn some bread.

As a whole, Bolivia, the so-called jewel of the Andes, is not just a desperately poor country, it is the poorest and least developed country in South America. The size of France and Spain combined, and Britain's biggest export market for bowler hats, it is, according to some statistics, the poorest country in the entire western hemisphere, poorer even than Haiti. The World Health Organisation goes even further: they reckon it is worse than either Ethiopia or Burkina Faso. Ninety-seven per cent of the rural population live below the poverty line, the highest percentage of rural poverty anywhere in the world. Mortality is unbelievably high. Nearly 10 per cent of all babies who die do so before they are a year old. Adults, too, die much earlier than elsewhere – few live beyond the age of forty-six.

I know both Ethiopia and Burkina Faso, so I know what poverty looks like. This seems worse, maybe because it isn't desert and it isn't Africa. Not that the government, or rather governments, have done much to solve the problem, even though there have been, according to my calculations, only 200 of them in Bolivia's brief 160-year history as a nation. Most of them have been corrupt, inefficient and totally incompetent; the others have just been bad. At one stage the only way you could tell the time in Bolivia was by the number of revolutions per minute. The country has had enormous financial problems. Inflation was once as high as the Andes itself, but it has now come crashing down from 26,000 per cent to less than 10, the lowest in South America.

But the crazy thing is that Bolivia is potentially one of the richest countries in the whole of South America. Their nuts are famous all over the world – not as Bolivian nuts, but as Brazil nuts. The Brazilians have cut down so many trees in recent years that over 60 per cent of the Brazil nuts you buy in the shops now are grown in Bolivia. On top of that they have not only oil, but also tin, copper, silver and gold. Indeed, they have so much gold that *garim peiros*, unlicensed illegal Brazilian miners, have swarmed all over the San Simon region on Bolivia's eastern border to search for it and smuggle it back across the border. Anybody with a pick, a sieve and a mountain is out there scouring the length and breadth and height of the country for the yellow stuff. So, too, are all the big mining multinationals in Canada, Australia and America, and even the odd British company.

As if that is not enough to be getting on with, Bolivia is also the biggest producer of the most profitable commodity in the world: drugs. Way over 50 per cent of their exports are represented by drugs. In fact, it's touch and go whether the white covering you see on all those mountaintops is snow or cocaine. Whether this is good or bad I don't know, because as far as the Bolivians are concerned, coca is both legal and illegal. It's legal when grown for chewing and drinking as tea. It's illegal when used for the production of drugs. In theory, at least. What it is when the leaves are used to foretell whether you'll make a fortune, be caught by the police or end up as a respectable member of the community, I'll let you know as soon as my brain stops popping.

Corner a government official at a reception or meeting and he will tell you that around 10 per cent of the population is in the coca trade, most of them ex-miners living in red-raw, freezing cold poverty and forced into growing the stuff to make ends meet. That, however, was not the impression I got. It seemed to me that most of the people growing coca were farmers whose families had been cultivating it for generations. A few, the really big operators, the guys with thousands and thousands of hectares, are in it for the huge returns.

Down in Santa Cruz, the gateway to the Amazon, a safe haven, no doubt, for many a Nazi war criminal, and where there is more than enough oxygen to go round, things are slightly different. To the east are some of the world's most successful and productive soya farms, run not by Bolivians but by Japanese. To the north, south and west is a whole fix of some of the world's most successful and productive farms full stop. Run not by the Japanese, but by the Bolivians. These are the coca farms. Some, like those in the jungle around the Chapare River, north-east of Cochabamba, the principal coca-growing region in Bolivia, are so large they employ as many as 20,000 people, most of them down at heel *cocaleros*. Indeed, I was told, some of them are expanding so fast that they are not only causing untold damage in the back streets of Chicago, Baltimore and practically every other back street in the world, they are now beginning to damage their own environment. It's the old low-input high-output story. They plant enormous areas of coca and refuse to put any fertiliser back into the soil. When the coca plants begin to get exhausted, as inevitably they do, the big farmers simply move on to a fresh patch of dirt and start all over again and the old areas are just left to go to waste. But the truly amazing thing is that the whole business is no coke-and-dagger affair. It's wide open for all the world, as well as CIA spy satellites, to see.

The principal coca area is one hell of a joint. It's like driving through vast vineyards or tea plantations. There are the bushes, all in straight lines, growing away like mad in the subtropical climate. Like tea plants, the smaller the bush the better, and the smaller the leaves, better still. In the good old days, at least for the coca-growers, a 50-kilo sack of the very best dried coca leaves would fetch around US$1,000, a fortune for your ordinary farmer. Today, however, it can be as low as US$50, which hardly pays for the sack, let alone the cost of production. Somebody else – and this is where things become hazy – collects all the leaves together and turns them into a brown paste. The brown paste is then transported or smuggled out, in 1-kilo balls or rolled up and stuffed inside the handlebars of your bike, packed into the back of your car or moulded into any shape you like. Where and how the paste is then turned into the real thing I have no idea. However, everybody kept telling me there were over 1,200 airports in the country, not to mention thousands of landing strips, open fields and straight roads which could all handle small light aircraft, and São Paulo is less than two hours away.

Whether this has got anything to do with the fact Santa Cruz is the richest town in the whole of Bolivia, I wouldn't know. What I do know is that it's a cross between a grown-up spaghetti western, with those high, wooden walkways and hitching posts, and Dallas. And it just oozes money. With only 22.5 per cent of the total population it is responsible for over 30 per cent of the GDP, and annual incomes are 30 per cent higher than the national average.

On the outer of the eight rings which make up the town, you can hardly cross the road for huge trucks heading west loaded with enormous trunks of tropical timber from Bolivia's vast Amazon rainforests. On the inner of the eight rings, you can hardly cross the road for the gleaming, brand-new four-wheel-drives and stolen Japanese cars shipped in from Brazil, Peru and Argentina. You can tell they're stolen because not only are they all body-filler and no car, but the steering wheels have been switched from one side to the other, so that although the wheel is in front of the driver, luckily, the instrument panel is in front of the passenger. Hurtling through town, therefore, becomes a novel experience. The driver is always asking you if he is breaking the speed limit, whether the indicator worked and if you can see anything in the mirror. Worse still, because the switching of the wheel from one side to the other has inevitably been carried out by a cheap back-street Bolivian garage where the mechanics are none too hot, the steering often leaves something to be desired. It took one taxi I used – it had so much filler all over the place that I couldn't tell whether it was one of those old American classics or a Hillman Imp – eight turns of the steering wheel to get round a corner. I counted them each time.

The main square in the centre of town, the Plaza 24 de Septiembre, is quite picturesque with its colourful native *tajibos* trees which, for some reason or other, are home to a colony of sloths. One day I was strolling around the square (where, incidentally, I spotted a Body Shop at which Anita Roddick, never one to miss an opportunity, was raising funds to save the English rainforests) when I came upon a demented British export manager shouting, screaming, jumping up and down and complaining that one of the sloths had been following him around all day.

The crazy thing about the coca business is that the more

everybody tries to stop it, the more production expands
and the more money pours into Santa Cruz. And I mean
money. One evening, for various reasons I can't remember
at present, I accidentally on purpose gatecrashed an
enormous party in one of the big, swish hotels. There
must have been over 1,000 people there, all drinking
chin-chin like mad. Short of going to an end-of-term ball
in, say, Dallas or Monte Carlo, or I suppose, the Fontainbleu
in Florida, I doubt you'd see so much conspicuous
consumption on high heels anywhere. Everybody was in
a designer this, that or the other – in fact most of them
were practically out of their designer this, that or the
other, but that's a different matter. The point is there was
no way they could make all that money by sitting on the
pavement all day long selling bowls of hot llama stew and
T-shirts saying, 'My pa went to San Francisco with his new
partner and all they brought me back was this wonderful
T-shirt'. I don't know whether it was significant or not, but
the place where the party was being held was smothered
in signs saying, '*Gracias por no fumar*'.

What really gets up my nose, especially with the aid of
a tube and a hand mirror; what really makes my mouth go
dry, my teeth chatter, my ears pop, my eyes squint, my
eyeballs shoot out of their sockets, my lips peel back in a
sickly grin, my brain explode with poison gas, my head
swell, my back lock itself in a shudder of ice and the
whole of my body go into freefall, spinning wildly out of
control, grunting, screaming and howling at the moon, is
the hypocritical way everybody goes around pushing
needles into Bolivia when it comes to drugs. The US are
saying that the country must wipe out over 1,750 hectares
of coca and agree to extradite any criminals dealing in
cocaine. The British are lecturing them about cutting
production. Other countries are following suit. Which to
me is wrong, because the drug problem is not just a

question of production, it's a question of consumption as well. It's a bit like the way Britain and the European Union go on and on about cigarette-smoking, the damage it does to your health and why all cigarette advertising and promotion should be banned, and at the same time, continue to hand out a colossal US$1.2 billion to subsidise tobacco production. For the US to push little old Bolivia around is like the school bully blaming the little guy for always being beaten up.

In Bolivia coca is a habit, almost a sacred tradition. For generations they've grown the stuff, chewed it and enjoyed themselves on it. Go into the marketplaces any-where in the country and you will see great sacks of the stuff all over the place. It's also a means of earning a living, a pretty miserable living, I admit, for the poor *cocaleros* at the bottom of the heap, but at least it's a living. Take that away from them and how are they going to earn a crust? The US, meanwhile, is the world's biggest consumer of drugs. They should do something practical about con-trolling drugs in their own country rather than hounding people in the streets and then going off to Washington cocktail parties where they chop it up, sniff it and shove great gobs of the stuff down their throats while 'A Perfect Day' plays non-stop in the background. If you're ever looking for a cheap high, stand downwind of an American politician at a Washington cocktail party. You'll be singing and dancing all week. And whenever you go into an American law firm nowadays the whole place seems to smell of something like burned toast, or skunk. Funny, that. It ill behoves a country where every day 135,000 children take guns to school to protect themselves, where doctors are more likely to be punished for overcharging a patient than for killing him, and where the labour conditions in the Californian strawberry fields are as appalling as anything on earth to lecture anybody on anything. Indeed, in defence of poor little Bolivia, I'd go a stage further. I reckon that because the Americans have let drugs infiltrate virtually the whole of American society without taking any really serious steps to stop it, they ought to indemnify all the producers for the disastrous repercussions their increased consumption has brought on the economics, societies and environments of those countries.

If the Americans were really serious about stamping out drugs, it would be the easiest thing in the world for them to stop supplying all the drug-making equipment and materials to the drug-producers. And I don't just mean the occasional test tube and the odd second-hand Bunsen burner, I mean the big stuff. Methyl ethyl ketone. Acetone. Toluene potassium permanganate. Ethyl ether. They are all used to extract the crystalline powder from the raw coca leaves, so why don't the Americans prevent them from being shipped to Bolivia, or any drug-producing country come to that? I'll tell you why. Because it's big business for them. Over 10,000 tons of drug-producing equipment, I was told, are shipped every year from the States. That's why they won't do anything about it.

My solution to the drug problem? Easy. At present we are spending billions around the world on drug-related programmes. In the UK alone we shower £800 million a year on advertising and education campaigns, so just think how much is being spent in the rest of Europe, in the States and elsewhere. Yet everybody, apart, maybe, from the occasional customs and excise guy at Heathrow, agrees that it's not working because every year the situation grows worse and worse. Production increases, consumption increases, drugs-related problems increase. In Bolivia, for example, despite a massive voluntary and forced eradication programme by the government, production actually rose from 78,200 tons in 1989 to 80,300 tons in 1992, the last year for which figures are available.

What I would do is split the funds being spent on all these programmes around the world into two parts. One half I would continue to spend on education, re-education, looking after addicts and so on, because we can't stop trying or helping drug victims. The other half I would distribute among the poor coca farmers, so much per hectare, for them to switch to another crop. The sum each farmer would receive would have to be generous, but overall we wouldn't be spending any more than we are now. And it couldn't be any more of a total waste of money than the present scheme.

You think that's a stupid idea? Well, a number of organisations are already doing exactly that, if not in such a dramatic way. One farmer I met told me that under some United Nations Drug Control programme he'd switched to growing bananas. Was it better than growing coca? I asked him.

'Yes, of course.'

'Why?'

'Because my wife, she has stopped to nag me. When I grow coca all the time it is nag, nag, nag. The police here again. The police, they search house, they search kitchen. Police, they make mess. Who to clean up mess? Nag, nag, nag. Now bananas. *Fantastico*. No more nagging.'

I have to admit he is an exception: most farmers don't reckon they're given enough money under existing schemes to make it worth their while to stop altogether. So they're signing all the bits of paper, taking the money, grubbing up their plants and then replanting them elsewhere, which doesn't help anybody.

For the moment, though, according to a big guy in a big hat I was talking to one evening, production has increased to such an extent that twice a year, when they harvest the coca leaves, roads through the Chapare Valley have to be closed.

'What, by the police?' I guessed. 'To stop them getting the crop out?'

'No, by the farmers. They need all the roads to be empty so they can spread the leaves out in the sun to dry. It's the only space they've got that will handle the quantity.'

'So what happens to the traffic?' That's me, practical as ever.

'It goes along the edge of the fields.'

'Nobody minds?'

'They don't mind. Why should they? It is for us tradition.'

'What do the police do if they find out?'

'The police, they never find out.'

'What, you mean even if whole stretches of road are blocked off for days on end?'

'No. Never.'

'Tradition?' I guessed.

'Tradition.'

But don't worry, the farmers don't have it all their own way. They still have to cope with Umopar, the big anti-drugs battalion.

'Why, what do they do?' I asked.

'They tear-gas the plants.'